AF411947

Vladimir Putin and Central Asia

Culture and Society in Western and Central Asia

Series Editors: Annika Rabo and Bo Utas

1.   Vladimir Putin and Central Asia: 1 85043 628 2
     The Shaping of Russian Foreign Policy
     Lena Jonson

2.   Trade, Industrialization and the Firm in Iran: 1 85043 681 9
     The impact of Government Policy on Business
     Javad Amid and Amjad Hadjikhani

3.   The Unwelcome Neighbour: 1 85043 682 7
     Turkey's Kurdish Policy
     Asa Lundgren

4.   A Shop of One's Own: 1 85043 683 5
     Independence, Trust and Reputation among Traders
     in Aleppo
     Annika Rabo

Vladimir Putin and Central Asia
The Shaping of Russian Foreign Policy

LENA JONSON

Reprinted in 2006 by I.B.Tauris & Co Ltd
6 Salem Road, London W2 4BU
175 Fifth Avenue, New York NY 10010
www.ibtauris.com

In the United States of America and in Canada distributed by Palgrave Macmillan, a division of St Martins Press, 175 Fifth Avenue, New York, NY 10010

Published with generous support from the Swedish Research Council

First published in 2004 by I.B.Tauris & Co Ltd

Culture and Society in Western and Central Asia 1

ISBN 1 85043 628 2
EAN 978 1 85043 628 7

A full CIP record for this book is available from the British Library
A full CIP record for this book is available from the Library of Congress

Library of Congress Catalog Card: available

Printed and bound in India by Replika Press Pvt. Ltd

CONTENTS

LIST OF MAPS

ABBREVIATIONS

ABM	Anti-Ballistic Missile (Treaty)
ADB	Asian Development Bank
CAEC	Central Asian Economic Community
CACO	Central Asian Cooperation Organization
CIS	Commonwealth of Independent States
CP	Communist Party (Tajikistan)
CST	Collective Security Treaty
CSTO	Collective Security Treaty Organization
EAPC	Euro-Atlantic Partnership and Cooperation Council
EBRD	European Bank for Reconstruction and Development
EEC	Eurasian Economic Community
EU	European Union
FPS	Federalnaya Pogranichnaya Sluzhba (Federal Border Service)
FSB	Federalnaya Sluzhba Bezopasnosti (Federal Security Service)
G8	Group of Eight industrialized countries
GUUAM	Georgia, Ukraine, Uzbekistan, Azerbaijan and Moldova
IMF	International Monetary Fund
IMU	Islamic Movement of Uzbekistan
IRP	Islamic Revival Party
ISAF	International Security Assistance Force (Afghanistan)
KGB	Komitet Gosudarstvennoi Bezopasnosti (Committee of State Security)
MRD	Motorized Rifle Division
NATO	North Atlantic Treaty Organization
NGO	Non-governmental organization
NMD	National Missile Defense
OSCE	Organization for Security and Co-operation in Europe
PDP	People's Democratic Party (Tajikistan)
PFP	Partnership for Peace
PJC	Permanent Joint Council (Russia and NATO)
SCO	Shanghai Cooperation Organization
SVR	Sluzhba Vneshnei Razvedki (Foreign Intelligence Service)
TRACECA	Transport Corridor Europe Caucasus Asia
UES	Unified Energy Systems
UN	United Nations
UNMOVIC	UN Monitoring, Verification and Inspection Commission
UTO	United Tajik Opposition
WMD	Weapons of mass destruction
WTO	World Trade Organization

ACKNOWLEDGEMENTS

Some periods in history are more open to structural change than others. Existing relationships between states in the international system change, end, accommodate to new conditions and find new forms. Some events provide windows of opportunity for policy makers to adjust and revise previous policy and, in responding to the most burning challenges, a state's relationship with other states. Vladimir Putin saw and acted upon these opportunities during his first period in office—from his appointment as Prime Minister in August 1999, becoming President in March 2000, until his re-election as President in March 2004. After 11 September 2001 Central Asia became the area where the reconfiguration of international politics and Russian–US relations combined. After remaining in the background for most of the twentieth century, Central Asia, at the turn of the new century, became the centre of international attention.

This book was born out of the author's long-standing interest in the Central Asian countries and Russian foreign policy. The study of press reports and articles, and discussions with Russian and Tajik friends, led me to address the question 'How will Russia find its way in the post-Soviet world?' At conferences in the past few years I had the opportunity to discuss my ideas with colleagues in the USA, Europe and Russia. I am indebted to a large number of friends for taking the time to respond to my detailed questions, give me additional ideas, and both encourage and challenge my own. I cannot name them all but I am sure that they know who they are. Among them are Russian and Tajik friends and colleagues primarily from academia but also from my time at the OSCE Mission in Dushanbe in 2002.

A few people deserve special mention for their constant support, encouragement and constructive comment and criticism: Olav Knudsen, Gunnar Sjöstedt, Björn Hagelin, Gudrun Persson, Daniel Tarschys, Gösta Lavén, Torgny Hinnemo and Ingmar Oldberg. I am also grateful to the late Alvin Rubinstein who encouraged me to write this book, and Bruce Parrott, who included me in a fruitful seminar at Johns Hopkin University.

I want to extend my thanks to the Swedish Research Council for their financial support. Without the support of my home institute, The Swedish Institute of International Affairs, I would not have had the opportunity to concentrate on writing this book. Writing in a foreign language, the text would not have made sense had it not been for Eve Johansson and Andy Mash. I express my gratitude to all of these people, but I alone am responsible for any errors that remain.

Last, but certainly not least, I want to express my gratitude for the personal encouragement and support I received from those closest to me—Puck and Björn.

Stockholm 15 March 2004
Lena Jonson

Map 1: The Russian conquest of Turkestan

After B. Wehlman, in Otto Hoetzsch, *Russland in Asien. Geschichte einer Expansion* (Stuttgart: Deutsche Verlags-Anstalt, 1966)

Map 2: Kyrgyzstan, Tajikistan, Uzbekistan, Turkmenistan: main railroads and roads

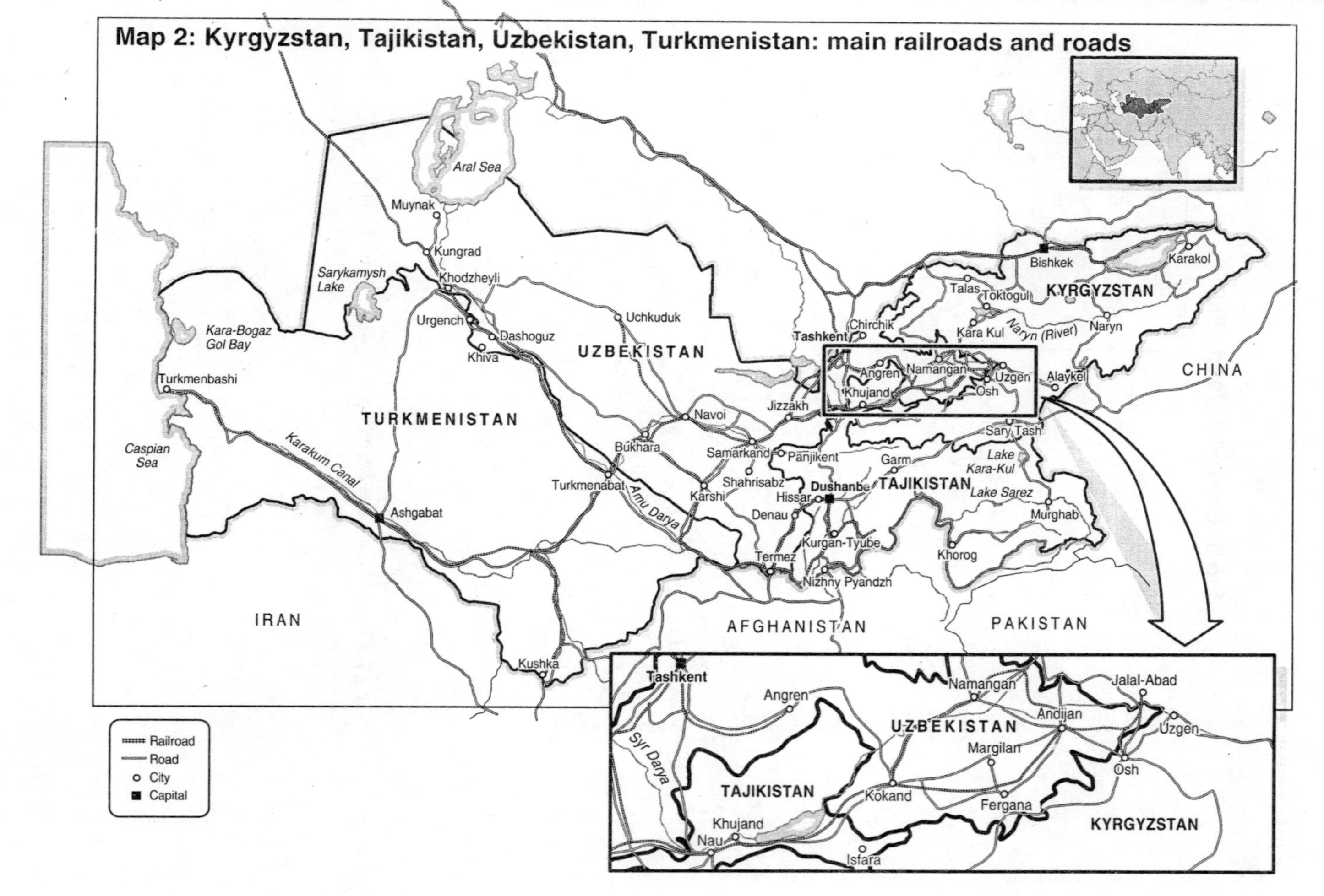

Map 3: Central Asia in 1868

1

INTRODUCTION

The terrorist attacks of 11 September 2001 put Central Asia back on the world map as the world's attention came to focus on terrorism, Afghanistan, and Osama bin Laden. President of the Russian Federation Vladimir Putin's consent in late September to the deployment of Western forces in Central Asia and to the US military's use of Central Asian airfields during the US-led operations in Afghanistan represented a dramatic turn in Russian Central Asian policy. His Central Asian policy of 1999, after he was appointed prime minister in August that year, had already seen a shift as terrorism was given top priority on the Russian agenda in Central Asia. Putin's policy at that time represented an effort to respond to the security challenges of the region, but it also addressed the growing US engagement in the area. This policy appeared to be diametrically reversed in 2001 as Putin extended the anti-terrorist agenda and included the USA and the Western states, making them Russian partners in Central Asia. The policies of 1999 and 2001 were both turning points and reflected continuity in the history of Russian Central Asian policy.

The Shaping of Foreign Policy under Putin

How to interpret these changes? The purpose of this book is to analyse Russia's Central Asian policy as an example of its efforts to find a role and a policy while trying to adapt to the post-Soviet world.[1] It focuses on the period from 1999 to 2004, which includes President Putin's first term of office. The aim is threefold: (a) to analyse the changes in the Russian Central Asian policies of 1999 and 2001, and explain why these changes took place; (b) to analyse Russian policy in the region since then; and (c) to discuss the implications for the overall revision of Russian foreign policy.

The collapse of the Soviet Union left Russia bereft of its former great-power status and desperately searching for a new policy.[2] Like many other former great powers it faced tremendous challenges in accommodating to its new position as a declining state in the international system and searching for a course of action corresponding to its new status. Russia's problems in this respect were not unique. Both France and the United Kingdom went through similar processes after the Second World War. For them it was not only a matter of recognizing the fact that their status had been lost with the loss of their former territories and accepting a more modest position in the international system; it was also a question of making the best of the situation to create favourable conditions for domestic recovery and a return to international influence. The complex post-imperial readjustment process took several decades in each case.

In 2001, ten years after the break up of the Soviet Union, Russia had come a long way in defining the main direction of its foreign policy towards Europe and the West. However, it was still struggling to formulate a policy on the territory of the former Soviet Union. This was particularly true of its policy towards Central Asia.[3] Like most other former Soviet territories, post-Soviet Central Asia has been characterized by a drastic reduction of Russian influence accompanied by a growing foreign engagement. In addition, Central Asia has become a scene of growing security concern.[4] It has been under constant threat from the turmoil and radical Islamism emanating from Afghanistan. The Afghan situation brought several other threats, including drug trafficking, as Afghanistan became one of the largest producers of opium in the world. The threat to security culminated with the Taliban takeover of power in Afghanistan 1996 and led Putin to reactivate Russia's Central Asian policy in 1999. The greater US engagement in Central Asia, after 11 September 2001, accelerated Russia's decline in Central Asia.

In 1998 the present author wrote that the extent to which Russia is marginalized in the present transformation process in Central Asia will depend on its own capacity to adapt and to formulate policies adequate to the new situation.[5] Although the US-led military operations in late 2001 removed the Taliban regime and thereby improved the security situation in Central Asia, the domestic security situation remained complex and unstable, and Russia continued to lose influence. The new situation after 11 September 2001 made Russia one of many external actors in Central Asia as foreign governments, international organizations and private companies became engaged in the region. As a consequence, the new conditions in Central Asia placed new demands on Russian policy making. It is argued here that, in order to secure a future in the region, Russia must prove itself useful to the governments of the Central Asian states by addressing the problems of these countries. Furthermore, the Russian Government has to define its new role and policy in the region while, at the same time, it is under pressure to balance strategic and security concerns outside Russia with Russian domestic policy priorities.

Russia's problems in finding a policy in Central Asia can be said to encapsulate the problems of a general foreign policy revision after the break up of an empire. In the opening sentence of *Anna Karenina*, Leo Tolstoy wrote that there is nothing unique about a happy family, but each unhappy family is unhappy in its own way. To some extent, this seems to apply to empires as well. While Russia may share the experience of searching for a new position in the world—and for a sound balance between commitments and resources—with several other states that are in the process of transforming from great power status to a minor position in the international system, Russia's quest for a new role is in one respect unique. Throughout history, Russia has been able on many occasions to return to a great power position after defeats and losses of territory. This gives it a specific and different experience, distancing it from most other states. Why should a return to great power status not be possible again? The Russian philosopher Ivan Ilin wrote: 'With each attempt to divide [Russia] and after each disintegration it restores itself again by the mysterious ancient power of its spiritual identity (*bytiya*)'.[6]

Although this dream is still alive, Russia has to come to grips with a new international situation.

Policy Change and Revision

In what sense can Putin's policies of 1999 and 2001 be considered turning points? How can they be characterized?

In Western academic literature, policy change has been defined as both the minor, natural adjustments to changing conditions, which governments always undertake, and changes which alter a country's policy more fundamentally.[7] Charles Hermann identifies four levels or degrees of change: (a) adjustment changes or refinements, while policy remains unchanged; (b) programme changes, that is, changes of methods and means (instruments of statecraft) while the purposes remain the same; (c) problem or goal changes, which mean that the initial problem or goal that the policy addresses is replaced or simply lost; and (d) international orientation changes, which involve the redirection of the actor's entire orientation towards world affairs, and require a basic shift in the actor's international role and activities.[8] Of most interest to the present study are changes which amount to a revision of foreign policy. The three latter levels are therefore included in the study. The fourth level where fundamental revision to the orientation of a state is enacted, is of particular interest. Minor adjustments may with hindsight be regarded as determining steps in the direction of fundamental change. This aspect is also taken into consideration in the following analysis.

Since the break up of the Soviet Union, Russia can be defined as a state in decline in the international system. In his study *War and Change in World Politics*, Robert Gilpin discusses different courses of action possible for states in decline. A state in decline tries hard to maintain the status quo for as long as possible. A principal problem, however, is the contrast between its high ambitions and its lack of power. When this conflict proves irreconcilable under the existing structure, policy must be revised if the dilemma is to be resolved. Gilpin identifies two possible and analytically different courses of action for a state in decline: (a) to devote more resources to maintaining its commitments and position in the international system; and (b) to reduce its commitments (and associated costs) while trying not to jeopardize its international position.[9] Although the two courses of action can be considered analytically as separate policies, they are not mutually exclusive. The general strategy of the last Soviet leader, Mikhail Gorbachev, as well as the post-Soviet leaders has been to increase efficiency through domestic reform while trying to reduce costs.

The first type of response—to devote more resources—can involve mobilizing resources within the country, for example, through taxation, inflationary policies, manipulating the terms of trade with other countries, or by increasing efficiency in the use of existing resources; or it can involve increasing the total amount of disposable resources through organizational, technological or other types of innovation and reform. According to Gilpin, a second type of response—to reduce costs—can be attempted in three general ways. Of most relevance to the discussion here are: (a) expansion into more secure and less costly defensive boundaries;[10] and (b) political, territorial or economic retrenchment. Gilpin's option of reducing costs through political, territorial or economic retrenchment is of special interest to this study of policy in Central Asia. Gilpin describes three possible directions for this alternative. A state may: (a) unilaterally abandon certain of its economic, political or military commitments; (b) enter into alliances with or seek rapprochement with less threatening powers; or (c) make concessions to the rising power and thereby seek to appease its ambitions.

Gilpin gives historical examples of successful appeasement: 'Contending states have not only avoided conflict but also achieved a relationship satisfactory to both. A notable example was British appeasement of the rising US in the decades prior to World War I. The two countries ended a century-long hostility and laid the basis for what has come to be known as the "special relationship" between the two Anglo-Saxon powers.'[11]

The policy of appeasement is politically difficult and delicate, Gilpin says, and the fundamental problem of appeasement 'is to find a way to pursue it that does not lead to continuing deterioration in a state's prestige and international position'.[12] Retrenchment may have a damaging effect on relations with allies, which sense the decline of their protector and try to obtain the best deal from the rising power, and generate new pressure from rivals, which are encouraged to 'close in'. The success of retrenchment therefore depends greatly on timing and circumstances.

Gilpin discusses the options that are available to a state in decline that is trying to maintain the status quo. However, a state may come to the point where it is forced by circumstances to revise its main foreign policy goal (in this case, maintaining the status quo) and accept its reduced international status. Although, initially, the goal of the government is to maintain its international position, at the end of the day it may have to radically reduce its foreign policy ambitions in order to achieve a better fit with its present resources and capabilities and to adapt to the new situation. From a new, more modest, international position the state may be able to increase its international influence, which adds another alternative to the foreign policy options presented by Gilpin.

Russia's Experiences of Foreign Policy Revision

Under Gorbachev and Yeltsin

When in the late 1980s Mikhail Gorbachev introduced perestroika and 'New Foreign Policy Thinking', the initial declared purpose was to prevent the Soviet Union from lagging behind the developed West in the economic and technological spheres in order to maintain its international status. Gorbachev introduced a revision of foreign policy and also of the goals of foreign policy because he realized that the Soviet Union was losing its capacity to wield international influence. Initially, the strategic goal of a return to the international arena as a great power was maintained. Gorbachev's major contribution was to de-ideologize foreign policy and reduce commitments in order to concentrate on domestic reform. He abandoned the concept of the Soviet Union as a superpower and started a process of adaptation to the more modest role of a great power. He stressed international interdependence, international cooperation and good relations with the West.[13] He introduced an emphasis on non-military tools of foreign policy—in particular economic aspects and economic means—in contrast to the strong tradition in Soviet/Russian foreign policy of relying on security aspects and military means. Thus, the policy aimed to increase resources by means of domestic reform while reducing costs by reducing on international commitments and appeasing the USA and its European allies. Gorbachev was, however, overtaken by events and the process of revision he initiated resulted in the break up of the Soviet bloc and the Soviet Union itself.

President Boris Yeltsin continued what Gorbachev had started. The pillars of his strategy were the same: economic and political reforms; international cooperation; and a rapprochement with the West. Yet, during Yeltsin's presidency the strategic direction of Russian foreign policy—to provide the external conditions for domestic reform—were lost in a battle for power, influence and money in the circles around the president. Foreign policy became a battleground with vested interests competing for influence. Policy was in flux as the government remained passive and institutional interests were able to push themselves forward. Russia's policy on the armed conflicts on former Soviet territory in the first half of the 1990s is an illustration of this. While the government stood by and was reluctant to intervene when armed conflicts erupted in former Soviet republics, the Russian military took action.[14] In the early 1990s the democrats around Yeltsin tried to avoid discussion of a Russian return to great power status for fear of being criticized for 'new imperialism' or 'great-power syndrome'.[15] Yet, in 1993, under pressure from their critics for not defending Russian national interests and for giving in to the West, Yeltsin and his foreign minister, Andrei Kozyrev, retreated into great power rhetoric and the pretension of being the leader of an integrated bloc of former Soviet republics and an equal of the USA.[16] The Russian Government adopted a more militant rhetoric, and the strategy of retrenchment for the purposes of domestic reform seemed to have moved into the background. As a result, Russian policy on the territory of members of the Commonwealth of Independent States (CIS) increased the uncertainty about what Russia's intentions were, and was sometimes directly destabilizing.

By January 1996 a wide gap had opened up between ambition and capacity, largely because Russia had failed to live up to its own rhetoric to become the economic and military integrator and guarantor of security on former Soviet territory. Thus, there was a need to temporarily curtail Russia's ambitions in order to achieve a better fit between resources and what was actually possible. It was Yevgeny Primakov (foreign minister 1996–98 and prime minister 1998–99) who turned Russia towards a more pragmatic and low-profile policy on former Soviet territory in order to narrow the gap between policy declarations and actual capacity, although he was viewed by the West as anti-Western and an old-style Soviet thinker in his Western policy. At the same time, Primakov tried to restore a more strategic direction to Russian foreign policy by reintroducing the vision of a Russian return to great power status, made possible after the success of domestic reforms. For this purpose Primakov introduced the name of Alexander Gorchakov into the Russian debate—the tsarist foreign minister who had restructured Russian policy after the Russian defeat in the Crimean War and the severe terms of the 1856 Treaty of Paris.[17] Gorchakov was Primakov's main legacy to Putin when he came to power in 1999.

Alexander Gorchakov as a Point of Reference

Alexander Gorchakov (born in 1798 and foreign minister 1856–82) was given the task of rethinking Russian foreign policy after defeat in the Crimean War and the Paris Peace Treaty.[18] Forty years earlier Russia had developed into the most powerful state on the European continent. Entering the Crimean War as a strong power, Russia came out of it having been shown to be seriously lagging behind other European powers both economically and militarily. The 1856 peace terms were humiliating, demanding Russian demilitarization of the Black Sea. By this time it was obvious that Russia needed a radical change of foreign policy, above all of the interventionist policy under Nicholas I. The policy that Gorchakov proposed, and which characterized his years as foreign minister, was an effort to reorient foreign policy in order to give Russia a chance to recover and build up its strength. Gorchakov combined an agenda for domestic reform with a long-term foreign policy aim of a return to great power status. He coined the phrase 'Russia does not sulk, she concentrates' to summarize the idea behind his agenda.[19]

Gorchakov concentrated on creating the external conditions for economic recovery and development. In his domestic policy, he was in favour of modernization and reform. As he said: 'The first duty of Russia is to accomplish the work of her internal reorganization, which contains the germ of her destiny'.[20] The period of Tsar Alexander II, 1856–74, became known as the 'era of Great Reforms' because of the amount of legislation the regime sponsored to improve and transform Russian society. The abolition of serfdom in 1861 was one of the most important reforms. Gorchakov pursued a careful, risk-averse foreign policy towards the European powers but combined it with active diplomacy in an effort to strengthen Russia's influence in European politics.

A first task was to create the international conditions necessary for domestic reform by ensuring that the anti-Russian alliances of the Crimean War did not last into peacetime. Gorchakov tried to make policy predictable and non-aggressive in order not to provoke or confront the other European powers. He also pursued an active diplomacy, trying to build coalitions and alliances not only to put an end to the constraints imposed by the Treaty of Paris but also to strengthen Russia's international influence. He advocated cooperation with France and supported a wide range of French interests, primarily in southern and south-eastern Europe, in order to gain French support for ending the restrictions of the Paris Peace Treaty. While this policy failed—when cooperation ended in 1863 Russia had not achieved French support to free itself of the conditions of the peace treaty—Russia acted unilaterally after France was defeated in its war against Prussia in 1870. Generally, Gorchakov's policy was successful and it helped to return Russia to a position of strong international influence. Gorchakov's policy included the unilateral abandonment of commitments in Europe, alliances with less threatening powers and concessions to the rising power. It was an example of the classic art of the balance of power.

The programme for domestic recovery created a base for the strategic objective of making Russia a powerful European state with extensive international influence. Gorchakov's policy can be described as 'revisionist' in the sense that he wanted to 'reduce and eliminate the distance between the existing status quo and the acceptable order'.[21] This did not necessarily imply 'aggressive' and 'immoral' policies. As Barry Buzan writes, revisionist states, for whatever reason, simply feel 'alienated from [the status quo], threatened by it and oppose its continuation'.[22] Gorchakov's primary purpose was to change not the international system but Russia's position in that system.

Yet Gorchakov's policy was not without its dilemmas. He emphasised the domestic reform agenda, but also encouraged every opportunity for Russia to increase both its visibility and its influence internationally. His policy opened the way for a serious foreign policy revision aimed at closing the gap between ambition and capacity—but it also included the risk that this gap would increase if ambitions remained the same or expanded beyond Russia's capabilities. It was in this general context of Gorchakov's foreign policy agenda that the Russian territorial expansion into Central Asia took place from the 1860s.

Under Putin

The heritage of Gorchakov is contradictory when used as a point of reference for Russian policy in the late twentieth century, and it does not solve the problem of setting strategic priorities. As demonstrated above, under Yeltsin the combination of a declared intention to carry out domestic reforms and a foreign policy retrenchment, on the one hand, with a desire to restore Russia's great power status, on the other, contained fundamental contradictions. The desire to concentrate on domestic reform and economic development clashed with the old reflex—to try to win international influence even at the risk of an overstretch of Russia's capabilities.[23] Russia's desire to participate in international cooperative structures clashed with measures taken to enhance its international status, and this resulted in tensions with the West. Thus, policy remained contradictory and there was a need to revise foreign policy further in order to achieve a better fit with Russia's limited capacities, and to create the external conditions for domestic reform. The strategic direction of policy, that is, what comes first on the list of priorities, had to be more directly spelled out. Did the declared aims of domestic reform and economic growth or the desire for a return to international influence have top priority? How could these rival aims be best combined?

Vladimir Putin was appointed by Yeltsin. He was unknown to the public but came to represent a contrast to the 'old regime' and all that Yeltsin had been unable to achieve—a strong state and domestic reforms; a strong Russian international position and international cooperation; respect for Russia's national interests; and good relations with the West. He represented a young, determined mind and a capacity to implement policy, in contrast to the old Yeltsin. He was a mystery to the outside world in so far as his priorities were concerned. Nevertheless, he managed, intentionally or not, to be a kind of mirror in which supporters of most of the different views on the Russian domestic scene saw what they wanted to see.

This was reflected in the elections of 1999 and 2000, when the name of Putin attracted both liberal reformers and nationalists, including communists. Putin gave the impression of standing up firmly to the West, both in European politics and on matters related to former Soviet territory. He strongly defended Russian territorial integrity (in Chechnya) and Russian national interests. Yet, in his 'Internet speech' of December 1999, just before becoming acting president, he emphasized that domestic reform and the economic development of Russia was his priority and, to this end, the improvement of relations with the West, in particular the United States.[24] From the beginning of his rule Putin cultivated the image of a leader concentrating on strengthening the Russian state and restoring Russia's leadership on former Soviet territory. He used Alexander Gorchakov as his reference point for restructuring Russian foreign policy. Elected president in March 2000, Putin asked his foreign minister, Igor Ivanov, to explore the lessons of Gorchakov for the twenty-first century as he edged his way towards a resolution to the dilemma of setting priorities in foreign policy. Western suspicion about him remained strong, however, and he was not able to make a breakthrough in relations with the West.

Central Asia in Russian Foreign Policy

How does Central Asia enter the discussion of Russia's overall revision of foreign policy?

In the late nineteenth century, at the same time as Russia adopted a policy of increasing resources through domestic reform and reducing commitments and associated costs in Europe, it also carried out a large-scale territorial expansion into Central Asia. This seems contradictory but can be explained by the tension between Russia's overall goal of reducing costs while doing its best to maintain international influence. Applying the policy options described by Gilpin, the territorial expansion into Central Asia can be understood as a policy to secure long-term resources for Russia but also as a retreat to a more secure perimeter at a time when its influence in Europe was blocked.

This tension reappeared in the late twentieth century. After the break up of the Soviet bloc and the Soviet Union, Russia had to come to terms with its reduced role and status in Europe. During the 1990s it accepted that it had to withdraw politically, economically and militarily from Eastern Europe, the Baltic states and the western CIS states.[25] Gradually, Russia found a new policy for this new situation by developing new relations with these countries. Military cooperation no longer constituted the major area for Russia's proposals for cooperation. Instead, economic, and above all energy, cooperation moved to the forefront of Russian European policy.

The situation was different in Central Asia. While Russia quickly accepted that the Central Asian states were independent and as such did not automatically follow its dictates, it nevertheless wanted to maintain a role as a security guarantor for the region and a leader with regard to economic integration. Central Asia was regarded as a Russian sphere of interest, and Russia tried to deny other states access to the region through its efforts to integrate the CIS economically and militarily. For most of the 1990s Russia pursued a foreign policy in Central Asia that was very different from its policy in Europe. While advocating international cooperation and the crucial role of the United Nations and its Security Council, and that of the Organization for Security and Co-operation in Europe (OSCE), in conflict resolution in general, Russia remained sceptical about these organizations' activities on former Soviet territory.[26] Gradually, however, it came to accept them as valuable for conflict resolution in the CIS, but refused to allow foreign soldiers on former Soviet territory.

Thus, the way in which Russia relates to and behaves in Central Asia constitutes an interesting example of its foreign policy restructuring. This is because the traditional Russian view of Central Asia as its 'backyard' made the process of the restructuring of Russian policy in the region more complicated. Moreover, Russia's own national security is directly linked to Central Asian security since proper border and customs controls on the borders between Russia and Kazakhstan and between the former Soviet republics, which have only been international borders since December 1991, are still not established.

Russia's policy towards Central Asia involves fundamental aspects of Russian foreign policy such as: (a) the way Russia perceives its interests in Central Asia (how and why Central Asia matters) and understands its own role in the region; (b) the way Russia reacts to Western (above all the US) engagement in Central Asia and defines its own interests in relation to Western actors in the region; (c) its choice of means and instruments in its policy responses in Central Asia and its general understanding of means and instruments in foreign policy. How do the changes brought in by Putin's 1999 and 2001 policies in Central Asia relate to the overall revision of Russian foreign policy? These two cases of self-correcting change—Why did they take place? Nothing has been said so far about the reasons for change, or whether the changes were planned or made under pressure. At this point it is enough to say that the Russian leadership had realized that its policy in Central Asia did not accurately respond to the challenges, and that therefore policy had to change.

What Policy Change?

The Russian policy shifts at the two turning points of 1999 and 2001 are analysed in the context of Russian Central Asian policy since 1991 and the way Russia handled the challenges on the ground in Central Asia. This analysis uses a modified version of Charles Hermann's definition of policy change referred to above, and includes: (a) the way problems and concerns are defined; (b) the means by which Russia responds to major problems; and (c) overall orientation.[27] The latter aspect includes not only the approach towards Western states engaging in Central Asia but also Russia's own image of its role and commitments in Central Asia.

The Way Problems and Concerns Are Defined

Major problems and concerns that Russia identifies directly with its interests at the local level in Central Asia are described analytically as belonging to one or other of the following categories: (a) strategic concerns about the growing engagement of foreign actors in Central Asian countries; and (b) security concerns about the threats to the security of the region. Economic concerns are included in both these categories.

Russian governments have always viewed foreign influence in Central Asia with suspicion. The governments concerned with the security of the region feared a possible 'Muslim threat' above all. Russia proper was itself vulnerable in this regard and Central Asia was viewed as a buffer between the Muslim South (Turkey, Iran, Afghanistan) and Russia's own Muslim 'underbelly' of the North Caucasus and central parts of Russia (Tatarstan, Bashkortostan and other Russian Muslim regions). After the break up of the Soviet Union, Central Asia became an immediate security concern to Russia as civil war erupted in Tajikistan, thereby confirming the Russian fear of a Muslim revival. Neighbouring Afghanistan, which collapsed and became a 'failed state' when Soviet troops withdrew in 1989 after years of occupation and war, threatened to spread instability to Central Asia. The 'Islamic threat' grew as the Taliban took control of Kabul in 1996, extended their control to northern Afghanistan almost up to the Tajik and Uzbek borders in 1998, and gave support to Chechen separatists—the security issue of most direct concern to Russia.

The lens through which the region is viewed determines the way policy is framed. The framing of policy implies what is at issue and also what is to be done.[28]

The Means by Which Russia Responds to Major Patterns

The relative weight given to the military and economic means of statecraft is crucial to determining the means and methods of policy.

Traditionally, military and security aspects have dominated Russia's relations with Central Asian countries.[29] As mentioned above, in the late 1990s Russia was strengthened in its conviction that more emphasis had to be given to the economic and diplomatic levers of foreign policy because the value of military and military–political instruments was perceived as limited. Nevertheless, in Central Asia the security sector continued to be the area where Russia had its strongest assets.

The concepts of 'securitization' and 'economization' are used here to characterize the government's choice of policy instruments.

Bobo Lo has provided very convenient definitions of these two concepts in his studies of Russian foreign policy towards the West.[30] Economization implies the primacy of economic rather than security matters, and Lo concludes that 'the emphasis Putin has assigned to economic priorities has emerged as one of the most distinctive and important features of his foreign policy management'.[31] Lo discerns four themes to the economic dimension: (a) the direct linkage between an active foreign policy and domestic socio-economic transformation and prosperity; (b) the campaign to integrate Russia into ongoing international economic processes; (c) the profit motive; and (d) the inter-relationship between geo-economics and geopolitics, between Moscow's pursuit of economic objectives and its continuing ambitions to project itself as a regional and global power. Lo defines securitization as: (a) the enhanced role of the security apparatus in foreign policy making; and (b) the primacy of political–military priorities over economic priorities and the dominance of security objectives in the interplay with economic interests.[32]

In this study, the concepts are defined as different ways of framing policy in a security context and an economic context. Securitization will be interpreted more in line with its original definition, coined by Ole Waever, et al., as the process by which an issue is lifted out of the general political agenda and framed as an issue that is crucial for 'life and death'.[33] In order to move an issue up the agenda and mobilize resources, including resources for the use of force, it has to be defined as an 'existential threat, requiring emergency measures and justifying actions outside the normal bounds of political procedure'.[34] Securitization does not require that a real threat actually exists but only that it is presented as such and accepted as such. As the chapters below demonstrate, the issue of terrorism and extremism was made the top priority issue on the Russian agenda in Central Asia in 1999, and thereby framed Russian policy towards Central Asia. In the context of Russia's relations with the Central Asian states this meant that among the different threats, problems and challenges, this specific issue was presented as the most crucial. The concept of economization will be treated accordingly. It implies that economic issues are lifted out of the general agenda and defined as the most crucial for relations between states. Russia's new focus on energy cooperation with Central Asia is discussed in this context.

For Russian policy makers there is a choice between relying mainly on cooperation in the traditional security sector and emphasizing the economic and energy spheres for cooperation.

Russia's Overall Orientation

Russia's overall orientation includes its approach to the main foreign actor in the region (the USA) as part of its general approach to the West, but also the way Russia views its own role and commitments.

Russia's approach to the USA is analysed in relation to its perception and policies with regard to the USA at the global level and in the Central Asian arena. Of special interest here is the question of whether there is any movement in the Russian official approach away from a zero-sum perspective towards a cooperative perspective.[35] The zero-sum perspective has a long and strong tradition in Russia. It implies that in the competition between state interests the gains of one side are the losses of the other. The essence of international politics is thus reduced to a struggle between the main centres of power for control over territories. From a zero-sum perspective, for instance, Russia observes with concern all processes in Central Asia whereby states that are not part of the Commonwealth of Independent States (CIS) gain influence, and regards this as a loss of its own position and influence. A cooperative perspective is different in that it also appreciates the opportunities for Russia that result from greater international interest in Central Asia. In a cooperative perspective there can be win–win situations. In practice, two options exist for Russian policy with regard to the US presence in the region—to counter it or to accept it and cooperate. In reality, policy will include parts of both options, although analytically they appear to be alternatives.

Measuring Foreign Policy Change

It is often claimed that Russia has no Central Asian policy. It is true that there was no conscious policy planning for years, although Russia is not unique in this respect. Most states formulate policy through a process of trial and error. Foreign policy is therefore defined here as the pattern which evolves from both the statements and actions of a state. Policy change is indicated by shifts in pattern. Official statements may reflect policy changes, but they do not always correspond to the actual behaviour of a government. Government statements are not always implemented and, equally, not all actions are reflected in official speeches and statements. This study therefore considers both the words and the deeds of the Russian Government. Changes are identified as deviations from the overall pattern composed of the statements and the actual behaviour of government actors.

Why These Policy Changes?

What caused policy to change the way it did at the time of the two turning points for Russian policy in Central Asia in 1999 and 2001? The general answer to the question why policy changed has already been indicated: Russia is in the process of adapting to the new international situation after the break up of the Soviet Union. To this can be added that dramatic events took place in 1999 and 2001, which created a 'policy window' for the Russian leadership.[36] Yet these responses do not answer the question: Why did policy change *in the way that it did?*

External and Internal Factors

Three sets of factors stand out as central to explaining foreign policy—external factors, internal factors and historical–cultural factors.[37]

External factors relate to the international environment and include both Russia's relations with other powers—primarily the USA—and the situation for Russia on the local Central Asian stage.

Relations with other powers, in particular the USA, are analysed here at the global level and within the Central Asian sphere. When Putin was appointed prime minister in August 1999, Russian–US relations were at a low ebb after the 1994 and 1999 decisions to enlarge the North Atlantic Treaty Organization (NATO) to the East; NATO's bombing of Kosovo and Serbia in April–May 1999 without the authorization of the UN Security Council; and Western criticism of the Russian military campaign in Chechnya of September 1999. In September 2001 Putin, who had inherited a tense relationship with the West, saw an opportunity to improve relations.

The term 'local scene in Central Asia' refers to developments relevant to Russia in and between the four Central Asian states. Uzbekistan and Tajikistan are central to this study because they were the first to suffer from the war, turmoil and radical Islamism in Afghanistan. The common denominator of the instability in the area was radical Islam, linked to Afghanistan. The Batken events of August 1999, when Uzbek Islamist rebels from the Islamic Movement of Uzbekistan (IMU) intruded into Kyrgyzstan and took hostages, had a direct link to Afghanistan. So too had the terrorist attacks on the USA in September 2001. It can be argued that Russia's weakened role and lack of capacity to respond to the challenges in Central Asia caused Putin to adopt a more determined policy in the region in 1999 and to give his consent to a US military presence in 2001.

Internal factors include Russia's domestic security situation, foreign policy making process, official perceptions and ideological concepts and, finally, the attitudes of elites. Among internal factors economic conditions are most often included as crucial to the capacity of a state to act beyond its borders. Russia's economic situation is not examined in detail in this study. Instead, Russia's economic and financial constraints are regarded as the general background against which Russian Central Asian policy is carried out. The Chechnya factor is regarded as the major internal security problem creating restrictions on foreign policy and a defining factor for the way in which events in Central Asia were perceived by the Russian leadership. The policy making process and the role and influence of different institutions in this process are also decisive. The way that the terrorist issue was moved to the forefront of Russia's agenda can be related to the rise of institutional groups and interests, while the way that Putin was able to carry out his 2001 change of policy can be explained by the 'correlation of forces' on the domestic scene. Decision making under Yeltsin has most often been described as a competition between sectional agendas without a strategic policy direction. In contrast to Yeltsin, Putin seems to be able to get the structures and mechanisms of foreign policy making under control, although a contest persists between the institutions for influence and for the ear of the president.

Official perceptions and rhetoric form the ideological concepts through which policy makers formulate their policies and explain and legitimize policy. The way in which these concepts change and relate to each other contributes to an understanding of policy change. They explain the basis on which international cooperation can be carried out and common interests develop between a country and its former adversaries. They also reveal the government's image of Russia. Russia traditionally defines itself as a great power, but it has to clarify for itself in what capacity it is still to be counted as a great power, how to act in order to be perceived as such, and with whom to ally itself in order to be regarded so. What is required may be a shift in psyche from a sense of 'great powerness' to one that places primary value on Russia's 'normalness'—or, the development of a new identity as a nation state 'like the others'.[38] Many analysts have concluded that the ideological component in Russian foreign policy disappeared with its Communist ideology. Yet, ideology is still alive and can be identified in alternative positions in the foreign policy debate, and as a state ideology in the making. The way in which Gorchakov was introduced into the Russian policy debate suggests that a new state ideology is being constructed. The analysis of Russian internal factors also includes the analysis of elite attitudes with regard to policy in Central Asia, that is, the degree of disagreement or criticism as opposed to consensus and unity evoked by Russian Government's Central Asian policy.

Background historical and cultural factors constitute the third set of factors. They include first and foremost the history of the Russian territorial expansion into Central Asia during the nineteenth century. History explains why Russia has been prepared to take on commitments in the region. Although history never repeats itself, and the history of the expansion into Central Asia cannot be read as a blueprint for contemporary policy, the historical memory of expansion may be a reminder of and the inspiration behind Russia's long-term interest in Central Asia.

These three sets of factors are used to structure the below analysis. The relationships between them have not yet been indicated. Which of them is most important? The discussion of their relative weight is left for the concluding chapter, where they are included in different theoretical approaches in order to explain why Russian Central Asian policy changed in the way it did and what implications this had for an overall revision of Russian foreign policy.

Four Possible Explanations

The relationship between the structure of the international system and the individual state as an agent for change is a fundamental theoretical question.[39] While the two extremes in this discussion—Russian policy change as the result of changes in the international environment or as the result of a conscious effort by the state to change the international environment—are inadequate as a description of reality, the discussion here seeks a way to balance the two.

Chapter 8 examines the 1999 and 2001 shifts in Russian Central Asian policy from the angle of four different groups of explanations. Without diving too deeply into theories of foreign policy change or international relations theory, and without attempting to test hypotheses, these explanations are used to shed light on why Russian policy changed in the way it did. They are: (a) the *international structure* explanation; b) the *instrumental* explanation; (c) the *institutional rivalry* explanation; and (d) the *socialization* explanation. They all view the state as the major actor in foreign policy, but using varying theoretical premises they explain policy change differently.

The first explanation views international conditions as having the greatest explanatory strength. According to the basic premises of classical realism and neo-realism theories, a state's policy and position in the international system are determined by its powers and capabilities compared to those of other states. Realist thinkers usually analyse the international system and its change rather than the foreign policy changes of individual states. In this study, realist theories are used as an inspiration for creating an explanation of the policy change of one single state—Russia. Kenneth Waltz has said that the economic and technological basis of the state will define its military power and its place among other states.[40] In a 1981 study of Soviet foreign policy, Waltz called for attention to be focused 'on the Soviet Union's situation rather than on her motives' or 'on the outcomes of her actions rather than her often disturbing behavior'.[41] The first explanation thus emphasizes the international structure, which is characterized as anarchic, where questions of power, capacity and the balance between states set the conditions for individual states and define the limits of government policy. The weak position of Russia in the present international balance of states and in Central Asia thus sets the limits of Russian foreign policy. The government of a weak state, such as Russia, reacts to events without having the capacity to exert influence, while a strong state may be proactive and able to influence the rules without necessarily changing the basic character of the system.

The second explanation regards the state as an autonomous and unitary actor. Policy is an instrument of the state for international change and influence. It also ascribes to the actor a certain rationality as a basic characteristic, and the state is assumed to have a fixed set of preferences and to behave in order to maximize the attainment of these preferences. The state is expected to follow its self-interest in an effort to increase gains (absolute or relative). In order for a government to evaluate gains and losses, a general understanding can be assumed to exist of what the strategic values and goals of the state are. This approach explains policy change as a reformulation by the state leadership of its strategic goals, tactics and instruments.

Although the third explanation accepts the state as the major actor, it explains policy as the outcome of a contest between different groups with vested interests. The explanation indicates institutional rivalry and has its roots in the bureaucratic model, which Graham Allison elegantly formulated in 1971.[42] The state is not a unitary actor, and policy is the result of the priorities of those institutions or groups which prevail at the time.

The fourth explanation indicates a process where Russia finds it to be in its own interests to be drawn into an international and institutional framework of accepted norms and rules of behaviour. Structures are to be understood here as social institutions in the form of international regimes and norms and rules instead of material values such as 'military power'. In the late 1980s Joseph Nye introduced 'learning' as an important factor,[43] and Robert Keohane wrote that international regimes can affect both the capabilities and the interests of states: they can alter bureaucratic practices or habits; promote an understanding of cause-and-effect relations; alter ideas about the legitimacy and value of practices; become embedded in higher-level normative networks; increase the political salience of certain issues; change the balance of political influence in domestic politics; and enhance the political or administrative capacity of government or non-governmental organizations in countries.[44]

This explanation has its roots in both neo-liberal institutionalist and constructivist theories. States change their values and norms by participating in international cooperation and multilateral institutions. Thus, states find that there are potential gains from cooperation as well as possible costs if they violate norms, rules and commitments. These specific norms, rules and commitments also influence state behaviour. Moreover, a state such as Russia makes cost-benefit calculations but may also take into account the wider implications or longer-term costs of non-compliance.[45] Once states accept the long-term benefits of participating in an international legal system, the idea of obligation and the normative nature of rules can be given tangible form. It is the existence of shared interests, common values and expectations that matters.[46] Constructivists stress that the behaviour of states changes with their practice of normative structures. As Alexander Wendt writes, the first steps may be motivated by egoistic reasons, but cooperation and the practice of actors may, in the best case, transform essentially egoistic reasoning into collective identity.[47]

The socializing explanation thus indicates that a state makes decisions in order to fall in line with what could be expected of a state—in this instance Russia—which wants to be on a par with and cooperate with Western states and participate as an equal in the international community.

These four explanations are not mutually exclusive but instead complement each other. Yet the explanatory force of one or other may vary over time, as the discussion below demonstrates.

What Is Central Asia?

Central Asia is defined in this study as the four states of Tajikistan, Uzbekistan, Kyrgyzstan and Turkmenistan.[48] This follows the Soviet definition of Central Asia, which excluded Kazakhstan. It roughly covers the territories of the former khanates of Bukhara, Khiva and Kokand. They were latecomers to the Russian Empire. In the 1860s Russia conquered parts of the Kokand Khanate and set up a Russian administration with a centre in Tashkent. The Bukhara Emirate (consisting of large parts of present-day Uzbekistan and Tajikistan) and the Khiva Khanate (located in present-day Turkmenistan and part of Uzbekistan) continued as independent principalities, although they became de facto Russian protectorates in the 1870s. While southern Kazakhstan, around the Syrdarya river and the cities of Chimkent and Dzhambul, can also be regarded as Central Asia proper, Kazakhstan is not included in the analysis.

The Bukhara Emirate and the Khiva Khanate existed until the early 1920s. Bukhara was the largest and strongest. It was protected in the east by the mountains of the Pamir and in the west by the vast deserts of Kyzylkum and Karakum. The emirate was made up of two quite distinct parts. In western Bukhara life was organized on the plains flanking the great rivers, the Zarafshan and the Amudarya (the Oxus of the ancient Greeks). In the eastern mountainous part of the emirate, settlements were concentrated in the narrow valleys along the rivers and streams. When Bukhara was incorporated into the Soviet Union, the Tajik territories became an autonomous oblast within an Uzbek republic administered from Tashkent, remaining so until 1929 when Tajikistan gained the status of a Soviet Socialist Republic. After the break up of the Soviet Union, Tajikistan and Uzbekistan remained, as an inheritance from their history, closely locked into each other's security. The Kokand Khanate, which appeared in the late eighteenth century and was incorporated into the Russian Empire in the 1870s, included the Fergana Valley and thereby parts of the territories of present-day Uzbekistan, Kyrgyzstan and Tajikistan.

Afghanistan is discussed in this study as an area directly relevant to the development of Central Asia. After the break up of the Soviet Union, the independent Uzbekistan, Tajikistan and Kyrgyzstan became highly vulnerable to developments in Afghanistan, while Turkmenistan managed, until September 2001, to keep out of the maelstrom emanating from Afghanistan. Turkmenistan went its own way, declaring its neutrality and cutting its contacts with the outside world, including the other Central Asian states. Although Turkmenistan managed to avoid the worst effects of the Afghan turmoil, it did not remain unaffected. In the future, after the rigid control of Turkmen society is gone, Turkmenistan may become more directly involved in the political development of the region. Taking the proximity of Afghanistan into consideration, these four Central Asian states, together with northern Afghanistan, may be regarded as a 'regional security complex'.

A security complex has been defined as 'a group of states whose primary security concerns link together sufficiently closely that their national securities cannot realistically be considered apart from one another'.[49] The states in a regional complex are locked into common security concerns and linked to each other in such a way that the actions of one state to advance its security are likely to have consequences for other parts of the complex. The factor of radical Islamism is taken here to be one major common denominator in this security complex, that is, radical Islamism as a perceived or real threat to security. Thus, this study pays close attention to radical Islamism as a factor crucial to the dynamics of the development of security in the Central Asian region.

Special attention is paid here to Tajikistan. It is not as large and powerful a state as Uzbekistan, but it has become a key state for the security of the region and for Russia's multilateral security arrangement, the Collective Security Treaty (CST) of 1992. Tajikistan is vulnerable because it borders Afghanistan, and fragile as a consequence of the civil war of 1992–97, yet its geographical proximity to Afghanistan and Uzbekistan gives it the potential to be a key channel for countering influences from these countries. This is especially so with regard to Afghanistan. Russia, after 1998, increased its support for the remaining ethnic Tajik-based wing of the anti-Taliban Northern Alliance, and the Tajik leadership became a strong supporter of Putin's anti-terrorist agenda of 1999. It is therefore of special interest to study how relations between Russia and Tajikistan were influenced by the post-11 September situation when the dynamics of the entire region shifted under the impact of the US-led anti-terrorist coalition.

The Structure of the Book

Part I of this volume gives the background to Putin's policy. Chapter 2 presents the Russian conquest of Central Asia and chapter 3 Russia's policy under Boris Yeltsin after the break up of the Soviet Union, when Russia lost Central Asia. Part II analyses the changes of policy in Central Asia under Vladimir Putin. Chapter 4 deals with policy after 1999, when terrorism became a top priority for Russia's Central Asia policy and Russia aimed to resist the growing US presence. Chapter 5 analyses the policy shift of September 2001 when Putin extended his anti-terrorist agenda to include the USA as a partner. The chapter traces the contours of a new Russian foreign policy after September 2001. Part III is an analysis of the factors behind Russian foreign policy making. Chapter 6 discusses possible Russian internal factors. Chapter 7 analyses the dynamics of the domestic scene in Central Asian countries as a factor for Russian policy change in the future. Chapter 8 summarizes the chapters on the change of Russian policy, presents four possible explanations, relates the policy changes to the issue of the overall revision of Russian foreign policy, and discusses the possible impact of developments in Central Asia on Russian policy towards the West.

PART I

BACKGROUND

2

CENTRAL ASIA GAINED
The Russian Conquest

In the 1860s, after the Crimean War, Russia set out on a military expansion into Central Asia, which surpassed any previous Russian conquest of territory.[1] It took place against the background of a growing British presence in Asia, including Central Asia, Russia's defeat in the Crimean War and a Russian domestic crisis, which led to strong demands for economic and political reform. Russia advanced into Central Asia and took Tashkent in 1865. Although Russia officially had a policy of non-intervention in the internal affairs of the independent khanates, and Khiva and Bukhara formally remained independent state entities until the early 1920s, they became de facto Russian protectorates in the 1870s. The Kokand Khanate was subsumed into the Russian Empire in 1876.

Three sets of questions are discussed in this chapter. First, what made Russia expand into Central Asia? It is true that Russia had been constantly expanding its territory since the sixteenth century. Yet, how is the conquest of large Central Asian territories in a short period of time at what was a moment of weakness to be explained? Second, what were the main factors behind this expansion? Was it the result of government policy, or, as is often claimed, the result of insubordinate officers? Third, how did Russia influence and control Bukhara when it officially pursued a policy of non-intervention in Bukhara's internal affairs?

The Bukhara Emirate along the Zerafshan Valley and the Khiva Khanate on the lower stretches of the Amudarya River each had long histories. At the end of the eighteenth century a third khanate, the Kokand Khanate, was consolidated in the Fergana Valley after taking control of Kazakh and Kyrgyz tribes and building fortifications along the Syrdarya, Chu and Ili rivers.[2] The Bukhara Emirate—which included the famous religious and trading centres, the cities of Bukhara and Samarkand—was the largest khanate with a population of almost 3 million people out of a total Central Asian population of 5 million in the mid-nineteenth century (Khiva's and Kokand's populations were 0.5 million and 1.5 million, respectively).[3] Early on, Bukhara had become Russia's most important trading partner among the khanates. At the beginning of the nineteenth century the Kokand Khanate conquered Tashkent, which was by then an independent city state and as important a trade and political centre as Bukhara. No distinct borders existed between the khanates. Beyond them, and especially to the south and east of Bukhara, were small principalities that were to different degrees dependent or semi-dependent on the larger khanates.

Factors behind Russia's Policy of Expansion into Central Asia

Step by step over 150 years Russia built fortifications and expanded defence lines that took it closer to Central Asia. Scholars have pointed to a continuity in Russian policy towards Central Asia from the time when Tsar Peter I sent an expedition to Khiva in 1717. The expedition had been part of a fact-finding mission for the tsar's future India project. Its purpose was to force the khanate to recognize Russian suzerainty and permit the stationing of Russian troops there.[4] The expedition failed and all its members were slaughtered. In the 1820s, Russia began its expansion from Omsk and Semipalatinsk and the empire expanded deeper into the Kazakh Steppes during the 1830s–50s.[5]

Its expansion brought Russia into military conflict with Kokand. As the Soviet scholar V. V. Bartold wrote more than 100 years later, efforts to reconcile Russia and Kokand were impossible at that time: the Russian Government had to make the choice either to completely give up its power over the steppes or to force out the Kokands.[6] In 1847 Russia established the fortification at Raim, at the delta of the Syrdarya, which opened the way to both Khiva and Kokand for the Russian military. By 1853 the Russians had already reached Ak-Mechet (renamed Perovsk) and established a chain of fortifications along the lower Syrdarya. In 1854 the territory was conquered and the Russian fortress (and town) was named Vernyi (now Almaty) in the Semirechye in what is today eastern Kazakhstan.

The Crimean War of 1854–56 slowed the process. However, on 20 December 1863 the Tsar confirmed a plan for advancing south, and this became official government policy in the spring of 1864. This was followed by a wave of intense Russian conquest during the 1860s–1880s even deeper into Central Asia.

Several factors combine to explain Russia's policy shift towards military expansion into Central Asia in the 1860s. These factors are grouped into political–strategic factors and domestic factors, in particular economic interests, in the analysis below.[7]

Political–Strategic Factors

In his famous dispatch of 21 November–3 December 1864, Russian Foreign Minister Alexander Gorchakov wrote to the heads of the European powers in an effort to explain why Colonel Mikhail Chernaev was encamped with his troops outside Tashkent. The argument he used referred to the security situation at the border, which forced Russian troops to take measures:

> The position of Russia in Central Asia is that of all civilized States which are brought into contact with half savage, nomad populations, possessing no fixed social organization. In such cases it always happens that the more civilized State is forced, in the interests of the security of its frontier and its commercial relations, to exercise a certain ascendancy over those whom their turbulent and unsettled character make most undesirable neighbours. First there are raids and acts of pillage to put down. To put a stop to them, the tribes on the frontier have to be reduced to a state of more or less perfect submission.

He continued: 'Like the United States in America, France in Africa, Holland in her colonies, and England in East India' Russia was driven 'less out of ambition than absolute necessity' down a path 'where it is extremely difficult to stand pat'.[8]

There were several aspects to Russian security concerns. Robbery of caravans and raids along the borders were permanent problems, especially in the initial stages of Russian expansion, and had motivated the Russian conquest of the Kazakh Steppe between 1824 and 1854. Kazakh nomads, who were nominally Russian vassals, raided both the Russian frontier and caravans trading between Russia and Central Asia. Russian expansion into the Kazakh Steppe aggravated tensions with the Khiva Khanate by raising the problem of conflicting Russian and Kokand claims to authority over the Kazakh tribes between the Caspian Sea and the lower Syrdarya. In 1839–40 Russia launched an unsuccessful offensive against Khiva. Russia pushed further and further into Central Asian territory.

Another crucial aspect of security concerned the two Russian extensions of its lines of defence linked to its advance south. Until the mid-1850s Russia built fortifications to defend it against attacks from the steppe. These lines of defence stretched from the Caspian Sea to Orenburg along the Ural River; to Ishim; along the river Irtysh to Semipalatinsk; and down to Vernyi. The so-called Orenburg Line and the West Siberian Line were separated from each other by 900 kilometres of barren steppe, and would have to be connected in order to create a safe border. This became even more necessary as Russia expanded south along the two extensions.

In March 1863 preparations started on a plan of action to connect the Orenburg line and the West Siberian line. The plan was worked out by the so-called Special Committee (Osobyi komitet), the highest policy making body regarding Central Asian affairs, and signed by the Tsar on 20 December 1863.[9] Military operations were initiated in the spring of 1864. Russia's conquest of the Caucasus that year made penetration into Central Asia easier. Converging columns from the east and the west took Turkestan and Dzhambul (now Taraz) and met in Chimkent (now Shymkent) in October 1864—thereby joining the lines of defence. In this way Russia gained control of 'the granary of the entire country between the Chu River and the Syrdarya'.[10] The conquest in June 1865 of Tashkent, however, was an expansion beyond this connecting line. Tashkent was regarded as crucial to the defence of Russia's new border and Russian control over the Central Asian independent khanates. However, the conquest of Tashkent had not been included in the tsar's decree. Foreign Minister Gorchakov, who sought to justify the Russian advance to an international audience played down the responsibility of the government, thereby creating the myth that the officers on the ground were responsible for the expansion in Central Asia—that they had exceeded their instructions to gain distinction and advance their career. However, it is highly unlikely that Russian officers would have advanced unless there had been a basic consensus over the final objective, and had they not expected credit for achieving it.

Following the military expansion, Russia's security considerations gradually shifted south. Russia's expansion into Central Asia in the 1860s can therefore be explained as a kind of compensation in the East for the losses in the West. As mentioned above, the Treaty of Paris (30 March 1856), which ended the war, had deprived the Russian Empire of the importance it had gained in Europe at the time of Catherine II and still enjoyed under Nicholas I. The treaty seriously undermined Russia's imperial role and the prestige of its government. The conquest of Central Asia reflected a psychological hunger for compensation since Central Asia offered an opportunity at a time when Europe was closed to Russian influence.[11] It made it possible for Russia to regain military–political prestige and to better protect the empire's holdings in Asia against attacks by the state which had allied itself against Russia in the west—Britain. Russian officials and military representatives argued that Russia should use its influence in Central Asia as a means to put pressure on Britain and force it to maintain a restrained policy in relation to Russia and Europe in general.[12]

Britain's expansion in Asia is considered a crucial factor behind the Russian policy in Central Asia.[13] The Russian and British Governments each feared the expansion of the other in Asia. India was Britain's 'jewel in the crown' and Britain feared a Russian advance towards Afghanistan, and thereby towards India. Russia feared British expansion into Central Asia. At the beginning of the nineteenth century Britain had cast its eyes over the Caspian Sea region. As early as 1810 the commander of the Russian troops in Georgia informed St Petersburg that the British representative in Teheran had asked permission from the Shah to go to Enzel, Astrabad and other places along the south Caspian Sea coast to choose a place for building ships.[14] The request was turned down, but Britain repeated the request in the 1830s and again in the 1850s. The first Anglo-Afghan War (1838–42) cut Britain's contacts with Afghanistan for several years. However, during the Crimean War Britain established diplomatic contacts with the Afghan Emir and the Anglo-Afghan agreement, signed in 1855, was very favourable to Britain. In the 1830s and 1840s the penetration of British products into the markets of Central Asia increased. By the time the first Anglo-Afghan War ended, the Russian Government had become seriously worried about the activities of the British in Central Asia.[15] Both Russia and Britain tried to exploit contradictions between, and within, the khanates in order to gain influence.[16] Russia feared that the weak khanates would be easy targets for the British. British and Turkish agents tried to stir up anti-Russian feeling, and Russia tried to squeeze the British out.[17] In 1855 the Russian commander of the Siberian contingent, G. Kh. Gasford, warned about British support for an offensive by Kokand forces against Russian positions. At the same time, Russia exploited Bukhara's fear of British support for the Afghan Khan, who was trying to conquer territories on the left bank of the Amudarya, where Uzbeks and Tajiks lived who had previously been subordinated to the Bukhara Emirate.[18]

The British expansion can thus be viewed as a crucial factor behind Russia's expansion. However, the presence of Britain in Asia also made the Russian Government more cautious when expanding into Central Asia, to avoid provoking a British reaction. Even so, the conflicting interests of Russia and Britain pushed them to the brink of war in the spring of 1885, after Russia's capture of Merv.[19]

Domestic Factors

Economic Conditions. Like Britain, Russia tried to expand its trade with and exports of manufactured goods to the Central Asian markets. To Soviet scholars, economic interests were the major factor behind Russia's expansion into Central Asia. They analysed the Tsar's policy in accordance with Soviet theories on capitalism and classical imperialism, and thus drew the conclusion that the quest for markets and for natural resources was the determining factor. Most Western scholars denied that economic considerations were behind the Russian expansion.[20] Their scepticism seems to be confirmed by statistics. As the German scholar Dietrich Geyer argues, only later did economic interests become an important factor. Initially, they played no major role in the expansion.[21] A Russian study in the 1990s came to the same conclusion by analysing government documents from the late nineteenth century, which referred to political factors, first and foremost rivalry with Britain. Nevertheless, as the authors of the study point out, this does not exclude the possibility that economic factors also played a role.[22]

A strong component of economic interest certainly did exist. Articles, studies and speeches from the 1850s arguing in favour of expansion into Central Asia referred to the economic benefits. In the early nineteenth century, when Russian merchants had just begun to penetrate Central Asia, they were met with discrimination in the Central Asian khanates.[23] The Russian Government therefore placed a strong emphasis on improving trade relations. Military representatives also used economic arguments when pleading for a more active Russian policy in Central Asia. The US scholar Seymour Becker therefore seems to be on safe ground when he argues that Russia's aims in Central Asia in the 1840s and 1850s can best be described as both political and economic.[24]

The economic history of relations between Russia and Central Asia demonstrates a long-term economic interest in the region.[25] Regular exchange of commodities by means of caravans date back to at least the eighth century and were highly developed between the eighth and tenth centuries and the thirteenth and fourteenth centuries (the periods of the Khazar Kaganate and the Golden Horde).[26] In 1557, the year after the Russian conquest of the Astrakhan Khanate, both Bukhara and Kharizm sent embassies to Ivan IV (1553–84) to ask for permission to trade freely in Russia. The main concern of the Russian embassies in Central Asia in the seventeenth century was commerce. At that time almost no Russians were trading in Central Asia. Instead, Bukharan and Khivan merchants carried their goods to Astrakhan, Samara, Kazan, Nizhnii Novgorod, Yaroslavl and Moscow. The Bukhara Emirate was especially important. It was Russia's largest Central Asian trading partner and also acted as middleman in Russia's trade with the small principalities in the Amudarya Valley, in Afghanistan and in north-west India.[27]

Russian industrial production started to expand during the first quarter of the nineteenth century. The cotton industry in the central parts of Russia was first to expand while industrial production lagged behind. Russia's industry was less developed than in the rest of Europe, and its products could not compete in European markets. In the 1830s, Russian exports of cotton textiles to the USA started to decline.[28] While Russia exported mainly agricultural produce to the West, it exported manufactured metal and textile products, leather products, and so on, to Central Asia.[29] Against this background, the Central Asian markets became of interest to a growing number of Russian industrialists and merchants.

In 1836 Tsar Nicholas I set up a Special Committee to investigate the conditions for trade relations between Russia and Asia, particularly Persia, Asian Turkey and other neighbouring countries in the East. In the same year a specialist on trade with Asia, General A. I. Verigin, requested that unrestricted economic contacts with the Central Asian khanates be secured, since Russia faced no competition from European powers there.[30] However, following the British expansion in Asia, by 1830 British products were finding their way to northern Persia and Bukhara. At this point, British textiles were only a minor threat to Russian products on the Central Asian market but, as the British influence in Asia expanded, the threat became more real. In the 1840s British and Indian exports to Bukhara, particularly of textiles, increased. The Russian Department for Foreign Trade watched this development with concern. The market for British goods expanded because prices were kept low. Britain's active policy of penetrating the Central Asian market worried the Russian Government deeply. Therefore, in 1841–42 the Tsar sent an expedition to Bukhara under K. F. Butenev.[31]

Over the following years Central Asia received a great deal of attention in the policy discussions of the Russian Government. Several Russian specialists pointed out the advantages of developing trade relations with the Central Asian khanates.[32] In 1850, G. P. Nebolsin came out strongly in favour of an active Russian policy of developing trade with Central Asia in his *Statisticheskoe obozrenie o vneshnei torgovle Rossii* ('Statistical Overview of Russian Foreign Trade').[33] Although Central Asia's share (including Kazakhstan) in Russia's total imports was only about 2.5 per cent at the time, government and business people claimed that its potential was huge. Moreover, after the Manchu Government closed its border to Russian merchants at the beginning of the nineteenth century, Russia's access to the markets of western China was through Central Asia. The restoration of direct trade relations with Chinese Xinjiang was one of the goals of the Tsar's foreign policy.[34]

By the early 1850s interest in Central Asia had grown in Russian business circles. Trade associations (*tovarishchestva*) were created. The end of the Crimean War brought high expectations of the benefits from trade and economic exchange with Central Asia. Although these expectations were only partially realized, Russia's exports of metal and textiles to Central Asia increased dramatically between 1858 and 1859, while exports to Europe fell.[35]

After the reforms of 1861 the Russian economy expanded. Petitions and reports were sent to the ministries of finance and foreign affairs on 'the creation in Central Asia of conditions favourable for Russian merchants'.[36] Business representatives saw good prospects for Russian trade and pleaded for government measures in order to improve conditions for their trade in Central Asia.[37] They pointed out that Russian merchants were discriminated against with regard to customs and movement, while conditions for Central Asian traders in Russia were much better.

The American Civil War of 1861–65 reduced the export of raw cotton to Russia. Until then, the United States had been Russia's largest single supplier. There was therefore an urgent need for raw cotton for the Russian textile industry, prices rose and Russia had to look for other sources. In this context, Central Asia became more interesting and the Russian media started to speak of Central Asia in terms of a base for Russia's supply of raw cotton, although Becker claims that: 'Although Central Asian cotton had acquired a new importance for Russia on the eve of the conquest, and considerable sentiment existed for an advance into Central Asia to protect and promote Russian manufacturing and trading interests, the influence of these factors on policy-formation was minimal'.[38]

Ideological Perceptions and the Policy Making Process. As early as 1827 the Tsar created an Asian Committee as the supreme body for determining state policy with regard to Asia. In 1847 this was replaced by the Special Committee, led by the Tsar himself, as the highest policy making body dealing with Central Asian affairs.[39] The Tsar was the ultimate decision maker.

There was no such thing as public opinion with regard to policy towards Central Asia: the general population had neither an opinion nor a voice. The Russian media, however, began to pay a great deal of attention to Central Asia. In the early 1850s academics, members of the government, civil servants, representatives of the armed forces, merchants and people from business circles all urged the government to turn its attention to the opening up of Central Asia to economic penetration.

Although Central Asia was not given much attention in the political–ideological debate, there was a general consensus in support of expansion. Conservative ideas dominated the debate, and conservative ideologues presented the most developed foreign policy concepts. To conservatives, nationalists and pan-Slavists the importance of Central Asia derived from the role it played in European affairs.[40] By itself it played only a subsidiary role. Fyodor Dostoevsky, for example, applauded the victories in Central Asia because they helped to dispel disappointments on the European front and the depressing news concerning the inner state of the Russian Empire.[41] The general conviction was that only the West mattered. Asia was only a means to increase Russia's status in the West. History was written in Europe, not in Asia. Aware of Russia's humiliation in the Crimea, Slavophile thinkers called for Russia to push its historic advantage in the East.[42]

There were other voices advocating the importance of Central Asia, and claiming that Russia's future was in Asia. Nonetheless, few believed that the Russian Empire's existence was at stake over events in Asia.[43] 'The English tremble over India, but need we tremble over Tashkent? Russia would remain Russia even without Central Asia but what would England be without India?' wrote the newspaper *Moskovskie vedomosti* in 1879.[44] It was not until the early twentieth century that the Eurasianists would identify Russia fully or partly with Asia and view Central Asia as highly important to Russia.

The liberals shared the belief that expansion into Central Asia was necessary and demanded the conquest of further territories—Khiva, Bukhara, Merv and even northern Afghanistan—citing, again, the economic benefits[45] but also that Russia had a 'civilizing mission' in Central Asia. The idea that Russia brought 'civilization' and European values to Asia was especially strong among the liberals.[46]

The government was not a monolithic bloc of ideological allies. Instead, 'liberal, conservative and Slavophile proclivities or convictions gave rise to controversial opinions'.[47] Nevertheless, by the 1850s a basic consensus had developed within the government concerning Russia's objectives in Central Asia, taking into consideration commercial interests, military–strategic interests, and the wish to deny influence to Britain.

It is interesting to note that the strongest advocates of domestic reform in the government also strongly advocated a policy of expansion in Central Asia. Dmitrii Milyutin, Minister of War from 1861, and Foreign Minister Gorchakov are both good examples. However, they disagreed over tactics—and especially the form and the timing of an advance. Neither of them was as impatient and hot-headed as some of the Russian officers on the ground, who advocated direct military conquest. Instead both Milyutin and Gorchakov favoured a policy of gaining control of Central Asian territories by diplomatic and economic means. If military pressure had to be used, they argued, direct force should be avoided. Nonetheless, while Gorchakov favoured a more cautious policy, Milyutin preferred a much more straightforward one.

Disagreement over policies, tactics and timing caused a certain amount of wavering within the government. As a result, there was some room for manoeuvre, and the officers on the ground took advantage of this. They considered that they knew the situation, the risks and the possibilities better than the government and acted in the conviction that they would find support from their superiors. If successful, they would be decorated, as indeed Chernaev was when he conquered Tashkent. Seymour Becker explains: 'Throughout the period of conquest the Russian Government persisted in adhering to the principles of Gorchakov's circular, although in practice St Petersburg often willingly sanctioned *faits accomplis* that departed from those principles. The end result was a compromise between the cautious and the expansive schemes of the military'. Becker continues: 'Although they [Alexander II and Prince Gorchakov] consistently refused to sanction in advance military and political moves that involved great risk or great expenditures, they applauded enthusiastically when a daring commander like Chernaev took a risk and achieved success with the forces available'.[48]

Although Russia was economically weak and in need of domestic reform (and such reforms were introduced in the immediate post-Crimean war period), no one within the government doubted that Russia was bound to regain its status as a great power. Those very people who urged reform wanted an expansion of Russia's influence in Central Asia and were preparing for a strong Russian return to the international scene.

The Conquest of Tashkent

Close readings of the development of the Russian Government's decisions, statements and measures with regard to Central Asia confirm that, while there was disagreement over tactics, a basic consensus existed that Russia should take control of Central Asia.[49]

The new, expanded Russian interest in Central Asia was reflected when, in 1856, the Asian Department of the Foreign Ministry commissioned studies of the Central Asian khanates and their economic relations with Russia. When Alexander Gorchakov replaced K. B. Nesselrode as foreign minister that year, he appointed Kovalevskii head of the Asian Department and, under Kovalevskii's leadership, the department made it its task to develop Russia's economic relations with Central Asia and increase Russian influence in the region.[50]

On 16 October 1857 Tsar Alexander II approved Foreign Minister Gorchakov's proposal to send N. P. Ignatiev on a fact-finding mission to Khiva and Bukhara. Ignatiev was a specialist on Asia and, as a former military attaché in London, also familiar with the British political debate on Asia. His delegation, which was the first since 1841–42, made a considerable contribution to Russia's knowledge of Khiva and Bukhara. His instructions from Kovalevskii reflected the three main purposes of the mission: (a) to analyse the situation in Central Asia; (b) to strengthen the influence of Russia in Khiva and Bukhara and improve trade with the khanates; and (c) to prevent the penetration of British goods into Central Asia.[51] The specific request that Ignatiev brought to the Emir of Bukhara included the freeing of Russian captives, permission for Russian vessels to sail freely on the Amudarya, and improved conditions for commercial relations between the two states.[52]

Ignatiev returned to Russia in December 1858 arguing in favour of offensive action in Central Asia. He was of the opinion that there was no purpose in signing formal trade agreements with the Bukhara Emirate since it did not respect international agreements or abide by domestic regulations. He drew the conclusion that it was time to move from diplomatic negotiations with the Central Asian governments to direct pressure in order to open up the Central

Asian market to Russia. Ignatiev claimed that Russia should use the British experience of colonial wars in the East and subordinate the Central Asian khanates to Russia. Already, in his letter to the Russian Foreign Ministry of May 1858, he had argued that Russia should exploit tensions between the khanates, support the Emir of Bukhara against the Khan of Kokand, and make an advance to connect its Syrdarya line of defence with the West Siberian line by conquering Turkestan and Tashkent. In 1858, he also called for an opening of the way for Russian ships up the Amudarya River all the way to Afghanistan. This, he said, would strengthen Russian economic and military–political positions, and 'make England value our friendship'.[53] Moreover, for the first time since the Crimean War an official in such a responsible position decisively recommended an alliance with Bukhara for the purpose of partitioning Kokand and pushing Russia's state borders beyond Tashkent.[54] In its initial response to Ignatiev the Foreign Ministry turned down the proposals for an alliance with Bukhara and the advance of the Russian border.[55]

Ignatiev's mission gave the Russian Government considerable knowledge of the Central Asian khanates, and it drew the conclusion from his analyses that the khanates would be feeble adversaries.[56] An open proponent of direct military force was Chernaev, who was to conquer Tashkent some years later. In 1858 he was only at the beginning of his career, and he argued in favour of a broad offensive against the Kokand Khanate. 'Did we really come here to comfortably settle down and make business? For this there is plenty of land and more than enough land in Russia. We need this territory to spread our influence in Central Asia … Why this outdated embassy to Khiva? … We are dwelling on details and losing sight of the main idea.'[57]

The Governors-General of Orenburg and Siberia, A. A. Katenin and G. Kh. Gasford, strongly supported a 'firm policy' in Central Asia. In December 1858 Katenin proposed a plan of action for Russian expansion, which included, first and foremost, an offensive against the Kokand Khanate by establishing a fortress in Dzhulek in order to prepare to take Turkestan, Chimkent, Aulie-Ata, and, finally, Tashkent. He also suggested strengthening the Aral Sea flotilla building a new fortress at Embe on the way to Khiva.[58] Katenin's plan had been worked out by a special commission in Orenburg, which included officers and officials from the Orenburg Provincial Government; Ignatiev and some of his colleagues; and Chernaev.[59] Although there were different opinions within this group, the majority agreed that the Russian lines had to be connected, that special attention had to be paid to Tashkent, and that fortifications should be built at Dzhulek as a first step in the conquest of Tashkent.

In January 1859 a 'consultative meeting' took place at the highest level of state to discuss the suggestions presented by the Ignatiev mission and the Orenburg Government, including Katenin's proposal. Foreign Minister Gorchakov; Minister of War N. O. Sukhozanet; the Governors-General of Orenburg and Siberia; the head of the Asian Department, Kovalevskii; and, of course, Ignatiev participated. The meeting expressed support for the development of Russian trade on the eastern bank of the Caspian Sea, as suggested by Ignatiev, but was against any expansion by military means towards the Central Asian khanates. It formed the opinion that Khiva and Kokand should be subordinated to Russian influence and that trade should be expanded in Central Asia. However, the proposals for a military offensive were considered premature and turned down with the words that the government 'at present does not have any aggressive acts for this part of Asia'.[60] Instead, Ignatiev proposed another plan of action, which was adopted.

Ignatiev's plan included a call: to strengthen Russia's relations with the Emir of Bukhara 'in order to prevent British involvement'; to exploit internal tensions within Khiva and the enmity between the Khiva and Bukhara Khanates; to incorporate the Kazakhs and Karakalpaks of Khiva into the Russian Empire; to conquer the town of Kungad and set up a Russian administration there; to end Kokand's hold over the towns of Turkestan and Tashkent; and, finally, to establish Russia's domination of Central Asian markets. He suggested that military operations against the Kokand Khanate be postponed until 'the time when it is possible to continue the Syrdarya line without meeting the united forces of Kokand and Bukhara and any special publicity to our offensive move'.[61] Thus, in principle, Katenin and Ignatiev agreed to take control of parts of Kokand, including Tashkent, in order to expand Russian influence and control southwards. They disagreed, however, on the timing of the use of military means.

The consultative meeting of January 1859 thus did not support immediate military action against the Central Asian khanates, but it clearly favoured Russian expansion into the area This 'cautious' policy by the Russian Government can be explained by Russia's fear, at the time, of provoking Britain in Asia.

In the early 1860s serious divisions continued within the Russian military and administrative leaderships concerning plans and action in Central Asia. The new Governor-General of Orenburg, A. P. Besak, supported the idea of a military offensive against Tashkent. Different papers and projects of the Tsarist administration mention Tashkent, Turkestan, Chimkent and Aulie-Ata as crucial to connecting the Syrdarya and West Siberia lines. On the other hand, the new Governor-General of West Siberia, Lieutenant General A. O. Dyugamel, appointed in February 1861, was opposed to all plans for further territorial conquests.[62] He warned that further military operations against the Kokand Khanate would undermine Russia's positions in Central Asia and called instead for the strengthening of existing positions, such as the fortress of Vernyi, and the opening of peaceful negotiations with the Kokand Khanate.

Opinions were also divided at government level. The Minister of War, Milyutin, did not exclude the use of military force or military conquest.[63] Foreign Minister Gorchakov preferred the use of diplomatic and economic means. Milyutin later wrote his memoirs, accusing Gorchakov of not paying enough attention to Asian affairs, of not getting to the heart of issues, and of ascribing every military operation to the wilfulness of local commanders and their eagerness for decorations and rewards.[64]

Thus, very different views were to be found within the administration. Even so, military expansion became the policy outcome.[65] The Tsar's decisions of March and December 1863 initiated a new era in Russian–Central Asian relations.[66] The plan prepared by Milyutin and confirmed in December 1863 argued that it was necessary to exploit the favourable situation indicated by the information collected by new expeditions to Central Asia in 1863—the state of domestic turmoil in Kokand and the war between Kokand and Bukhara—and to start a military offensive in spring 1864 in order to 'connect the lines'. In May 1864 Colonel Chernaev set out from Vernyi in the east, and in June Colonel Verevkin left Perovsk in the west. By the end of June they had taken Aulie-Ata and Turkestan and, in September, Chimkent. On 21 November 1864 Foreign Minister Gorchakov dispatched his famous circular to the European powers in order to minimize Western reaction to the Russian offensive.

The plan of action of December 1863 did not explicitly mention military conquest of Tashkent. On this issue there was still disagreement in the Russian Government. Gorchakov wanted Russian control of Tashkent but did not explicitly spell out direct military conquest. He proposed instead that Russia foment a revolt against Kokand in Tashkent and that, after that, Russian troops should enter Tashkent to guarantee the success of the rebels. His goal was a nominally independent Tashkent under Russian influence.[67] In June 1865 Chernaev's troops took control of Tashkent. With Tashkent now under Russian military control, disagreement continued within the Russian Government for several months as to whether the conquered Tashkent should be incorporated into the Russian Empire or constitute a 'neutral zone' under Russian influence. The issue was not resolved until July 1867, when Tashkent was, in reality, incorporated into the Russian Empire as a new administrative region, Turkestan, which consisted of the Russian conquests in Central Asia at the time. Russian policy from 1864 was the beginning of the end of the khanates' independence.

Policy towards the Bukhara Emirate after the Crimean War

The Russian Government had agreed that Tashkent under Russian control would serve as a buffer against surprise attacks from the khanates and a convenient base for further action in Central Asia with regard not only to the Kokand Khanate but also to the Bukhara Emirate. Russia had been playing on the contradictions and clashes between and within the khanates, waiting for the weakest party to turn to Russia for support.[68] Now Russia decided to take decisive measures against Bukhara—and three difficult years followed.

There had already been military clashes between Russian and Bukharan troops along the border in the steppes between the Syrdarya and Dzhizak when, in 1866, Russian troops invaded the emirate and conquered Irdzhar on the road to Samarkand and Khodzhent further to the east. Russian dominance of Bukhara was seen as a necessity by Moscow. There was no middle way, asserted one of the officers of the General Staff in a memorandum of July 1866. It was necessary 'either to take possession of the Central Asiatic khanates, or else to put the khans in such a position that they would not dare to take a step without the agreement of Russia'.[69] The Amudarya, rather than the Syrdarya, had now become the preferable southern border. In May 1866 Russian troops took

Khodzhent and in October 1866 Ura-Tyube and Dzhizak.

The external pressure on Bukhara from Russia increased internal contradictions within the emirate, and thereby the pressure on the emir. The Islamic clergy demanded stronger resistance to the Russians and issued a *fatwa*, of a 'holy war', against the Russian troops, while others within Bukhara wanted to regularize the situation with the Russians as soon as possible. In the autumn of 1867 Russian proposed a draft of a bilateral treaty with the Bukhara Emirate that the emir, after five months, refused to sign. Instead, he declared a holy war against Russia. When, in April 1868, Bukharan troops went on the offensive against the small principalities in the Zerafshan Valley, they weakened their own defence of the city of Samarkand by diverting the troops. Following a plan of action to take Samarkand that had been confirmed by the Russian Ministry of War, the new Governor-General and military commander of the newly organized Turkestan Government, General K. P. Kaufman crossed the river and conquered Samarkand using the pretext that Bukharan troops had not withdrawn from the Zerafshan Valley.[70] Bukharan troops capitulated in May 1868.

Thus, after two military campaigns against the Bukhara Emirate, a peace agreement was signed between Russia and Bukhara in June 1868. Russia demanded that the Emir of Bukhara recognize Russian territorial conquests; cede Khodzhent, Ura-Tyube and Dzhizak; open Bukhara up to privileges for Russian merchants on an equal footing with local merchants, and guarantee their security; and pay a huge sum of money as military reparations. As a guarantee that the money would be paid, Russia continued to occupy Samarkand and Kattakurgan. Because the Emir could not pay that amount specified, these areas were ceded to Russia and became the basis of the Zerafshan District of Russian Turkestan, formed in June 1868 and formalized in 1872.

Russia considered Samarkand to be highly important strategically for control of the Bukhara Emirate, since Samarkand supplied the city of Bukhara with water. The control of the water resources of the upper Zerafshan River was an important lever for influence. Kaufman wrote:

> Our possession of Samarkand, 'the Mittpunkt of the world' and the most important city in Central Asia in historical and religious regards, completely destroyed the dominant influence of the Bukharan Emir in this part of the Islamic world, and moreover made the city of Bukhara and its surroundings fully dependent on us with regard to water supply, since by the destruction of the dams at Zerafshan near Samarkand we would be able to reduce the city to a ruinous condition.[71]

Different opinions persisted in the Russian leadership over whether or not to take the emirate by force. The Russian Army prepared for an offensive against Bukhara but was not allowed to launch it.[72] The orders from St Petersburg to the Russian troops were to take firm action against Bukhara but avoid military confrontation. Both Milyutin and Gorchakov stressed, however, that its relations with the Bukhara Emirate were decisive for Russia's future position in Central Asia. Russia's treaty of 1868 with the Bukhara Emirate was formally a trade agreement and did not touch upon the issue of Bukhara's status as an independent state.[73] It gave Russia control, but without the formal right to intervene in domestic affairs. Since the emirate bordered on the British zone of influence, the Russian Government did not want to take further measures which would complicate relations with Britain at that time. The treaty gave Russia all the conquered territories (Khodzhent, Ura-Tyube, Dzhizak, Samarkand and Kattakurgan) and great commercial advantages (taxes on Russian goods reduced to 2.5 per cent, free passage across the khanate for Russian merchants, and the right to create commercial agencies)—as Hélène Carrère d'Encausse has said, it gave them 'everything that for almost three centuries Russia's envoys had been unable to obtain'.[74]

In March 1868 Russia signed a treaty with what remained of the Kokand Khanate. This treaty also included all the privileges for Russian merchants for which they had been calling. Kokand became a de facto Russian protectorate, although it formally remained an independent khanate for eight more years.[75] Thus, by 1868 Russia had gained substantial control of the two largest khanates. The smaller Khiva Khanate and the territories to the south-east of the Caspian Sea remained outside Russian control until Russia forced it to sign a treaty in 1873.

Russian Policy towards the Bukhara Emirate after the 1868 Treaty

Because of its geographical location the Bukhara Emirate was strategically important for Russia not only in relation to Afghanistan and the expanding influence of Britain but also for Russia's plans to conquer the Khiva Khanate. An important goal for Russian policy was to influence the Bukharan Emir in dealings with Khiva and Afghanistan without provoking a British reaction. Russia therefore chose to keep the Bukharan Emir in power after 1868 and to help him maintain control of his territory. To conquer the emirate was considered too costly and was thought likely to lead to too much bloodshed because of the strong anti-Russian feelings in Bukhara and the generally turbulent internal state of the emirate.[76] Against this background, the Russian Government preferred to help the emir bring order to his country.

Russia avoided intervening directly in the domestic affairs of the emirate, although there were repeated tensions between Bukhara and Tashkent, the political and administrative centre of Russian Turkestan, over several issues. The Emir flirted with the anti-Russian rulers of Afghanistan, Khiva and Turkey; the slave trade continued in Bukhara; and Russian merchants had difficulty expanding their businesses in the emirate. Inside the emirate discontent grew. Four-and-a-half years after the treaty was signed the Russian Governor of Turkestan therefore worked to have the treaty with Bukhara replaced by a new one, more favourable to Russia.[77] The Russian Government was cautious, however, wishing neither to strain Russia's finances and military manpower nor to provoke Britain.

In 1873 a second treaty was signed between Russia and Bukhara which had the official character of a treaty of friendship and dealt with commercial affairs. Formally, the Emirate maintained its sovereignty. In reality, it became a Russian protectorate without a foreign policy of its own. Russia left domestic policy to the emir but maintained the final say over top appointments.[78] This second treaty was more favourable to the Russian side but was not as far-reaching as the Russian treaty with Khiva. Bukhara was allowed to pursue own foreign relations, while the Khiva Khanate was deprived of this right. The Russian–Bukharan treaty restricted Bukharan *caranvanserais* to Russian Turkestan, instead of allowing them access to the whole of Russia as previously; opened up the Amudarya River to Russian vessels; allowed Russian subjects to engage in industry and to acquire land and property in Bukhara; and obliged the khanate to extradite fugitive Russian criminals. The slave trade in the khanate was abolished, although only on paper; the exchange of permanent envoys was arranged, in contrast to the ad hoc arrangements provided for in the previous treaty; and, last but not least, the Russian–Bukharan boundary of 1868 was reaffirmed.

The Emir of Bukhara 'voluntarily' submitted to Russian policy in 1873, when he realized how weak his position was in relation to his larger neighbour. As a vassal, Russia allowed him to conquer the small principalities to the east. The independent principalities of Shahrisabz and Kitab were incorporated in the emirate, as were Karategin and Darvaz.[79] Russia was happy to see the Emir strengthen his position, hoping this would reduce the risk of domestic turmoil in the khanate.[80] Russia gave Bukhara Chordzhui, which it had conquered from Khiva. Moreover, Russia helped the emir to stay in power when his own citizens revolted. Russian troops also crushed the revolt led by the feudal lords of Hisar and Shahrisabz, who had been waging a holy war against the Emir to free themselves from his rule.[81]

In May 1873 Russian troops invaded the Khiva Khanate. The Treaty of Amnest 1873 made Khiva a de facto Russian protectorate, explicitly forbidding an independent foreign policy.

The Kokand Khanate was abolished in 1876 when Russian troops intervened after it had erupted in domestic turmoil. In 1875, a revolt had started in the Fergana Valley in which the Muslim clergy played a leading role. The revolt spread and soon approached Tashkent. The clergy called for a holy war (*gazavat*) against Russia, and emissaries went to Bukhara, Khiva and Afghanistan to seek support for the struggle.[82] Russian troops invaded, and the Kokand Khanate was occupied and incorporated into Russia as the Fergana Region of Turkestan.[83] Russia's treaties with Bukhara and Khiva remained in force until 1917.

Russia further strengthened its control in the region in the 1880s expanding southwards towards Afghanistan over the territory of Turkmen tribes down to Merv. In 1884 Bukhara was included in Russia's customs frontier by an agreement signed between the two states, and Russian troops took control of Bukhara's borders with Afghanistan, which were now to be guarded by Russian troops and customs officials.[84] After the establishment of the Russian customs frontier on the Amudarya River in 1885, the Bukharan army was reduced under informal pressure from Russia.[85] Russian analysts had come to the conclusion that the army of the emir could not control the situation in the country.

In early 1895 Britain and Russia signed an agreement in London defining 'the Spheres of Influence of the Two Countries in the Region of the Pamirs'. According to the agreement Roshan, Shugnan and northern Vakhan, to the east of the Afghan–Bukharan border, would be transferred to the Bukhara Emirate, while southern Darvaz, on the left bank of the River Pyandzh, was to be transferred to Afghanistan. Russia gained direct control of the eastern Pamirs, and Russian garrisons were established in 1897–98 at Khorog in Shugnan and in two locations in Vakhan.[86]

Bukhara's role as a dependency of Russia did not increase its trade with Russia. Between 1868 and the mid-1880s trade did not rise much above the levels of the 1860s, at just over 10 million roubles per year,[87] and in the 1870s Russian merchants focused their attention on Tashkent, which soon overtook Bukhara as the commercial centre of Central Asia. The building of the Central Asian railway in 1886–88 did bring about an improvement: Bukhara's annual trade with Russia doubled in the first six years after the railway opened, and tripled between the early 1890s and the eve of World War I. The railway brought Russian merchants to Bukhara, although their activity was still restricted by a great many regulations imposed by the Bukharan Government.[88]

Nor did the treaties result in a Russian monopoly of Central Asian markets. In the period 1873–85, Russia's share in Bukhara's total foreign trade was only about one-third. Bukhara also traded with India, Afghanistan and Persia. In the 1870s English muslin, cotton prints, calico and brocade, as well as Indian tea and rice, were sold widely in Bukhara.[89]In 1887, one year after the opening of th e Central Asian railway, 83 per cent of Bukhara's exports went to Russia, but 63 per cent of its imports came from Britain.[90] By 1913 the corresponding figures were 88 per cent and 89 per cent.[91] Cotton accounted for about three-quarters of the total value of Bukhara's and Khiva's exports to Russia. Almost the entire cotton crop was exported to Russia, as it had been before the conquest.[92] By 1890 Central Asia had become the major supplier of cotton to Russia.[93]

Russia continued its policy of non-intervention in the domestic affairs of Bukhara. The tolerance of General Kaufman, Governor-General of Russian Turkestan, towards the autonomy of Bukhara can be explained by his conviction that the emirate would collapse sooner or later. He believed that the example of good government and material prosperity in Russian Turkestan would create stress and tensions within the khanates which they would not be able to survive, and therefore they would sooner or later be incorporated into the Russian Empire. Many Bukharans emigrated to Russian Turkestan.[94]

As a consequence of Russia's policy of non-interference in the domestic affairs of Bukhara, its isolation from the rest of the world increased. The emir's and the clergy's strong opposition to the modern world maintained Bukhara in its old-fashioned, feudal condition. The emir at first even opposed Russian suggestions that a postal system should be established and a railway built. Thus, Western influence on Bukhara before 1868 was limited to the few occasions when Bukharan merchants went to Russia and Russian merchants to Bukhara.

Khiva was even more isolated and almost completely unaffected by the passing of time. The decade following the 1873 treaties with Bukhara and Khiva have been called a period of Russian 'neglect' in its relations with them. Russia mainly pursued its aim of frontier security and the internal stability of the khanates, and helped both the emir and the khan to keep down revolts.[95] The railway did bring stimuli from the outside world, however, and set off a desire for change and reform among the local intelligentsia. Unrest was building up in Bukhara and the Russian Government waited for it to fall as a result of internal stresses and tensions.

The Muslim clergy—acting as political leaders—played a considerable political role over the years both in putting pressure on the emir to take a firmer stand in relation to the Russians and in resisting the advances of the modern world. Russia viewed religious radicalism mainly through the lens of its geopolitical rivalry with Britain and feared that it would undermine the emirate and make British access easier. As early as 1854 the then Russian Minister of War, V. A. Dolgorukov, claimed that outbursts of religious fanaticism in Turkey and the Caucasus were damaging relations between Russia and the Central Asian khanates and that this favoured Britain. Britain, he said, was trying to give the revolts a religious character, and there would always be a basis for this in such important Islamic centres as Bukhara and Samarkand.[96]

The final breakdown of the emirate from within did not come until October 1920, when it was replaced by the Bukharan People's Soviet Republic, established with the help of Russian troops intervening in the domestic turmoil of the emirate.[97] The academic literature most often claims that the overthrow of the emir was the result of domestic opposition, which was supported by the Russian Red Army. Later research in the archives has shown that the Red Army was the principal actor behind the revolt and not merely supporting domestic opposition against the emir. A polarization had taken place in society but the local population generally abstained from engagement.[98] The Bukharan People's Soviet Republic existed for four years until it was finally incorporated into the Soviet Union. The supporters of incorporation in the Russian leadership had finally got their way.

Summary

The Russian expansion of the 1860s took place at a period when the Russian state was both internationally and internally weak after its defeat in the Crimean war. Against the background of the declared policy of Foreign Minister Alexander Gorchakov, prioritizing domestic reform and a cautious foreign policy towards the European powers, Russia set off on a course of outright military expansion into Central Asia. Although anxious not to provoke Britain, which was also expanding in Asia, Russia enlarged its territory into the steppes and the mountainous areas to its south, and east of the Caspian Sea. In 1863 the Tsar gave the green light to operations to connect the two Russian defence lines, which stretched like two arms into Central Asia. The wave of military conquest in Central Asia did not abate until the mid-1880s.

The Russian expansion was successful. The Central Asian troops were badly equipped and trained and ill-prepared for a war with the comparatively well trained and well equipped Russian troops. Casualties on the Central Asian side were large, while Russian losses were minimal. Although the Russian troops met some strong resistance, especially among the Turkmen tribes in the late 1870s and 1880s, and were compelled to crush armed revolts against Russian rule in the Fergana Valley in the 1890s, generally, resistance was weak. From the Central Asian perspective this is a bloody and brutal period in history.

The first question posed at the beginning of this chapter was: what explains the change to such a determined expansionist policy from the 1860s? The academic literature picks out two major factors: (a) political–strategic factors, in particular the rivalry with Britain; and (b) domestic, primarily economic, factors.

Although the general public at the time was uninvolved in and unconcerned about the destiny of Russia in Central Asia, the government was clearly interested in expanding Russian influence and had the support of large sections of the political elite. The failure of Russian policy in the West created a 'hunger' for compensation in the east. The powerful rivalry with Britain, with other European states shifting between being allies and adversaries, contributed to Russia's concern over Britain's advances in Asia.

Among the domestic factors the political or ideological perception of Russia's international status played a role. The political establishment perceived Russia as a great power, and what was achieved in Central Asia was a back up for strengthening Russia's position in Europe. Economic factors were also relevant. The potential economic value of Central Asia to Russia was a key argument in the Russian debate during 1840–1870. Yet, this argument does not stand up to closer examination. The distance of the Central Asian market from Russia, the dangerous trading routes, the low purchasing power of the Central Asian population and the size of the domestic Russian market were obstacles to any significant increase in trade between Russia and the Central Asian territories. 'In contrast to England, in Russia the flag did not follow the merchant, but the merchant followed the flag', wrote A. Ignatiev and his colleagues in a study from the late 1990s—thereby underlining the comparatively minor role of economic factors for Russian expansion into Central Asia.[99] The study even concludes that the annexation of Central Asia was unprofitable for Russia. During the years 1868–80, the state's expenditure on the conquered territories in Central Asia was almost three times larger than the revenue it gained from them. This did not change until the 1890s, when the situation in Central Asia stabilized.[100] Yet it cannot be denied that *perceptions* of the future economic benefits from Central Asia constituted a component of Russian interest in Central Asia.

The next question posed in the introduction was: how did policy change? How much of a consensus existed in the Russian Government over policy aims in Central Asia? To what extent is it true that Russian generals acted independently, against the will of the government?

There was a basic consensus over ends. There had long been basic agreement that Russia should expand its influence in Central Asia. The government did not see any dilemma over balancing commitments with resources, or any contradiction between giving priority to the domestic reform agenda while, at the same time, pursuing an active policy in Central Asia. The revision of policy towards the European powers did not constitute any constraint on policy in Central Asia. Disagreement in the Russian Government reflected concerns about tactics, particularly the form and timing of expansion in a manner that would not provoke Britain. Thus, the British presence in Asia constituted a constraining factor on Russian policy towards the Bukhara Emirate. The British presence did not prevent Russia from pursuing what it considered to be its national interest—yet it influenced Russia's behaviour and the Russian timeframe for expansion.

The final question asked at the beginning of this chapter was: how did Russia influence and control the khanates after 1868—particularly the Bukhara Emirate? Although officially Russia did not intervene in the domestic affairs of Bukhara, it did use the classic methods of power politics. The exploitation and manipulation of tensions and contradictions between the khanates belong to this arsenal of policy instruments. Interested in both control and stability in the region, Russia supported revolts when necessary in order to take control of an area, but otherwise helped the emir to control the territory. The Russians bided their time, waiting for the internal tensions in feudal Bukharan society to cause the emirate to break up.

Looking at policy in Central Asia as part of Russia's general foreign policy in the 1860s, it is possible to conclude that, although Russia did try to reduce its commitments through political, territorial and economic retrenchment in Europe, in Asia it pursued a policy of territorial expansion. In general, Europe did not pay much attention to what was going on in Central Asia—apart from Britain, which became seriously concerned when Russia expanded down the east coast of the Caspian Sea towards Afghanistan, which Britain considered crucial to its control of India. The Central Asians themselves were unable to put up any strong resistance to the Russian troops.

Thus, the cautious foreign policy prescribed by Gorchakov did not exclude expansion into Central Asia. Russia followed the example of those European states that had become colonial powers. Expansion was regarded as a natural part of the conditions for regaining international status and influence as a great power. Russia defined its international position and influence in relation to the European powers, and the expansion into Central Asia assisted that goal. The Russian Government had a long-term interest in Central Asia and had been planning for expansion for many years before Russian troops entered Tashkent.

As a model for Russian foreign policy today the policy of the Russian Government at the time of Gorchakov seems to carry a double message—that, although the declared priority of the government is domestic reform, this does not exclude an active policy to enlarge Russia's international status or its influence in Central Asia. Although the world today is very different, and so is Russia, the Gorchakov model reflects the potent dream of and desire for an international return to prominence that existed 150 years ago. The question remains, what does this model mean for Russian policy in the very different international circumstances of the early twenty-first century.

After the Bukhara Emirate and the Khiva Khanate were incorporated into the Soviet Union, the further development of Central Asia became an internal Soviet affair. It took time, well into the 1930s, before the Basmachi rebellions against Soviet rule were brought under control. During the period 1917–1924 the peoples of Central Asia were looked upon by the Bolsheviks as one nation, and the Turkestan Autonomous Soviet republic was created covering all conquered territory. However, Stalin soon set about dividing this territory in order to prevent the development of a single nationalist coalition that was antagonistic to socialism.[101] By the time the Soviet Constitution of 1936 was adopted four separate Central Asian Soviet socialist republics (excluding Kazakhstan) had been created. Under Soviet rule a modernization process was initiated. An offensive was launched against Muslim leaders and infrastructure and, by the outbreak of World War II, the traditional Muslim religious establishment in Central Asia had been destroyed.[102]

The Soviet leadership made it their objective to cut Central Asia off from the Muslim world and from its neighbours to the south—Afghanistan and Iran.[103] Afghanistan maintained its status as a buffer state between Britain and Russia after the Soviets secured power in Central Asia. Lenin, and later Stalin, followed a 'relatively stand-offish policy' with regard to Afghanistan, avoiding confrontation with Britain and a provocative intervention in the internal affairs of that country.[104] As a result of the great powers' interest in maintaining the status quo in Afghanistan, economic and political conditions were preserved within the country. The coup of 1973 installed a reform-oriented regime under president Muhammad Daud, who received considerable support from the Soviet Union. The modernization process evoked strong domestic resistance from the traditionalists and Islamic fundamentalists. The coup of April 1978, intended to speed up reforms, further increased tensions in society. In February 1979 a wave of Islamist activity in neighbouring Iran brought about an Islamic revolution, which increased Russia's concern over the geopolitical situation in the wider region, and its own position in the unstable Afghanistan. The Soviet Politburo hastily decided to secure influence in Afghanistan and Soviet troops intervened on 27 December 1979. Moscow had always looked on Afghanistan as a dependent and underdeveloped country and did not expect its military intervention to create any great problem.[105] This turned out to be a serious miscalculation. The material and symbolic losses suffered by Soviet power in the drawn-out war in Afghanistan contributed to the break up of the Soviet Union. Mikhail Gorbachev decided to end the war in Afghanistan and Soviet troops were withdrawn in 1989. By then, the process leading up to the dissolution of the Soviet state was already well under way. Two years later, the Soviet Union was dissolved and the Central Asian republics became independent states.

3

CENTRAL ASIA LOST
Policy under Yeltsin

Although the Central Asian republics experienced the policy of perestroika in the 1980s and there was a growing demand for reform, the break up of the Soviet Union in December 1991 was not a welcome event in Central Asia. In common with all other Soviet republics, including the Russian republic, those in Central Asia declared their sovereignty in 1990. However, Central Asian leaders feared the consequences of independence because they were used to relying on large subsidies from the federal centre. The creation of the Commonwealth of Independent States (CIS) in late 1991 seemed to offer the possibility of maintaining a common framework after the republics became independent states. However, Russian President Boris Yeltsin and his group of supporters, who would have been able to make something out of the CIS, were too preoccupied with Russia's own national state-building problems to give any degree of priority to transforming the remnants of what had once been the Soviet Union.

Although Central Asia had been part of the Russian Empire and the Soviet Union, and in that sense was familiar to Russian leaders, as independent states they represented completely unknown territory. Russian Government structures lacked the The capacity to deal with the newly independent states. Attempting to work out a policy for the new, loose entity that was the CIS was like jumping into the unknown.

During the Yeltsin era Russian policy towards Central Asia followed the general shifts of Russian policy towards former Soviet territory, but it also had its specific elements. The first Russian Government under Acting Prime Minister Yegor Gaidar shared the widespread belief among Russian reformers that Central Asia was an economic burden to Russia. They feared that Russia would be left with only Central Asian allies as the European states on former Soviet territory went their own way.[1] The policy proposals 'A Strategy for Russia', written in August 1992 by the unofficial but politically influential Council on Foreign and Defence Policy, advised the Russian Government to concentrate on relations with Kazakhstan, Belarus and Georgia as countries of key interest to Russia.[2] The main preoccupation of Foreign Minister Andrei Kozyrev at that time was relations with the West. As a result, Russian policy towards Central Asia during 1991–92 can best be described as 'withdrawal and confusion'. The opposition to Yeltsin, which formed in 1992, accused the government of abandoning Russian interests in its 'near abroad'[3]

Adapting to his critics in 1993–1995 Yeltsin and his foreign minister became more vocal on Russian national interests, Russia as a great power, and Russia as a leader of the CIS. Thus, by the mid-1990s a general consensus had developed among the Russian elite around a strategic vision for Russian foreign policy— Russia as the great power and the nucleus of CIS integration. However, the question of how to make a breakthrough with regard to the integration of CIS territory became a major headache for Russian policy makers. There was no common understanding of what specific policy should be pursued with regard to the CIS, or towards Central Asia, in order to accomplish the strategic vision. In spite of President Yeltsin's decree of September 1995 on Russia's policy towards CIS military and economic integration, there was no common understanding within the Russian political establishment—inside government or outside— about what policy would best protect Russian interests. The mechanisms for translating long term objectives into practical policy for the here and now remained unclear.

Moreover, the Russian debate on policy towards CIS countries was linked to the priority given to domestic reform in Russia, and Russia was unwilling to take on costly obligations that would harm its own economic interests. President Yeltsin's words in February 1994 reflected this concern when he described the government's dilemma when trying to combine a wish for the integration of former Soviet territory, on the one hand, with efforts to avoid all obligations that might be costly or harmful to Russia's own economic development, on the other: 'Integration must not bring harm to Russia itself or lead to overstretch of our forces and resources, material as well as financial'.[4]

In spite of the acknowledgement that Russia should avoid overstretching its resources, a great power rhetoric developed during 1993–95. Russia, which had been drawn into the Tajik civil war in a heavy military engagement, was not capable of pursuing an actively interventionist policy on former Soviet territory. A gap developed between ambitions and capabilities—rhetoric and reality.

A new period of Russian Central Asian policy was initiated when, in January 1996, Yevgenii Primakov replaced Kozyrev as foreign minister. Primakov, a former head of the foreign intelligence service (Sluzhba Vneshnei Razvedki, SVR), an Orientalist, and a former director of one of the most famous Moscow research institutes (IMEMO) was well aware of the weakness of Russia. The years 1996–99 can be described as a 'pragmatic search' for solutions to problems on CIS territory. They involved political accommodation between the parties in the Tajik civil war and included a 'wait and see' policy on many of the issues of CIS integration.

In Central Asia, Russia followed a policy that had no linkage to its policy towards the West. Policy for the Central Asian arena was separated from the European or Western arena. In his Western policy, Yeltsin wanted Russia to become a recognized member of European organizations. He was therefore conciliatory in Europe. Central Asia, on the other hand, was regarded as Russia's 'backyard' where Russia still had special rights and obligations. Primakov and the Russian Government viewed the small but growing Western engagement in Central Asia from the 1990s with growing suspicion.

This chapter analyses the changing strategic and security situation in Central Asia and the Russian policy response from 1992 until Vladimir Putin became prime minister, in 1999.

The Strategic Situation and the Russian Response

The break up of the Soviet Union and the desire of most of the new states, including the Central Asian states, to orient themselves towards new partners presaged a rapid loss of Russian influence in the years to come.[5] While this development was not initially something that worried all parts of the Russian political elite, the May 1992 draft document and the November 1993 final version of the Russian Military Doctrine expressed clear concern in this regard. The draft outlined the risk of foreign military bases being set up in neighbouring countries, and of former Soviet republics entering into hostile military alliances.[6] In the political debate during 1993–95 this issue became a salient one, and Russian politicians closed ranks over their concern about the consequences of Russia's rapid loss of influence on former Soviet territory.

In 1992 the Russian military became involved in armed conflicts in Moldova, Azerbaijan, Georgia and Tajikistan. The civil war in Tajikistan (1992–97) led to a larger Russian military presence in Tajikistan than in any other hot spot on former Soviet territory. In spite of this military engagement, Russian policy towards the Central Asian states during Yeltsin's first presidential term (1991–96) can at best be characterized as ambivalent, and Central Asia played a subordinate role in Russian policy on the CIS. In September 1994 a report by the Russian Foreign Intelligence Service (SVR) under Director Yevgenii Primakov warned in dramatic terms of the ongoing disintegration on CIS territory and the interest shown by Western and Muslim states in furthering the process.[7] During Yeltsin's second term (1996–99), the Russian Government became more concerned about the rapidly changing strategic situation in Central Asia.

Although Russia remained the most important economic and military partner of the Central Asian states during the 1990s, its fears that these states might orient themselves away from Russia were not without foundation.[8] Turkmenistan declared itself a neutral country in 1993, and the UN General Assembly recognized its status of 'permanent neutrality' in 1995. The state did not sign the 1992 Collective Security Treaty and avoided signing multilateral CIS military agreements. From the mid-1990s it reduced its bilateral military cooperation with Russia and went its own way in foreign policy but remained dependent on Russian outlets for its gas exports. In May 1999 the Turkmen side unilaterally announced its decision to end the 1993 Russian–Turkmen agreement on border cooperation. Russian border troops left Turkmenistan and at the end of the year, there were no Russian troops left in the country.[9]

In the first half of the 1990s, Uzbekistan seemed to be developing into a close military ally of Russia. For example, in 1992 it cooperated with Russia to bring President Emomali Rakhmonov to power in Tajikistan. After 1995, however, Uzbekistan distanced itself from Russia, ceased to participate in multilateral CIS structures on both military and economic issues and initiated a foreign policy that sought assistance and investment from the West, in particular the USA. Uzbek President Islam Karimov became openly critical of multilateral CIS efforts—military as well as economic. Towards the end of the 1990s, Uzbekistan withdrew from CIS military cooperation and it left the CST in April 1999. It also criticized the extension of the Russian military presence in Tajikistan and the 1999 Russian–Tajik agreement in this regard. By the time Uzbekistan left the CST it had already extended its cooperation with the USA and with the North Atlantic Treaty Organization (NATO) Partnership for Peace (PFP) programme. In April 1999 it joined GUAM, the sub-regional association of Georgia, Ukraine, Azerbaijan and Moldova (which therefore became GUUAM). Uzbekistan had no border with Russia and no Russian soldiers or border guards on its territory. It was not dependent on Russian energy supplies, or for their transportation. Russia feared the consequences if it were to 'lose' Uzbekistan as the latter was a strategically key state and a potential regional leader.

Kyrgyzstan and Tajikistan were also bent on a diversification of their foreign policies, but here the process was not so strong. Kyrgyzstan, small and squeezed between Uzbekistan, Kazakhstan, China and unstable Tajikistan, was dependent on Russia for its security. Nonetheless, in January 1999 a Kyrgyz national border service was set up and Russian border troops had left Kyrgyzstan by the end of the year.[10] Tajikistan remained heavily dependent on Russia as a consequence of the civil war, with Russian soldiers acting as CIS peacekeeping troops from September 1993. Tajikistan therefore constituted Russia's most loyal ally in Central Asia. Nonetheless, with a Persian language, in contrast to the other Turkic-speaking Central Asian states, and with a large group of ethnic kinfolk in northern Afghanistan, Tajikistan also seemed to have the potential for a future foreign policy reorientation away from Russia.

Russia responded to the disintegration process taking place on former Soviet territory with initiatives to integrate the CIS, but without success. The Central Asian states had a direct interest in maintaining and developing economic relations with Russia and, in principle, Russia also needed the Central Asian states. Nevertheless, Russia's economic dealings with these states stagnated—the volume of trade fell and cross-border investment was reduced to almost nothing.[11] The planned CIS Economic Union never materialized. Instead, in 1995, the CIS Customs Union was created by the states most interested—among them two Central Asian states, Kazakhstan and Kyrgyzstan. Tajikistan joined in 1998.[12] Although the Customs Union was supposed to be at the CIS cutting edge with regard to economic cooperation, trade between the member states fell.

Russia remained the Central Asian states' largest trading partner—but at a much lower level. Its share of total trade between the countries fell. This was part of the general pattern on former Soviet territory: in all the Central Asian states, except Tajikistan, there was a general reorientation of trade towards non-CIS states during the 1990s and the percentage of imports and exports accounted for by other CIS states fell. The share of other CIS countries in Russia's total foreign trade fell from 54.6 per cent in 1991 to 18.7 per cent in 1999.[13] The reasons for the decline are to be found not only in the different quotas placed on goods but also in the lack of purchasing power, the different systems for the taxation of trade, the increase in barter trade and the instability of currencies.[14] These problems made it difficult to reach agreement on abandoning national tariffs, quotas and regulations in favour of a joint policy.

The CIS summit in Chishinau, Moldova, in 1997 demonstrated that the CIS had run into a profound crisis. Russia's immediate response to the organization's problems was to propose administrative reform. In April 1998 Russian oligarch Boris Berezovsky was appointed secretary of the CIS and his main task was to come up with suggestions for reform. The choice of Berezovsky indicated the emphasis on economic aspects and economic cooperation, which was also a priority for most CIS leaders. At the April 1998 summit meeting, the CIS member states declared their support for making the CIS more effective— primarily in the economic sphere.[15] Berezovsky, however, failed to reform the CIS. His proposals to slim down the organization, centralize it and give its executive bodies more authority were rejected. Centralization was contrary to the wishes of most other CIS leaders and Berezovsky was replaced. The difficulties of developing multilateral cooperation increased scepticism about the future of the CIS as an organization.

While both economic and military integration were goals for Russian policy makers, and were intended to develop on parallel tracks, economic cooperation was explicitly given priority in Russia's CIS policy. All CIS member states were in serious economic difficulties. At summit meetings both Russian and CIS leaders stressed the development of economic cooperation and official documents and statements, including those from Russia, requested a focus on economic issues. Foreign Minister Yevgenii Primakov said in the summer of 1998: 'Thus, problems of economic integration and the creation of a united economic space have the highest priority and are among the most important tasks of Russian foreign policy today'.[16]

Economic cooperation did not develop, however, and Russian debate remained focused on how, and around which issues, a breakthrough could be made in order to trigger a process of integration. With regard to military cooperation, Russia had signed bilateral agreements to supplement the multilateral cooperation that was not developing as rapidly or as easily as planned. The CIS was unable to develop joint military forces, which was one of its declared aims, and was only able to set up consultative bodies for military coordination. From 1993 Russia tried to make peacekeeping and the handling of conflicts the major issue around which permanent CIS military structures could be built, but without success. The Collective Peacekeeping Force in Tajikistan (1993–2000) was a CIS mission in name only and consisted mainly of Russian troops. The Collective Security Treaty (CST), which had been signed in 1992 by six states with three more states joining the following year, remained mainly a paper organization.

Voices among the Russian military argued that military issues were best suited to promote integration on CIS territory.[17] In December 1996 then Defence Minister Igor Rodionov echoed the warnings of the earlier SVR report about the process of disintegration on CIS territory and suggested the creation of a CIS defence union as the remedy.[18] Rodionov believed that there was an 'evil master plan' by Western and Muslim states purposely working for the disintegration of the CIS and of individual CIS member states. From time to time, Russian military leaders aired the idea of creating joint military forces. In March 1997 Russia suggested a system of CIS coalition forces in so-called 'collective security regions', but without eliciting any positive response from the Central Asian states.[19] Vladimir Zemskii, General Secretary of the Collective Security Council of the CST, admitted at the time that 'the task of achieving fully fledged military–political integration stretches far beyond the immediate future'.[20] The Central Asian states were not attracted to the idea of developing common military structures.

In January 1996 Yevgenii Primakov became foreign minister, and he adjusted policy to Russia's limited resources and means. He replaced the previous declaratory policy of integrating the Central Asian states into a multilateral CIS framework with a more diversified policy allowing for functional and issue-oriented cooperation and different speeds of integration, with stronger emphasis on bilateral relations.

Nonetheless, Russia still had a problem with identifying a common denominator for developing military cooperation. The CST dealt with external threats—and Russia and the Central Asian states did not agree on what and who constituted an external threat. The Central Asian states did not share the Russian view that increased engagement by Western states—above all the USA—was a threat. To the Central Asian leaders, greater involvement by the USA, Turkey, Iran or China offered instead a guarantee of their independence and a promise of future economic development. The main threats they perceived were those emanating from within society—from economic underdevelopment—and Russia had little to offer in this regard. Up to 1999, none of the Central Asian leaders (except President Rakhmonov of Tajikistan) responded with any enthusiasm to Russian proposals for military cooperation.

By the summer of 1999 only Kazakhstan, Tajikistan, and Kyrgyzstan were CST members among the Central Asian states. Russian troops had been withdrawn from all states except Tajikistan. Russia's role and influence were reduced and the states in the region were reorienting their foreign policies away from Russia.

The Russian retreat opened the way for investors from other countries. Trade increased between the Central Asian states and China, Iran, Turkey, the USA and the European Union, among others.[21] New prospects for the exploitation of the energy resources of the Caspian Sea raised the stakes and the level of interest from external powers. The prospect of, and plans for, the construction of oil and gas pipelines circumventing Russian territory threatened Russia's future role and influence in the region. The states of Central Asia reoriented themselves politically, economically and with regard to security. Russia had neither the policy nor the means to counter this trend.

Events outside Central Asia increased Russia's concern at the processes going on in the southern Caucasus and Central Asia. Russia reacted strongly to NATO's 1994 decision to enlarge. The 1999 NATO Strategic Concept, providing for out-of-area operations, and the bombing of Kosovo and Serbia, which began in April the same year, left Russia extremely frustrated.[22] Russian commentators perceived this as a warning that the measures the US Government took in the Balkans could be repeated in the Caucasus under the pretext of support for human rights but with the real purpose of squeezing

Russia out of the Caucasus and cutting it off from the Europe–Caucasus–Asia transport corridor that was under construction.[23] They warned that NATO, by defining the conflicts in Abkhazia, Nagorno-Karabakh and Transdniestr in terms of violations of human rights, was preparing to support the Georgian, Azerbaijani and Moldovan Governments in these conflicts in order to expand NATO's influence, and primarily US influence. In September 1999 Russia initiated its second Chechnya campaign and Western reaction was strongly negative. Then Defence Minister Igor Sergeev asked in November 1999: 'Has the anti-Russian campaign over Chechnya been launched to force Russia out of the Caucasus, and then out of Central Asia?'[24] He added: 'The question often raised in Moscow is whether Kosovo and Chechnya are links in a chain of steps toward the creation of a one-dimensional, NATO-centred world. Is Chechnya being used as a smokescreen for preparing NATO to assume the role of world policeman, for undermining the fundamental components of strategic stability and reversing the disarmament process?' The Chief of the Russian General Staff, General Anatolii Kvashnin, did not exclude the possibility that NATO in the future would use force on former Soviet territory.[25]

The anti-Western, and above all anti-US, rhetoric peaked as the Russian parliamentary and presidential elections (December 1999 and March 2000) came closer. Russia watched with concern as the security cooperation between Central Asian states and NATO countries developed first of all within the framework of the PFP programme and later through bilateral agreements with individual NATO members. Since 1997 US and NATO troops participated in military exercises on Central Asian soil organized by the Central Asian Peacekeeping Battalion (CentrasBat). CentrasBat was created in 1996 by Uzbekistan, Kazakhstan and Kyrgyzstan. Russia participated in 1998 but not in 1999. Russian–US strategic tensions were clearly reflected in Central Asia.

The Security Situation in Central Asia and the Russian Response

Quite soon after the break up of the Soviet Union, security in Central Asia became a matter of urgent concern for Russian officials. The weakest security link was Tajikistan, where the domestic situation deteriorated during the first half of the 1990s under the impact of the turmoil in Afghanistan.

After the Soviet withdrawal from Afghanistan in 1989, Moscow kept a low profile in the country. Soviet troops had invaded Afghanistan in December 1979 when the pro-Soviet Afghan regime, which came to power in April 1978, was threatened by its opposition, and against the background of the Islamist Iranian revolution of February 1979. Three years after the Soviet withdrawal the pro-communist Najibullah regime was toppled and, in April 1992, the Islamic State of Afghanistan was declared. When Burhanuddin Rabbani took over as President of Afghanistan in June 1992 he received the backing of Russia. However, rival Islamic factions continued their fight for power and the country fragmented into a cluster of self-ruled and self-sustaining regions.[26] Turmoil, war and religious extremism exploded during the 1990s and Afghanistan became a 'black hole', which threatened to swallow neighbouring Central Asian societies. Russia watched these developments, fearing the influence that turmoil in

Afghanistan would have on the Tajik conflict.[27] When civil war erupted in Tajikistan in 1992, the Islamic State of Afghanistan declared its neutrality but, as the civil war raged in Afghanistan, various factions there supported the Tajik opposition. Tajik opposition leaders found refuge and were allowed bases on Afghan territory. Rival political factions in Afghanistan played the 'Tajik card' in their own favour.[28]

When the Taliban movement took control of Kabul in September 1996, Russia feared that it would develop close relations with the Tajik opposition, especially those in exile in Afghanistan.[29]

Tajikistan

When the Soviet Union broke up, armed conflicts erupted on former Soviet territory. The conflict in Tajikistan was the most violent. Russia's 1993 Military Doctrine pointed to armed conflicts and local wars in the vicinity of Russia's borders as the most serious threat to Russian security. The main reasons for local wars were identified as 'social, political, territorial, religious and national–ethnic contradictions' and 'the desire of a number of states and political forces to resolve them by means of armed struggle'. In particular, the doctrine singled out aggressive nationalism and religious intolerance.[30] According to Vladimir Lukin, writing in *Foreign Affairs* in the spring of 1992, there was a fear that 'Islamic fundamentalism' would 'reverberate within Russia's own Muslim areas'.[31]

The roots of the Tajik civil war were regional–political in character rather than ethnic or religious.[32] Although the Islamic factor played a crucial role in the Afghan civil war, it was not of major importance in the case of Tajikistan. However, Russia viewed the conflict through the prism of its fear of Islamic extremism. The Tajik opposition, the United Tajik Opposition (UTO), was a coalition of Islamic and democratic organizations, and its strongest force was the Islamic Revival Party (IRP), created in 1990, which participated in the 1991 elections but was forced underground when the civil war broke out. As Yevgenii Ambartsumov of the Foreign Policy Committee of the Russian parliament said in late July 1993: 'If Russia leaves Tajikistan … Tajikistan will have been sacrificed to the Islamists'.[33] Foreign Minister Andrei Kozyrev followed this up, speaking of 'the establishment of a shield against the spread of regional clan and Islamic extremism in Central Asia. Around Tajikistan there is an abundance of inflammable material…It is impossible to allow the zone of complete instability and violence to move from the southern borders, to other borders of Tajikistan, right up to Uzbekistan and Kyrgyzstan, threatening the entire Central Asian part of the CIS.' He also pointed out that: 'Those same political–extremist forces that are active today not only in Afghanistan, but in Iran and Pakistan as well, are causing havoc on the Tajik border. These very forces are recklessly driving the waves of instability towards the north; they are whipping up religious extremism, conflicts and international terrorism'.[34]

The 1994 report of the SVR under its Director, Primakov, explicitly expounded the growing threat of Islamic extremism and warned that Muslim states might use Islamic organizations to promote the disintegration of former

Soviet territory. 'Recently, Islamic extremism has been gaining strength as a movement with the aim of spreading Islam by force and suppressing all who oppose this, and of changing the secular character of the state. A 'breath' of this extremism appeared in Tajikistan and in the Caucasus conflict zone. Furthermore, the problem of the spread of Islamic extremism is not a local phenomenon.'[35] Primakov was careful to distinguish between Islamic fundamentalism and Islamic extremism, and the report defined the former as using neither violence nor terrorism. In one possible scenario outlined in the SVR report, the position of 'Islamic extremists in CIS states with a Muslim population' would grow stronger in a situation of social and economic crisis, thereby posing a threat to Russia and to Central Asian states.[36] Eight years later, one of the authors of the SVR report commented on this early warning of the threat of radical Islam, that the trend of Islamic extremism had been clearly visible in the Fergana Valley at that time.[37] Russia considered the proximity of Afghanistan to be a major factor influencing the situation in Tajikistan in particular but also in the rest of Central Asia.

The SVR report also warned of the ethnic aspect of the Afghan situation, and its consequences for Tajikistan, by claiming that forces in Afghanistan were trying to associate northern Afghanistan with Tajikistan in order to create a new state of Persian-speaking people across the border. Above all, the report pointed to the growing threat of Islamic extremism and warned that Muslim states might use Islamic organizations to promote the further disintegration of former Soviet territory.

When the Tajik conflict erupted into civil war in May 1992 former Soviet troops were deployed in the country. Russia's policy was hesitant and passive in the initial stages but soon changed into active involvement. Russian troops assisted in the rise to power of Rakhmonov. Russian border troops also replaced Soviet border troops in 1992. Tajikistan was linked to Russia by treaties and agreements, among them the multilateral 1992 CST and the bilateral 1993 Treaty of Friendship, Cooperation and Mutual Assistance. An attack on 13 July 1993 on a Russian border post on the border between Tajikistan and Afghanistan, when 25 Russians were killed, was a watershed in the Russian involvement in the Tajik civil war. It was the motivation behind the major Russian military involvement that followed. The threat posed by turmoil, war and Islamic extremism in Afghanistan was cited when Russia and three Central Asian states (Kazakhstan, Kyrgyzstan and Uzbekistan) decided to deploy CIS peacekeeping troops in Tajikistan in September 1993 and to reinvigorate the CST. The 201st Motorized Rifle Division (MRD) was reorganized into the core of the CIS Collective Peacekeeping Force on mission in Tajikistan.

Russia's approach to peacekeeping had more characteristics in common with a counter-insurgency operation, or at least peace enforcement. Russian peacekeeping troops were introduced to an environment where no ceasefire agreement existed, and their tasks and functions went beyond peacekeeping in the UN tradition, as it was at that time. As peacekeeping troops, members of the 201st MRD were not allowed to directly engage in combat and were supposed to be impartial. Even so, the troops were part of a Russian package of measures supportive of the Tajik Government in the latter's struggle against the UTO. Russia played a crucial role in initiating and leading the negotiation process, which started in April 1994, and in mediating the ceasefire agreement of October 1994. Yet, in spite of its efforts to act as a 'third party' mediator and peacekeeper, Russia continued to support the Rakhmonov regime and its struggle against its opponents. The Russian 'double' approach to its mission in Tajikistan coloured the negotiation process, which soon ran into a dead end.

In 1996 Russia's policy changed to one of actively bringing an end to the Tajik civil war and finding a political solution based on political compromise, which would allow a place for the former enemy, the UTO, in Tajik political life. This change of policy was of tremendous importance and, thanks to Russian diplomacy, the inter-Tajik General Peace Agreement was signed in June 1997.[38] The Taliban takeover of Kabul in September 1996 was an important factor behind the Russian change of policy in Tajikistan. The inter-Tajik negotiations took a new turn. Russia's new policy should be viewed against the background of the Taliban's advance in Afghanistan and Russia's fear of the influence of religious extremism on Tajikistan—although the military stalemate on the ground in Tajikistan was equally important. No side saw a prospect of victory, but attacks by the opposition were felt on the Russian and Tajik Government side. The end to the first Chechnya war in August 1996, when Russian General Alexander Lebed and Chechen leader Aslan Maskhadov signed a ceasefire, also offered the lesson that only a political solution could bring an end to the war.

The General Peace Agreement of June 1997 prescribed that a National Reconciliation Commission was to be set up, consisting of representatives of the government and the Tajik Opposition (UTO), to lead the country through a transition period. The UTO was to be integrated into the political and military life of Tajikistan and given a 30 per cent representation in the national government as well as in executive organs at all administrative levels.[39] Before the end of the transition period, a new constitution was to be adopted and presidential and parliamentary elections were to take place.

The Tajik peace agreement was based on national conciliation with the former political and military enemy—the UTO, and especially its Islamic wing, the IRP. Conflict resolution in Tajikistan thereby set an example for other armed conflicts on former Soviet territory. However, representatives of the Leninabad region in the north (today the Sughd region) were not allowed to join. Many feared that the peace agreement would not work unless all major regional interests and groups were represented. However, the National Reconciliation Commission was designed to include representatives of the two warring parties, and Leninabad had never directly participated in the civil war. More importantly, there was an interest on both the Russian and the Tajik side in reducing Uzbekistan's influence on the formula for post-conflict peace building in Tajikistan. With a large Uzbek population and close links to Uzbekistan, the exclusion of Leninabad reduced Uzbekistan's influence on the peace process. Tajikistan accused Uzbekistan of intervening in Tajik domestic politics by supporting rebel warlords. The Tajik Government feared Uzbek involvement in 1995 and 1996, periods of increased discontent with the Rakhmonov regime. Revolts by local warlords, the ethnic-Uzbek Makhmud Khudoberdiyev and Ibod Boimatov in Tursunzade and Kurgan-Tyube added to these suspicions.[40] In 1998 Khudoberdiyev staged a revolt demanding *inter alia* representation for Leninabad in Tajik governing bodies.

The peace agreement changed Russia's role in Tajikistan. By being impartial and loyal to the agreement, Russia was able to guarantee that the former opposition was integrated in Tajik political life and its structures. The implementation of the peace agreement was not without problems to Russia since it created a precedent in Central Asia, and the Russian and Tajik Governments were hesitant to implement the agreement. On the other hand, the failure of the peace process would have radicalized the UTO and made radical Islamism a political force in Tajikistan. In the post-conflict situation, Russia was expected to carry out three functions as (a) guarantor of the political process; (b) stabilizer of the military security situation; and (c) contributor to post-conflict economic reconstruction.

The political situation in Tajikistan remained fragile, however. A tentative integration was initiated of former UTO representatives into executive structures and military units, attracting criticism from the opposition that the Tajik Government was delaying the process. Mistrust between the parties in government and mistrust of the IRP did not dissipate quickly. Many in Russia and elsewhere in Central Asia regarded Tajikistan with suspicion as a 'dark horse' with regard to regional security, since the peace agreement had brought Islamists into the government. In July 1999 the previous ban on opposition political parties was lifted and the IRP was legalized.

Further developments in Afghanistan increased the importance of Tajikistan to Russia. When the Taliban took control of Kabul in September 1996, the northern part of Afghanistan remained under the control of the ethnic-Tajik Akhmed Shah Massoud in the north-east, and Abdurrashid Dostum, an ethnic-Uzbek, in the north-west. As the Taliban advanced to the north of Afghanistan in 1998, Dostum was ousted and Massoud was squeezed into the north-east corner of Afghanistan. Russia intensified its political and material support for Massoud, and this was done mainly through Tajikistan. Tajikistan remained politically fragile but still became a crucial ally for Russia. The Tajik Government was not in full control of its territory, and parts of the country were controlled by Tajik warlords, which recognized neither the government nor the peace agreement, and Uzbek Islamists. After the car bombs in central Tashkent in February 1999, of which the Uzbek Islamic opposition was accused, and during the following crackdown on the opposition, several opposition members fled to Tajikistan.

Stability in Tajikistan was crucial to regional security. Most Russian politicians and commentators believed that a continued Russian military presence was required. Even so, there were some arguments for, and proponents within Russia of, reducing that presence. A long-term reduction and reorganization of Russian troops, including the border troops, started after the signing of the General Peace Agreement. Russian border troops in Tajikistan had been reduced from 16,000 in 1997 to 11,000 by July 1999. In order to prepare for the future withdrawal of its troops, Russia built up and trained the Tajik national army and contributed troops to the creation of a national border service. Russian border troops also transferred tasks along a limited part of the Tajik-Afghan border to Tajik border troops. However, national Tajik forces were only seen as capable of taking over border defence and national security in the long term. The ranks of both the Russian border troops and the 201st MRD were filled by Tajik nationals and, after 1998, the Tajik ethnic component in the officer corps also increased. In an effort to secure a Russian military presence in the future—after the peace process had come to an end and the mandate of the peacekeeping troops had expired—an agreement was signed in April 1999 reorganizing the 201st MRD into a military base, with fewer soldiers, for a period of 25 years.

The war and turmoil in Afghanistan continued to have a negative impact on the situation in Tajikistan. The Tajik Government was not capable of fully controlling the country's territory. Tajikistan continued to be viewed as a 'black hole' and accused of offering transit routes for drug trafficking, arms smuggling and all manners of illegal activities.

Uzbekistan

As the strongest power in Central Asia, Uzbekistan was an important ally for Russia. However, its strength which Russia sought to contain also made it a potential competitor for influence in the region. In the turbulence that followed the break up of the Soviet Union, Uzbekistan played a central role in Russia's policy in Central Asia.[41] Uzbekistan acted as Russia's regional policeman in Tajikistan, but also looked after its own interests. It provided logistical supplies, military training and air support to the Tajik paramilitary pro-communist factions. Uzbek units participated actively in the civil war in Tajikistan, and the Uzbek air force bombed opposition strongholds in Garm and Gorno-Badakhshan.

President Karimov was extremely concerned about the threat from 'Islamic fundamentalism' and about the toppling in September 1992 of his counterpart in Tajikistan, President Rahmon Nabiev, by a coalition of secular and Islamic forces. He was also concerned about the position of the large Uzbek minority in the Leninabad region of Tajikistan. Therefore, Uzbekistan abandoned its support for Rakhmonov in 1993 when the latter initiated a process of 'kulyabization' of senior administrative and political posts in Tajikistan, thereby squeezing out those from all other regions, including Leninabad, from senior positions and replacing them with people from his home region, Kulyab.

As Uzbekistan distanced itself from Rakhmonov after 1993, it could no longer play the role of Moscow's 'arm' in Tajikistan. Instead, it became a rival to Russia in Central Asia. Trying to influence the Tajik domestic scene, Uzbekistan exploited Tajikistan's economic and energy dependence upon itself and gave support to local warlords in their revolts against Rakhmonov, particularly Khudoberdiev.

The deterioration in relations between Russia and Uzbekistan after 1993–94 was followed by an increasingly pronounced Uzbek policy of increasing its independence from Russia. Uzbekistan set up its own national border service, did not accept Russian troops on its territory, and started to build up its national army. In September 1996 the Uzbek defence minister declared that his country did not intend to participate further in CIS peacekeeping missions, and withdrew its troops from the CIS peacekeeping force in Tajikistan.[42]

In 1998 Russia intensified efforts to improve relations with Uzbekistan. President Karimov visited Moscow in early May 1998 and the security situation, economic relations, military–industrial cooperation (within the aerospace industry) and military–technical cooperation (including deliveries of weapons) were all discussed. The joint communiqué issued by presidents Karimov and Yeltsin mentioned Afghanistan and highlighted the danger coming from 'further escalation of tension, fraught with the spread of religious extremism and terrorism, the growth of smuggling of arms and drugs, and refugees …'[43]

Uzbekistan's role in the local dynamics of its neighbouring countries added to Russia's concerns.[44] Growing tensions within Uzbek society between the regime and its critics—first and foremost radical Islamists—added a source of tension to the region as a whole. Karimov had already clamped down on the opposition in 1992–93. From the mid-1990s, repression of the opposition increased. Uzbekistan also continued to influence the domestic life of its neighbours, each of which had large Uzbek minority groups in their populations. As long as Uzbekistan remained an ally of Russia, Russia accepted its involvement in neighbouring countries. However, when Uzbekistan became more independent, Uzbek influence threatened to shift the balance of power in the region and Russia tried to prevent it from spreading.

There was a risk that conflicts would spread across the state borders of the Central Asian states. Given the ethnically complex composition of their populations, as well as regional differences, harsh socio–economic conditions and an ongoing Islamic revival, the area represented a possible breeding ground for conflicts and extremism. Large diasporas constituted a source of conflict. The Uzbek population of Tajikistan, which made up 24 per cent of the total population, lived mainly in the north and along the border with Uzbekistan. There were also large Uzbek diasporas in border areas of Kyrgyzstan (which made up 16 per cent of its population), Turkmenistan (9 per cent) and Kazakhstan (2 per cent) as well as in the north of Afghanistan.[45] The severe social and economic situation in these countries accompanied by widespread corruption created conditions in which social and political discontent linked to national, regional or religious affiliation threatened to flourish.

The car bombs in central Tashkent on 16 February 1999, which targeted government buildings, killed several people, wounded more than 100 and nearly killed Karimov, increased government concern over the terrorist threat. The Islamic Movement of Uzbekistan (IMU) and its leaders, Juma Namangani and Takhir Yuldashev, were immediately accused, but domestic repression also targeted members of the moderate opposition far removed from the extremism of the IMU. Fear of the Islamists led the Uzbek security service to intervene in Kyrgyzstan and Kazakhstan in the spring and summer of 1999 to pursue ethnic Uzbeks suspected of Wahhabism.[46] After the Tashkent bombings, Uzbekistan closed its border with Tajikistan alleging a Tajik connection to the bombings.[47] The February 1999 bombing in Tashkent demonstrated that Uzbekistan was vulnerable and the target of extremists. Although deeply concerned, President Karimov did not turn to Russia for assistance.

In August 1999 Uzbek Islamic fighters from the IMU intruded into Kyrgyzstan en route to Uzbekistan—the threat from Islamic extremism seemed to have seriously increased. IMU groups moved into the area around Batken and captured, among others, a mayor and three of his employees. The Kyrgyz authorities gave in to the fighters' demands, paid a ransom and supplied a helicopter to fly the hostage takers to Afghanistan. The fighters then entered three villages and captured, among others, a major general in the Kyrgyz Interior Ministry. On 23 August, seven more hostages were captured, including four Japanese geologists working for a mining company.[48] The IMU declared from Afghanistan that it had launched a *jihad* to topple the Karimov regime and capture the Fergana Valley.[49] The hostages were gradually freed. The Japanese geologists were freed in late October after a large ransom had been paid. The IMU retreated into Tajikistan from where they were given safe passage by Russian helicopters to Afghanistan with the agreement of the Tajik Government.[50] Russia immediately branded the incursions international terrorism and, because the group took not only Kyrgyz hostages but also internationals, the IMU was branded a 'terrorist' group by the US authorities. Thus, the Batken events brought a new element into the security situation in Central Asia. For the first time radical extremists from the region had resorted to weapons in a direct fight with Central Asian military and interior troops. The incursions increased tensions between the Central Asian states. The Uzbek Government accused the Kyrgyz and Tajik Governments of passivity. Karimov criticized the Kyrgyz authorities for not demonstrating greater urgency and 'resolution' in resisting the militants and said: 'These things are happening because of the weak policy carried out by the Kyrgyz Government. This kind of humane attitude towards terrorists will lead to this kind of incident'.[51] The Tajik Government was accused of not taking measures to prevent Islamic fighters from maintaining camps on Tajik territory. Several IMU fighters had participated in the Tajik civil war on the side of the UTO. Uzbekistan thus took an active role and Uzbek aircraft bombed areas in southern Kyrgyzstan (with the permission of the Kyrgyz authorities) and also villages on the Tajik side of the border, which led to protests from the Tajik Government.[52] The events in Kyrgyzstan created renewed tensions in relations between the Central Asian states. The internal problems of Uzbekistan had become a cause of instability for its neighbours.

The Russian approach to Uzbekistan remained ambivalent. On the one hand, Russia tried to counter Uzbek influence in its neighbouring countries. On the other hand, it tried to find common ground for cooperation with Uzbekistan. The struggle against religious extremism and international terrorism offered a common denominator.

Afghanistan

There was an Afghan factor in the Tajik civil war from its very beginning. Just before the Communist regime of Najibulla fell in Kabul, the situation in Dushanbe had become more tense and a demonstration by many thousands of people gathered in central Dushanbe in the Shakhidon Square. Along with slogans such as 'Down with the USA', and 'Down with Russia' there were also shouts of 'We have an army of 27,000 Mujaheddin' and 'In Afghanistan our brothers have taken power'.[53] At the end of December 1992 armed units belonging to the Tajik opposition fled to Afghanistan where they stayed as refugees for several years. In Afghanistan, Rabbani and his Tajik-dominated government mediated two important meetings between Tajik President Rakhmonov and UTO (and IRP) leader Nuri.[54]

The Taliban takeover created a serious challenge for Russia and the security of Central Asia. How should it respond? On 4 October 1996, Russian Prime Minister Viktor Chernomyrdin and Central Asian CIS leaders met in Almaty, Kazakhstan, and later in Dushanbe, Tajikistan, to discuss the new situation presented by the Taliban offensive. They declared their readiness to take measures if necessary but did not decide on any troop increases along the Tajik-Afghan border, in spite of demands from President Rakhmonov. While the Government of Uzbekistan spoke in favour of active support for Dostum's troops in Afghanistan, the Kyrgyz and Kazakh governments declared that they did not wish to become involved in the internal affairs of Afghanistan. Turkmenistan did not attend the meeting and abstained from any joint measures, citing its status as a neutral country, calling the issue an internal Afghan matter, and trying instead to find a role as a possible arbitrator between the warring Afghan factions.

In spite of its declared preparedness to act, the official Russian reaction had been low-key. Primakov's immediate reaction was that no support would be given to any party in the Afghan conflict.[55] Opinion was divided within the Russian leadership. The Russian media reiterated the fear that the Taliban would cross the border into Central Asia. Immediately after the Taliban takeover of Kabul in September 1996, Alexander Lebed, at the time Secretary of the Russian National Security Council, suggested that Russia provides active support for the anti-Taliban forces. He warned that the route to Bukhara lay open to the Taliban to continue their advance all the way into the Russian city of Orenburg, in the heart of Russia but close to the Kazakh border. In contrast, the head of the Russian Federal Border Guard Service, Andrei Nikolaev, declared there was no need to increase the number of Russian border guards.[56] Russian commanders along the Tajik-Afghan border expressed neither fear nor expectation of any Taliban territorial expansion across the borders into Central Asia.[57] Russian Defence Minister Rodionov stated that the troops of the 201st Division were not to be increased.[58]

Russia did, however, exploit the Taliban threat to promote Russian military integration with Central Asian states and suggested sharing the defence costs of CIS external borders, but the results were limited.

When Taliban troops advanced north in the summer and autumn of 1996, Russia initiated its support for the anti-Taliban commanders, Dostum and Massoud, of the Northern Alliance led by Burhanuddin Rabbani, who remained the legitimate president in the eyes of the international community. Uzbekistan initiated active measures to fortify its southern frontier. At that time Russia's General Staff, in cooperation with Uzbekistan's Defence Ministry, began to elaborate plans to resist possible aggression by the Taliban. Over the next few years, Russia assisted Uzbekistan with equipping Dostum's forces. However, when in 1998 the Taliban took control of areas in northern Afghanistan held by Dostum, and he was ousted, Uzbekistan stopped referring to a 'Taliban threat'. In August 1998, it joined Turkmenistan in claiming that the war in Afghanistan was of a domestic character and that the only real reason for concern was the possibility of an influx of refugees into the CIS countries. Uzbekistan became a firm supporter of a negotiated solution to the war.[59] Russia, which had previously had common interests with both Uzbekistan and Iran in ousting the Taliban from power, therefore lost the chance to influence events in Kabul with the help of Uzbekistan. Thus, Akhmed Shah Massoud became all the more important—and so did Tajikistan. Tajikistan was also important for Massoud as a retreat, and he was allowed to use an airfield on Tajik territory close to the border with Afghanistan.

In 1998 Massoud was left in control of a shrinking strip of land in the northeast of Afghanistan, close to the Tajik border. By the end of 1999, the Taliban authorities claimed control of more than 80 per cent of Afghan territory.

An Evolving Anti-Extremist Agenda

Fear of the destabilizing effect that the Taliban victory might have on Central Asia led Russia to take new initiatives to strengthen military cooperation with Central Asian states, but without much success. When, in 1998, the Taliban offensive almost ousted the anti-Taliban Northern Alliance from Afghanistan, Russia presented a new initiative for security cooperation—a 'troika' with Uzbekistan and Tajikistan, the states most concerned by the Taliban threat.

In 1998 the issue of combating Islamic extremism and terrorism was introduced as a matter for trilateral cooperation with Uzbekistan and Tajikistan. As a result of Russian efforts, in May 1998 Russia and Uzbekistan signed an agreement, which Tajikistan joined, on cooperation to fight 'aggressive religious and other extremism'. On 12 October this was followed up by a declaration providing for military support in the event of a situation arising which one of the signatories regarded as a threat to its security, territorial integrity and sovereignty. The declaration explicitly stated that, in the event of an act of aggression against any one of the parties, the other parties would give necessary assistance, including military assistance, as an act of collective self-defence, referring to Article 51 of the Charter of the United Nations. In such a case 'consultations' would follow with the purpose of coordinating positions and taking necessary measures to remove the threat. The declaration also stated that the parties would develop a dialogue in the field of security and defence; show each other all-round support as and when needed; and coordinate their efforts to prevent the spread of aggressive religious and other extremism, and attempts from inside or outside these countries to change the constitutional and social order by the use of force. Furthermore, each party would abstain from supporting or participating in acts directed against the other two, and agreed not to allow its territory to be used for preparations for such acts. Finally, it stated that the parties would 'ensure close cooperation between the law enforcement and other competent bodies in the fight against terrorism, organized transborder crime, illegal drug trafficking and smuggling'.[60] The term 'terrorism' was used only in the context of cooperation between law enforcement bodies.

Although the agreement was signed it was not implemented. Mutual confidence between the three states was weak. In late October Karimov criticized Russia for attempting 'to create here, on the southern borders of the CIS, some sort of association or a bloc of states that will be under Russia's control'.[61] There also seemed to be disagreement concerning the target of the declaration. While Russia and Tajikistan wished to highlight the threat emanating from the Taliban, Uzbekistan was less interested in spelling this out.

Central Asian leaders who were not part of the 'troika' were suspicious. Turkmen President Saparmurad Niyazov dismissed the idea that there was any threat of Islamic fundamentalism spilling over from Afghanistan. President Nazarbaev of Kazakhstan was also reported to have been unenthusiastic about the initiative.[62] The agreement did not stop Uzbekistan from leaving the CST in April 1999—even though it expressed general apprehension about the Afghan situation and by then had experienced the car bombs in the centre of Tashkent.[63]

When Uzbek Islamists intruded into southern Kyrgyzstan in August 1999, the 1998 troika agreement was not referred to. Thus, the effort by Russia to create a kind of anti-extremist alliance in Central Asia was not successful. Nevertheless, in his speech to the Federal Parliament in April 1999, President Yeltsin reported that cooperation with the Central Asian states with the purpose of 'fighting political and religious extremism' had strengthened.[64] A first important step had been taken towards defining the threat to Central Asian security in terms of 'terrorism'.

Summary

After the break up of the Soviet Union the position and influence of Russia were undermined in the independent Central Asian states of Uzbekistan, Tajikistan, Turkmenistan and Kyrgyzstan. Russia became increasingly concerned with the changing strategic and security situation in the region. Russian Central Asian policy remained for most of the decade passive, fragmented, and without focus or political will (apart from its military involvement in the Tajik civil war). There was no clear understanding of what Russia would do in Central Asia, what the purpose of policy was to be, or what Russia's goals and interests were. The vagueness surrounding these issues was soon covered by a great-power rhetoric, which awarded Russia a leading role in an integrated CIS. The lofty declarations about CIS economic and military integration were not implemented in practical politics.

During the 1990s, the Russian Government officially gave priority to bringing about economic cooperation in the CIS, but no adequate policy was developed to achieve this objective. The problems on the ground in Central Asia drew Russia into commitments and cooperation in the security field. In Tajikistan, Russian troops acted formally as CIS peacekeeping troops but were simultaneously part of the Russian Government's support for the Rakhmonov regime against the United Tajik Opposition. Old networks of the military and security structures of the former Soviet Union remained intact, although they were divided and reorganized as national institutions, and this made military cooperation easier compared with economic cooperation. Even so, a wide gap emerged between Russian policy declarations and policy implementation.

The year 1996 brought a change to Russian Central Asia policy. Appointed foreign minister in January 1996, Yevgenii Primakov brought knowledge about Central Asia to the ministry and gave the area priority in foreign-policy making. With a background in academia and as a former director of the Foreign Intelligence Service, Primakov introduced a more realistic and pragmatic policy on CIS territory in general, and particularly on Central Asia, by taking into account Russia's reduced capacity. Western observers often underestimated him and denounced him as first and foremost a Soviet-type ideologue with an anti-US bent. Primakov contributed personally to bring the Tajik civil war to a political solution by integrating the adversary, the UTO, into the peace plan. Primakov advocated down to earth policies and narrowed the gap between Russia's words and its deeds, its declarations and its capabilities.

Primakov understood the limits to Russia's resources. Nevertheless, he was the one who reintroduced into Russian foreign policy debate the strategic goal of a Russian return to the international scene as a great power, while at the same time emphasizing domestic reforms. While he shifted to a policy more in line with Russia's reduced capability, the basic dilemma of the Gorchakov model remained—whether to concentrate on domestic reforms or on an active foreign policy, and how to avoid overstretch.

From the mid-1990s, Russia rapidly lost influence, and no efforts by the Russian Government seemed to take the CIS any further towards integration or cooperation. At the same time, the security threats to Central Asia increased under the impact of civil war and the Taliban takeover in Afghanistan. Moreover, Uzbekistan, the strongest state in the region, was orienting itself away from Russia. Russia's efforts in 1998 to develop security cooperation with Uzbekistan and Tajikistan through the 'troika' on the basis of the common threat of religious extremism were unsuccessful. In the same way that Russia lost control over developments in Afghanistan, it was now rapidly losing influence over local dynamics in Uzbekistan and Tajikistan, which had been triggered by radical Islamism in Afghanistan. At the same time, US and Western engagement increased in the second half of the 1990s. Russia, which regarded Central Asia as its 'backyard', remained hostile to this process. Increasingly concerned with the strategic and security situation, Russia could not find a policy to respond to the challenges in the region.

By 1999 the ground was prepared for a full redefinition of Russian policy in Central Asia and the Batken events provided the pretext for a change of policy.

PART II

PUTIN AND CENTRAL ASIA

4

THE POLICY CHANGE OF 1999

After Putin came to power the issue of terrorism was placed at the top of Russia's policy agenda in Central Asia.

In August 1999 Chechen rebels invaded Dagestan, took control of two Dagestani villages close to the border, and declared their intention to set up an Islamic state on Chechen and Dagestani territory. It was this crisis in August 1999 that led to Putin's appointment as prime minister—replacing Sergei Stepashin who had wavered over how to respond to the new situation. Putin immediately branded the event a case of terrorism. In the same month rebels from the Islamic Movement of Uzbekistan (IMU), led by Juma Namangani, made incursions into the Batken Region in southern Kyrgyzstan from bases in Tajikistan and Afghanistan, and took hostages including four Japanese geologists.[1]

This chapter examines Russia's policy in the region from August 1999 until September 2001.

The Policy Shift

The events in Batken gave Putin the opportunity to make the issue of anti-terrorism the top priority in Russia's relations with the Central Asian states and to make it a platform for the development of military and security cooperation. Russian's policy in Central Asia was framed by the terrorist threat.

The new policy framework and the way the anti-terrorist struggle moved up the Russian agenda can be understood as a reaction to events on the ground. It can also be viewed as an effort to use the opportunity—'the policy window' created by the Batken events—to give new impetus to Russian-led cooperation with the states in the region. The concept of 'securitization' is used here to highlight the process of the issues of terrorism and extremism being raised on the Russian agenda and introduced to the Central Asian states as a 'genuine existential threat' requiring closer cooperation with Russia. Among the different threats, problems and challenges, this specific issue was presented as the most crucial.

The term 'international terrorism' had already found its way into the official Russian lexicon. The threat of 'international terrorism' had been mentioned briefly in the 1993 military doctrine but not given special attention. In his June

1996 speech on national security, Yeltsin described the sources of external military threat and reiterated the threat of local conflicts but added international terrorism: 'existing and potential hotbeds of local wars and armed conflicts, first of all in the vicinity of Russian borders; international terrorism and its development of links with political extremist groups inside Russia and former Soviet republics'.[2] For his speech, Yeltsin used the draft document on national security, prepared by Yeltsin's security adviser Yurii Baturin, that had been published in May 1996. Baturin's draft did not point to terrorism as a specific threat. Instead, it highlighted 'separatism' as the major evil and the Chechnya conflict was viewed from that perspective. The final version of the National Security Concept, prepared by Secretary of the Russian Security Council Ivan Rybkin and published in December 1997, included terrorism in the context of an 'intensified struggle for power on the basis of group, political–ideological and ethno–nationalistic interests' on former Soviet territory.[3] The authors of the final version also had Chechnya in mind. The 1998 troika agreement between Russia, Uzbekistan and Tajikistan only mentioned terrorism as one problem among many. Terrorism was not yet the prism through which Central Asia was viewed and not a basic component of Russian policy in the CIS.[4]

The terrorist issue was introduced in the general CIS context in early 1999.[5] When, in October 1997, the CIS prime ministers decided to create a Committee on Conflict Situations, the main issue was conflict resolution and peacekeeping. The issue of organized crime was also discussed, but not the issue of terrorism.[6] When, in early March 1998, the CIS foreign ministers agreed on a draft programme on developing military cooperation up to 2001, the problems of conflict regulation and peacekeeping were again on the agenda. So was the issue of organized crime and a document was adopted on cooperation against crime, but no references were made to the issue of terrorism in the reports of the meeting.[7] Nevertheless, when on 4 February 1999 the CIS foreign ministers met to discuss economic cooperation and a future economic free trade zone, 12 days before the car bombs in Tashkent, the issue of terrorism was intensively discussed. The ministers agreed to present a draft programme on cooperation against the terrorist threat at the following summit meeting of heads of state to take place in June in Minsk.[8] Terrorism as such was not defined, and no direct references were made to Central Asia. One year later such a draft programme found its way to the CIS Council of Heads of State, by which time the Batken events had already taken place.

Thus, while terrorism had been on the Russian agenda at CIS meetings before Putin, Putin made it a top-priority issue. The Batken events opened a 'policy window' and he used it to move a full-scale common anti-terrorist struggle into the CIS arena, although primarily into Central Asia.

A meeting of signatories to the Collective Security Treaty on 7 September 1999 branded the Batken events as 'international terrorism'.[9] The term international terrorism was also used at the 15 September emergency session of the CIS Council of Defence Ministers in Moscow, with representatives of Russia, Uzbekistan, Kyrgyzstan, Tajikistan, Kazakhstan, Armenia and Belarus present, which agreed on joint efforts.[10] Putin announced the establishment of an 'anti-criminal coalition', the main purpose of which was to handle extremists 'everywhere from the Caucasus to the Pamir'.[11]

The terrorist theme was repeated on 28 September 1999 in the speech by Deputy Foreign Minister Vasilii Sredin on the main directions of Russian foreign policy. Islamic extremism was now explicitly the target, and responsible for world terrorism:

> A serious challenge to the world community is religious extremism, in particular that which uses Islam as a cover. Islamic extremists are trying to create a whole chain of hot spots in the world in order to destabilize the situation in individual states. This is confirmed by their acts in Afghanistan, Algeria, Bosnia, Kosovo and now also in Russia (Chechnya and Dagestan) and Kyrgyzstan. Religious extremism together with separatism and terrorism harbours *an especially* dangerous threat to international security and stability.[12]

In the following months, Russian policy shifted noticeably towards a stronger emphasis on relations with Central Asia in general and some Central Asian states in particular.

This new focus was a radical shift compared with Moscow's initial lack of interest in Central Asian affairs (apart from Tajikistan) immediately after the break up of the Soviet Union, and its ambivalence during the years that followed. Visits to Central Asia by Prime Minister Putin in the autumn of 1999 reflected this new attention. Putin's first foreign trip as prime minister was to Tajikistan in November 1999, just before the Tajik presidential election, and demonstrated continued Russian support for its ally, President Rakhmonov. The weighty Russian delegation also included Defence Minister Igor Sergeev, the Minister for CIS Affairs, and the Director of the Russian Federal Border Guard Service.[13] The visit to Uzbekistan, which followed in December, was no less important. Uzbek President Islam Karimov responded positively to the Russian Government's proposals for cooperation, and a series of bilateral agreements on security and military–technical cooperation were signed. The Russian Government also became more active with regard to Turkmenistan and issues connected with the export of energy from Central Asia. Discussions with Turkmenistan, which were initiated in autumn 1999, resulted in an agreement on the restoration of gas exports from Turkmenistan to Russia and indicated a willingness to allow the transportation across Russia (to Ukraine) of larger quantities of Turkmen gas in the future.

Putin's address to the Russian Federation Council on 22 December also signalled this new emphasis on Central Asia in general, and Uzbekistan in particular. Putin mentioned three levels of 'integration' between Russia and CIS countries. He placed relations with Belarus on the first level, with the countries of the CIS Customs Union on the second, which apart from Russia and Belarus included Kazakhstan, Kyrgyzstan and Tajikistan, and on the third level he placed Russia's relations with Uzbekistan.[14] With regard to Uzbekistan, not only did he describe the bilateral treaty on military and military–technical cooperation of 11–12 December 1999 as a 'turn for the better' but he also described Russian–Uzbek relations as a 'strategic partnership'. He even suggested that the bilateral agreement 'in its scope and in terms of integration processes ... is more significant than the Collective Security Treaty' from which Uzbekistan had withdrawn in April 1999.

At the same time the Russian Government made it clear that it did not want to take on major new commitments. Torn between its wish to strengthen its influence through the fight against 'international terrorism', on the one hand, and the constraints imposed by limited resources, on the other, the Russian Government resolved the dilemma by choosing the 'collective' option and called for increased military and security cooperation with the Central Asian states. When the Islamic rebels advanced into the Batken district and took hostages, and on 31 August the Kyrgyz Government requested assistance from Russia and the CIS, Defence Minister Sergeev replied that Russia would send military–technical assistance to Kyrgyzstan but no soldiers and that the Central Asian states themselves had to play the leading role in removing the terrorists. He stated that 'the question of sending Russian ground units to the theatre of combat operations is not being discussed'.[15] Russia's assistance was limited to help from Russian Generals and officers sent to the conflict zone, the Osh and Batken regions, to analyse the situation, work out proposals and participate in planning.[16] As a result, no troops from the Russian 201st Motorized Rifle Division (MRD), based in Tajikistan, were transferred to Kyrgyzstan. Because Russia did not send soldiers or aircraft to the area, Uzbek troops and aircraft played the critical role in defeating the Islamists. Russia delivered attack helicopters to Uzbekistan, which used them against the IMU fighters. At his meeting with Kyrgyz Prime Minister Amangeldy Muraliev in late October, Putin promised Russian assistance against terrorist threats in the future.[17]

With a new focus on terrorism it was logical that the 2000 Russian Military Doctrine, the 2000 National Security Concept and the 2000 Foreign Policy Concept, which were all finalized under Vladimir Putin, would emphasise the terrorist threat. The Military Doctrine gave terrorism more prominence among the potentially destabilizing factors that could affect the military–political situation than had its predecessor of 1993: 'the activities of extremist nationalist, religious, separatist and terrorist movements, organizations and structures; the expansion of the scale of organized crime, terrorism, and weapons and drug trafficking; and the multinational nature of these activities'.[18] The National Security Concept called terrorism a 'serious threat to the national security of the Russian Federation.'[19] The Foreign Policy Concept mentioned military–security cooperation to fight international terrorism and extremism as a priority task for Russian policy within the CIS.[20]

By January 2001 the terrorist threat was defined as an existential threat to Russian and Central Asian security and the prism through which the world was viewed. Putin outlined, at a meeting with senior diplomatic officials at the Foreign Ministry, that:

> Our country has to face a whole range of acute questions. They include regional conflicts, separatism, terrorism, uncontrolled migration, organized crime and others. I would like to stress the danger of international terrorism and fundamentalism of any, absolutely any, stripe. We have said this on many occasions and we are responsible for it becoming part of the international vocabulary. Quite obviously a Terrorist International is emerging and together with our partners we should proceed in a concerted and coordinated way. It is in our direct interest to contribute to the establishment of effective mechanisms of international cooperation in every area.[21]

A wave of Russian activity was initiated in Central Asia not only to respond to the new threat but also to find a new basis for future security and military cooperation. The Russian newspaper *Vedomosti* commented, 'It seems that Russia is ready to take revenge in Central Asia for what it is losing in the Caucasus'.[22]

In August and September 2000, one year after the Batken events, around 200 IMU fighters launched a well-coordinated, multi-pronged offensive. Fighting took place in the valley close to the Sokh and Vorukh enclaves in south Kyrgyzstan and also in south-eastern Uzbekistan—in the mountains of the Surkhandarya region and the mountains north of Tashkent, around Jangrabad and Bostanlyk.[23] This time the Kyrgyz authorities were better prepared. By the end of October IMU commander Namangani had withdrawn his forces and retreated to Tajikistan and Afghanistan.[24]

Policy on Russian-led Multilateral Cooperation

Putin's new emphasis on 'international terrorism' and the anti-terrorist struggle brought a focus and direction to Russia's Central Asia policy which had previously been lacking. The struggle against terrorism was an issue to which the Central Asian leaders responded positively, although the number of terrorist actions was still very small. They agreed with the way Putin framed the issue and to Russian efforts to develop multilateral security cooperation within the CIS (of twelve members) and the CST (with six signatories).[25]

At the CIS summit meeting in January 2000 the decision was taken to prepare a CIS Anti-Terrorist Programme and examine the idea of a CIS Anti-Terrorist Centre. This was followed up on 20-21 June 2000 when the 'Programme on the Struggle Against International Terrorism and other Forms of Extremism', covering the period until 2003 was adopted, and the decision to set up the CIS Anti-Terrorist Centre was taken.[26]

The Anti-Terrorist Programme called for the coordination and harmonization of national laws on combating terrorism and other forms of extremism, joint research projects and information exchanges. The functions of the Anti-Terrorist Centre were described as primarily information analysis and the building up of an integrated databank of the different countries' security and special services. The centre was given the function of coordinating the 'competent bodies' of CIS member states to work out joint measures and assist with carrying them out. This was to be managed by a council consisting of the heads of the security bodies and special services of the CIS member states.[27]

While the CIS was thus to focus on analysis and information exchange, the CST was made the main instrument for the fight against terrorism. Its Collective Security Council, which had not been prominent hitherto, now became a crucial agent in this common fight. At its inception in 1992 the treaty had been defined as a defence treaty dealing with external threats. In early 1999 preparations were made to revise it in order to include domestic threats to security.[28] Thus, in April 1999, a declaration was adopted stating the intention to adapt the treaty to the 'new geopolitical situation' and to include domestic threats with international connotations in the threats covered by the treaty. At the summit of

24 May in Minsk a memorandum was adopted which referred to the fight against terrorism and religious extremism as a crucial task for the CST.[29] The final declaration of the session stated that the treaty was 'adapting to new geopolitical realities', was an important instrument, and provided a solid basis for collective measures to ward off 'any kind of aggression, including the especially pressing international terrorism and extremism'.[30] The threat of international terrorism was said to be increasing rapidly. 'It is closing ranks with aggressive separatism, religious intolerance and organized crime.' In Central Asia and the Caucasus there was 'a continued danger of aggravation of the situation'.[31] In an effort to coordinate policy towards third countries (for which read Western countries) the declaration stated that military–political relations between the parties to the CST had priority over military contacts with third countries.[32]

The CST summit meeting in Bishkek on 11 October 2000 decided to establish a joint military force intended for Central Asia.[33] It concluded that international terrorism and extremism in Central Asia constituted the main threat to the security of the region and were leading to long-term destabilization. According to the concluding document, troops can be sent to the territory of a member state in order to avert external aggression and carry out joint counter-terrorist operations—if requested by the state concerned. Participation must be governed by national legislation.[34] However, the October 2000 summit only agreed on general principles and the general staffs were given the task of working out the specifics concerning the composition of troops, their state of readiness and financing.[35] The Central Asian states seemed, however, as reluctant to enter permanent military structures and take on obligations as they had been in previous discussions on creating a permanent CIS peacekeeping force.[36]

Under the label of the anti-terrorist struggle, bilateral agreements were signed between Russia and individual Central Asian states in 2000 on cooperation between national militaries, border troops, security services, and interior ministries. Agreements were also signed on the training of Central Asian military forces at Russian military colleges. Large-scale military exercises were carried out in Central Asia, starting in October with Southern Shield 1999, which was based on the scenarios of anti-terrorist operations.

Thus the issue of terrorism and the focus on the fight against terrorism paved the way for a new wave of Russian military cooperation with the Central Asian states. By October 2000 the issue of terrorism had made it possible for Russia to gain acceptance of its proposal to create 'regional security systems' and 'joint groups of forces' in the Western, Caucasian and Central Asian directions. While the future Russian–Belarussian and Russian–Armenian groups were to consist of general-purpose forces, the Central Asian group was designed specifically to be a rapid deployment force for anti-terrorist operations.[37]

Russian and Central Asian security cooperation also paved the way for a modernization of the Central Asian militaries and the delivery of Russian arms and military hardware to Central Asian states. In June 2000, the CST parties signed an agreement on military–technical cooperation, which made it possible for the member states to buy equipment at a reduced cost, that is, at the same price as the army of the producing country. This was intended to speed up a process of Russian-led modernization.[38] At the CST summit meeting in Bishkek in October 2000, it was decided that Russia would deliver armaments—aircraft (Su-25s and attack helicopters) and armoured vehicles suitable for mountain warfare.[39] Russia entered bilateral agreements, for example, with Kyrgyzstan on the provision of Russian technical equipment in order to strengthen Kyrgyzstan's southern border and to modernize and repair communications equipment along its border with China.[40]

The activation of the CST was also reflected in Russian efforts to turn the treaty and its Collective Security Council into internationally recognized representative bodies and to encourage the parties to close ranks in relation to third countries, coordinate their positions and speak with one voice. In April 2001 the Secretary of the Collective Security Council, Valerii Nikolaenko, also suggested that direct formalized relations be established with China, Iran, the Organization of the Islamic Conference and other international bodies.[41]

Moscow tried to extend this new emphasis on security cooperation within the CST to the CIS. In May 2001, at a meeting in Baku with CIS defence ministers, Russian Defence Minister Sergei Ivanov proposed that a 'single defence policy' for all other eleven CIS countries be drawn up under the banner of anti-terrorism. He argued that all the CIS countries faced terrorist threats of a similar nature and that this required a CIS-wide response.[42] Thus, the issue of terrorism was exploited in order to legitimize Russia's urge for military integration not only in Central Asia but also in the CIS area as a whole.

The final decision to create a CST rapid deployment force for Central Asia was taken in Yerevan in May 2001. The troops were to consist of c. 1500 men provided by Russia, Kazakhstan, Kyrgyzstan and Tajikistan and to be deployed at the request of any of the signatory states.[43] The Coordination Staff were to be located in Bishkek and consist of two representatives from each signatory. Each national contingent was to be financed by the home country and personnel expenses would therefore be minimal. In order to guarantee mobility, the core of the Central Asian force would be different kinds of airborne troops.

From time to time voices were heard in Russia in favour of a stronger Russian military presence in Central Asia and there were signs that this might come about, although no reinforcements were decided on. In August 2000, Defence Minister Sergeev seemed to concur when he suggested that Russia's positions in Central Asia should be strengthened and that Russia should take a more active stance on Islamic extremists in Uzbekistan and Kyrgyzstan. On 1 September 2000, the Military News Agency reported that Sergeev had sent the president a report on the joint tactical exercise, Combat Commonwealth 2000, and consultations with the CIS member states. Sergeev's conclusions were interpreted as an open call for military intervention in Central Asia. The Foreign Ministry was reported to have been startled by this initiative,[44] yet the Chief of the General Staff, General Anatolii Kvashnin—Sergeev's main rival in the struggle for military reform—was already in favour of the idea. The third actor in the Russian security establishment and the one who was closest to Putin at the time, Sergei Ivanov (at this time Secretary of the Russian Security Council), was of the opposite opinion. In December 2000 he declared that it was not so much a question of increasing the number of men as of increasing the level of combat readiness.[45] Instead of increasing the number of troops, the Russian

Government continued along the road of creating a sub-regional security system and a collective rapid deployment force in Central Asia as a way to share the responsibilities for and the costs of missions in Central Asia.

Putin exploited the terrorist issue in order to legitimize Russia's urge for military integration in the CIS area as a whole. However, although he seemed successful at first in drawing Uzbekistan into closer security cooperation, Putin did not succeed in orienting it back into the multilateral framework of the CIS or the CST. Instead, relations with Uzbekistan were to develop within a bilateral framework.

Policy on the Ground

Uzbekistan

Following the 1999 Batken incursions, Russia initiated a rapprochement with Uzbekistan. Putin's preparedness to respond immediately at CIS forums and to send weapons and equipment to Kyrgyzstan was also a signal to Uzbekistan. The bilateral treaty of 11–12 December 1999 referred directly to the common struggle against the new threat. After his talks with President Karimov, Putin stated: 'We are ready by joint efforts to place a barrier to the spread of terrorism and extremism'. Karimov responded: 'We are convinced that Russia's help and presence in the region will allow us to repel the rampant expansion of extremism and terrorism'.[46] The agreement envisaged cooperation between the defence ministries and armed forces of the two countries on security issues, the joint development and production of military equipment and armaments, and the training of military personnel.[47] The rapprochement was described in the Russian media as a reorientation by Uzbekistan back to Russia and a sign that Uzbekistan had concluded that only Russia (in contrast to the USA) could offer assistance in fighting the Islamists.

Uzbekistan started to participate in the series of large military exercises of both staff and troops that Russia initiated under the name Southern Shield in October 1999. Although Uzbekistan had not joined the CIS multilateral agreement on air defence, it participated in a major air defence exercise, held in early April 2000, based on the scenario of an aircraft being hijacked. Both Uzbekistan and Tajikistan agreed to take a more active role in 'anti-aircraft defence initiatives' and Kyrgyzstan joined the joint combat anti-aircraft defence roster of the CIS member states.[48]

After a time, however, it became obvious that Uzbekistan maintained its earlier interest in also developing relations with the West and GUAM.[49] Uzbekistan intensified its cooperation with Russia but only on a bilateral basis. It did not return to multilateral CIS military and security cooperation.

In March 2001 the Russian Parliament ratified the agreements with Uzbekistan.[50] However, by then signs of friction had developed in the Russian–Uzbek cooperation. Although Uzbekistan had participated in military exercises with Russia and the Central Asian states in late 1999 and 2000, it did not allow its forces to participate outside Uzbek territory and remained categorically against any foreign military presence in Uzbekistan. Observers interpreted these restrictions as a sign of friction in relations.[51] When the April 2001 Southern Shield command-and-staff exercise took place in Moscow, with participation from Russia, Kazakhstan, Kyrgyzstan and Tajikistan, Uzbekistan did not participate.

In May 2000 Putin, now President of Russia, again visited Uzbekistan at the head of a high-level Russian delegation, which included both Defence Minister Sergeev and Foreign Minister Igor Ivanov. They had a 'frank exchange of opinions' with their Uzbek counterparts on issues of world and regional politics, including the situation in Central Asia. Also on the agenda were bilateral trade policy and military–technical, cultural and humanitarian issues. Here, there was clear interest on both sides in developing economic contacts[52] and they succeeded in reaching agreement on military–industrial and military–technical deliveries. Security issues, however, remained the most important. They again stressed the need for the two countries to coordinate efforts against international terrorism and religious extremism, but nothing specific was agreed.[53] Uzbekistan continued to take unilateral measures against Tajikistan and Kyrgyzstan in order to increase its own security. Early in 2000 Uzbekistan started to mine parts of its border with these countries. Uzbekistan's suspicion of Tajikistan increased when members of the former United Tajik Opposition, among them a military commander, became members of the Tajik Government.

In October 2000 the trial began of those accused of the February 1999 bombings in Tashkent as well other bombings in towns during 1991–99. Twelve leaders of the IMU (including Namangani and Yuldashev) and the Erk (Mohammad Solikh) were tried, although most were tried in absentia.[54]

Looking back at the cooperation on terrorism between Russia and Uzbekistan, it is obvious that a major disagreement developed as to how to define the enemy—in particular whether it was the Taliban regime or Central Asian terrorists finding shelter and support in Afghanistan. While Uzbekistan wanted to fight its home-bred terrorists, it became less willing after 1998 to fight the Taliban regime. After the incursions of 1999 and 2000, IMU fighters, who had been 'deported' from Tajikistan and then retreated to Afghanistan, intensified their contacts with the Taliban.

Having already become less militant in its stance against the Taliban in 1998, Uzbekistan became more conciliatory towards them as they advanced further north during the summer of 2000. In this situation, because of the attitude of the Central Asian states in general and Uzbekistan in particular, it became increasingly difficult for Moscow to deal with the issue of Afghanistan. On 23 May 2000 Putin's spokesman, Sergei Yastrzhembskii, warned of the possibility of a preventive air strike against what were said to be training camps for terrorists in Afghanistan. The warning was repeated by such senior Russian officials as Secretary of the Russian Security Council Sergei Ivanov, Defence Minister Sergeev and Deputy Prime Minister Ilya Klebanov.[55] Ivanov declared that Russia might consider bombing Afghanistan in order to prevent it from supporting and encouraging terrorist activities in Central Asia, adding that Russia would not rule out any type of action.

Uzbekistan, however, seemed to be adapting to the fact that the Taliban were in power in Afghanistan.[56] On 22 September 2000, at the UN Millennium Summit, President Karimov declared that it was necessary to study the influence and the potential of the Taliban and to reach agreements with them.[57] In October, talks were initiated between the Uzbek and Afghan ambassadors in Pakistan on the possibilities for trade and for opening up a crossing on the Uzbek–Afghan border.[58]

Senior Russian officials stated repeatedly that the struggle against international terrorism and religious extremism within the CIS would not be successful without the participation of Uzbekistan.

Tajikistan

The transition period prescribed in the peace agreement formally came to an end[59] after the presidential elections in Tajikistan in November 1999 and the parliamentary elections of February and March 2000. Consequently, the CIS peacekeeping mandate expired in June 2000. Neither set of elections was considered fair by international observers, yet, the UTO chose to accept the outcome. The political situation in the country remained fragile and the country unstable. Murders of high-ranking politicians and well-known personalities were part of everyday life. Among the former members of the Islamic wing of the UTO to become members of the government were Akbar Turazhonzoda, one of the two previous leaders of the UTO and now the new First Deputy Prime Minister, and Mirzo Ziyoyev, a former commander and now the minister for emergency situations. Ziyoyev had fought together with Namangani during the Tajik civil war and therefore became a special target of criticism from the Uzbek Government. The IRP and Ziyoyev played a crucial role in convincing the IMU fighters to be 'deported' from Tajikistan to Afghanistan in 2000.

By January 2000 Russian border troops had been withdrawn from Uzbekistan, Turkmenistan and Kyrgyzstan, and replaced by their respective national border guards. Russian border guards only remained in Tajikistan, where a national border force service had just started to function.[60] The porosity of borders was a serious problem for the states of the region. The borders between the Central Asian states were not yet functioning as state borders. There was no proper border control and the borders were therefore more or less open to the illegal movement of people. Against this background, the presence of Russian border troops at the Tajik–Afghan border was all the more important as a factor for stability.

The Tajik Government lacked control over large parts of its territory, especially in Garm and Tavildara which were old strongholds of the Islamic wing of the UTO. Fearing an influx of Islamic rebels from Afghanistan through Tajikistan, Uzbekistan accused Tajikistan of harbouring Uzbek militants in its interior and resorted to unilateral measures against Tajikistan.

Tajikistan's dependence on the Uzbek economy was used as a source of leverage. In 2000, after repeated incursions by Islamic militants from across Tajikistan and Kyrgyzstan, Uzbekistan introduced a visa regime for Tajik citizens, including the inhabitants of districts bordering Uzbekistan. Several border-crossing points were closed completely and Tajikistan felt the effects immediately.

Northern Tajikistan had always been closely linked to the Uzbek economy as part of the Fergana Valley, a natural economic unit for hundreds of years. The new post-Soviet state borders seriously hampered trade and economic development in the area. The common infrastructures for transport, gas and electricity, inherited from the Soviet system, made Tajikistan especially vulnerable. Tajikistan's dependence on Uzbekistan for the supply of gas was an instrument of Uzbek control over Tajikistan. From time to time Uzbekistan cut gas deliveries, citing unpaid Tajik debts. The main exit roads out of the country and the only railway connections with the outside world run across Uzbekistan.

Tajikistan accused Uzbekistan of exploiting the discontent of the Uzbek population in Tajikistan, which is heavily concentrated in the north and along the border with Uzbekistan in the west and south-west (Hissar and Khatlon), and supporting the rebellious colonel and ethnic-Tajik, Uzbek Makhmud Khudoberdiyev, who twice staged a revolt against Dushanbe in the 1990s.

In spite of Tajikistan's weakness and vulnerability, however, it became an increasingly important ally to Russia as the anti-terrorist struggle became the top priority on Putin's agenda, and especially important as a transit country for military materiel to the anti-Taliban Northern Alliance. Participating in a power-sharing agreement with the government, the IRP maintained no contacts with the Taliban. By 2000, all the Central Asian countries, except Tajikistan, had become more inclined to expand contacts with the Taliban regime because of the Taliban de facto control of Afghanistan. While no government suggested full diplomatic recognition, they were considering the prospect of normalization.

Afghanistan

The question of whether Russia would increase its support for Akhmed Shah Massoud was raised once again by the incursion of terrorists into Kyrgyzstan in 1999. The debate was reflected in the Russian media, where articles argued in favour of increased assistance to Massoud and his troops.

When, in the spring of 2000, the Taliban successfully intensified their offensive against Massoud in the north, Russia became even more frustrated in its search for a response to the situation. The new Taliban offensive drove Massoud's forces from the town of Taloqan and parts of the provinces of Baghlan and Takhar. Russia feared that the Taliban was making its final offensive against the Northern Alliance.

The Taliban offensive added to the contradictions and interdepartmental struggles within the Russian leadership over the response to the Afghan threat. It also increased disagreements in relation to the Central Asian states, which did not agree that air strikes were an option, even though they shared the view that Afghanistan was the primary source of instability in Central Asia. It therefore came as no surprise when Ivanov had to backtrack on his warning of Russian air strikes against Afghanistan. When the October 2000 CIS summit meeting in Bishkek decided to create a collective CIS rapid-reaction force, Ivanov stressed that this decision did not indicate any intention to attack Afghanistan and that preventive measures with regard to Afghanistan would only be of a political or diplomatic nature.[61]

It became increasingly difficult for Moscow to deal with the issue of Afghanistan because the Central Asian states in general, and Uzbekistan in particular, distanced themselves from Russia's position and seemed instead to adapt to the fact of Taliban power in Afghanistan. Turkmenistan continued its policy of maintaining normal relations with the Taliban and did not join CIS declarations or activities directed against the Taliban. Kazakhstan, from its distance, had never been especially concerned about the 'Taliban threat', but in the autumn of 2000 it urged talks and contacts with the Taliban.[62] In common with Turkmenistan and Uzbekistan, the Kazakh Government called for pacification in northern Afghanistan, accommodation with the Taliban authorities and internationally sponsored economic reconstruction in Afghanistan as a whole.[63] In October 2000 the Tajik Government, which had not been interested in either recognizing the Taliban or initiating a dialogue, said it considered the Taliban to be no direct threat to Tajik national security. Most Tajik political commentators were of the opinion that the Taliban would not cross the border from Afghanistan.[64]

In the autumn of 2000 there were reports that Russian officials and military personnel were establishing contacts with the Taliban on the Tajik-Afghan border.[65] Sergei Yastrzhembskii's trip in September 2000 to Central Asia and Pakistan also raised speculation in the Russian media that he had discussed the issue of initiating talks with the Taliban. This was, of course, denied by the Russian side.[66] During the autumn of 2000 individual voices within Russia, among them some politicians, made statements in favour of recognizing the regime in Kabul,[67] but the Taliban regime's recognition of Chechnya as an independent state made it unrealistic to believe that Russia would do so.

Instead, Moscow found ways to increase pressure on the Taliban regime. In the United Nations, it lobbied in favour of a Security Council resolution on strengthening sanctions against Afghanistan.[68] In December 2000, Russia and the USA won a vote in the UN Security Council for a resolution on sanctions against the Taliban regime. The USA was increasingly concerned about the presence of the international terrorist Osama bin Laden, who had been operating from Afghanistan since 1996.

At the same time, Moscow stepped up its direct military pressure on the Taliban regime. On 26 October 2000, Defence Minister Igor Sergeev met the leader of the Northern Alliance, Akhmed Shah Massoud, in Dushanbe to discuss the situation in northern Afghanistan and measures to be taken against the Taliban.[69] Russia increased its support for Massoud in the form of deliveries of military equipment and hardware and, according to Russian military analyst Pavel Felgengauer, its support for the Northern Alliance in Afghanistan took on more intrusive and overt forms.[70] The delivery via Tajikistan, by the Russian Ministry of Emergency Situations, of two plane loads of what it described as humanitarian supplies to the Massoud-controlled corner of Afghanistan was made public by the Russian media. In fact, the two flights seem to have been designed to inaugurate and legitimize supply lines to Massoud from Moscow and Tehran.[71]

Turkmenistan and Uzbekistan were critical of international sanctions against Afghanistan. The Turkmen representative at the UN announced at the 55th session of the General Assembly that 'dialogue and cooperation with the Taleban in Afghanistan will be much more productive than international isolation'. He argued that sanctions would be counterproductive because they hurt ordinary Afghans and instead recommended inter-Afghan negotiations under the aegis of the UN. Uzbek President Karimov echoed these ideas during a trip to Ashgabat, 'We want the Afghani people themselves to solve the existing problem. It will happen as soon as external meddling stops'.[72]

The Russian tone towards the Central Asian states sharpened as their approaches diverged on how to deal with the Taliban regime. On 9 November 2000 Sergei Ivanov, Secretary of the Russian Security Council, warned that states that assisted the Taliban financially and militarily or entered into talks with them risked 'severe sanctions' from Russia. The warning was understood by observers to be partly directed at Central Asian states moving towards talks with the Taliban regime in the hope of establishing economic relations with it.[73]

UN Security Council resolution 1333 of 21 December 2000, initiated by Russia and the USA, called for the introduction of limited sanctions against Afghanistan if the Taliban regime failed to extradite Osama bin Laden.[74] The sanctions included a ban on air traffic to and from Afghanistan and an arms embargo. The resolution demonstrated that Russia and the USA had come to an understanding on the issue of Afghanistan and international terrorism. This was the result of high-level diplomatic talks, which had started at the meeting between Russian Deputy Foreign Minister Trubnikov and US Deputy Secretary of State Armitage in August 2000.[75]

Russia seemed to have found common interests and a common approach with the US Government on the issue of the Taliban, but the Afghan factor continued to pose a dilemma for Russian policy making with regard to the Central Asian states.

To Russia, the Taliban regime could not be understood in isolation from its support for and financing of international terrorism. Afghanistan was viewed as the centre of a terrorist network, especially after bin Laden increased his financial support of the Taliban regime and of terrorist groups outside of Afghanistan. The Taliban regime was accused of making the country a refuge for terrorists from Central Asia, Chechnya and Xinjiang, and of hosting training camps for terrorists.[76] Russia saw a worldwide terrorist network and in 2000 Putin extended the area previously covered by the concept of an 'arc of instability' to stretch all the way from the Philippines to Kosovo.[77]

Dilemmas for Russian Policy

Under Putin, Russian policy towards Uzbekistan, Tajikistan and Afghanistan underwent a change of emphasis. The effects of this policy, however, increased some of the ambiguities and contradictions in Russian policy in the region, thereby creating new dilemmas.

First, there was the dilemma created by Russia's emphasis on the struggle against 'international terrorism' as a main theme for developing security cooperation with the states of the region. The label 'terrorism' addressed one very narrow aspect of a much wider problem, that of radicalism and extremism, and indicated a very strong emphasis on military means when instead a broad package of measures with the emphasis on non-military means might have been more appropriate to respond to the challenge.[78]

The second dilemma was the gap between commitments and limited capacity. While Russia made commitments to provide military assistance, it was not certain that it was capable of living up to those commitments. The defeat in late October 1999 of the Uzbek Islamists' incursion into Kyrgyzstan under Juma Namangani was used in the Russian media to illustrate Russia's capacity to provide military security assistance in the event of a crisis in Central Asia. The USA, the NATO and other foreign actors engaged in Central Asia were described as being incapable of providing any assistance in such situations. Yet, the question of whether Russia itself would be capable of assisting if serious conflict erupted again in the region remained unanswered.

The constraints on future Russian military assistance had been reflected in the statements of September 1999 by Defence Minister Sergeev that the Central Asian states would have to cooperate mainly between themselves to solve the crisis in Kyrgyzstan. In this way, he indicated that Russia was not prepared to take on the burden and the responsibility in the same way as it had in Tajikistan in the early 1990s. Kyrgyzstan was offered only military–technical assistance and no troops. Russian elite troops were concentrated in the northern Caucasus in order to secure control of Chechen territory, would have to remain there for a long time, and could not be sent to Central Asia. If a serious crisis developed in Central Asia, Russia would not be prepared to engage in a Central Asian 'Chechnya scenario', and would only be able to provide assistance in minor crises in the region.

At the same time, Putin's anti-terrorist policy for CIS territory in general, and for Central Asia in particular, was understood within Russia as a step towards a more interventionist policy on CIS territory in the sense that Russia was taking on much larger responsibilities and costs. Some people in Russia questioned such new responsibilities. The following view, published in a debate in the military supplement of *Nezavisimaya gazeta*, was in no way the dominant view in the media at the time. However, it demonstrated that there was deep concern, not least among the military, about Russia taking on too large a burden in Central Asia.

> It is time to understand that Russia is at present too weak, too damaged and lags much too far behind the rest of the world to load itself down with heavy sacks of Central Asian problems and once again play the role of the older brother all the more in a defence organization of which the purposes are unclear. The only possible alternative for our country is the following: to keep away as much as possible from all possible conflicts, from all possible military alliances, and not to engage in any adventures in Europe of the Kosovo kind, and especially not in Asia. It is time to release it from the utterly dangerous and absolutely unnecessary illusion that not a single issue in world politics can be solved without Russia.[79]

A third dilemma was created by Russia's emphasis on a 'strategic partnership' with Uzbekistan and its regional consequences. Several Russian commentators pointed out that Russia could not expect a long-lasting alliance with Uzbekistan—Uzbekistan's cooperation with Russia was tactical and Uzbekistan was not interested in revising its foreign policy in favour of Russia or in damaging its relations with the West.

There was also a regional dimension to the emphasis on Uzbekistan. Serious regional consequences could follow if Russia were to support Uzbekistan and be bound to accept Uzbekistan's involvement in the domestic affairs of neighbouring countries. The incursions by Islamic extremists into Kyrgyzstan had seriously aggravated relations between Uzbekistan, Tajikistan and Kyrgyzstan. Russian press reports had warned that a 'Dagestan scenario' could follow from events in Batken, in the sense that Uzbek forces enter into Tajikistan to destroy rebel bases and camps with artillery fire and air raids.[80] Karimov declared that Uzbekistan was 'quite within its rights' to conduct an operation against terrorists in Tajikistan. He severly criticized the Kyrgyz authorities for their passivity and lack of capacity to handle the crisis. In his view, the terrorists had crossed the Kyrgyz border not in August 1999 but two years before, which explained 'all these criminal raids and the tons of explosives we discovered in the cities of Kokand, Andizhan and Namangan. It was all brought there through the territory of Kyrgyzstan'.[81] During the spring and summer of 1999, when the Uzbek secret service was pursuing Islamists on Kyrgyz territory, President Askar Akaev of Kyrgyzstan and the Kyrgyz Government tried to play down the Islamic threat. In the summer of 1999 Akaev argued, more or less, that Kyrgyzstan was a small country unable to do much when a larger neighbour behaves as the Uzbek security service did in Kyrgyzstan.[82] His words reflected his concern over Uzbek involvement.

Neighbouring Tajikistan, completely vulnerable to Uzbekistan's involvement and influence, accused Uzbekistan of supporting anti-government forces in Tajikistan. If Russian policy prioritized Uzbekistan it would be more difficult for Russia to restrain Uzbek influence in Tajikistan. A close partnership between Russia and Uzbekistan would weaken the constraints on Uzbek power and influence and trigger a reaction from Uzbekistan's neighbours that, in the end, would be harmful to Russian influence in the region. It was therefore a tricky balancing act for Russia to support Uzbekistan in a partnership relationship and at the same time counter Uzbekistan's growing influence.

The fourth dilemma followed from the Taliban's advance into northern Afghanistan, up to its border with the Central Asian states, and the Central Asian responses to the new situation. While Russia wanted the Central Asian states to join forces against the Taliban regime, their leaders, in varying degrees, thought of normalizing relations with the Taliban to encourage them close down Uzbek rebel camps on Afghan territory. One option for Russia was to take on the task of countering the Taliban itself. There were suggestions in Russian debate that Russia should increase its support to the Northern Alliance. Among those voices was the chief of the operational department of the Russian border troops in Tajikistan, who published such a recommendation in the military supplement to *Nezavisimaya gazeta* in February 2000.[83] A second option was to normalize relations with the Taliban. However, it was not possible for Russia to recognize a Taliban government—especially after the Taliban had, in January 2000, recognized the independence of Chechnya. It was argued, however, that Russian recognition of the Taliban regime would have prevented the Taliban from recognizing Chechnya.[84] Instead, Russia chose to continue its support for Massoud of the Northern Alliance and rely on Tajikistan for assistance with delivering the arms.

While the dilemma following on from the rapprochement with Uzbekistan soon vanished, because Uzbekistan maintained a distance to Russian policy, the other dilemmas remained unresolved.

In order to carry out policy with regard to Central Asia, and the CIS states generally, Putin had to give more emphasis to bilateral relations than Primakov had done. In January 2000, as acting president, he outlined the main principles, objectives and tasks of Russian policy with regard to the CIS states in two policy directives.[85] While multilateral integration was defined as the long-term goal bilateral relations were presented as the way forward. Central Asia illustrated to this dilemma.

Policy towards the Major Powers in Central Asia

Russia and the USA

Putin retained the suspicious attitude to US engagement in Central Asia that had characterized the Russian approach since the early 1990s. Nonetheless, Putin indicated an early interest in improving Russia's relations with the West in general and the USA in particular in his so-called Internet Speech of 28 December 1999, just before he was appointed acting president. [86] The desire to improve relations with the USA did not, however, stop Russia from trying to prevent it from gaining a foothold in Central Asia.

Putin invited NATO Secretary-General George Robertson to visit Moscow in February 2000. Relations with NATO had been broken off in March 1999 after NATO's air campaign against Serbia when Russia withdrew from participation in the NATO–Russia Permanent Joint Council. Meetings of the PJC resumed in July 1999 but, at Russia's insistence, they dealt only with the joint NATO–Russian peacekeeping mission in Kosovo. By inviting Robertson, Putin signalled a Russian return to contacts with NATO. In February 2000, after Robertson's visit to Moscow, Defence Minister Sergeev indicated that future discussions of the PJC would include Russia's military doctrine, NATO's Strategic Concept, disarmament, the implementation of UN Security Council resolution 1244 on Kosovo, and the fight against terrorism as a global problem.[87] The first PJC meeting for almost a year was held on 15 March 2000. Thus, Russian–Western relations improved somewhat but the wars in the Balkans and the NATO bombing during the Kosovo conflict still dominated relations.

In Central Asia the strategic rivalry between Russia and the USA had become more visible. The rich supplies of oil and gas in the Caspian region had fuelled rivalry but also increased their willingness to engage in resolving conflicts in the region. When the US Government engaged in the Caucasus and Central Asia during the second half of the 1990s, it became interested in maintaining security in the area. It made a series of security assistance commitments to the states of the Caspian region, thereby demonstrating that it did not want to leave security issues in the region to Russia. Cooperation developed in the form of bilateral agreements under the Partnership for Peace Programme, of which all Central Asian states were members except Tajikistan. Many US commentators questioned the seriousness of these commitments, and whether the US Government was not over committing itself.[88]

US engagement in the security of the Central Asian states increased first and foremost in relation to Uzbekistan, which was considered the strategic state in the region. Cooperation also developed with Kazakhstan and Kyrgyzstan. The US Administration responded to increased Central Asian concern about the terrorist issue and, in April 2000, Louis Freeh, the Director of the US Federal Bureau of Investigation (FBI), went to Tashkent to discuss how to fight crime and terrorism.[89] The FBI opened an office in Almaty, which was to cover all of Central Asia and coordinate operations between the FBI and law enforcement bodies in the region.[90] In the same month, Secretary of State Madeleine Albright visited Central Asia and issues of regional security in general and combating terrorism in particular were high on her agenda in talks with the presidents of Kazakhstan, Uzbekistan and Kyrgyzstan.

However, many commentators argued that no single state would be able to provide military assistance if a violent conflict were to erupt in Central Asia or the South Caucasus—neither Russia nor the USA alone would have the capacity. International cooperation therefore seemed to be the only option if states were to defend themselves against the new threats to security coming from international terrorism and organized crime, the drugs and arms trade, and the proliferation of weapons. However, even if this general insight was accepted in the Russian and US administrations, there was no sign of evolving Russian–US or Russian–NATO cooperation in the handling of conflicts on former Soviet territory.

No forum was created for discussing joint efforts for conflict prevention and security cooperation on former Soviet territory. The PJC agenda did not include former Soviet territory, although it had a potential of including joint efforts in the Caucasus and Central Asia. Dmitri Trenin of the Moscow Carnegie Center wrote in the *NATO Review* in April 2000 that: 'A close joint review of the provisions of the PJC would allow each side to identify real needs and set priorities, which could then be harmonized and developed into a feasible work plan'. He suggested that the security situation in Central Asia and Afghanistan be a subject for dialogue but stressed that such a dialogue would only take place provided that 'NATO could calm Russian fears that it sought to supplant Moscow as the security patron of the region'.[91]

The increasing crisis over Afghanistan resulted in intensified contacts between Russia and the US Administration. In 1999 two meetings took place within the so-called '6+2 formula' talks in which Russia and the USA together with the six states bordering Afghanistan (Iran, China, Pakistan, Tajikistan, Turkmenistan and Uzbekistan) participated. The group tried to create favourable external conditions to involve the warring parties in Afghanistan in a negotiation process.[92] In August 2000, the first meeting took place of what were to become regular bilateral talks on Afghanistan between the Russian first deputy foreign minister and the US Secretary of State. The declaration issued after the meeting stated that Moscow and Washington envisaged joint, even active, efforts to achieve a radical change in the situation in Afghanistan, the formation of a government with a broad base, and measures to fight international terrorism emanating from Afghanistan.[93] When Russia and the USA introduced and lobbied for a joint proposal on UN sanctions against Afghanistan in December 2000, this was the first time in the modern political history of Afghanistan that they had acted together to coordinate policies on the Afghan question.[94]

The summit meeting between presidents George W. Bush and Vladimir Putin in Ljubljana in the summer of 2001 was a clear demonstration of Putin's desire to improve relations with the West. The meeting ended the period of intense Russian scepticism following the wars in the former Yugoslavia. Russian concern over the increasing US engagement in Central Asia did not abate, however.

One important disagreement between Russia and the USA remained—the role of the UN Security Council on issues of the use of force to end or prevent armed conflict. Russia had come to strongly emphasize the importance of multilateral structures and the authority of the UN to decide this issue. This remained a principal issue of disagreement between Russia and the USA. Their different views also reflected the asymmetry in power relations between the two nations.

Russia and China

As the anti-terrorist struggle became top priority on the Russian agenda in Central Asia, Russia invited China to cooperate multilaterally on issues of Central Asian security. China became an accepted actor in former Soviet Central Asia and a natural partner with regard to the security of the area. The organizational framework was provided by the so-called Shanghai Five, which had developed from agreements signed in 1996 between Russia, China and China's Central Asian neighbours (Kazakhstan, Kyrgyzstan and Tajikistan). Events in Batken made it a forum for anti-terrorism.

A summit of the five states had already discussed, in July 1998, the strengthening of regional peace, stability and economic cooperation—thereby focusing on common efforts to fight separatism, religious fundamentalism, terrorism, illegal arms trafficking and the illegal drugs trade.[95] Initiated by Russia, a summit took place in Bishkek in August 1999 and a declaration was adopted on fighting 'separatism, religious extremism and terrorism'.[96] The Bishkek Declaration reflected the shift in emphasis of the group. During the following summit meetings in Astana and Dushanbe the themes from Bishkek were reaffirmed and developed. At the Dushanbe session in July 2000 the name of the group was changed to the Shanghai Forum when Uzbekistan joined as an observer. It was decided to form a Council of National Coordinators of the Shanghai Forum and to regularize the meetings of the five heads of government, foreign ministers and defence ministers.[97]

At the 15 June 2001 summit meeting in Shanghai the organization changed its name again, to the Shanghai Cooperation Organization (SCO), and

Uzbekistan became a member.[98] Although some interest was expressed, no further states joined the organization. This was explained by Kazakh President Nursultan Nazarbaev: 'It is necessary to strengthen the organization first, achieve results and then consider requests for accession'.[99] The SCO summit also decided to create an anti-terrorist centre.

Russia and China tried together to use the SCO as a vehicle for an anti-Western front directed first and foremost against the USA and its growing engagement in Central Asia. Such an approach was not supported by the Central Asian states, which saw US engagement in the region as an opportunity rather than a threat. At the same time, although strongly critical of US policy in Europe and concerned by increasing US engagement in Central Asia, neither Russia nor China was prepared to destroy its relations with the USA by developing the SCO into a direct anti-US front.

Summary

Under Putin Russia's Central Asia policy changed. Putin skilfully used the 'policy window' that the Batken events opened in August 1999 and resolutely moved the anti-terrorist struggle to the top of the Russian agenda in Central Asia. This gave him a platform for developing military and security cooperation with Central Asian governments and rapprochement with Uzbekistan. Putin's policy followed the traditional Russian emphasis on security issues. Yet, when the terrorist threat was used to frame Russian Central Asian policy, problems and concerns became more pronounced, and the means of conducting policy shifted. Russian policy became more focused and Central Asia received more attention than had previously been the case. Taken together, this meant a dramatic policy change.

Putin's anti-terrorist policy also aimed to counter US engagement in the region. The strategic situation in Central Asia had become more complex for Russia in the sense that foreign engagement was rapidly increasing and Uzbekistan quickly distanced itself from Russia. Thus, Putin spelled out the goal of Russia's policy more clearly—to integrate Central Asia under Russian leadership. Putin pursued Russia's previous policy of developing CIS economic cooperation but spent more time on establishing bilateral economic relations in order to compensate for the multilateral integration that never took place. However, it was as a security guarantor that the Russian Government believed it had something to offer.

At the time that anti-terrorism became first priority in Russian policy no one knew the exact scope of the terrorist threat or whether it was correct to talk about a serious terrorist threat to Central Asia. Before 11 September 2001 several Western scholars were of the opinion that the terrorist threat in Central Asia was being exaggerated.[100] Without doubt the general security situation on the ground in the region had deteriorated—in particular as Afghan territory was being used as a refuge for Central Asian radical Islamists. Russia feared the threat of Islamic extremism spreading to Central Asian countries.

Putin's policy of securitizing relations with the Central Asian states, which seemed so successful at first, no longer looked successful by the end of the summer of 2001. Although the anti-terrorist agenda was given priority at summits and meetings as a basis for multilateral and bilateral cooperation between Russia and Central Asia, neither the security situation nor the strategic situation in the region had improved. Instead, Afghanistan constituted a 'black hole' of instability for a large part of Asia, with direct implications for Uzbekistan and Tajikistan. Moreover, Putin's Central Asian policy, which had been an effort to counter the growing engagement by the West—and the USA most of all—had not prevented Uzbekistan from continuing its reorientation away from Russia. Russia's opposition to US engagement in the region was also reflected in its policy towards China—primarily within the Shanghai Five, later to become the Shanghai Cooperation Organization. Both Russia and China were strongly critical of US foreign policy in Europe and Central Asia. The SCO therefore took on an anti-US character, although neither Russia nor China was prepared to sacrifice its relations with the USA. Russia seemed to have few means with which to respond to the security situation and counter the diversification process going on in the foreign policies of the Central Asian states.

5

POST-SEPTEMBER 2001
The Contours of a New Russian Policy

On the morning of Tuesday 11 September 2001 two US aircraft were hijacked during domestic flights and deliberately crashed into the World Trade Center in New York and the Pentagon, near Washington, DC—two major symbols of US economic and military power. The news shocked the world and fundamentally altered the international situation. President Putin faced his most difficult decision: his reaction would have a determining influence on Russia's future and international standing. This chapter examines Russia's policy response, the changing strategic and security situation in Central Asia, and the evolution of Russian policy in Central Asia in the light of the attacks of 11 September.

The Policy Shift

In his phone call to US President George W. Bush in the evening of 11 September, Putin, after consulting his power ministries, was the first foreign head of state to express sympathy and condemn the attacks. In a telegram to Bush sent later the same night he wrote: 'Without doubt such inhuman acts should not stand without punishment'.[1] Thus, Putin immediately took a position that acknowledged the US Administration's right to take measures in self defence.

In the days that followed it remained unclear how and against whom the US would direct its response, but a massive strike was expected. Because Osama bin Laden was immediately accused of the attacks it seemed most likely that US forces would strike against al-Qaeda camps in Afghanistan. In the new international situation, Putin had to decide how Russia would react to a US attack, how it could contribute to a US operation, if at all, and how to take account of the degree of interest expressed by Central Asian leaders in cooperating with the USA in the case of military operations in Afghanistan. Moreover, Putin had to build basic agreement for his policy within Russia. During the following two-week period, Putin undertook intensive consultations.

After paying a state visit to Armenia on 14–15 September, Putin went to his summer house at Sochi on the Black Sea coast, where he stayed for a week. What was intended to be a holiday became instead a period of intensive work.

On his return to Moscow on 24 September he made Russia's policy response public. The strategic choice faced by Putin, as the analyst Andrei Fyodorov described it in an article on 14 September, was either to support the West in a struggle against terrorism on a global scale, thereby risking relations with the Muslim world, or to step aside to avoid siding with the West, in which case relations with the West would deteriorate. He argued that active Russian cooperation with the West in a joint anti-terrorist operation would have positive political and economic implications, and speed up the process of rapprochement with the EU and achieve a wider understanding with NATO. Russia's decision, Fedorov concluded, would determine whether or not it would remain among the world powers.[2]

On 14 September the *New York Times* alleged that there had been negotiations between US and Russian officials over the use by US forces of Russian military facilities in Tajikistan and a former Soviet airfield in territory controlled by anti-Taliban forces in northern Afghanistan for attacks on Afghanistan. Russian Defence Minister Sergei Ivanov and Chief of General Staff Anatolii Kvashnin denied that any such discussions had taken place.[3] Sergei Ivanov excluded the possibility that US forces would be allowed to use Central Asian territory stating: 'Central Asia is within the zone of competence of the CIS Collective Security Treaty. I see no reasons whatsoever, even hypothetical, for any suppositions about NATO operations being conducted from the territories of Central Asian countries which are members of the CIS'.[4] The Russian media, when interviewing politicians and commentators, displayed a general caution about getting too involved on the US side or becoming a 'hostage to US policy'.[5] For example, Gleb Pavlovskii at the Foundation for Effective Policy stated that: 'We have to demonstrate all necessary cooperation without falling into an awkward situation'.[6] Deep scepticism was also expressed about the USA using military force in revenge for the terrorist attacks, for example, by Grigorii Yavlinskii in *Nezavisimaya gazeta* on 13 September. Once Sergei Ivanov had excluded operations conducted from CIS territory, it seemed probable that Russia would instead provide intelligence information in support of US operations in Afghanistan, without the participation of its troops.[7] The Russian media discussed what else Russia could contribute in order to advance rapprochement with the West.[8]

The next difficult issue was how Russia should react to the keenness shown by Central Asian leaders to participate in US-led operations and how Russia could act to encourage them to fall in line with Russian policy. On 16 September, Uzbek Foreign Minister Abdulaziz Kamilov declared that Uzbekistan was open to 'any form of anti-terrorist cooperation with the United States', including the possible use of Uzbek territory for strikes on terrorist camps in Afghanistan.[9] The Tajik foreign minister also indicated an interest in cooperating with the USA but, because he was uncertain of what Moscow's policy would be, announced that talks with Moscow would take place first.[10]

On his arrival in Sochi on Sunday 16 September, Putin had long and detailed consultations with his 'siloviki' (representatives of the power ministries) and general guidelines were agreed. The following day, Putin discussed over the phone with all the Central Asian presidents, including the Kazakh President Nazarbayev.[11] At the same time, the Secretary of the Russian Security Council,

Vladimir Rushailo, was sent to Central Asia for consultations and a meeting of security officials of the Collective Security Treaty in Astana.[12] The Chief of the Russian General Staff, Anatolii Kvashnin, was also sent to Central Asia and, on 19 September, met with Tajik President Rakhmonov. Kyrgyzstan and Tajikistan were members of the CST and had to coordinate their responses with Moscow. Nevertheless, both leaders were eager to allow a US presence. This created a dilemma for Putin, described at the time by two Russian analysts—Russia either makes specific promises to participate in US operations against Afghanistan and achieves the status of a major US ally, which makes the decisions by Central Asian leaders look like consequences that flow from Russia's choice, or Russia gives vague answers to the USA and does not provide military support, in which case all acts by Central Asian leaders will be interpreted as if they were leaving the Russian sphere of influence.[13]

On 20 September the Russian media reported a statement by Foreign Minister Igor Ivanov that the Central Asian states would themselves decide whether or not to contribute to the US military operation.[14] Yet Sergei Ivanov had already excluded the possibility that their territory would be used for offensive operations. Putin tried to coordinate a joint position with Central Asian leaders. On Saturday 22 September, in Sochi, Putin met with representatives of his own power ministries in a meeting that lasted for six hours.[15] The following day he again held further phone consultations with all Central Asian presidents.[16] On Monday 24 September, returning to Moscow four days after President Bush had announced the impending war to Congress, Putin gave Russia's consent to US troops in Central Asia during military operations against Afghanistan. With regard to the upcoming operation, his statement outlined that Russia would: (a) provide intelligence information concerning infrastructure and the locations of terrorists and their camps; (b) open its airspace to flights with humanitarian cargoes to Afghanistan; (c) give its consent to the Central Asian states opening their airspace and air bases for the USA and its allies; (d) be prepared to participate in international search and rescue operations; and (e) increase its material support of weapons and military technology to the Northern Alliance and the Government of President Rabbani.[17]

Putin's decision was a compromise. He declared full support for the US operation but without the participation of Russian troops. He gave his consent for the Central Asian states to open their territories to US forces but with the proviso that offensive operations were not to start from this territory. The Central Asians were sympathetic to the last point because they initially feared repercussions from the Taliban if their cooperation with the USA was too far-reaching. Putin thus gained the acceptance of the Russian military and at the same time created the impression that Russia and the Central Asian states shared the same view on these policy issues. Putin's statement was the outcome of intensive discussions, as pointed out by Sergei Ivanov.[18] When the CIS prime ministers convened on 28 September, they backed Putin's formula.

Putin used the opportunity created by the terrorist acts of 11 September to make a breakthrough in relations with the West. The day after his statement he left for an official visit to Germany. His speeches at the German Parliament on 26 September and at NATO headquarters shortly thereafter clearly reflected his intention to improve relations with the US Government and with Europe.[19] From the Russian side there were great expectations regarding what would follow from closer cooperation with the USA. Reports from the meeting between Putin and NATO Secretary-General, George Robertson, on 3 October seemed to support such expectations: 'The global threat from international terrorism and interests in building a long-term and balanced system of European and global security demand deep changes in the format and content of cooperation between Russia and NATO'.[20] The Russian media speculated that Russian support for the USA at this difficult moment would improve Russian–US cooperation, enhance Russia's international role, bring it closer to membership of the World Trade Organization (WTO) and contribute to a more understanding approach by the West towards Russia's war in Chechnya.

Although Putin in his statement of 24 September explicitly spelled out that no offensive operations would take place from these countries, his announcement was sensational. US troops had participated in exercises on Central Asian soil as part of the NATO Partnership for Peace (PFP) programme since 1997. This, however, was something completely different.

By his September 2001 policy turn, Putin inverted his 1999 anti-terrorist agenda by extending it to include Western states as partners in Central Asia. Previously, Moscow had regarded policy towards Central Asia as separate from its policy towards the West. Central Asia had been perceived as being within the Russian sphere of interest, from which foreign powers should stay away. Now, by extending the 1999 agenda, Putin made Central Asia part of his Western agenda.

The New Situation in Central Asia

The Strategic Situation

The first US troops arrived in Uzbekistan in late September and were deployed at the Khanabad base (90 miles from Afghanistan). On 5 October President Islam Karimov repeated that these troops would be deployed only for humanitarian and 'search and rescue' operations.[21] The Taliban had issued warnings to Karimov on the consequences of Uzbek participation in offensive acts. Taliban units were located on the Uzbek–Afghan border not far from the Uzbek town of Termez. More US and Western troops were sent to Central Asia. By February 2002 there were about 1500 in Uzbekistan, 2000 in Kyrgyzstan and 300 in Tajikistan.

On 7 October US bombing of Afghan territory was initiated. Although Russia decided to stay out of the bombing campaign and not to send military personnel to the international anti-terrorist coalition force, Russian contributions were crucial to the overthrow of the Taliban. Russia gave the US Command crucial intelligence information and increased its support in the form of military materiel to the anti-Taliban Northern Alliance. Russia's main ally in Afghanistan, Akhmed Shah Massoud, had been murdered two days before the 11 September attacks but Moscow maintained contact with his successor—the ethnic Tajik commander Muhammad Fahim. On 13 September senior Russian,

Iranian, Uzbek and Tajik officials gathered in Dushanbe for an extraordinary meeting to discuss the new situation now that their ally was dead.[22] On 20 September Kvashnin met with Muhammad Fahim in Dushanbe.[23]

When the USA started to support the Northern Alliance as the force on the ground to overthrow the Taliban regime, its support went mainly to the Uzbek part of the alliance under Commander Abdurrashid Dostum. Russia, on the other hand, continued its support for the Tajik section. When US bombing paved the way for Northern Alliance troops to advance, voices within the Russian military demanded that Russia radically increase its financial support for Fahim to enable him to expand his and to neutralize the growing US influence.[24]

The strategy behind Operation Enduring Freedom (the name given to the US-led military operations in Afghanistan) involved air strikes, building alliances with anti-Taliban Afghan forces, deploying special operations units to improve the capabilities of the opposition forces, and creating a system of sensors and strike aircraft to execute precision strikes on Taliban military formations.[25] In late October, US efforts concentrated on capturing the city of Mazar-e Sharif in the north of the country in order to split the Taliban forces. On 9 November the city fell and the Northern Alliance forces took control of northern Afghanistan, major east–west and north–south highways, and turned its attention to Kabul in the south.[26] President Bush requested, and the Northern Alliance leaders agreed, that the Northern Alliance would not enter Kabul until an agreement had been made on a temporary government. However, on 12 November the Northern Alliance captured Kabul.

Disagreements over the composition of a new Afghan Government to replace the Taliban regime surfaced at an early stage. Putin stated that a new government should be open to all ethnic groups but reiterated that former President Burhanuddin Rabbani was the legitimate leader of Afghanistan. On 22 October a meeting took place between the Russian and Tajik Presidents together with Afghan representatives led by Rabbani. The different interests of the USA, Russia and the neighbouring states with regard to the composition of a new Afghan Government became evident when the USA and Pakistan claimed that a new government should be open to moderate members of the Taliban, while Russia, Rabbani and Tajikistan explicitly ruled out Taliban participation of any kind. [27] The capture of Kabul by the Northern Alliance shifted the balance of power on the ground. General Fahim moved quickly to create a political–military *fait accompli* and appointed his people to all senior posts. On 17 November, Rabbani returned to Kabul and reasserted his status as head of state.

The UN-sponsored Bonn meeting at the end of November, where representatives from four Afghan factions participated, appointed an Interim Administration under Hamid Karzai. The Northern Alliance was allotted 17 of 30 cabinet positions but the ethnic composition of the government was broadened. The Bonn Agreement established a political process: a *loya jirga* (grand national council) was to be convened within six months. Its task was to create a transitional government that would oversee the writing of a new constitution. A permanent government was to be elected within two years. On 22 December 2001 the interim administration under Karzai took power.

Although Russia and the USA were on the same side in Afghanistan it seemed for some time that their interests clashed. The rush to Kabul in late

November 2001 by Russian military transport aircraft and personnel from the Ministry of Emergency Situations—before international coalition forces had entered the city—seemed at first to the outside world to be a repetition of the Russian rush to Slatina Airport in Kosovo in 1999.[28] In spite of this incident Russia demonstrated its will to cooperate with the USA over Afghanistan and soon switched to a more flexible approach with regard to the composition of the Afghan interim government. In spite of its old contacts with Rabbani, Moscow soon supported the temporary administration of Hamid Karzai.

Russia continued to play a role in Afghanistan—particularly through its close contacts with the Tajik faction of the Northern Alliance, which dominated the Karzai Administration. The Panjshiri Tajiks held the posts of minister of defence, minister of the interior and minister of foreign affairs (Muhammad Fahim, Yunis Qanoori, and Abdullah Abdullah, respectively) and provided 36 of the initial 38 generals.[29] While this influence gave Russia a voice in the internal Afghan power struggle, it was not enough to influence the situation in Afghanistan. The US Government did not neglect Russian interests in Afghanistan, but the USA was the major actor in setting the agenda and priorities for Afghanistan and Russia's role was only secondary. Russia kept a low profile and adopted a 'wait and see' attitude.

Russia prepared for the peaceful development of Afghanistan, and Russian representatives declared that it was interested in participating in the future economic reconstruction of the country. In the meantime, Russia played a crucial role in providing humanitarian assistance to Afghanistan through Tajik territory. Tajikistan was already the main route for military assistance to the Northern Alliance and also maintained a crucial position with regard to humanitarian assistance to Afghanistan. In early 2002 a temporary crossing was built with German funding over the Pyandzh River at Nizhnii Pyanzh in Tajikistan. Russia repaired the Salang tunnel connecting the north and south of Afghanistan. Foreign Minister Igor Ivanov visited Kabul on 5 February 2002 to discuss economic and political cooperation in the reconstruction of Afghanistan. Russia continued its military support to the Northern Alliance, and military cooperation and Russian weapon deliveries to the new Afghan Administration were discussed during the visit to Moscow by Afghan Defence Minister Fahim on 12 February. Also discussed were Russian help with relief work and rebuilding Afghanistan's agricultural base. Hamid Karzai visited Moscow on 11 March and discussed with President Putin the main principles for bilateral cooperation. Moreover, Russia supported initiatives taken by Tajikistan as a mediator in the international assistance effort to Afghanistan, in particular in supplying electricity to northern Afghanistan.

In Central Asia developments after 11 September 2001 meant a breakthrough for the US and Western presence. The Central Asian states were quick to respond to the new situation. In the same way as Putin had caught the moment, so did they. The strategic scene in Central Asia completely changed. Uzbekistan was the most willing to cooperate with the USA. On 12 October the US Government, in a joint statement with President Karimov, gave extended security guarantees to Uzbekistan.[30] As many as 1500 US troops were deployed at the Uzbek military base at Khanabad.[31] For Uzbekistan, cooperation with the USA and NATO countries provided an opportunity for both economic and security assistance. Uzbekistan also saw a chance to equip its army with modern types of arms and military equipment. Not only the USA but also the UK and Turkey promised assistance with the development of a military training centre within the framework of the PFP programme.[32]

President Karimov made a clear decision to pursue the options of increased security cooperation with the USA and Western-oriented military cooperation. Consequently, he was not prepared to give any deadline for the US presence in the country to end. The USA was there to carry out a mission and would stay as long as was needed. One year after the terrorist attacks on New York and Washington Karimov stated:

> They came here to carry out their mission and function which they had made known to the entire world, that is, to create a coalition the main aim of which is to destroy the machine of terrorism. … In this situation the Americans came and only they, thanks to their military power—I am saying this with full responsibility—only they played the leading role here. Only their operations made it possible to liquidate camps and bases and the machine of the Taleban, to deal a blow and break the backbone of terrorist organizations and gangs. … My opinion is that they will be here for as long as it takes to ensure … security in the region, peace in the process of restoring Afghanistan, so that Afghanistan is an independent, sovereign and neutral state that poses no threat to its neighbours.[33]

The increased US presence in Uzbekistan meant that the role of security guarantor for Uzbekistan was transferred to the USA. This also meant that the task of controlling the Uzbek factor in Central Asia was de facto transferred to the USA. Russia now had no means of influencing Uzbek policy. Although Uzbekistan remained a member of the CIS and participated in certain operational border and security operations with Russia and Central Asian CST states, it was now outside the institutional Russian-led security cooperation. In official statements Karimov repeatedly stressed the importance of Russia for Central Asian stability. However, it became obvious that in reality Tashkent regarded the Russian-led CIS and the CST as paper organizations only—with policies that were purely declaratory, lacking in substance, and insignificant for Uzbekistan's future.

In Kyrgyzstan on 28 December 2001 the parliament agreed to allow the US military to set up a base at Manas International Airport, outside Bishkek, for one year.[34] In January 2002 President Askar Akaev declared that he was prepared to prolong the agreement for a US military presence on Kyrgyz territory.[35] About 2000 soldiers from NATO countries were located at the base, although the agreement allowed for as many as 5000. In mid-March 2002, the Kyrgyz parliament followed its previous decision with approval of a one-year deployment at Manas of troops from Australia, Canada, Denmark, France, Italy, Spain and Turkey. The French troops participated in operations in Afghanistan while the others provided technical and logistical support to the anti-terrorist campaign.[36]

On 14 September 2001 Turkmenistan President Saparmurad Niyazov had responded positively to a US request for support for retaliatory strikes on the Taliban regime because 'organizers of the terrorist assault prove to be in Afghanistan'.[37] Niyazov pointed out that the US-led coalition's goals, mandate, procedures and missions had to be clearly defined and function under the aegis of the United Nations.[38] He had to reconcile his actions with Turkmenistan's status as a permanently neutral country and did not allow foreign troops on its territory. Turkmenistan came to play an important role in the transport of international humanitarian aid to Afghanistan, but the new situation did not do much to increase the presence of international organizations or to end the isolation of Turkmenistan.

The change with regard to Tajikistan, however, was remarkable. As Russia's most loyal ally in Central Asia, Tajikistan had been an exclusively Russian domain before 11 September 2001. In late September the Tajik Government announced to the US Government its willingness to open up its territory, if needed, for overflights, landing and basing, offered all available sites and left it to the USA to state its preferences.[39] After a telephone conversation between Putin and Rakhmonov on 5 October, the Tajik Government made its offer public on 8 October. In mid-October, Foreign Minister Talbak Nazarov declared that Tajikistan 'does not rule out the stationing of US forces in the country'.[40] On 3 November 2001, during a visit to Dushanbe by US Defense Secretary Donald Rumsfeld, Tajikistan publicly gave its consent to the use of three military airfields by the US-led coalition.[41] A US assessment team found, however, that of the three airfields under discussion (Dushanbe, Kulyab and Kurgan-Tyube) only Dushanbe could be used but, because it was not suitable for heavy aircraft, it was only used to refuel cargo planes. During Rumsfeld's visit, President Rakhmonov agreed to initiate regular exchanges of information on anti-terrorist operations and to establish permanent military-to-military contacts between the USA and Tajikistan. Rumsfeld confirmed that Tajikistan would provide assistance with regard to 'overflights, intelligence gathering and various types of military-to-military cooperation'.[42] Troops began arriving in December. Among the first were French Marines, arriving on 6 December en route to Afghanistan.

The US Government offered Tajikistan support and assistance to strengthen its border security system, although Russian troops had the main responsibility for guarding the Tajik–Afghan border. Under a bilateral agreement, signed on 5 February 2002, the USA was to provide support to the Tajik Border Force with training and the purchase of technical and communications equipment. As part of Tajikistan's participation in the US-led anti-terrorist coalition, Tajikistan and the USA also developed full cooperation in intelligence–gathering, especially with regard to movements and events on both sides of the Tajik—Afghan border.

Although Tajikistan still remained Russia's most loyal ally, and the numbers of coalition troops involved were small, the US presence brought a new element into the Tajik political debate. The new international attention on Tajikistan brought hopes and expectations—and the beginning of a more critical stance towards Russia within Tajikistan. Problems in bilateral relations developed when Russia in early 2002 initiated a policy of regulating the presence of foreign migrant labour in Russia and deported Tajiks later in the year. Tajikistan reacted strongly. Rumours surfaced from time to time that the Tajik authorities had started to claim compensation for the presence of Russian troops, although this was officially denied.

In January 2002 the USA lifted its ban on the export of weapons to Tajikistan. On 22 February Tajikistan formally joined the PFP programme—the last of the states of Central Asia to do so—and this provided further impetus to cooperation with the USA and the NATO countries. It was expected that Tajikistan would work together with the PFP in civil emergency planning, scientific affairs, environmental programmes and military reform.[43] Although the Western military presence in Tajikistan was small (150 US troops at the most, and in September 2002 only 50; and 500 French at the most, and 150 in September 2002), the strategic situation in the country shifted markedly.[44]

Thus, the trends for an increasing foreign engagement in the region since the mid-1990s suddenly took a leap forward as US and NATO military personnel became part of everyday life in Central Asia.

The Security Situation

Tensions increased in Central Asia in the immediate aftermath of the 11 September 2001 terrorist attacks, primarily between Uzbekistan and Tajikistan. Most Uzbek border crossing points were closed. Strict regulations were introduced for the transit of goods.[45] For Tajikistan the costs were considerable: freight traffic was stopped at the Uzbek border and the costs for transit through Uzbekistan were damaging to Tajikistan's exports.[46] The strict visa regime introduced by Uzbekistan created effective barriers to the transit of people and goods, and to shuttle traders and local merchants. Formally, Tajiks could enter Uzbekistan but, in reality, it was difficult and expensive to get a visa, there were various taxes on goods, and the procedure at the border crossing points was humiliating. On 25 September 2001 Kazakhstan suspended passenger trains from Tajikistan to Moscow via Kazakhstan.[47] There were also several unresolved issues between Tajikistan and Uzbekistan over the supply of energy, the customs regulations for transit shipments, and water use. Uzbekistan had repeatedly cut off the supply of gas to Tajikistan, Kyrgyzstan and Kazakhstan, demanding immediate payment of debts. Now gas to Tajikistan was again cut because debts had built up. Uzbek landmines in the Fergana Valley along the borders with Tajikistan and Kyrgyzstan continued to take lives. By early 2002 almost 100 Tajik civilians had been killed or injured.[48] Most victims were women and children gathering firewood along the border or shepherds pasturing cattle in the area.

The fall of the Taliban regime in November improved the general security situation in Central Asia. Although tensions between the states in the region did not disappear, they abated when the external threat declined. The power struggle between different groups and clans within the anti-Taliban alliance indicated that instability would continue in Afghanistan for many years to come, but there was a chance that the Central Asian states would follow a different trajectory. The new and important Western factor contributed to the stability of Central Asia.

In November 2001, Juma Namangani, leader of the Islamic Movement of Uzbekistan (IMU), was reported killed in combat in northern Afghanistan. Since most of the IMU members had fought on the side of the Taliban, the organization went underground. The overthrow of the Taliban regime thus contributed to the removal of IMU fighters from the scene, at least temporarily. The Russian media reported from time to time during the spring of 2002 that groups of IMU fighters were illegally entering Gorno-Badakhshan and Tavildara, in the heart of Tajikistan, from Afghanistan, but this could not be confirmed. The Uzbek authorities, however, continued to refer to the threat from the IMU when defending the country's policy of restrictions on Tajikistan.

In late December 2001 a process of normalization of bilateral relations between Tajikistan and Uzbekistan was initiated. The two presidents met in Tashkent on 27–28 December on the eve of the summit meeting of the Central Asian Economic Community. The two leaders decided that more than 25 border crossing points were to be opened, the fees paid at the border by those travelling in cars and trucks would be reduced, and 10 per cent of the Tajik debt to Uzbekistan would be written off. Their meeting restarted the work of the existing but inactive Tajik–Uzbek Intergovernmental Commission and, on 12 February 2002, several agreements were signed when Tajikistan Prime Minister Akil Akilov visited Tashkent. Among them was one on the reopening of more border crossing points.[49] According to comments in the Tajik press during the spring of 2002, the US presence had made Karimov more willing to make agreements with Tajikistan. It seemed logical to many commentators that the stimulus for a cooperative framework was provided by an external actor, the USA. Thus, the USA had partly begun functioning as a regulator of bilateral relations in the region

The process of normalization continued, but slowly. In August 2002, the prime ministers of the two countries signed agreements and protocols on rail transport, television broadcasting, Tajikistan's debt to Uzbekistan, the functioning of border checkpoints and the delimitation of the border.[50] Severe disappointment with the slow progress of normalization was reflected in an article in March 2002 in the Tajik newspaper *Biznis i Politika*—accusing certain circles in Uzbekistan of hegemonic ambitions in Central Asia and calling Uzbekistan's mining of the border and the harsh treatment by the Uzbek authorities of Tajik transit passengers 'a kind of terrorism with regional means and on a regional scale'.[51] Nevertheless, by August 2002 about 70 per cent of Tajikistan's border with Uzbekistan had been delineated[52] and by early October 2002 an agreement had been signed demarcating the 1050 km-long border, apart from four disputed areas.[53] The issue of de-mining was not discussed. Several practical issues relating to the Tajik-Kyrzyz border and the situation in Tajik enclaves on Kyrgyzstan's territory were resolved in early October 2002 at a meeting between local representatives from the Batken (in Kyrgyzstan) and Sughd (in Tajikistan) regional administrations.[54] Yet, disputed border areas remained.

No agreement was achieved on the delimitation of the Uzbek–Kyrgyz border on which there were 39 points of dispute. The most complex section along the 1400 km-long border was located in the Jalal-Abad region and in the area of the Andizhan water reservoir. Border delineation negotiations between Kyrgyzstan and Uzbekistan had started in February 2000. When delegations from the two countries met in late September 2002, the Kyrgyz side offered delineation on the basis of work carried out by a commission in 1955. Uzbekistan, on the other hand, came out in favour of delineating the border on the basis of documents dating from 1924–27.[55]

Thus, the overthrow of the Taliban reduced the external threat to the Central Asian states, partly improved relations between the states in the region, and helped a little to progress the negotiations on border issues. Once the external threat was reduced domestic problems moved to the forefront. The domestic situation in the Central Asian states is discussed in Chapter 7.

Policy on Multilateral Security Cooperation with Central Asia

If Russia had expected the USA to use Russian-led security structures such as the CST to coordinate anti-terrorist measures in Central Asia, it was disappointed. Instead, the USA built up direct contacts with Uzbekistan, Kyrgyzstan and Tajikistan. When the US-led bombing of Afghanistan was initiated on 7 October 2001, this clearly demonstrated the new dilemma for Russian foreign policy. Neither the CIS nor the CST was given a direct role in the US-led anti-terrorist coalition.

It therefore became important for Russia to try to coordinate a common approach to the international fight against terrorism and to define the role of the CIS in this approach. As mentioned above, the Chief of the Russian General Staff, Kvashnin, and the secretary of the Russian Security Council, Rushailo, were sent for discussions with Central Asian leaders in September 2001. At the meeting of the CIS prime ministers on 28 September, Putin stressed how crucial it was to join forces against terrorism, and he declared that the active participation of the CIS states was to form the new security architecture of the world.[56] In parallel with the growing US presence in Central Asia, Russia continued to develop multilateral cooperation within the CST on the issue of anti-terrorism. At the CST meetings that followed in the aftermath of the 11 September terrorist attacks, the member states discussed the new international situation and its consequences for the CST's zone of responsibility, the role of Russia in the international fight against terrorism, and how participation in the US-led coalition could be coordinated within the CIS.[57] On 5 October, against the background of US troops being sent to Central Asia, Russian and Kyrgyz Parliamentarians suggested that a Russian military base be created in southern Kyrgyzstan under the responsibility of the CST.[58]

On the initiative of Tajikistan, on 8–9 October 2001, an extraordinary meeting of the Committee of the Secretaries of the National Security Councils of the CST member states was held in Dushanbe to discuss the specific situation in Central Asia and 'joint measures to counter international terrorism and religious extremism'.[59] The declaration from the meeting reflected a wish to make the CST part of UN-led international measures while at the same time encouraging the Central Asian states to stick to a common CST approach when cooperating with the USA and its allies. Preparations for the CST rapid deployment force continued. There were problems with making the CIS Anti-Terrorist Centre in Moscow operational: although it had started to function, the issue of its financing was not yet resolved. As before, the principal incentive

Russia could offer the Central Asian states in order to encourage them to enter security cooperation was subsidized weapons and military equipment.[60]

The sessions of the CST foreign ministers on 19 November and the defence ministers on 21 November took place against the background of the changing situation in Afghanistan.[61] Additional decisions were taken regarding the CST Rapid Reaction Force, but no forces were committed. At the 10th anniversary of the CIS in November 2001 declarations and statements repeated the importance of coordinated efforts and policies in the fight against terrorism, but the CIS again demonstrated its inability to go beyond statements.

As the bombing of Afghanistan continued and the US military presence strengthened in Uzbekistan, Kyrgyzstan and Tajikistan, Russian concern increased. Visits in January 2002 by delegations from the US Congress to the capitals of Central Asia indicated a growing US interest in economic and military assistance to the region. A delegation from US Central Command followed in February. In response, Russia dispatched government representatives to the Central Asian states to discuss the situation. In early January, Foreign Minister Ivanov went to Turkmenistan and Uzbekistan, while Deputy Foreign Minister Vyacheslav Trubnikov went to Kyrgyzstan and Kazakhstan.[62] The Director of the Russian Federal Border Service, General Totskii, and the Speaker of the Russian Parliament, Gennadii Seleznev, visited Dushanbe at the head of a delegation of Russian parliamentarians. While officially, Russian concern about the US military presence was muted, and official representatives only repeated that they expected the US military presence to be temporary and to last only as long as the military operations in Afghanistan continued, Seleznev was more outspoken. His criticism was direct, and he declared that he was in favour of an increased Russian military presence. His statements, however, reflected the mood among the Russian political elite rather than any plans of the Russian Government, since the Duma has no real influence over foreign policy making.

Criticism of Putin's foreign policy in the media became louder. On 15 March the Russian Security Council held a special meeting to discuss how to strengthen cooperation with the CIS countries, especially in the fields of security and fighting terrorism.[63] Russia was losing ground in Central Asia and had to counter the trend.

In May 2002, at ceremonies to mark the 10th anniversary of the signing of the CST, the six member states agreed in a joint declaration to raise the status of the organization by formalizing and reorganizing it, and to seek international recognition as a regional organization according to Chapter VIII of the UN Charter.[64] In its application to the UN, the description of the tasks of the CST confirmed the new direction that the organization had taken since 1999. Its remit was no longer limited to external threats but included defence against new threats to 'national, regional and international security' mentioning international terrorism, drugs and arms trafficking, and organized crime.

The joint declaration of the May 2002 session presented the CST as a coordinating mechanism for the foreign and security policies of the member states as well as their relations with the outside world, and stressed that military–political relations between the member states should have priority over relations with non-member states.[65] In Chishinau on 7 October 2002 the member states finalized the Collective Security Treaty Organization (CSTO) by signing its charter and agreeing on its legal status.[66] It was recommended that the national parliaments of the CSTO member states should complete the procedure for ratification by May 2003. According to Sergei Prikhodko, deputy chief of the Russian presidential administration, 'A collective mechanism has been created, which is, both politically and militarily, a major step forward' he added that the CSTO was to be a 'fully fledged, proper and well-structured international body with clear rules' and the 'ability to respond in reality to new global challenges, in particular the threat of international terrorism'.[67]

The purpose of the reorganization was to strengthen the CST and make it a potential partner for the West while at the same time rallying the Central Asian countries. Russian Ambassador Vadim Lukin explained this in an article in which he argued that the West should regard the CST as a partner for cooperation in Central Asia:

> The course of the antiterrorist operation in Afghanistan has supplied the West with a reason to have another look at the regional security structures to be successfully employed in the antiterrorist struggle and the efforts to stabilize the situation in Central Asia and the adjacent regions. Here I have in mind the Collective Security Treaty and the Shanghai Cooperation Organization ...the current antiterrorist operation has testified that it is not in the interests of the West to continue ignoring the security structures set up in the former Soviet Union. They should be treated seriously and with due attention as potentially useful collective partners.[68]

Yet neither the USA nor NATO was interested in developing institutional contacts with the CST. In June 2002 head of the CIS Anti-Terrorist Centre Colonel General Boris Mylnikov complained that, although the centre sought closer ties with its Western partners, the exchange of information between it and the secret services of the USA and NATO members was minimal: 'The antiterrorist centre does not have direct contacts with the secret services of the United States and NATO, and this is not our fault. We have announced our openness and readiness for the exchange of information. The CIA has been reserved in the discussion of the antiterrorist fight'.[69]

The post-11 September developments seemed to undermine the rationale for the CST. As US troops remained in Central Asia two parallel security arrangements appeared in the region—the old Russian-led one and a new US-led one. All Central Asian states sent their representatives to the NATO summit meeting in Prague in November 2002, when seven former Soviet bloc countries were invited to become members of NATO in May 2004. The Presidents of Kazakhstan, Uzbekistan and Tajikistan were present in person at the ceremony, while Kyrgyzstan and Turkmenistan sent their foreign and defence ministers.[70] Although they had no direct role at the meeting, the mere fact that they were present reflected a completely new international situation. The Central Asian Governments showed no interest in setting a deadline for US military withdrawal from their countries. In August 2002 President of Uzbekistan, Karimov declared that the US troops could stay as long as they needed. In this he expressed, to a great extent, the attitudes of Kyrgyzstan and Tajikistan. During 2002 Karimov, and Presidents Emomali Rakhmonov of Tajikistan and Askar Akaev of Kyrgyzstan visited the USA.[71] For Rakhmonov the visit in early

December 2002 was his first to the USA. It was successful, and Tajikistan's role in the international anti-terrorist coalition was much praised in Washington. The Tajik Foreign Ministry reported that the prospects for 'long-term strategic partnership' were the main focus of the talks.[72]

Russia continued its efforts to build up the CST. To demonstrate its determination in this regard, a Russian military base opened at Kant outside Bishkek, Kyrgyzstan, in early December 2002. Kant was a former Soviet base, situated not far from Manas International Airport where US and other Western troops were based. The main part of the Kant airbase became the responsibility of the CST and its Rapid Reaction Force but Russia was to finance the base and maintain operational control. The base was de facto part of the Russian military district of Ural and its centre in Ekaterinburg.[73] The agreement defining the status of the Russian troops on Kyrgyz territory was signed in September 2003. It will run for 15 years, with the possibility of an automatic extension for further five years.[74] Five aircraft arrived in time for the opening ceremony in December 2002 but left a few days later. The base became operational only in October 2003. According to the Russian Defence Ministry it hosted 12 Russian aircraft and 500 personnel.[75] Together with the existing Russian military base in Dushanbe, the Kant airbase enables the Russian Air Force to cover the Fergana Valley shared by Kyrgyzstan, Tajikistan, Uzbekistan and Kazakhstan. The opening of the Kant base indicates Russia's long-term interest in maintaining influence in Central Asia. Although the opening was officially declared not to be a move against the NATO presence at the Manas airbase, the Russian media interpreted it differently.[76]

The official role of the base was clearly stated, but its real purpose was far from clear. The designated aircraft did not seem appropriate for fighting terrorism and, should a serious terrorist threat arise, their number seemed insufficient. President Karimov reflected the general scepticism about the base in his comments in December 2002, when Russia transferred military aircraft from the CST Rapid Reaction Force to the Kant airfield. Karimov asked whether the deployment was for strategic purposes:

> I would like to say that if all this is being done—and better late than never as the saying goes—to ensure stability, peace and prevent possible incursions, the Uzbeks say—welcome, no problem. But if it is being done as part of a competition [for dominance in the region given the US presence there] … I think that this kind of competition is absolutely counter-productive.[77]

Karimov asked, rhetorically, why Russia was now prepared to fight Islamic intruders when, in 1999, 2000 and 2001, it had not wanted to participate directly. He continued, 'I didn't get any support other than general words: "Yes, we'll be there, yes it's necessary"'. Russia only wanted to get out of a difficult situation, he argued, but added that it would be a 'positive' development if such bases could help to avert future attacks in the region.[78] The Government in Tashkent continued to regard the CST as a paper organization of no relevance to the future of Uzbekistan.

According to plans for the CST Rapid Reaction Force for Central Asia, which had been agreed as early as May 2001, not only Russia but also Kyrgyzstan, Tajikistan and Kazakhstan were to contribute troops. Such commitments amounted to up to 5000 troops. However, when the force became operational in November 2002 it consisted of about 1000 men, most of whom were from the Russian 201st Division located in Tajikistan with the rest located in their home countries.[79] With the CST Rapid Reaction Force and the Kant Base, Russia, at least symbolically, demonstrated that it was still a factor to reckon with in Central Asia—and that the CST was developing as an organization.

The summit meeting of the CST parties in Dushanbe on 28 April 2003 completed the transformation of the alliance into an international security organization—a process which had started in May 2002.[80] By institutionalizing the treaty, the CSTO could be recognized as a legitimate regional organisation by the UN, which occurred later in 2003. In line with the original 1992 defence treaty, the charter of the CSTO, signed in Chisinau in October 2002, specifically stipulated that an act of aggression against one member state would be considered an attack on all member states. In an interview in May 2003 the new Secretary-General, Nikolai Bordyuzha stressed CSTO's character as a defence organization and briefly defined the threats it was defending against as 'terrorism, narcotics, and organized crime'.[81]

The Dushanbe summit decided to create a Permanent Council and a Joint Staff.[82] The Joint Staff was to start work in January 2004 with its headquarters in Moscow and led by the Head of Russia's General Staff, Anatolii Kvashnin. The Joint Staff appoints the operational command of the Rapid Reaction Force which will be located in Kyrgyzstan. There will be a rotating chairmanship of the Joint Staff but the Secretary-General will always be Russian.[83] The highest body of the CSTO is the Council of Collective Security, whose all six presidents are represented and which meets annually. The organizational structure of the CSTO includes councils of the foreign ministers and defence ministers, a committee of secretaries of the national security councils, a permanent council with national representatives, and a secretariat led by the Secretary-General (appointed for a period of three years).

In spite of this gradual CSTO build up process, Russia was concerned with what it perceived as the Central Asian states distancing themselves from Russia. As mentioned above, Russia offered arms deliveries at subsidized prices to CSTO member states in order to make membership of the organization more attractive.[84] Even so, it felt threatened by growing US-NATO exports of arms, equipment and training to Central Asian states.[85] Moreover, Russia encountered problems with reaching all practical agreements with Tajik authorities on the reorganization of the 201st Division in Tajikistan into a military base, and these problems were interpreted in the context of the larger US presence. To Moscow, a politically more distant Tajikistan would be a serious blow to the Russian presence in the area.[86] According to one media commentator, 'The weathercock policy characterizing many CIS member states in relation to the USA quite naturally irritates the Kremlin'.[87]

The post-11 September developments in Central Asia radically changed the strategic situation in the region. Two parallel security arrangements were in the making—one led by Russia, the other by the USA. This unusual situation had become part of the new realities that Russia had to take into account.

A New Policy in the Making

By the summer of 2002 there were signs that Russian policy was becoming more active on CIS territory in general and in Central Asia in particular. While the US military presence in Central Asia might have given the impression that Russia would become a passive spectator in the region, in fact the opposite was the case. This new policy was based on cooperation with the West, was US-centric, but also included a more active policy in Central Asia. In March 2002 Foreign Minister Igor Ivanov indicated such a Central Asia-policy when he said in the Duma:

> I want to tell you that most will depend not on how much hot air we talk but how we act in real terms in these regions. If we actively develop relations with Central Asian countries, build long-term economic ties, give credits to serious projects, train cadres (including military cadres) cost-free, and develop military-technical cooperation, our positions will not weaken. If we only talk but do little substantial in Central Asia, then, of course, the vacuum will be filled by others.[88]

How did this more active policy in Central Asia manifest itself? Did it follow the previous emphasis on security issues, or was there a new interest in economic issues as instruments of government policy? Were there any signs that could point to an 'economization' of foreign policy?

From the summer of 2002 there were signs that the Russian Government was 'getting its act together' regarding its policy response to the post-11 September situation on CIS territory. President Putin's speech of 12 July 2002 at the Russian Foreign Ministry outlined the strategic guidelines of Russian policy. He mentioned nothing about the US military presence in Central Asia. Instead, he stressed that Russia was to give particular attention to relations with the West, above all the USA. He also made it clear that he regarded Russia as a great power with responsibilities in world affairs and, in this sense, on the same level as the USA.[89] His statement on Russia's role was more forceful than usual and seemed to indicate that a policy shift of some kind was on the way. At the very least, the speech reflected a new determination. Although Russia's international position had not improved, and its capabilities were as limited as before, the government seemed to be acting with a new self-confidence.

A series of events in the Caspian Sea region and southern Caucasus in early autumn 2002 were interpreted as signs that Russia would counter the expansion of US influence on CIS territory. During the first two weeks of August 2002, the Russian Caspian Sea flotilla held its largest ever exercise. A total of 10,500 Russian military personnel, 60 vessels and over 30 aircraft participated.[90] Although officially the object of the exercise was to fight international terrorism, commentators viewed it as a demonstration that Russia saw the Caspian Sea and its resources as vital to Russian national interests. It was also thought to reflect frustration at Russia's loss of influence in the Caspian region.

By September Russian frustration over the security situation in the Pankisi Gorge in Georgia had increased. US military instructors had arrived in May and, although the Russian Government had already declared that it was not concerned about the US presence, the Russian military viewed the situation differently. When Putin demanded that Georgian troops clear the Pankisi Gorge

of Chechen rebels who were using it for transit and shelter, and threatened that
Russian aircraft would otherwise bomb the gorge, the world was surprised and
concerned at the new situation.[91]

Putin's ultimatum to Georgia did not directly affect policy towards Central
Asia, but it was interpreted as the sign of a general change in Russian policy on
former Soviet territory. Some in the Russian media felt that:

> The Russian president correctly exploited the foreign policy conditions which he
> had partly created himself in order to compel the CIS states to turn to him for
> assistance or just accept Russia's conditions. All approaches seemed timely—from
> using the political juncture to direct economic blackmail and threat.[92]

Russian policy on CIS territory was described as becoming a 'minor model of
US behaviour', in other words, that Russia was now prepared to take a tough
stance in defence of its interests. Putin's threat to Georgia in September raised
questions about the purpose of his statement—whether he wanted to frighten
Georgia into a generally more conciliatory approach towards Russia, or whether
he only required Georgia to clear the Pankisi Gorge of Chechen rebels. The
vagueness of Putin's message reflected the fact that the government had yet to
find a proper form for its policy. Nonetheless, there seemed to be a new policy
in the making.

New Attention to the Economic Sector

Putin's emphasis on economic priorities and objectives emerged as one of the
most distinctive and important features of his foreign policy towards the West.
There was a strong emphasis on the economic aspects of foreign policy in
Putin's speech to the Russian Parliament in April 2002. He presented a view of
the world according to which economic strength and economic factors
determine the international status of a country and described competition as a
basic characteristic of the world:

> I wish to draw attention to another thing: norms in the international community,
> norms in the modern world, also mean harsh competition—for markets, for
> investment, for political and economic influence. And in the struggle—in this
> struggle—Russia has to be strong and competitive.[93]

In his speech he upgraded the importance of CIS states to Russia's economy.
He said the CIS was crucial to Russia in securing competitive advantages on the
world market.

> The Commonwealth of Independent States is a genuine factor in stability across an
> extensive part of the world's territory, an influential group of states with a wide
> range of objectives and interests. Work with the countries of the CIS is Russia's
> main foreign policy priority. This priority is linked, among other things, to the
> securing of competitive advantages on world markets. The CIS countries have
> many opportunities to carry out large-scale, joint, infrastructure, transport and
> energy projects. I am sure that their implementation will increase the solidity of

our integration, and will provide new opportunities for the Russian economy, and for others besides.[94]

Although the Central Asian states were not mentioned by name they were implied in his references to CIS energy and transport projects. Thus, the economic importance of Central Asia to Russia was recognized for the first time—in the context of international economic competition. Putin's words were in stark contrast to the reality of Russia's economic relations with Central Asia. To what extent did these words reflect a genuine change of policy?[95]

Ever since the break up of the Soviet Union, economic integration within the CIS had been declared a priority task for Russian policy, and yet decisions had not been implemented. In spite of numerous declarations and decisions there was no coordination of economic, credit, or tax policies—and no system of responsibility for the implementation of decisions. The reason was fairly simple.[96] There was no genuine economic interest in Russia in developing economic cooperation with Central Asia. Central Asia was regarded as of economic interest to Russia only in general terms and in a long-term perspective. It did not seem to offer any economic benefit in the short term. Russia therefore remained passive in the economic field in Central Asia and, in the meantime, the Central Asian economies reoriented themselves in other directions.[97]

When Putin came to power he tried to breathe new life into CIS economic integration and came up with the proposal in October 2000 to launch a new organization, the Eurasian Economic Community (EEC), to replace the CIS Customs Union.[98] The EEC was given a federal element in its decision-making structures in order to make it more effective.[99] Putin declared in the same way as Yeltsin had, that he intended to create a Russian-led economic bloc similar to the EU. The difficulties in developing the EEC made it seem stillborn. Putin therefore gave more emphasis to bilateral relations, since they had a better chance of success.

In a previous study, the present author concludes that Russia since 1997 placed more emphasis on developing cooperation in relation to the strategically important energy resources of the Caspian Sea region, and that this reflected a new tendency towards a geo-economic orientation. The greater focus on energy issues aims to secure Russian interests with regard to investment, exploitation, and transportation of energy resources on former Soviet territory. The first sign in this regard was a statement in November 1997 by then Deputy Prime Minister Boris Nemtsov calling for more active Russian involvement in the development of the Caspian oilfields in order to counter growing Western influence in the region. The study concluded that: 'The new Russian focus on energy issues can … be viewed as an effort to concentrate resources and efforts on a few key sectors vital for maintaining Russian control over Central Asia'.[100] As Putin came to power, energy issues moved to the fore. In April 2000, Putin stated in the Russian Security Council that Russia should become more active in the Caspian Sea Region. He called for greater Russian engagement in the exploitation of the Caspian energy resources and the coordination of Russian policy by companies and ministries. The position of Representative of the President in the Caspian region was created, with responsibility for coordinating policy and dealing with all foreign policy issues concerning the region, including the legal division of the Caspian Sea.[101] The former Minister for Energy, Viktor Kalyuzhnin, was given the post. Turkmenistan, as a Caspian coast state with large gas deposits, formed part of this Russian interest.

The post-11 September situation gave a new impetus to Russian efforts in the energy sector. At the EEC summit meeting on 27 April 2003, a four-year strategy document was adopted with a large focus on energy cooperation.[102] To most observers, the programme seemed too ambitious. However, it reflected a new Russian emphasis on energy and transport links with Central Asian states, and thus indicated this new component of Russia's view of its strategic interests in Central Asia.

After September 2001 Russia gave stronger emphasis to the energy assets of all four Central Asian states. Previously, its interest had focused on the oil and gas resources of the Caspian Sea region. However, interest was now extended to the non-Caspian states of Central Asia—Uzbekistan, Tajikistan and Kyrgyzstan—and also to include hydro-energy.

The crucial role of energy cooperation in Russian foreign policy became more pronounced.[103] Putin moved the energy issue up the Russian agenda for cooperation with Central Asia. In 2000 he had launched the idea of a gas alliance between Russia, Turkmenistan, Uzbekistan and Kazakhstan. In January 2002, he presented a proposal for a Eurasian Alliance of Natural Gas Producers, to include these four states. On 1 March 2002, the leaders of Russia, Kazakhstan, Turkmenistan and Uzbekistan agreed on a statement of intent on Cooperation in Energy Policy and Measures to Defend the Interests of Natural Gas Producers. According to joint statement, cooperation over natural gas would ensure 'stable supplies to the world and CIS markets'.[104] Another statement signed on 23 October confirmed this intention, although the final agreement was left for further negotiation. Putin stressed the importance of uniting the efforts of Russia and Turkmenistan, the major gas producers, and Kazakhstan and Uzbekistan, which provide their gas pipelines for transit. The four countries intended to coordinate their import–export and investment policies and to promote a common 'energy security strategy'.

A gas alliance would open up the Russian natural gas pipeline network to Central Asian producers, which are eager to access European markets. A new pipeline through Ukraine would run along an existing route from the Kazakhstan border with Russia, at Alexandrov-Gay, to Novopskov in the north of Lugansk Oblast, Ukraine. Because the pipeline infrastructure in Central Asia already exists, the main question was an agreement on the access point to the European market. However, the Central Asia–Center pipeline system was deteriorating, with decrepit pipes and limited capacity, and therefore needed investment on a large scale.[105]

Russia had strong economic reasons to push for the alliance, which would enable it to boost energy exports to its Western customers with the help of the Central Asian countries. Gazprom was rapidly running out of easily accessible resources on its own territory and experts warned that the company's mainstay Siberian fields were declining fast.[106] The new Zapolyarnoe field, which opened in 2001 and reversed Gazprom's decline in output, was not expected to reach peak production before 2006. Gazprom was planning substantial investment in new Arctic fields in order to double energy exports to Europe by 2020, but in the meantime Central Asia represented a ready source of supply. Another advantage of the gas alliance for Russia related to its agreements with Turkmenistan. It was announced in October 2002 that Gazprom and Turkmenistan's state oil and gas company, Turkmenneftegaz, were finally to sign a long-term contract on gas sales and transport.[107] This deal would not be viable unless the wider-ranging gas alliance was also formed with other Central Asian states since the existing Central Asia–Center trunk line crosses Turkmenistan, Uzbekistan and Kazakhstan before linking up with the Russian distribution network.

Russia's interest in forming a gas alliance should also be seen against the background of the revival of plans for a gas pipeline from Turkmenistan across Afghanistan to Pakistan. Although Russia had demonstrated interest in the project,[108] it was a priority of Russian policy to prevent it from becoming Turkmenistan's first choice in the future. In early 2002 a Memorandum of Understanding was signed between Turkmenistan, Afghanistan and Pakistan on a feasibility study in preparation for building a 1500-km long gas export pipeline from Dovletabat in Turkmenistan via Kandahar in Afghanistan to Multan in Pakistan.[109] On 17 October 2002 officials from Afghanistan, Pakistan and Turkmenistan drew up an intergovernmental agreement on the construction of the gas pipeline. It was to supply 30 billion cubic metres of Turkmen gas to Pakistan annually.[110]

Russia's Itera oil and gas company declared an interest in taking part in the trans-Afghan pipeline project.[111] Russian Deputy Foreign Minister Andrei Denisov welcomed the forthcoming summit meeting of the participating countries, stating that the Russian Foreign Ministry believed that 'any initiative of this type will promote Afghanistan's speedy reconstruction and the development of regional cooperation on the whole'.[112] On 27 December 2002 a framework agreement to build the pipeline was signed which defined the legal mechanisms for setting up the consortium that was to build and operate the pipeline.[113] The Asian Development Bank was to finance the feasibility study. However, the political situation in Afghanistan did not allow the project to proceed.

The Baku–Ceyhan pipeline project to transport gas from Azerbaijan across the Caspian Sea to the Turkish Mediterranean port of Ceyhan could have provided an alternative outlet for Turkmen gas, but these plans were also abandoned. The plans step towards realization when on 1 August 2002 representatives of Azerbaijan, Georgia and Turkey signed the documents setting up the Baku–Tbilisi–Ceyhan (BTC) company.[114] However, the project for a gas pipeline across the Caspian Sea was considered unrealistic.

For Russia to succeed in creating a gas alliance with the Central Asian states it had to ensure that the pipeline system became operational. Russia had managed a few years before to extend the northern route for oil from Kazakhstan to Novorossiisk, even before the formal documents on the Baku–Ceyhan oil pipeline were concluded. Repeating this success story, by joining with Turkmenistan and Uzbekistan in a gas alliance, would secure a strong position for Russia in the international gas market.

Russia thus tried to place more emphasis on economic cooperation with the Central Asian states in response to the post-11 September situation, first and foremost in the energy sector. This was also reflected in bilateral economic relations with the Central Asian states.

Bilateral Relations

In 2002 Russia made active, and in many ways successful, efforts to improve bilateral economic and security relations with the Central Asian states. However, there was still an underlying trend for Central Asian states to distance themselves from Russia in order to develop relations with Western countries.

Kyrgyzstan

Relations between Russia and Kyrgyzstan improved during 2002. Kyrgyzstan, which is a member of both the CSTO and the EEC, remained close to Russia but its desire to diversify its foreign policy resulted in a certain distancing from Russia, and this tendency accelerated after the US military presence.

President Akaev's hold on power was seriously challenged when demonstrations in March 2002 resulted in the police shooting five people dead. The domestic situation erupted in protest and the opposition united its forces. The Kyrgyz regime thus became more vulnerable and in need of support to strengthen its domestic security. Putin seized the opportunity to strengthen relations with Kyrgyzstan. During the spring and summer of 2002 Russian visits and contacts with the Kyrgyz authorities intensified. This increased interest culminated in a number of bilateral agreements in the economic, political and security fields, which were finalized during Putin's visit to Bishkek in early December 2002. As part of the December 2002 agreement, Russia rescheduled Kyrgyzstan's state debt to Russia, which was due to be repaid by the end of 2004. It was rescheduled over 20 years and one-fifth of the overall debt was converted into Russian investments in environmental protection projects, as well as in the Kant airfield for use by the Russian military.[115] Military–technical production was also resumed. The two countries had cooperated since Soviet times, primarily with regard to the production and testing of torpedo rockets at Lake Issyk-Kul.[116]

Kyrgyzstan, which together with Tajikistan is the major source of water in Central Asia, sought foreign assistance to complete the construction work, begun in Soviet times, on a series of hydroelectric installations on the Naryn River, notably the Kambarata hydroelectric plant, and also to begin new projects. In March 2002 the secretary of the EEC, Grigorii Rapota, discussed possible Russian investment.[117] In October 2002 an agreement was signed according to which the Russian state-controlled company, Unified Energy Systems, would upgrade five major power stations over the next 10 years.[118] At the EEC summit in April 2003, contracts were signed on the completion of the construction work with Russia and Kazakhstan as main investors.[119] In May 2003, Gazprom signed a 25-year agreement with Kyrgyzstan on repairing and modernizing existing gas pipelines and developing the joint production of oil and gas in the country. Gazprom also signed an agreement on the joint development of oil and gas fields. Gazprom intends to renew and modernize gas fields in Kyrgyzstan and increase the amount of gas extracted to 300 million cubic meters, which would cover half of the population's needs. [120] Under the terms of the agreement, Kyrgyzstan hopes to receive a reliable supply of gas throughout the year, which it has not enjoyed since independence. Like Tajikistan, Kyrgyzstan is dependent on Uzbek gas for the larger part of its consumption. Uzbekistan has used this dependence to put pressure on Kyrgyzstan and keep it in line.[121] In August 2003 Russia started to buy electricity from both Tajikistan and Kyrgyzstan through the energy grids across Uzbekistan and Kazakhstan.[122]

The Russian Government also made efforts to develop trade and economic cooperation. When Putin went to Kyrgyzstan to open the Kant military base in October 2003 he brought Russian businessmen along in his delegation, and a Russian–Kyrgyz economic forum took place to demonstrate the new Russian interest in Kyrgyzstan's economy. Although Russian investment increased in Kyrgyzstan during 2002, it was still lower than the level of US direct investment in the country.[123] Nevertheless, Russia signalled a new policy in the region.[124]

Although Russia put more emphasis on cooperation with Kyrgyzstan in the economic sphere, primarily in the energy sector, military–security cooperation remained a high priority. With the Kant and Manas bases Kyrgyzstan acquired the unique position of having two different countries' military bases on its territory. Although it might seem difficult for Kyrgyzstan to balance the presence of two different security arrangements, Kyrgyz Foreign Minister Askar Aitmatov, commenting in April 2003, declared: 'This region and Kyrgyzstan are in the sphere of the strategic interests of both Russia and the United States. In my opinion ... [the two bases] ... will complement one another'. Aitmatov made undirect criticism of Russia, saying that he regretted that the CST airbase was being established in 2003 and not 1999. If it had been set up in 1999, he said, 'we could have avoided many problems with international terrorism'.[125]

Regardless of whether the Kant airbase was of more political–symbolic than military–practical importance for its stated purpose, it was a step towards a larger Russian presence in Kyrgyzstan and increased military cooperation there.

Turkmenistan

With regard to Turkmenistan, Putin also skilfully exploited a moment of weakness of the Niyazov regime to improve relations. The first signs of a serious domestic crisis were already visible in the spring of 2002 (see chapter 7). An opposition developed within the state structures and the crisis culminated in November 2002, when former Foreign Minister Boris Shikhmuradov was arrested and charged in connection with an unsuccessful attempt on the life of Niyazov. In this delicate situation, Niyazov turned to Putin and Russia for support.

The situation offered Putin the possibility of making a breakthrough in relations with Turkmenistan. Niyazov had not only been generally unpredictable; he had also played the card of the USA's interest in alternative gas pipeline projects—with routes across the Caspian Sea to Baku and further to Ceyhan—or through Afghanistan. Russia had few channels of influence in Turkmenistan and little access to information about what was going on there. Although preliminary documents had been signed on increased gas exports to Russia, disagreements over prices had prevented an agreement from being concluded. With Niyazov weakened by the domestic situation, the Russian Government now managed to press for an agreement.

A 25-year agreement was finally concluded during President Niyazov's visit to Moscow in April 2003. Gazprom was given the right to buy all Turkmenistan's gas, excluding what was already committed under existing agreements with other partners.[126] Turkmenistan's current export obligations—notably with Ukraine and Iran—expire in 2006.

Turkmenistan is not a member of the CSTO or the EEC. Niyazov reduced contacts with the outside world through his inward-looking foreign policy. Energy plays the dominant role in Russia's relations with Turkmenistan, and Turkmenistan is dependent on Russian pipeline systems for its gas exports. In spite of this dependence, however, the two countries found it difficult to agree on conditions for the export of Turkmen gas. The behaviour had often been contradictory of the both sides.[127] Disagreement between Gazprom and the Russian Government characterized Russian policy in Turkmenistan during most of the Yeltsin years.

The Central Asia–Center pipeline is the major export pipeline for Turkmen gas. Only one additional gas pipeline, from Turkmenistan south to Iran, is in place but its capacity is limited. Several pipeline projects for exports bypassing the Russian pipeline system have been proposed over the years, including one from Turkmenistan to Pakistan and India across Afghanistan. When Putin came to power in autumn 1999 he renewed the discussions over increasing Russia's imports of Turkmen gas. During his visit to Turkmenistan in May 2000 a statement of intent was signed whereby Russia was to increase its purchases of Turkmen gas by 10 billion cubic metres per year from 2001 to a level of 60 billion cubic metres per year by 2004. This was a long-term agreement to cover a period of 30 years. The questions of prices and payment mechanisms were left for further negotiations,[128] not least because the two countries could not agree over prices.

In May 2002 negotiations intensified. In September 2002 Russia announced a 15-year agreement with Turkmenistan, planned to begin in 2005, but again the two countries were unable to agree on the price of gas. A Turkmen Foreign Ministry press release on 17 August 2002 stated that the price of the gas should be not less than US$44–45 per 1000 cubic metres at the border.[129] Prior to Putin's visit in May 2002 Turkmenistan had been asking for US$40 per 1000 cubic metres, while Russia was holding out for US$32–33. The press release stated it was 'quite reasonable' to sell the gas at the higher price, especially because Russia was selling its gas to European markets at a price three times as high.

In September 2002 a Russian delegation visited Ashgabat for a meeting with the Russian–Turkmen Intergovernmental Economic Commission.[130] The head of the delegation, the Russian energy minister, stated that the commission would work in many areas, including agriculture and transport, but first of all in the energy sector. He reiterated Russia's interest in increasing its import of Turkmen gas and said that President Niyazov supported the Russian proposals on gas purchases for the period up to 2020. Russia intended to restore the sectors that cross Uzbek and Kazakh territory and to make huge investments to expand the gas pipeline system. Russia also expressed an interest in taking part in the exploitation of hydrocarbon resources on the Turkmen part of the Caspian Sea shelf, in which the Russian companies Gazprom and Zarubezhneft were planning to participate.

The Russian–Turkmen agreement of April 2003 was a victory for Putin. However, the Russian media, commenting on the April agreement, claimed that Niyazov had won the negotiations on the price of gas, which at US$44 per cubic metre was the rate that Niyazov had been holding out for over several years of negotiations and higher than Russian observers had expected.[131] Nevertheless, for Russia the deal was crucial in several respects. It made it possible for Russia to meet its gas obligations to other countries, in spite of its own difficulties with production and investment in its own gas fields. The agreement covered not only Russian purchases of Turkmen gas but also Russian participation in the development of Turkmenistan's gas fields.

In parallel with the economic agreements, other agreements were signed on foreign policy coordination and security cooperation against terrorism. On 23 April 2002 the Russian and Turkmen Presidents extended the 1992 Treaty of Friendship and Cooperation, which covered political, economic, social and humanitarian aspects.[132] The new friendship and cooperation treaty stated that Russia and Turkmenistan would not allow their territories 'to be used in ways that damage the security of the other side'. The two countries also intended to expand cooperation 'in the sphere of the special services'. Both sides 'are cooperating in the fight against international terrorism, in intercepting the activities of terrorist and extremist organizations, acts of terrorism, their preparation and funding'. Consequently, Russia and Turkmenistan 'do not provide refuge for those revealed as members of terrorist organizations, are exchanging operational information on their plans, and are cooperating in the provision of legal assistance and the hand over of individuals who have committed and are planning terrorist acts on the territory of one of the sides'. In addition, they 'will inform each other, as the need arises, of measures taken in the fight against international terrorism, including participation in antiterrorist agreements, coalitions and associations'.[133] Thus, Putin secured a large Russian foothold east of the Caspian Sea down to Afghanistan.

There was, however, a political price related to the gas treaty. President Niyazov demanded and Putin accepted that the right to dual citizenship be scrapped. When the issue had first been raised in January 2003, Russian Prime Minister Mikhail Kasyanov had refused to abolish it.[134] The right to dual citizenship had been introduced in 1993, on the request of Turkmenistan, and Russian President Boris Yeltsin had been the first to acquire it. To scrap it in 2003 threatened not only members of the Turkmen opposition living in exile in Russia but also ethnic Russians living in Turkmenistan. A stream of Russian migrants from Turkmenistan could therefore be expected. On 10 April *Nezavisimaya gazeta* carried an article claiming that Turkmenistan had demanded the extradition from Moscow of two leading members of the Turkmen opposition who were accused of being among the organizers of the failed coup attempt.[135] The harsh treatment of the more than 100,000 Russians with dual citizenship raised the anger of the Russian opposition. On the day of Niyazov's visit to Moscow, members of the Union of Rightist Forces (SPS, Soyuz pravyukh sil), a Russian political party, demonstrated outside the Turkmen Embassy in Moscow to protest against the abuse of the rights of Russians in Turkmenistan. On 29 April, Boris Nemtsov of the URF attacked the government for 'making hundreds of thousands of our compatriots into outcasts, forced to lose their property and abandon Turkmenistan', thanks to what he described as a 'gas-for-people deal'. Nemtsov criticized the weak response of the Russian Foreign Ministry to the developments in Turkmenistan.[136]

Although the issue risked becoming a domestic liability to Putin, he had secured a favourable agreement and Russian influence in Turkmenistan. Soon the citizenship problem became a major political issue, and Putin came under heavy pressure to take steps and defend the rights of the Russians in Turkmenistan. After his visit to Moscow, Niyazov returned home and issued a decree that all citizens with dual citizenship would within two months have to choose to which country they wanted to belong or automatically become Turkmen citizens. Spokesmen for the Russian foreign ministry at first claimed that such a decree could have no retroactive effect. The Russian Duma became agitated, especially its foreign affairs committee under Dmitrii Rogozin. The deputy chairman of the committee on CIS affairs, Vyacheslav Irgunov, argued that Russia had an obligation to intervene in Turkmen affairs and cited human rights concerns.[137] On 20 June, as the two-month deadline ended, Putin declared that it was the duty of the Russian Government and Foreign Ministry to defend the rights of its citizens in Turkmenistan.[138] At the same time, Russia could not be sure of the status of the 25-year gas deal with Turkmenistan, since Niyazov had also discussed extendings of gas agreements with Ukraine—even though such an extension would be impossible under the agreement with Russia.[139] Russian–Turkmen relations became a serious concern to Moscow. The question was—how could Russia deal with the situation?

Tajikistan

Tajikistan remained Russia's closest ally in Central Asia, but relations were not entirely free of friction. Discussions on reorganizing the Russian military presence into a Russian military base, as agreed on in April 1999, were dragging on. When Putin visited Tajikistan in April 2003 the discussions seemed to be well on their way to completion, and the signing of final agreements on all the practicalities was to take place in May. However, it did not. The difficulties in reaching agreement seemed to indicate that Tajikistan was becoming more willing to tough it out in negotiations because it saw possibilities for more cooperation with NATO under the Partnership for Peace Programme, and for bilateral agreements with individual NATO countries. Media reports suggested that Tajikistan wanted to write-off part of its debt to Russia in return for allowing Moscow to have the base.[140]

Disagreement over Russia's military presence was demonstrated when in September 2003 the head of the Tajik border service demanded that the 'dual power' of responsibilities along the Afghan border end, and that the Russian troops hand over full responsibility for the border to their Tajik colleagues.[141] The Tajik Government was quick to declare, however, that this was his personal view and not the view of the government.[142]

In spite of the fact that Russia had a large military presence in Tajikistan its economic presence was minor.[143] In 2000 Russia's share of Tajikistan's exports was about 30 per cent and its share of Tajikistan's imports about 27 per cent.[144] Russian investment in Tajikistan was more or less non-existent. Different expectations therefore caused friction in relations. President Rakhmonov from time to time expressed Tajikistan's expectation of a more active Russian engagement with its economic development. At a meeting with President Putin in March 2002 he repeated his complaints that, while political and military–technical cooperation between the two countries was developing, cooperation in the economic sphere was lagging behind.[145] Thus, when in early 2002 Russian Minister for Emergency Situations Sergei Shoigu, a close ally of Putin, was appointed co-chairman of the Russian–Tajik Inter-Governmental Commission, this was interpreted as a sign that Russia was to give greater priority to its economic relations with Tajikistan. In March 2002 Shoigu went to Dushanbe as the head of a sizeable government delegation. Although more than 30 agreements were signed at the meeting, no breakthroughs were reported.

In an article in the Tajik newspaper (and news agency) *Asia Plus*, Rakhmonov's adviser, Sukhrob Sharipov, expressed both disillusionment and expectation before President Putin's visit to Dushanbe in late April 2003. The development of bilateral relations was 'quite contradictory', he wrote: 'I don't know why but our elite expects a kind of miracle from Russia'.[146] According to Sharipov, hundreds of documents on various aspects of cooperation had been signed but implementation remained the main problem. His explanation was that Russia's interests in Central Asia were first and foremost geopolitical, while Tajikistan was interested primarily in Russia's participation in the rehabilitation and development of its economy and in joint investment projects.

Sharipov's words clearly reflected Russia's emphasis on security issues in its relations with Tajikistan. During his visit to Tajikistan in April 2003 Putin confirmed that Russia was to maintain its military presence.[147] 'Russian–Tajik border interaction is an irreplaceable element in the joint struggle against international terrorism and international drug trafficking.' The Afghan conflict, he said, was far from being settled, and the Taliban movement and al-Qaeda network had intensified their activities in Afghanistan.[148] Whatever the outcome of these negotiations, Russia was determined to maintain a sizeable presence in Tajikistan. However, Tajikistan demonstrated a new willingness to assert its national interests.

There is one aspect of Russian–Tajik political and economic relations which should not be overlooked. According to unofficial statistics, about 650,000 Tajiks go to Russia every year as 'guest workers'.[149] Other Central Asian countries also send guest workers to Russia, but for Tajikistan, with its post-war economy, this contribution to the national income and to the incomes of many households is crucial. Labour migration has not helped the Tajik economy to progress but it has helped the population to survive. The presence of migrant workers in Russia also constitutes a vital link in relations between Russia and Tajikistan. However, since the majority of them are in Russia illegally, they also contribute to tensions in bilateral relations. Russia's revision of its regulations on labour migrants in 2002 hit the Tajik workers in Russia hard. Tensions between the two countries developed when the Duma discussed the new regulations. President Putin's representative in the Duma, Aleksandr Kotenkov, made ugly comments about the Tajiks and created a scandal when he claimed that 'Moscow is full of Tajik beggars' during the debate on the draft law on citizenship in February 2002.[150] The Mayor of Moscow, Yurii Luzhkov, followed suit accusing Tajiks in Moscow of crime and theft. After a strong reaction from the Tajik Government, Kotenkov was obliged to apologize and sent a letter to Rakhmonov. However, the conflict deepened when the Russian authorities started to deport Tajiks who did not have the necessary documentation to allow them to stay and work in Russia. What complicated the issue, as the Tajik media pointed out, was that Russia and Tajikistan had agreements on the free movement of labour. In November 2002 President Rakhmonov stated that Russia's deportation of Tajiks was 'a major violation of their rights, including their financial rights'.[151]

As part of Russia's increased overall interest in energy issues in 2002, Tajikistan's hydro-energy also received attention. Tajikistan is among the most richly endowed countries in the world as regards water resources. The large-scale investment and construction by the Soviet Union of hydro-energy complexes came to an end when the Soviet Union broke up. Construction works were left unfinished and, during the civil war, hydroelectric stations were not repaired.

In March 2002 the Russian–Tajik Inter-Governmental Commission discussed the issue in Dushanbe. The Russian representatives were interested in investing in Tajik hydro-energy in order to build an electricity capacity, which would also allow the export of electricity to Afghanistan. Much publicity was given to the grand plans for reconstructing and completing the Tajik hydroelectric power stations with the help of Russian expertise, although it was stated that international money would be needed for the project. The Sangtuda hydroelectric power station was of major interest, but Shoigu stressed that a third partner had to be found for financing. He spoke of developing a model of international cooperation by which Tajikistan would offer the object of cooperation (completion of the construction work or modernization of the energy infrastructure), Russia would provide the production and scientific–technical potential, and a third partner would provide the finance. If the Sangtuda project worked, Shoigu said, the model could be used to complete construction of the Rogun hydroelectric power station in central Tajikistan as well, but that would only be workable if the international community became involved in Afghan affairs.[152]

On 29 October 2002 Russia and Tajikistan struck a deal on the Rogun power station.[153] When it goes into operation it will have the capacity to provide the whole of Tajikistan with electricity and also allow it to export to other countries.

Work on the project was intended to continue until 2007. If completed, the plant will be the second-largest hydroelectric power station in the world and its construction will have a significant impact on the economy of the whole of Central Asia.[154] Experts predicted that US$1.3 billion would be needed to complete it. In March 2003 UES, the Russian partner, declared its interest in creating an electricity market and buying electric power generated by Tajik hydro-energy facilities.[155] In April 2003 documents were signed at the EEC summit meeting on a joint project to complete the construction of Sangtuda, with Russia and Kazakhstan as large investors.[156]

In May 2003 a 25-year agreement was signed between Gazprom and Tajikistan, which gave Gazprom the right to explore and develop the gas fields of Rangon and Sargazon. Tajikistan's reserves are considered small and will be used only within the country.[157] Gazprom began to repair Tajikistan's damaged energy infrastructure, gas and oil wells, and pipelines; and intended to participate in the exploitation and use of resources inside Tajikistan. Gazprom linked the agreements to the upgrading of the Central Asian pipeline system, which connects the Central Asian infrastructure with Russia.[158]

Tajikistan is expecting more of its economic relations with Russia than Russia is able to deliver, and this is a source of tension in their relations. Nevertheless, in 2002 Russia demonstrated its interest in the energy resources of Tajikistan. An economic dimension had been added to the traditional military–security dominance of Russia's relations with Tajikistan.

Uzbekistan

In common with Turkmenistan, Russia had no developed military cooperation with Uzbekistan—and nothing changed in this regard after September 2001. Russia was not able to substantially improve relations with Uzbekistan but became active in the economic field, primarily in the energy sector. Several previous agreements formed the basis for bilateral economic relations.[159] Nevertheless, Russia's trade with Uzbekistan fell throughout the 1990s. In 2000 it accounted for 15.8 per cent of Uzbekistan's imports and 16.7 per cent of its exports—mostly cotton, fruit and nuts.[160] Although Russia's investment in Uzbekistan was larger than its investment in Tajikistan, Kyrgyzstan and Turkmenistan, it still remained small.

In June 2002 a Russian–Uzbek Inter-Governmental Commission on trade and economic relations was reactivated with Deputy Prime Minister Viktor Khristenko in charge.[161] Russian–Uzbek cooperation within the defence industry had been crucial since Soviet times, above all in the construction of the Ilyushin military aircraft. Several problems had hampered cooperation in this sector during the 1990s. Nevertheless, in April 2003 Russia and Uzbekistan agreed on terms for the production and sale of aircraft at the Chkalovsk aircraft production centre in Tashkent.[162]

Uzbekistan was an energy importer during Soviet times but became self-sufficient in the mid-1990s. It is an exporter of gas, most notably to Tajikistan, Kyrgyzstan and Kazakhstan but also in smaller volumes to Russia. The Central Asian-Centre pipeline runs from Bukhara to Russia. Exports to other Central

Asian countries go through two pipelines. One runs from Tashkent through Bishkek to Almaty, Kazakhstan, and the other runs through northern Tajikistan and connects with the eastern part of Uzbekistan. Gazprom took on the task of reconstructing the gas pipeline system. Uzbekistan is the tenth-largest natural gas producer in the world and its reserves are substantial.[163] There are major natural gas fields in Kuanish, Shakhpakhty and Chembar. In May 2002 a Russian-Uzbek 'strategic' agreement was signed on cooperation in the gas sector. In January 2003 Gazprom and the Uzbek state-owned company Uzbekneftegaz decided to increase deliveries of Uzbek gas to Russia and signed an agreement on delivery covering the years 2003–12.[164] According to reports in the summer of 2003, Uzbekistan planned to double gas exports to Russia to 10 bcm by 2005.[165] Other Russian energy companies, in particular Lukoil and Itera, also engaged in exploiting Uzbekistan's energy resources and in September 2002 signed an agreement with Uzbekneftegaz to develop gas and condensate reserves in the Bukhara-Khiva and Gissar blocks in the south of Uzbekistan.[166] Gazprom and Lukoil also invested actively in oilfields in the north of the country.[167] When President Putin visited President Karimov on 6 August 2003, for the first time since September 2001, he stressed Russia's interest in economic exchange with Uzbekistan, especially in the gas sector. By then Russia was not only an importer of Uzbek gas but also in charge of the transportation of gas across Uzbek territory from Turkmenistan. Thus, in 2002–2003 Russian energy companies demonstrated an increased interest in the energy resources of Uzbekistan.

Uzbekistan did not want to develop security cooperation with Russia, but it became a more active member of the Shanghai Cooperation Organization and, by January 2004, the SCO Anti-Terrorist Centre had moved to Tashkent. Although Russia's presence in Uzbekistan continued to decline, Moscow made an active effort to maintain a future role by developing the strategic resource of energy.

In summary, Russia maintained an emphasis on military-security issues in its relations with Central Asian states. Anti-terrorism continued to provide the framework for cooperation within the CSTO, the SCO and at the bilateral level with Central Asian states. Nonetheless, there was a new emphasis on economic cooperation by the Russian Government. The Russian energy monopolies of Gazprom and Unified Electric Systems and the oil companies, especially Lukoil, made a breakthrough and long-term agreements were signed in the energy sector with all four Central Asian states. This meant that in spite of increased US engagement in the region, Russia secured its future influence in the production and transportation of gas and electricity. This was a new turn in Russian policy.

However, was this a trend towards 'economization' of Russia's relations with Central Asia? Were there commercial interests behind the new Russian drive into the economic sector? The energy companies undoubtedly acted in their own interests so this was partly true. However, they also shared with the Russian Government an interest in gaining a foothold in the region. These interests can best be described as geo-economic, that is, securing strategic assets for the future. Nevertheless, the government demonstrated a clear desire for Russian business to engage in Central Asia, although Russian investors were not yet ready. The Central Asian Governments, which expected Russian economic investments, were disappointed with the slow pace.

Policy towards the Major Powers in Central Asia

The political constellation of power in the wider Central Asian region before 11 September 2001 had been formed along an axis of Russia, China and Iran, on one side, and the USA, Uzbekistan and Pakistan, on the other. Even if Russia, China and Iran had not entered into any formal coalition or any deeper partnership relations, they shared a general fear of the growing US presence in Central Asia and the Caucasus.

China and the Shanghai Cooperation Organization

Although the SCO[168] was quick to make a statement after the terrorist attacks, inactivity seemed to be its main characteristic during the following month.[169] It was a new organization and it now seemed that events had pushed it to one side as US-led security cooperation took the lead. Moreover, to the SCO there was the risk that Russia would consider the organization irrelevant if Russia developed cooperation with the USA. The SCO had provided a platform for Russian–Chinese criticism of increased US engagement in Central Asia. Therefore, commentators argued, Russia now had to make the choice between improving relations with the USA and reducing cooperation with China—or the other way around.

Nevertheless, when on 11 October the heads of the law enforcement bodies and security services of the member countries (excluding Uzbekistan) met in Bishkek, they urged closer cooperation in the new international situation. Among the measures agreed were information exchange; the coordination of preventive measures and special operations for advance warning; measures to prevent member countries from being used for activities which violate other SCO members; and the intensification of work to find and stop channels for financing and supplying material, technical and other equipment to terrorist organizations. The setting up of the SCO Anti-Terrorist Centre was also to be speeded up.[170] Thus, for the SCO business went on as usual.

Russian efforts to build up the SCO continued. A charter was adopted at the June 2002 summit in St Petersburg.[171] The main objectives of the reorganized SCO were listed as:

> Consolidating mutual confidence, friendship and good-neighbourliness; strengthening multilateral interaction for the sake of maintaining and consolidating peace, security and stability in the region; responding jointly to new challenges and threats; encouraging effective and mutually beneficial cooperation in diverse fields; and facilitating the economic growth and social and cultural development of the member states of the organization.[172]

A final agreement was signed concerning the setting up of the Anti-Terrorist Centre in Bishkek, although the question of financing remained difficult and was not fully resolved.

However, the former anti-US bent of the CSO abated. Anti-US rhetoric was not pursued and Russia did not give up the SCO, which it considered crucial for the security of Central Asia. Russian officials instead spoke in favour of developing the cooperation between the SCO and the CSTO. When the Russian Security Council met on 31 October 2002 these organizations were yet not fully functioning, and Foreign Minister Igor Ivanov urged the anti-terrorist mechanisms of the SCO and the CST (the SCO Anti-Terrorist Centre, the CIS Anti-Terrorist Centre and the CST Rapid Reaction Force) to 'start working' and for their work to have 'real and specific content'.[173] At the CST meeting in November 2002, he urged the two organizations to closely coordinate their efforts and to act in accordance with a 'unified UN strategy'.[174]

While the CSO had from the start declared its interest to be mainly in issues of a political and security character, issues of economic cooperation between the member states became more pronounced during 2002. On 28 May 2002 trade ministers from the member states met in Shanghai to discuss mechanisms for expanding trade, investment and economic cooperation in the region of the SCO.[175] The meeting was reported as marking a shift in emphasis from the previous focus on security to include economic cooperation. Russian Deputy Minister of Economic Development and Trade, Dmitrii Sukhoparov, declared that the long-term aim was to create a free trade zone among the SCO states. China and Kyrgyzstan were already members of the WTO. Yet, the declaration from the summit meeting in June 2002 stressed the importance of economic cooperation, noting the member states' intention 'to step up negotiations on creating favourable conditions for trade and investment, and developing a long-term programme for multilateral economic cooperation'.[176]

In May 2002 the defence ministers of the member states agreed to pledge closer cooperation in the fight against terrorism and discussed plans for joint exercises in fighting those threats. The joint military exercise between China and Kyrgyzstan, which followed in August 2002, was the first to take place with China inside the SCO framework. It reflected a general tendency towards a greater Chinese involvement in the region. Looking at the long-term trends in the region, both China and the USA were increasing their influence in Central Asia. While China's bilateral relations with Central Asian states had previously concentrated on economic cooperation, cooperation now started to develop in the security field. Since Chinese engagement was embedded in the SCO, no open contradictions or tensions arose between Russia and China in this regard.

Thus, Putin's interest in the SCO remained. Although the SCO was still mainly a paper organization, it was endorsed as a regular security organization that was there to stay. Yet, it had to adapt in order to play a role in the future, as Putin pointed out in the summer of 2002: 'The effectiveness of the SCO is indissolubly linked to processes and trends that are taking place in the global dimension.'[177]

The tendency to formalize cooperation within the SCO met resistance—primarily on the extent of and the forms for developing military cooperation. Uzbekistan declared that the SCO 'should not be considered a military or political bloc' and that 'Its main task should be resolving global problems'. Putin therefore had to respond at the June 2002 summit to give assurances that the new organization was not to become a closed military bloc: 'I would like to stress here that the SCO is not a bloc, and not a closed association.'[178] The SCO seemed torn between the different interests of its members. Nevertheless, when the SCO Anti-Terrorism Centre opened at last in early 2004, Uzbekistan was its host country.

Although the SCO was sidestepped by the events following 11 September 2001, Russia pursued its previous efforts to develop cooperation with China in the SCO. Russia's rapprochement with the USA, however, reduced the previous anti-US bent of the organization.

The USA

Putin did not formulate any conditions for Russia siding with the USA after 11 September, but he expected it to bring about a rapprochement with the USA. His policy turn was made to bring about a breakthrough in Russia's relations with the West and, at least in the long run, to bring dividends for Russia. Russian media commentators made the comparison with the close US–Soviet cooperation in the alliance against Hitler during the Second World War, and articles in the media reflected the high expectations of what this new situation would bring.

One such issue was Chechnya on which several Russian commentators expected that the West would become more understanding of Moscow's policy. Another issue was the Russian application for membership of the World Trade Organization. Of special concern in Russian–US relations were the issues of anti-missile defence and strategic arms cuts. These were crucial in the eyes of the Russian military. The outcome of the two last issues, in particular, was a disappointment to Russia during the winter of 2001 and the spring of 2002.

At the Ljubljana Summit between Presidents Bush and Putin in the summer of 2001 discussions had touched on both anti-missile defence and strategic arms cuts. When the two met again in July in Genoa at the G8 summit, they agreed that that these two issues were related and therefore should be dealt with together. This meant that any modifications to the ABM Treaty would be accompanied by large cuts in offensive nuclear warheads. In contrast to the USA, Russia expected written agreements and verification procedures. Putin, who expressed his willingness to amend the treaty in such a way as to allow the development of the US Nuclear Missile Defence (NMD) programme, was not able 'to deliver the Moscow bureaucracy'.[179] The post-11 September Russian–US rapprochement therefore set off rumours that an agreement might be possible. Instead, on 10 December 2001 US Secretary of State Colin Powell informed Russia that the USA would be withdrawing from the ABM Treaty in six months' time, and that it would not be replaced by any new document. Putin maintained that Russia was not threatened by this move but sceptics within Russia were not reassured. During Putin's visit to President Bush in mid-November they called for the creation of a 'new effective mechanism for consultation, cooperation, joint discussion and coordinated joint action'.[180] In

May 2002 the Russian–US Strategic Offensive Reductions Treaty (SORT) was signed, a vague document that cut the number of strategic nuclear weapons. It foresaw a reduction of deployed strategic nuclear warheads by two-thirds by 2012, but it included no verification procedures and allowed the parties to store excess weapons.[181] The treaty also expressed a common interest in non-proliferation of nuclear weapons.[182]

In May 2002 a NATO–Russia Council was formally created at the Reykjavik Summit.[183] It had been decided on in December 2001 in order to give Russia a stronger voice than the 1997 Permanent Joint Council of Russia and NATO had allowed for. The Rome Declaration of 28 May 2002 constituted the basic document of the new council and was entitled 'NATO–Russia relations: a new quality'. It defined the following areas for cooperation: the fight against terrorism; crisis management; non-proliferation; arms control and confidence-building measures; theatre missile defence; search and rescue at sea; military-to-military cooperation and defence reform; civil emergencies; and new threats and challenges.[184] The Council was a symbol of a US–Russia rapprochement but the Council played no substantial role in subsequent developments. The US Administration was more responsive with regard to Russia's economic interests. The US administration recognized Russia as a market economy and supported its bid to join the World Trade Organization (WTO). Russia was also awarded full membership of the G8 in June 2002. However, the restrictions imposed by the Jackson-Vanik amendment on Russian exports to the USA were not lifted.

Putin's new policy contributed to a completely new political atmosphere of international cooperation. Yet, during the winter of 2001 and early spring 2002 there were few specific or visible rewards for Russia as a result of Putin's policy turn in relation to the USA. This constituted the basis for the increased criticism of his foreign policy. Late spring 2002 did bring something for Russia but not enough to silence Putin's critics.

In spite of the improved relations between Russia and the USA, and the consultations that continued on Afghanistan in the Russian–US Working Group, no direct cooperation developed between the two powers on issues relating to Central Asia. Although anti-terrorism remained the major theme in Russian–US relations, there was no direct Russian-US cooperation in Central Asia apart from what took place concerning Afghanistan.[185] Dmitrii Trenin argued that 'a convincing case can be made for Russian–American and Russian–European cooperation in Central Asia', and suggested a detailed programme for Russian–US cooperation in the security field. He wrote that both governments understood that a negative zero sum game would distract attention from the real security issues and that they shared an interest in regional stability in the region.[186] Trenin's recommendations for Russian–US security cooperation in Central Asia were relevant but they did not materialize. Mutual suspicion continued to constitute a barrier to any form of direct cooperation.

The fact that no initiatives were taken to develop structures for Russian–US security cooperation in Central Asia reflected the caution, suspicion and rivalry that remained between the two powers in Central Asia.

Summary

Although Putin was quick to express his sympathy in a phone call to President Bush after the terrorist attacks on the USA of 11 September 2001, he faced a very difficult decision over how Russia was to contribute to the US operation in response to the terrorist attacks. The answer to this question seemed likely to determine Russia's relations with the West and with the Central Asian states for years to come.

Working out his policy over a two-week period, Putin had intensive consultations with his own 'siloviki' and the Central Asian leaders. While he had to make the former comply with his proposal for a policy, he had to make the latter accommodate their cooperation with the USA to a general consensus with Russia. His policy, made public on 24 September, was a compromise in the sense that Russian would not participate in US military operations in Afghanistan but would provide the USA with intelligence information about Afghanistan, and increase its material support for the anti-Taliban Northern Alliance. Moreover, Russia did give its consent to the use by US forces of Central Asian territory, but only for humanitarian and search-and-rescue operations, not to launch offensive operations in Afghanistan. It was obvious that the Russian response was shaped to take account both of the Russian domestic scene and of the strong Central Asian interest in cooperation with the USA.

Although the security situation in Central Asia improved after the fall of the Taliban in November, the drastic increase in foreign engagement made the strategic situation more complicated for Russia. Russia continued its build up of the Collective Security Treaty and the Shanghai Cooperation Organization. Nonetheless, these organizations were sidestepped when the US Administration developed direct relationships with the Central Asian states. Russian policy towards the Central Asian states had to be shaped to take into account the large international presence in these countries.

Putin's response to the terrorist attacks of 11 September represented a continuation of his previous policy in the sense that it was in line with his anti-terrorist focus since 1999. At the same time, it represented a radical foreign policy turn—Moscow's approach to Western engagement in Central Asia shifted. Against the background of Putin's efforts in 1999 to rally Central Asian states and use the SCO against US engagement, his anti-terrorist policy was 'inverted'. Putin's interest in maintaining close relations with the USA meant that the previous anti-US character of the SCO abated.

Within the narrow perspective of policy in Central Asia, Putin's new policy indicated that his 1999 policy had failed—the anti-terrorist structures of the CST were never used by the US-led anti-terrorist coalition. His policy did not stand the test after the terrorist attacks against New York and Washington. However, Putin managed to make a breakthrough in relations with the West. To what extent Russia's change of approach to US engagement in Central Asia was a temporary move, and to what extent it was a fundamental revision, remained to be seen.

The Central Asian states willingly joined the US-led anti-terrorist coalition. To them the fall of the Taliban regime in Afghanistan, and the related increase in US engagement, brought stability to the region. New levels of international attention raised expectations of international economic aid and assistance.

Putin's consent to a US military presence might have given the impression that Russia would become a passive spectator of the growing US–Western engagement in Central Asia. This did not happen. Instead, Russia reactivated its policy in the region in an attempt to balance it within its overall pro-Western foreign policy. By autumn 2002 there were signs that a more active Russian policy was in the making after US forces had been deployed in Central Asia. Russia's reduced capabilities still constituted a constraint on its foreign policy. However, a new determination was reflected in government statements about regaining the initiative on CIS territory.

The contours of a new Russian policy towards Central Asia evolved. The previous emphasis on the security aspects of relations remained, as reflected in Russian efforts to develop both the CST and bilateral security relations. However, stronger attention was now given to economic aspects. The energy sector became the major focus and Russia's interests expanded to include not only Turkmen gas but also the resources of the other three countries, primarily Uzbekistan. Long-term agreements were signed under which Gazprom would exploit the resources, buy gas, repair pipelines and, together with Uzbekistan and Turkmenistan, provide gas to Europe through a common gas pipeline system. In Tajikistan and Kyrgyzstan agreements were signed on the development of the hydro-energy resources of these countries. Bilateral intergovernmental economic commissions were reactivated in 2002–2003, although no breakthrough took place with regard to trade and investment.

Thus, there was a shift in favour of a stronger emphasis on economic cooperation with Central Asian countries, although Russia's previous priority on military–security cooperation remained. A process towards 'economization' of foreign policy had started but economic interests did not yet constitute the driving force behind Russian policy. A Russian commercial interest in Central Asia was still something for the future, However, the government had indicated its desire that economic bonds should link Russia to Central Asia in the future.

Relations improved between Russia and Turkmenistan as well as between Russia and Kyrgyzstan. The Russian Government seized the opportunity to improve relations when domestic political crises developed in these countries, thereby making their governments more dependent on its support. As a result, Russia was able not only to sign a long-term gas contract with Turkmenistan but also to extend the Treaty of Friendship and Cooperation, which included, among other things, an agreement on security cooperation. In Kyrgyzstan, a Russian military airbase opened (formally under the responsibility of the CST Rapid Reaction Force) and Russia signed a series of cooperation agreements in both the economic and the security fields. Russia gave stronger emphasis to the economic dimension, in particular energy and transport systems, in its relations with all four countries.

More active in its policy towards Central Asia, Russia maintained a low profile with regard to the US military presence in the region. Russia and the USA had common interests in fighting terrorism, but they developed no joint cooperation in this regard in Central Asia.

PART III

FACTORS BEHIND RUSSIAN FOREIGN POLICY

6

RUSSIAN DOMESTIC FACTORS

What makes foreign policy change? Chapter 2 in this volume gives the historical background of Russia's conquest of Central Asia, and chapter 1 argues that history is a possible factor in any explanation of Russian foreign policy. History forms a collective memory which provides a backdrop for Russian strategic interests and great power rivalries in Central Asia—along with security concerns and the possible economic benefits to be gained from cooperation in the region. To this can be added the contemporary cultural aspect of the hundreds of thousands of ethnic Russians still living in Central Asia thereby upholding a Russian cultural influence in the region and also the interests of the Russian Government. Yet while an analysis of the Russian conquest in the late nineteenth century gives no clue as to why policy changed more than 100 years later, it does make it easier to understand why Russia wanted to maintain an influence in the region after a brief period of disengagement, immediately after the break up of the Soviet Union. The history of the Russian conquest of Central Asia also provides Russia with a point of reference for a policy of coming to terms with Western powers while, at the same time, increasing Russian influence in Central Asia and returning to the world stage as a great power. Thus, history gives the outside observer a better understanding of certain issues and why they matter to a government, However, it cannot explain the direction that policy takes. The external factors analysed in chapters 3 and 4 contribute more to explain the shifts in Russian policy. The developments on the ground in Central Asia—an increasing foreign engagement and Russia's rapid loss of control over regional dynamics and governments—provide the key to Russia's inability to handle the new challenges. The developments on the global scene—US dominance and its frosty relations with Russia—are part of that context.

This chapter focuses on possible domestic factors behind Russia's Central Asia policy. Chapter 7 discusses factors and dynamics within Central Asia and their importance to the shaping of Russian policy towards the region. An examination of the relative weight of different factors and the way they relate to each other is saved for the concluding chapter, as well as a discussion of alternative explanations for Russian policy.

Chapter 1 mentions four groups of Russian internal factors that could be assumed to influence Russian foreign policy—economic conditions, the domestic security situation, the specifics of the foreign policy making process and the political will as indicated by ideological concepts and elite attitudes.

Economic conditions are understood here to be part of the basic problem. They, along with the task of rebuilding the economy, constitute the general context of Russia's search for a new foreign policy. Economic conditions also explain why there have been constraints on Russian policy towards Central Asia. The state of the Russian economy did not allow the assumption of costly obligations beyond Russia's borders. Two wars in Chechnya during the 1990s drained Russian financial reserves and forced Russia to set firm priorities. The possible benefits had first to be weighed against the costs. This chapter discusses how Russian domestic factors influenced policy towards Central Asia—the major domestic security problem (Chechnya), the foreign policy making process, ideological concepts, and elite attitudes.

The Chechnya Factor

Developments in Chechnya were crucial to the development of Putin's anti-terrorist agenda of 1999. The crisis in Moscow's relations with Chechnya, which erupted into war in 1994–96 and resulted in the breakdown of social, economic and political structures in Chechnya and a process of rapid radicalization there, deeply influenced Russian perceptions of a terrorist threat emanating from chaos and fuelled by radical Islam. The Chechnya conflict constituted a major security problem for the Russian state, and it heavily influenced the way developments along Russia's southern flank were viewed.

The Chechnya conflict contributed to the reintroduction of the term 'terrorism' to the Russian vocabulary. When the first military campaign in Chechnya was initiated in December 1994, 'terrorism' was not used to legitimize the intervention. Instead, the campaign was justified in terms of the criminalization of Chechen life, the violation of the Russian constitution and federal law, and the danger of separatism. The years 1991–94 had witnessed what was called 'bandformirovanie' defined as groups of armed criminals engaged in kidnappings that were unconnected to political demands. During 1994–96, however, in parallel with these criminal activities, the phenomenon of terrorist acts with a political component entered the picture. They all emanated from the Chechnya conflict. In the summer of 1995 there was an attack on a hospital in Budennovsk, led by Chechen rebel Shamil Basaev, when more than 2000 people were held hostage. In December 1995, in Kizlyar, more than 2000 people were held hostage by another Chechen rebel Salman Raduev. These major terrorist operations were professionally carried out and had a military character. The number of hostage-taking incidents and explosions increased in the neighbourhood of Chechnya, and also in other parts of Russia. By 1998 kidnappings and individual acts of terrorism against civilians had changed the security situation in Chechnya to such a degree that the Organization for Security and Co-operation in Europe (OSCE) mission withdrew its office from Grozny. This development culminated in the explosions at two blocks of flats in Moscow in September 1999 when hundreds of people were killed. These, as well as other explosions in south Russia, were all blamed on Chechens.

In 1994, the same year as the first Chechen war started, the Russian Criminal Code, inherited from the Soviet period, was amended to include a special article on 'terrorism'.[1] As a result of the developments in Chechnya, a Russian federal law was adopted in July 1998 'On the Anti-Terrorist Struggle', which provided the legal–normative basis for the fight against terrorism within Russia and internationally.[2] It referred to 'terrorism' and to 'international terrorism' but without being specific. The law dealt with terrorist acts and did not associate them with any political purpose. International terrorism was defined as activities by organizations operating on the territory of more than one state or involving participants from more than one country.[3] In November 1998 the Russian Government decided to create a Federal Anti-Terrorist Commission with representatives from the departments concerned to work out a united policy and to coordinate the activities of government bodies. At the same time, similar commissions were also created in the Russian republics and the regions.[4]

The phenomenon of terrorism has a history in Russia. The late nineteenth and early twentieth centuries witnessed a series of terrorist acts by small radical groups in Russia.[5] By the time of the break up of the Soviet Union, the term 'terrorism' had gone out of use to describe the reality on former Soviet territory. It was not used to describe any of the armed conflicts that erupted at the time of the break up of the Soviet Union, even though they were violent. The 1993 military doctrine mentioned 'international terrorism' in general terms as a threat to Russian security but without specifying the nature of threat. The term 'terrorism' entered the political vocabulary in June 1996 in descriptions of conflicts in Russia and on former Soviet territory contained in President Yeltsin's message to parliament on national security.

The second military campaign in Chechnya followed the incursion by Chechen rebels into Dagestan in August 1999 to set up an Islamic state of Chechnya and Dagestan. Vladimir Putin, who had replaced Sergei Stepashin as prime minister, immediately characterized the conflict in terms of terrorism. From having previously been spoken of in terms of individual terrorist acts, the Chechnya conflict was now viewed through the lens of a terrorist threat—ignoring Chechnya's history of conflict that stretched back more than 100 years. The label of terrorism was now transferred to Central Asia when describing the situation there.

The second Chechnya campaign, initiated in September 1999, was unsuccessful—in spite of Putin's repeated declaration that the military situation in Chechnya was stabilizing as a result of Russian military operations. In January 2001, Putin declared that the task of bringing Chechnya under control was no longer that of the military, and that the number of Russian troops in Chechnya was to be radically reduced. The military phase was over, he said, and the task was now defined as defeating the remaining terrorists. Responsibility for the operation was transferred from the Defence Ministry to the Russian Federal Security Service (Federalnaya Sluzhba Bezopasnosti, FSB).[6] Putin presented a package of political, administrative and economic measures for rebuilding Chechen society and strengthening the Chechen administration, which had been set up in the summer of 2000 under Mufti Akhmed Kadyrov.

What on the surface seemed to be the result of a consistent and successful Russian policy was instead a policy without a strategy or a plan of action. Putin's

Chechnya policy, in common with his policy during the first Chechen war of 1994–6, was very much the result of a domestic power struggle at the top of Russian society.[7] Putin's policy did not bring any immediate results or bring society any closer to peace. Neither his military policy nor his efforts at political and administrative reform were successful.

The Chechnya factor presaged a large part of the terrorist agenda that Putin introduced to Central Asia in 1999. Chechnya also played a role in the 2001 redirection of Russia's Central Asian policy. Putin and the Russian media calculated that the US Administration and European Governments would be more understanding of Russia's problems in Chechnya after the al-Qaeda attacks on the USA. It was expected that Putin's definition of the Chechnya conflict as a case of terrorism would be more acceptable to the West and that the West would tone down its criticism of the methods used by the Russian authorities to handle the Chechnya problem. These expectations were not totally unfounded. The Bush Administration was less vocal in its criticism of Russia in the following years. European Governments, however, continued to criticize Russian violations of human rights in Chechnya.

On 23 October 2002, a group of Chechen fighters—many of them women—took hostage some 800 people in the audience at the Dubrovka theatre in central Moscow. After a two-day siege, Russian special forces stormed the building and shot the hostage-takers, while a large number of the hostages were killed by the gas used by the troops during the operation. The hostage-taking was branded a serious act of terrorism and seemed to confirm Putin's definition of terrorism—both domestic and international—as the main security threat.

This event demonstrated that what Russia needed most of all with regard to the CIS states in general and the Central Asian states in particular was practical down-to-earth cooperation to prevent terrorism. Although the Dubrovka hostage-taking had no direct links to Central Asia, it influenced Russian policy there in different ways. First, it resulted in a renewed discussion of Russian national security. During a Kremlin meeting on 29 October between Putin and the defence and foreign ministers, the chief of the General Staff and representatives of the different security organs, Putin ordered a revision of the national security doctrine.[8] This was reiterated in Putin's speech to the Russian Security Council on 31 October when he announced the revision of the National Security Concept and other essential doctrinal documents. The rewriting of these documents was explained by the threat of terrorism having become much more serious than the threat from the West—the Russian military therefore had to be organized in accordance with a proper understanding of the threats. The General Staff was given the task of revising the basic documents on national security.[9] Putin had thus been given another strong argument for speeding up military reform in order to strengthen the capacity for handling and preventing local and regional conflicts and wars, rather than the far less likely eventuality of a conventional attack from the West.[10] In this context, Central Asia seemed to be a natural area of continued concern for Russia and for security cooperation.

Second, with further emphasis on the terrorist threat, Putin declared at the Security Council meeting that greater priority was to be given to cooperation with the CIS states in order to prevent terrorism—which meant first of all cooperation with Central Asian states.[11] The Dubrovka hostage crisis had drawn attention to the fact that people could travel easily across CIS territory without passing customs and border controls. It thus gave impetus to increased cooperation on the ground between the Russian authorities and those of the CIS states, and especially the Central Asian states, with regard to borders, customs and financial control services. As Oleg Chernov, deputy secretary of the Security Council, said, similar hostage-taking actions could take place anywhere on CIS territory. The lack of proper border control on the transport of goods between CIS countries was being actively exploited by terrorists, and it was therefore necessary to create an international system for preventive measures and warnings.[12] This initiative was followed up at a meeting on 21 March 2003 of the secretaries of the national security councils of the parties to the Collective Security Treaty (CST), when further initiatives on cooperation between borders and customs services were discussed.[13] Third, the Dubrovka hostage crisis confirmed the priority given to the threat of international terrorism. It thereby confirmed the importance for Russia of cooperating above all with the USA in countering international terrorism.

The Chechnya factor had an immense importance for Putin's anti-terrorist agenda in Central Asia in 1999. It also played a key role in 2001 in the sense that Moscow expected a more understanding approach to Russia's Chechnya problem from Western governments after the events of 11 September. Chechnya continued in the following years to feed the strong Russian focus on anti-terrorism and to confirm to the Russian Government that its focus on countering terrorism was necessary.

The Foreign Policy Making Process

The Background: Foreign Policy Making under Yeltsin

While a consensus about the general strategic vision of Russian foreign policy—of Russia as a great power and the nucleus of an integrated CIS—had developed during 1993–95, there was no understanding of what specific policy should be pursued on CIS territory or towards Central Asia in order to accomplish these goals. Although President Yeltsin's decree of September 1995 'On Russian Strategy toward CIS Member States' declared the ideal of the creation of an economic, political and defence union,[14] there was no common understanding within the Russian political establishment, either inside the government or outside, as to what policy would best support Russia's national interests.

As there was no guidance from above, the floor was open for conflicting interests to influence and shape policy. There was room for manoeuvre for ministries, departments and agencies to intervene in the policy-making process where normally their responsibility and function were only to implement policy.[15] As is often the case in such situations, different institutions pursue their own agendas and informal interest groups gain a disproportionate influence. The consequence of such situations is usually 'a lack of balance between political policy making institutions and bureaucratic policy-implementing structures. The relative weakness of political organs means that the political function tends to be appropriated, in considerable measure, by bureaucrats. Intra-bureaucratic struggles become a primary focus of politics'.[16]

The 1993 Russian Constitution made it the prerogative of the president to formulate foreign policy. He was given extensive power to appoint the government, overrule parliament, issue laws by decree, and control the defence, interior, foreign and security ministries directly, without going through the prime minister. During the early 1990s, Yeltsin was mainly occupied with policy towards the West and the ministries were therefore left to formulate CIS policy themselves. The power of the Duma was circumscribed by the 1993 constitution and it was left without the opportunity to influence foreign policy except by changing moods and opinions through debates in the Duma and the work of its committees.

Responsibility for policy on the CIS countries was shared between the Foreign Minister and a Ministry for CIS Affairs. There was little expertise or knowledge about the newly independent Central Asian states in either of these ministries. Responsibility for CIS affairs shifted between them as repeated structural reorganizations took place, illustrating the structural weaknesses of the Russian Government and demonstrating that a consistent policy with regard to the CIS could hardly be carried out under such circumstances.[17] Their work was repeatedly criticized.[18]

The Foreign Ministry was weak on policy making towards the CIS countries during Yeltsin's first period in office, but its influence was strengthened when Primakov became foreign minister in January 1996.[19] He brought to his office knowledge of and interest in Central Asia, which the ministry had largely lacked under his predecessor, Andrei Kozyrev. Primakov demonstrated his concern about security developments in Central Asia in the 1994 report by the Foreign Intelligence Service (Sluzhba Vneshnei Razvedki, SVR).[20] His first trip as foreign minister was to Dushanbe, Tajikistan, as head of a delegation including the directors of both the Russian Federal Border Service (Federalnaya Pogranichnaya Sluzhba, FPS) and the SVR. Thanks to Primakov's efforts to find a solution to the Tajik conflict, Russia changed its policy on the United Tajik Opposition (UTO).

Yet, even if Primakov was able to bring greater attention to CIS problems in general and Central Asia in particular, the Russian foreign policy making structures remained fragmented not only between different ministries but also, and above all, between the government and the presidential apparatus.

As Eugene Huskey points out in his study of Russian presidential power, Yeltsin was unable to discipline his government and therefore 'resorted to a technique of executive leadership of long Russian pedigree—institutional redundancy'.[21] 'Instead of a presidency with a clear division of labour between offices, Yeltsin permitted the development of competing centres of presidential power, each with pretensions to expertise and influence on a wide range of policy. Thus, not only did presidential structures duplicate the functions of government, they duplicated each other.'[22] Another characteristic trait of Yeltsin as president was that he gave office to both reformists and traditionalists in order to balance these forces within the presidential apparatus.

Within the presidential administration three different agencies with foreign policy responsibilities existed: the Executive Office of the President

(Administratsiya Prezidenta), the Counsellors' Service, and the Security Council.[23] During Yeltsin's second term in office, the role of the Executive Office increased greatly, but in general it dealt mainly with domestic issues.[24] In December 1998 Nikolai Bordyuzha was appointed as its head. His professional training had taken place in the Federal Border Service, of which he became director in January 1998.[25] A few months before being appointed head of the Executive Office, he had been appointed Secretary of the Security Council. With this professional background, Bordyuzha was familiar with the security problems of Central Asia in general and the Tajik–Afghan border in particular, since Russian border troops at that time were still serving along the outer borders of all the Central Asian states apart from Uzbekistan, with an exceptionally large contingent in Tajikistan. Bordyuzha, however, did not hold these positions for long. He lacked the political skills necessary to survive in the Kremlin.[26] He was replaced as early as March 1999 by Alexander Voloshin, a loyal member of the Yeltsin 'Family'. The same month Vladimir Putin replaced Bordyuzha as secretary of the Security Council. The influence of the Security Council and its secretary varied from time to time. Created as a consultative body to provide a comprehensive view on external and internal security, it was as influential as the president wanted it to be. It prepared the final drafts of the 1993 and 2000 military doctrines and the national security concepts of 1993, 1997 and 2000. During Yeltsin's second term the Security Council mainly dealt with domestic security, above all with the Chechnya conflict.[27]

Huskey writes that after Bordyuzha's appointment as head of the Executive Office those with experience in the armed forces, the security and intelligence services—what became the FSB and the SVR, formed out of what had been the Committee of State Security (Komitet Gosudarstvoi Bezopasnosti, KGB)—came increasingly to supply the management of the presidential apparatus and government structures. Huskey explains that Yeltsin turned for administrative support to a group that was schooled in loyalty and discipline in response to 'mounting attacks on his rule by nationalists, communists, and democrats as well as an increasing insubordination in his own ranks'.[28] The appointment of Primakov a few months earlier reflected the same desire to secure loyal and disciplined people at the top.

Among the wider group of institutions and people which contributed to the process of securitization of Russia's Central Asia policy, a few agencies should be singled out. These directed their attention to the Central Asian region at an early stage. The General Staff drafted the Military Doctrine in 1992 and had pointed at the time to local armed conflicts spreading across borders as the greatest danger, but also briefly mentioned 'international terrorism'. The SVR was the first body to publicly point out the Islamic threat in Afghanistan and Central Asia in its 1994 report. As the military and the federal border service FPS was engaged from the beginning of the Tajik war, it reported on the security situation in the region. The role of the director of the FPS increased under Director Andrei Nikolaev, who sought to strengthen the FPS in order to have it play a much larger policy role in handling conflicts on CIS territory. However, in 1998 he was dismissed and the ambitions of the service were scaled back.

The military and security services thus acted as an important lobby group in pushing forward a security-dominated agenda with regard to policy on the CIS. For them Central Asia had a strategic position in this regard. Furthermore, people with a professional background in the security sector started to fill the ranks of government structures as a result of Yevgenii Primakov becoming prime minister in September 1998. He appointed many former colleagues from the intelligence and security services to key positions in the media and revenue-generating companies, such as the arms exporter Rosvooruzhenie, as well as in the executive branch.[29]

Foreign Policy Making by 1999

Vladimir Putin was appointed secretary of the Russian Security Council in March 1999 and thereby came to deal with Russia's major national security headache—Chechnya. With his professional background in the KGB and the FSB he seemed well prepared to take on this task. When he became prime minister in August 1999, against the background of the deteriorating security situation in Chechnya, foreign observers viewed this as the result of the influence of security and military interests within the presidential structures.[30] Primakov mentions in his memoirs that for the Yeltsin 'Family', whose choice Putin was, his background in the FSB did play a role.[31] With a solid background in the KGB, he had been brought into Yeltsin's Executive Office in 1996 as a deputy head of the property department—but by July 1998 he was back in the security service as head of the FSB.

Institutional interests were decisive in the shaping of Putin's Central Asian policy. When formulating a policy with which to respond to new and complex challenges in Central Asia, it was the institutions affiliated with traditional security that were able to provide a policy alternative. The security services, the military, the Ministry of the Interior and the Federal Border Troops service, all of which had already gained influence under Yeltsin, were more able to frame and define problems and come up with a solution. This paved the way for the anti-terrorist agenda as Putin was appointed prime minister in August 1999 and acting president in December the same year. The structural weakness of the foreign policy-making system since the break up of the Soviet Union also made it easier for the security organs, which remained more or less intact in spite of reorganizations and maintained old networks on post-Soviet territory, to make their priorities known.

When he became prime minister, Putin brought the FSB's focus on anti-terrorism to the government, and made it a top-priority issue on the political agenda in the general CIS context. The anti-terrorist agenda provided a convenient policy against the background of the difficulties experienced by both the governmental and the presidential structures in grasping the situation in Central Asia and the failure of policy so far. They welcomed the anti-terrorist focus because it provided a simple analysis and a simple answer.

Putin appointed people with a background in the security services. In May 2000 Vyacheslav Trubnikov, a former director of the SVR, was appointed first deputy foreign minister in charge of relations with CIS states and special representative of the president in the CIS states.[32] With Trubnikov in that position, more attention to the security aspects of Central Asian countries could be expected.

In November 1999 Sergei Ivanov replaced Putin as secretary of the Russian Security Council. Ivanov had a professional background in the KGB and later the FSB, and was a long-standing friend of Putin's. Under him the Security Council became an extremely active participant in Russian policy making with regard to the CIS states. Ivanov became instrumental in moving the anti-terrorist struggle up the Russian policy agenda. It was the Security Council that prepared the drafts of the military doctrine, the foreign policy, national security policy, and information doctrines which Putin signed in 2000. As the Security Council strengthened its influence, Ivanov also prepared for the creation of a new CIS structure to which the council would have direct access. Preparations to set up a new Committee of the Secretaries of the Security Councils of the parties to the CST intensified during the spring of 2000, and its first meeting finally took place in September 2000 in Bishkek, Kyrgyzstan.[33] It replaced earlier, more informal working sessions of the secretaries of the security councils. The new committee was created as a consultative body with the function of 'helping to create necessary mechanisms for the struggle with new challenges and threats to national, regional and international security'.[34] Its functions thus reflected the fact that the treaty organization had redefined its purpose and field of responsibility in order to include domestic threats as well.[35] The new committee consequently declared its first priority to be the fight against international terrorism and stressed the need to create sub-regional security systems, first of all in Central Asia. Sergei Ivanov was appointed chairman. The committee became an important mechanism for realizing Russian policy objectives on CIS territory.

As Sergei Ivanov strengthened his position, the Security Council became more involved in activities beyond what would normally be considered its field of responsibility. As a consequence of its larger role in foreign policy making and CIS affairs, an Inter-Departmental Commission on the Problems of the CIS was set up in April 2000 and had its first meeting in early October 2000.[36] Thus, in August 2000, with the second incursions by Islamic terrorists into Kyrgyz and Uzbek territory, Ivanov was sent as the special representative of President Putin to the summit meeting of Central Asian presidents (attended by all except the President of Turkmenistan).[37] The influence of the Security Council was not unlimited, however.[38] This was shown by the fact that when in 2000, at the peak of his influence, Ivanov addressed warnings to the Taliban regime of possible Russian air strikes on Afghan territory, these warnings were not followed up by practical policy.

Thus, the Security Council under Ivanov was a crucial institution in lobbying for and implementing Putin's anti-terrorist agenda. At that time the presidential administration played only a background role, since Putin did not yet have it under his full control. The Security Council played this central role until Sergei Ivanov was appointed minister of defence in March 2001 by which time Putin had gained control of the presidential administration.

The Russian Foreign Ministry lost the relatively strong role it had gained under Primakov. Foreign Minister Igor Ivanov was an experienced diplomat who had worked under Primakov, but he was more of a civil servant than an independent actor, as Primakov had tended to be.[39] Putin gave the Foreign Ministry the responsibility for coordinating CIS affairs.

While the Russian Parliament continued to have no direct influence in formulating foreign policy, it remained crucial to ratifying international agreements, sending troops abroad and allocating money. Individual Duma delegates, and especially the chairmen and members of Duma committees, played a key role in influencing the debate in Moscow, paving the way for the president's policy and reflecting changes in the predominant mood of the political elite, thereby influencing the basic parameters of the foreign policy consensus.

The appointments to the chairs of the Duma committees after the 1999 parliamentary elections were redolent of a new political mood and a more affirmative Russian self-image in international politics among the Duma majority. The chairmen of the foreign policy, defence and security committees were replaced by supporters of Putin, who were often from the security sector.[40] On the Committee on International Affairs, a civilian, Dmitrii Rogozin (Narodnyi Deputat), was appointed. He had become a close supporter of Putin and replaced Vladimir Lukin, a key figure from the 1993 and 1995 Duma.[41] As a Russian commentator said of Lukin: 'When under the second Yeltsin period the Foreign Ministry gradually became more patriotic under the leadership of Primakov and then [Igor] Ivanov, Lukin continued to express discontent but in his own way (*s svoeobraznom klyuch*)—alternating between "étatiste/Great Power" (*derzhavnicheskikh*) positions and "liberal" ones'.[42] Rogozin was explicit in his belief that 'the Russians should take back what belongs to them by right' and was considered an 'evident patriot'. He was also a strong supporter of a 'multi-vector' policy, sceptical about the West and in favour of close cooperation with Asian countries, above all China.[43] When Rogozin was appointed he said: 'Foreign policy is a fascinating lady. Once you approach her, you may become a "Gorchakovite"' ('Odin   raz   podoidesh,   a   potom   mozhno   stat "Gorchakovym"').[44]

During Putin's first year as president he remained an enigma to Russian and Western observers. He seemed to be giving little to anyone, yet all found in him what they wanted to find. The political fashion in Russia at the time was anti-Americanism and the political elite was filled with 'statists' and great-power advocates. Putin gave the impression that he was one of them but, according to Lilia Shevtsova, 'in developing his international agenda Putin definitely had some domestic priorities in mind, first of all an economic agenda'. However, at that time, she said, he seemed to be moving in all political directions simultaneously.[45]

In March 2001 Putin made changes in the government and, as a result, his ally Sergei Ivanov was appointed defence minister. By September 2001 he had managed to reduce tensions and rivalry between institutions—and to extend his control of the decision-making process. Moreover, he was building up his support among influential business circles as a consequence of his efforts to develop the market economy, and of signalling his desire that Russia integrate with the world economy. All this made possible his policy shift after 11 September 2001.

Foreign Policy Making since 2001

By 11 September 2001 Putin had more or less full control over foreign policy-making mechanisms, and the new foreign policy was formulated and pushed through by a narrow group of people around the president, primarily in the Presidential Administration. Putin was quick to react to the 11 September terrorist attacks on the USA, immediately telephoning President Bush, but he dragged his feet on the issue of what kind of support Russia would give to military operations against al-Qaeda, the Taliban and Afghanistan.[46]

The military was strongly against allowing the US military access to Central Asia. During October and November Putin had a series of talks with the General Staff and the generals. The military on these occasions expressed their concern about Putin's policy on several foreign policy issues and demanded a tougher Russian attitude. There were three issues in particular that the military raised: strategic parity with the USA; the geopolitical 'layout' in Afghanistan and Central Asia; and the living and social conditions of the military. The military feared that Putin would give in to President Bush on the issue of strategic nuclear weapons during his visit to the USA in November. There was criticism that Russia was losing influence in Afghanistan by not being active enough in its support for the Northern Alliance, and that Putin was paving the way for a permanent US military presence in Central Asia by allowing US troops to be stationed there.[47] The military was also discontented about the withdrawal of Russia's military bases from Vietnam and Cuba, the reduced number of Russian peacekeepers in Bosnia and Kosovo, and the shrinking Russian presence in the Caucasus and Transdniester. They warned that 'NATO is coming closer'.[48] According to opinion polls in February 2002 only one-third of military officers supported Putin's new foreign policy.[49]

Putin broke the resistance of the military by stating that the new situation would be temporary. US troops would stay only so long as operations in Afghanistan demanded. Russian military and security officials repeatedly stressed that Russia would not accept an extension of the US deployment or military bases in Central Asia after military operations in Afghanistan had been completed. Director of the FPS, General Totskii, while in Dushanbe in January 2002 thus declared that if the US forces remained there longer than demanded by the operations in Afghanistan 'we are unlikely to remain friends'.[50]

The general conclusion in the west at the time was that Putin was fairly isolated within the state structure because of his new pro-Western policy.[51] Not even his close entourage showed a particular desire to join the anti-terrorist campaign and the war in Afghanistan, according to Lilia Shevtsova.[52] For the first time, Putin had gone against the political class in Moscow. His policy had not been the result of any shift in the balance of power in Moscow. Nor could a change of personnel in the top posts explain the post-11 September policy change. In the group around the president three groupings were usually identified: people with a background in the security sector, mainly from St Petersburg; liberal economists, also from St Petersburg; and people representing the 'Family', the court of Boris Yeltsin. Sergei Ivanov represented the first category and had been publicly against US military deployment in Central Asia. Alexander Voloshin, already the head of the presidential administration at the time of Yeltsin, was a clear representative of the 'Family'. The 'Family' and the liberal economists supported Putin's new pro-US policy.[53] After September 2001, Putin's command consisted of the same people—Foreign Minister Igor Ivanov; Defence Minister Sergei Ivanov; the head of the Presidential Administration, Alexander Voloshin and his deputy Dimitrii Medvedev; presidential foreign policy adviser Sergei Prikhodko; the secretary of the Security Council, Vladimir Rushailo; Oleg Chernov, responsible for international affairs within the Security Council; the head of the FSB, Nikolai Patrushev; the head of the SVR, Sergei Lebedev; the head of the Military Intelligence Service (GRU), Valentin Korabelnikov; the director of the FPS, Colonel General Konstantin Totskii; and the chief of the General Staff, Anatolii Kvashnin. In the spring of 2003, Patrushev left this position in a major reorganization of the power structures.[54] In November the same year Voloshin also left his post as head of the presidential administration and as replaced by his deputy Medvedev.

Putin has usually been characterized as a cautious leader and, in Peter Reddaway's words, a 'balancer and principal implementer of the lowest common denominator of the interests of Russia's elite groups'.[55] This time he had to push through his policy. Nonetheless, he still had something to offer the different constituencies and, for this reason, he could be certain of maintaining support. His Western agenda had strong support among the Russian oligarchs and businessmen, and his anti-terrorist agenda had strong support among the military and the security sectors. Thus, neither of these constituencies would abandon him.

Putin also had the support of the most powerful economic interest groups in Russia. Already, in a speech on 26 January 2001, he had outlined the common interests between Russia's major business entities and the Russian state. He had called for a foreign policy that would take Russian business interests into consideration and asked business circles to pursue Russia's foreign policy interests. He declared this a task for the Russian business community in general but in particular, of course, for the energy sector because of its far-reaching interests abroad.[56] Putin said: 'I consider it to be extremely important that our Foreign Ministry pay particular attention to supporting the major foreign economic projects and linking them with state interests. It is necessary to create conditions abroad for Russian business that are at least as good as those that exist in Russia for foreign business.'[57]

In the spring of 2001 Putin increased his influence over the two state energy monopolies. He appointed his own man from St Petersburg as director of Gazprom: Alexei Miller replaced the all powerful Rem Vyakhirev. By initiating reforms of the electricity monopoly RAO UES, headed by the Anatolii Chubais, Putin wanted to avoid a repetition of the situation in the late 1990s when Gazprom fell out with the government over gas contracts with Turkmenistan.

As a result of Putin's declaration of the common interests between the government and Russian business, the business community agreed to act as a consultative group to the government through the Russian Union of Industrialists and Businessmen (the equivalent of the US Chamber of Commerce).[58] Moreover, in November 2002 the director of Lukoil, Vagit Alekperov, met for the first time with the military establishment at the Academy of the General Staff. In his speech he strongly stressed the common interests of the armed forces and the oil and gas companies, and claimed that the economic expansion of Russian companies promoted Russian state interests.[59] Thus, Putin's post-11 September policy was formulated in line with the general interests of Russian business circles. However, the business community could not expect to directly participate in decision making.[60]

The Foreign Ministry had little role to play in the formulation of foreign policy at the time. 'The foreign ministry these days provides little more than a delivery service for other people's messages', wrote *The Economist* in an analysis of February 2002.[61] Both the defence and foreign ministries were considered bastions of conservatism. From time to time, Putin complained that the foreign ministry was not properly carrying out its role as the coordinator of foreign policy.[62] Although Foreign Minister Igor Ivanov was considered a conservative with regard to Russia's relations with the West, and a reluctant supporter of Putin's policy, he nevertheless followed Putin's policy and implemented it. [63]

Nor did parliament have any influence over Putin's foreign policy turn in 2001. It played no part in foreign policy making either in general or on Central Asia and the US presence there. Putin did not talk to parliament until the morning of 24 September—just before he made public his decision on Russia's response to the upcoming US operation in Afghanistan. Even then he met only with the speakers of the two chambers, the leaders of parliamentary factions and of the groups of deputies in the Duma, and the members of the Presidium of the State Council. According to Grigorii Yavlinskii of the Yabloko party, who was present at the meeting, Putin made his pro-Western choice 'despite the views and the position of the majority of the Russian political elite'. Yavlinskii, describing the meeting, tells how one person advocated Russian support for the Taliban (Vladimir Zhirinovksii of the Liberal Democratic Party) and two called for unconditional support for the US-led anti-terrorist coalition (Grigorii Yavlinskii, and Boris Nemtsov from the Union of Rightist Forces), while the rest argued that Russia should adopt a neutral position.[64] The meeting was only an information exchange.[65] On 5 October 2001 a special session of the Collegium of the Foreign Ministry and the Duma Committee on International Affairs under Dmitrii Rogozin took place in order to defuse the criticism that was developing in the Duma and to increase support for the government.[66]

During the following months voices in the media complained repeatedly that foreign policy was decided only within the presidential apparatus and that neither the government and its individual ministries nor the parliament had any say over Russian policy in Central Asia. Not until 13 March 2002 did Foreign Minister Ivanov appear in the Duma to answer questions from the deputies at the government's Question Time.[67] Ivanov came mainly to explain why Russia, a few months before, had given up the former Soviet military bases in Vietnam and Cuba, but also to explain government policy in Central Asia. The presence of the foreign minister at Question Time was extraordinary, said Ivanov, but the 'dynamics of international events' demanded that such meetings take place more often in the future. He therefore suggested that future meetings should take place on a regular monthly basis, or at least every other month.

Thus, the crucial decision to give consent to a US military presence in Central Asia was taken by Putin and a narrow group of people within the presidential administration without any broader support from the policy establishment. His control of policy-making mechanisms, his strong rating in opinion polls and the fact that there was nobody to contest his hold on power made it possible for Putin to pursue the policy he had introduced in September 2001 in spite of strong criticism and a general atmosphere of disappointment over what Russia had gained.

Official Perceptions and Ideological Concepts

Putin had inherited from Yevgenii Primakov a conceptual framework of foreign policy that was based on Primakov's interpretation of the policy of Alexander Gorchakov. This conceptual framework constituted a kind of foreign policy paradigm and a lens through which the problems of Russian policy were understood. Putin modified the concepts he inherited from Primakov and used the framework to legitimize his own policy when approaching the West, first and foremost the USA.

Primakov's 1998 introduction of Gorchakov into the Russian policy debate had been an effort to set the debate on foreign policy and domestic reform and give it a strategic direction. It was a way of legitimizing retreats as temporary and in the interest of the larger strategic goal of a return to the international scene. The introduction of such an explicit vision had increased respect for Primakov in wider circles, including communists and nationalists, and the rehabilitation of Gorchakov has to be viewed in this context. Primakov pointed to Gorchakov's foreign policy as a model because Gorchakov pursued an active diplomacy that gave Russia a voice in European politics, albeit Russia was weak at that time.

In his interpretation of Gorchakov's foreign policy, Primakov gave strong emphasis to the concepts of 'multipolar' and 'multi-vector' policies. On the basis of his analysis—that a multipolar world was gradually developing, although the USA had developed into a 'dominant pole'—he urged Russia to find partners among the 'new poles' developing in the world in order to counter US dominance. Primakov said: 'A. M. Gorchakov was able to manoeuvre and use the contradictions between the different European powers and Turkey' and thereby to end the humiliating restrictions on Russia arising from the Treaty of Paris of 1856. Primakov pointed to two lessons to be learned from Gorchakov: that the definition of Russia's allies and adversaries must be flexible; and that a single great power should not be allowed to dominate.[68] Primakov's anti-Americanism was thereby given a historical point of reference. Primakov viewed Russia as a pole which alone or together with other poles could balance the US pole. It was through this ideological lens that Primakov and the Russian Government viewed the growing US engagement in Central Asia from the 1990s.

Although Putin took on the Gorchakov heritage from Primakov, he seldom made reference to Gorchakov. Foreign Minister Igor Ivanov, however, repeatedly referred to Gorchakov as a model for Russian foreign policy. Putin followed the path of Gorchakov in the sense that he also wanted to modernize Russia and at the same time strengthen Russia's international status and influence. However, Putin's interpretation differed from that of Primakov. Primakov was a Soviet scholar with experience of the Foreign Intelligence

Service. Putin, although trained as a security official, was more acquainted with the demands of the contemporary world. He was, and is, a *gosudarstvennik* (a proponent of the strong state) and a *derzhavnik* (a proponent of great-power status) but at the same time he is flexible enough to understand that the modern world of global and interdependent economies makes other demands on a state with ambitions to regain status as a great power.

On the Choice of Allies

For a proper perspective on Russia's foreign policy debate at the time of Gorchakov, it must also be remembered that there was a severe challenge to Gorchakov's Europe-oriented foreign policy during the 1870s in the shape of the 'aggressive, Panslav, Russia-first approach' of Nikolai Ignatiev, who by then was ambassador at Russia's influential embassy in Constantinople.[69] Putin's Western policy more than 100 years later was also challenged over the issue of allies.

When in June 2001 Foreign Minister Ivanov wrote in a long article that Russia would develop relations with any state as long as it was of benefit to Russia, he was indirectly taking issue with those who challenged Putin's views.[70] Although there was no strong panslavic lobby of the kind that existed at Gorchakov's time, Ivanov had to argue against critics from different camps. On the one hand, he had pro-Western and reform-minded people such as Viktor Sheinis, who was of the opinion that Russia should only make alliances with democratic countries.[71] On the other hand, he had radical Eurasianists, such as Aleksandr Dugin, who claimed that Russia's friends were to be found only on the Eurasian continent, or to the east and the south, but never on the other side of the Atlantic. Dugin regarded Europe as part of the Eurasian continent and despised the 'Atlanticist' values which predominate in Western Europe.[72] He had developed from a confused extremist thinker in the chauvinist journal *Den*, in the early 1990s, to a sophisticated ideologist working as an adviser to Gennadii Seleznev, the speaker of the State Duma, by the end of the 1990s. Some Western analysts claimed that he even had the ear of Putin in summer 2001 in his analyses of Russia as a Eurasian country.[73]

In his article, Ivanov argued in favour of a foreign policy free from moral and ideological aspects emphasizing only state interests or, as he said, 'realistic and pragmatic considerations'. As bad precedent he mentioned the policy of Tsar Nicholas I, whose obsession with ultra-conservative ideas of European absolutism had resulted in Russia's defeat in the Crimean War in 1855. After that, Ivanov said, a 'conceptual revolution' initiated by Gorchakov took place in Russian foreign policy. In Ivanov's words, Gorchakov understood that with its vast geography and underdeveloped economy Russia had to pursue 'an active but cautious foreign policy, avoiding adventures of any kind'. Thus, Tsar Alexander II rejected ideas of the 'solidarity of monarchies' (i.e., solidarity with Germany and Austria–Hungary). Instead, he entered into a close alliance with republican France, although its political–ideological ideas were far from his own, because such cooperation was believed to promote Russian state interests. 'For the sake of Russian security and the general balance of power in Europe',

Alexander II stood with his head uncovered for the *Marseillaise* 'in spite of the fact that the song was against his own ideological views', Ivanov wrote. Ivanov gave other examples of what he considered a realistic and pragmatic foreign policy, mentioning Prime Minister Pyotr Stolypin and his plans for modernizing Russia, and also the efforts made by Soviet diplomacy to prevent a nuclear conflict.

These were the words of a pragmatic politician, and Ivanov concluded in his June 2001 article that close cooperation with the West did not exclude close cooperation with other partners. 'All this convincingly disproves the stereotypes of our time, as if adherence to democratic values must mean that Russia cannot pursue an independent foreign policy, and as if such a policy would automatically result in either confrontation with Western countries or self-isolation.' Thus, by the time of the terrorist attacks on 11 September 2001, the way had been paved to allow the USA to be viewed as an ally.

On the Great Power Role

Both Primakov and Putin used Gorchakov to illustrate how Russia's return to great power status could be achieved. Foreign Minister Ivanov's account below of Russia's international status reflected a more general understanding of *why* Russia should already be seen as a great power:

> Whether it is a superpower or not, there is no shadow of a doubt that Russia is a great power. There are many factors which give it this status. It is not just its nuclear might, which is also taken into consideration. It is a question of geography, our natural resources, population, intellectual potential ... Different countries have a particular edge in different categories ... But a whole series of factors quite obviously mean that Russia is ranked as a great power. And that is precisely how Russia is treated in the world.[74]

Putin, convinced that Russia was bound to return to great power influence, argued that Russia had a special responsibility together with the USA for peace and stability in the world. This perspective on the role of Russia was reflected in his speech of 12 July 2002—at the first strategy discussion at the Russian Foreign Ministry since Mikhail Gorbachev had gathered Soviet ambassadors sixteen years before to explain to them what perestroika, glasnost and 'new thinking' were all about. Putin gave the outlines of Russia's foreign policy: the fight against terrorism was to remain the highest priority, it was 'a serious and long-term task', and would constitute the basis for cooperation not only in the international anti-terrorist coalition but also in relations with Russia's partners in international organizations'.[75] He concluded that 'Without doubt Russia and the USA have a special responsibility in strengthening global stability. And it is therefore important to know that at the basis of our present relations there is a new reading of the national interests of the two countries and also a similar notion of the very character of contemporary global threats'. Although a realist, pragmatic and modern in his understanding of the world, Putin assigned Russia and the USA status as *the* great powers of the world.

An interesting article in *Nezavisimaya gazeta* in March 2002 shed new light on

Russia's self-image as a great power and is of relevance to the policy debate on Central Asia.[76] The author Aleksander Yanov, a Russian historian who lived for several years in the USA, criticized the basic premises of most participants in the Russian foreign policy debate, whether they come from the liberal, nationalist or conservative camps and whether they are optimists or pessimists regarding the future of Russia. Yanov wrote that they are all influenced by Dostoevsky and his approach to Russia. Dostoevsky influenced generations of Russian policy makers to believe that a truly great nation can never be reconciled to a second-rank role or with being one among several in the first rank. They only accept being 'the absolute and exclusively first'. Yanov, arguing against this view, pointed to Germany as a country that through its post-Second World War policy had managed to gain 'great powerness' by accepting the status of one of several large powers in Europe. By abandoning its previous pretensions to be *the* great power, and by accepting a lower status, Germany had created for itself the conditions to develop 'great powerness'. If only Russia could accept a modified role as one among several large powers in Europe, Yanov argued, it would become a strong, prosperous and effective country in the future.[77] Putin held the belief that Russia was bound to return to great power status—but he also understood that he had to make compromises on that road.

On Multipolarity and Multi-vector Policy

Primakov had interpreted the world as divided into different centres or poles created out of concentrations of economic and military strength. While the USA was dominant, there was an underlying trend towards multipolarity. However, Primakov's multipolarity concept was not only an analytical tool for describing an observable tendency in the world. It also included a normative imperative that Russia has to develop as a pole in order to balance the US pole. If Russia is not strong enough itself, it has to ally itself with other states (e.g., Europe or China) against the USA. Thus, the multipolarity concept implied a direct policy recommendation very much along the old Soviet policy of splitting Europe from the USA. This was a Soviet-influenced version of classical theories of a balance of power, according to which the dominant state should be balanced by cooperation between other states. This gave the theoretical foundation for a Russian policy of cooperating with Europe against the USA and with other states that were critical of the USA. The multipolarity concept was heavily criticized within Russia in 2000 and 2001 not only because it defined Russia's position as against that of the USA but also because it ascribed to Russia a role which went far beyond its capacity.[78] The burden and costs of taking on the role of a 'pole' in the international system would result in serious 'overstretch', critics argued.

The multipolarity concept had already been toned down in Foreign Minister Ivanov's speeches before September 2001, and instead the 'multi-vector' concept had come to the foreground. The multi-vector concept referred to a policy in *tous azimuts* (in all geographical directions). In his speech to the 200th anniversary of the Russian Foreign Ministry, Ivanov claimed that Russia had a tradition of a multi-vectoral policy: 'The country's vital interests required

Russian diplomacy to actively promote relations with states in the West, East, and elsewhere.'[79]

Putin's post-11 September 2001 policy made the Primakov interpretation of the multipolarity concept irrelevant. There could be no poles when Russia and the USA shared fundamental security interests in combating terrorism. This became the basic theme in the post-11 September developments. It constitutes the basis for Putin's understanding of a new strategic Russian–US alliance.

Elite Attitudes

Throughout the 1990s, there were no political–ideological dividing lines in Russian policy debate on Central Asia. There was no public discussion about Russia's previous engagement in the Tajik civil war during the 1990s. In the mid-1990s, Alexei Arbatov, at the time vice-chairman of the Duma Committee on Defence, had pointed to certain differences over general political–ideological convictions. Arbatov wrote in 1997 that:

> Moderate-liberals are generally reluctant to approve direct Russian military intervention under the slogan of opposing the expansion of Muslim fundamentalism. Some neo-communist feudal regimes may try to secure Russian military support to fight local opposition movements by labelling them as Muslim fundamentalists, and in this way, indeed, push the opposition towards religious extremism. This process threatens to involve Russia in hopeless neocolonial wars that are against its foreign policy interests and domestic political preferences. Seemingly, this is what is now happening in Tajikistan.[80]

The Liberal Democratic Party had in 1997 demanded a Russian retreat from Tajikistan. Although there were people who were critical of heavy Russian engagement in Central Asian military affairs, and involvement in the problems of that region, this opinion did not follow rigid political–ideological lines.[81] In general, little discussion was heard on this kind of issue. The conclusion reached by Alex Pravda and Neil Malcolm, in their study at the end of the 1990s, that opinions about the 'near abroad' were 'less at odds politically than one might expect, given the differences in their basic stances', seemed to be confirmed.[82] When Putin introduced his anti-terrorist drive in Russian Central Asian policy in 1999, no objections were heard. The context of the deteriorating security situation in Chechnya coloured the way Central Asia was understood.

In contrast, the 2001 policy turn led to a tide of criticism. The media gave a good deal of space to views that were critical of Putin. *Nezavisimaya gazeta* expressed these feelings when commenting in December 2001 that the preliminary results of Russia's participation in the anti-terrorist operation had not been those expected, and that the 'new level of cooperation between Russia and the United States' had instantaneously destroyed Russia's efforts over the past 10 years to consolidate the CIS countries and create a collective security system within the CIS framework. 'The United States and the NATO countries brilliantly seized the opportunity to carry out the seemingly "soft" and "temporary" but in reality long-term occupation of the Central Asian region.'[83]

While criticism from official representatives remained muted, representatives of the parliament were more outspoken. Gennadii Seleznev, speaker of the State Duma, while on tour in Central Asia in January 2002 urged an increased Russian military presence because 'we are beginning to lose Central Asia'.[84] The same kind of concern was shared by the deputy chairman of the Committee on Defence and Security. He warned of the growing US presence in January 2002 and recommended an increase in the number of Russian border guards in Tajikistan.[85]

Some viewed the US military presence as contributing to the security of Russia in Central Asia, others saw it as part of an encroachment on Russia's 'turf' and demanded that Russia more forcefully request a deadline for the end of the US presence. The military daily newspaper *Krasnaya zvezda* blamed Putin's policy for the split within the political establishment.[86] The result of the split, according to Anatolii Adamyshin, former deputy foreign minister and a supporter of Putin's policy, was an 'almost Hamlet-like dilemma' in which, on the one hand, Russia would not get out of its present ruinous state without cooperation with the West while, on the other hand, the majority of the political, military and economic establishment did not want to approach the West.[87]

At the informal CIS summit on 1 March, Putin declared that the US presence was not harming Russia's interests. He was heavily criticized for this statement. *Nezavisimaya* wrote:

> Russia has lost the geopolitical game to America. … It has done so to a great extent because of its own political short-sightedness. We have lately stated too often and too loudly that everything the Americans do is beneficial for us. After all, it is obvious that the Kremlin can no longer ignore American actions and cannot constantly keep on saying that nothing terrible is happening. Actually, what is happening is something the Russian authorities cannot have failed to consider when in the past they chose their radical path to the West, namely, that this would be a serious blow to the image of Russia's president.[88]

During Government Question Time at the Duma on 13 March 2002, A. V. Mitrofanov of the Liberal Democratic Party asked Foreign Minister Igor Ivanov: 'Don't you feel that during the last year or year-and-a-half the situation [in Central Asia] has deteriorated to an extent that it never did even under Yeltsin? Would it have been possible to imagine that at the most secret Soviet airports there would be Americans? … Are you not, as a former Soviet person, going mad because of this? Can you sleep properly at night?'[89] Ivanov gave the expected answer—that the presence of US and Western military aircraft in Central Asia was a consequence of the international anti-terrorist coalition, in which both the Central Asian states and Russia had decided to participate.

In early April *Nezavisimaya gazeta* organized a round-table discussion with the US ambassador in Moscow and Russian specialists on Russian–US relations—including Colonel General Leonid Ivashov. Ivashov, who had retired from military duty and was active in one of the think tanks in Moscow, was one of the most public and outspoken critics of Putin's foreign policy. He argued that the strategic interests of Russia and the USA were diametrically opposed and that their interests could only overlap at the tactical level. He criticized Putin for being ignorant about geopolitics and geopolitical interests.[90]

The criticism of government policy in Central Asia did not abate. One year after the terrorist attacks, *Nezavisimaya gazeta*, evaluating the year that had passed, concluded that Russia had entered a mésalliance with the USA and had more to record on the minus side than the plus side, since it had been forced to let go of its geopolitical positions in Central Asia.[91] In January 2003 Leonid Ivashov again accused Putin of not understanding Russia's geopolitical interests. Ivashov's words were harsh—Putin had voluntarily given away Central Asia to the USA and abandoned the role of leader of integration on CIS territory, and the result of Putin's policy was withdrawal from all geographical directions. Furthermore, the prospects for the future were gloomy, and the disintegration of Russia itself was threatened as part of the process. He predicted that 2003 would be the prelude to major convulsions in Russia and ended his article 'It is necessary to unite all sound forces in the name of saving the Fatherland since otherwise the situation will become completely uncontrollable'.[92]

Nonetheless, in spite of all criticism, no foreign policy agenda was formulated as an alternative to Putin's policy: and Putin pursued his course.

Summary

What factors contributed to Russia's policy change? External factors governing Russian policy making were examined in chapters 4 and 5, including developments on the ground in Central Asia and in Russian–US relations on the global scene. These factors reflect the general trend of a reduced Russian role in the international system but also explain why Russia took the measures it did when dramatic events opened 'policy windows' in 1999 and in 2001. The historical–cultural factor of Russia's conquest of Central Asia in the late 19th century, presented in chapter 2, do not explain why policy changed under Putin. Yet, it contributes to a general understanding of why Russia maintains a desire to influence developments in Central Asia.

Among the internal factors examined in this chapter, the Chechnya conflict had a major impact on the way events in Central Asia were interpreted and defined by Moscow in 1999. In a worst-case scenario for the future, it was anticipated that the wave of terrorist acts in Chechnya during the second half of the 1990s would spread to Central Asia. The Chechnya factor also played a certain role when policy changed in 2001 in the sense that Moscow expected a more understanding approach to Russia's Chechnya problem from Western governments in exchange for Putin's consent to a US military presence in Central Asia.

The specifics of the policy making process also contribute to an understanding of Russia's Central Asia policy. By 1999 representatives of the security institutions had strengthened their influence in the state apparatus. In the policy 'vacuum' of Russia's relations with Central Asia in the early 1990s there was room for manoeuvre for institutions and people to influence policy. By the end of the 1990s, people from the traditional security sector had gained influence in top positions in the presidential administration, the government and the government apparatus. This can be explained by President Yeltsin's demand for professionally disciplined and loyal people as he felt more challenged towards the end of his presidency. Although Putin was not a candidate of the security services at the time of his appointment in 1999, he received their support thanks to his robust approach to the Chechnya conflict. The security and military structures had maintained their old contacts and networks with Central Asian colleagues when other networks had broken up after the fall of the Soviet Union. Their way of understanding and framing problems in Central Asia was simple to understand, and their remedies were easy for the Russian authorities to endorse. Their approach came to dominate as their influence was strengthened in the Russian Government and presidential structures. Putin himself made terrorism a top priority, moving it up the Russian policy agenda, and used it as an instrument to strengthen his own policy. By 2001 Putin was in command of foreign policy making mechanisms and therefore able to pursue his post-11 September policy, although his critics seriously challenged the policy.

The attitudes of the elites, and the widespread criticism in those circles, did not change Putin's post-2001 policy. Alex Pravda concluded in his 2003 analysis of Putin's foreign policy that the pro-US policy will continue for 'as long as the President himself remains committed to the post-September line'. Pravda argued that Putin's commitment depends not so much on the amount of elite grumblings but 'on how he personally assesses the balance of costs and benefits'.[93] Nonetheless, Putin has to take criticisms of his policy into account when formulating new policies and, in that way, elite attitudes could indirectly put pressure on the president.

Official perceptions and ideological concepts contribute to a broader understanding of why the policy turns of 1999 and 2001 were possible since they give the ideational context in which the situation was viewed on these occasions. While in 1999 Primakov's interpretation of the inheritance from Alexander Gorchakov was still dominant, by September 2001 Putin had already modified it. The pragmatic analysis of the lessons from Gorchakov presented by Igor Ivanov in the summer of 2001 demonstrated that the ground was prepared for the change of policy that was to come in September 2001.

Putin is usually characterized as a cautious leader anxious to have the support of several groups. Yet he demonstrated a skill and capacity for rapid decision making and a flexibility to use all possible situations to improve Russia's international position and influence as he thought best. Moreover, he demonstrated a great talent for turning what was an act of weakness into an act of forethought, strength and consistency—albeit that such forethought, strength and consistency might not always have existed at the time the decision was made.

Having said a great deal about the possible factors behind Putin's policy shifts, the question of *why policy changed in the way it did* has still to be addressed—and the relationships between the various factors have not been discussed. These questions are returned to in the concluding chapter, where possible alternative explanations based on different theoretical models are examined.

7

FACTORS WITHIN CENTRAL ASIA
Dynamics of Domestic Protest

At the same time as the external threat to Central Asian security was thought to be declining after the fall of the Taliban regime in November 2001, the threats from inside the region and from regional dynamics came to the forefront. The potential for instability and turmoil in these countries not only affects the future of these societies but also influences Russia's policy and future role in the region. This chapter discusses the internal dynamics of the region, dealing primarily with domestic political developments within the four Central Asian countries since September 2001. Chapter 8 returns to the discussion of the challenges these dynamics pose to Russian policy.

The dynamics of domestic protest follow from popular discontent and from demands for a political 'say' and a better standard of living. There are numerous problems in these societies which affect the daily life of the citizens. The decisive question for the future is how the population (governments and people) will respond to these problems. Who will take the lead in articulating demands, formulating a political agenda and drawing up a long-term vision for society? In this context, the political alternatives offered by different kinds of radicalism may determine the future chain of events. The Central Asian economies are lagging behind, and will do so for many years to come.[1] Thus, they are, and will remain, a possible breeding ground for radicalism and extremism of all kinds.

The issue of domestic protest is discussed here with regard to three possible political dimensions: the secular–political, the religious–political and the ethnonationalist. Within each of these dimensions there is a wide spectrum of opinion which includes moderate as well as extreme views. The first dimension includes efforts to form a secular opposition along the leftist–rightist spectrum—communist, centrist and liberal views. It continues the immediate post-Soviet discussion on how to carry out democratic and economic reforms in society after communism, including: demands for constitutional reform, free and fair elections, freedom of speech, and a free media; and issues of state policy in economic life such as the degree and form of privatization, and market freedom vis-à-vis state control. The religious–political dimension reflects the role of Islam in politics. Central Asian societies have a long tradition of keeping religion separate from government and the state. However, since the late 1980s there has been a general trend towards a politicization of Islam. The concept of 'political Islam' indicates that Islam is used for political purposes—either in the name of the authorities or of the opposition. The use of Islam for political purposes has enormous potential, especially for the opposition. The concept of 'Islamism' is used here as the normative political ideology that has at its core a programme for the establishment of an Islamic state, Islam as a state religion and the implementation of Islamic law (*sharia*).[2] The ethno-nationalistic dimension is the third approach. It is fed by the process of nation- and state-building under way in all the Central Asian states. The search for a national history, language and culture is part of the process of defining the titular ethnic group as separate from the other groups in society. There is a risk that the inability of authoritarian regimes to solve domestic political and economic problems could give rise to appeals on ethno-nationalist grounds either by groups or by governments. Such appeals would aggravate relations within states as well as between states. Conversely, deteriorating interstate relations may trigger ethno-nationalist expressions at the national level.

All four countries are authoritarian states to different degrees. In Freedom House's 2003 ranking of states according to the extent to which human and democratic rights exist, all Central Asian states scored badly. Kyrgyzstan and Tajikistan rank higher, however, than Uzbekistan and Turkmenistan.[3] In all four states the president holds executive power and dominates the legislative assembly and the judiciary. There is no real freedom of speech and the limitations on political debate are highly restrictive. Repression is a component of the political system and the violation of human rights a regular phenomenon. The wider political context includes drug trafficking from Afghanistan across Central Asian territory, with the support of powerful networks within these states. Corruption is widespread.

There is a serious risk that violence will erupt and the political process become distorted when normal channels for political discourse are blocked. At the same time, these societies have a potential for constructive development, which should not be underestimated. Within the state structures of these countries there are educated and reform-minded people who are willing to work for change. This is where the role of organizations such as the Organization for Security and Co-operation in Europe (OSCE) comes in, giving support and assistance for democratic institution-building, the rule of law and respect for human rights. The OSCE assists the governments while encouraging political parties and non-governmental organizations (NGOs) to develop.

The Secular–Political Dimension

The post-11 September situation raised the expectation that democratic and economic reforms were possible and would soon be initiated. There was a belief that the degree of interest and attention from international organizations and foreign governments—first and foremost the US Government—would create external pressures on the regimes and move them in the direction of reform, with the aid of both the carrot and the stick. In the short run such results could not be seen. Instead, authoritarian tendencies increased as the regimes tried to strengthen their hold on power.

Opposition groups in Central Asia had been formed on a secular-political basis during the disintegration of the Soviet Union. However, after a few years of freedom of speech and political activity, repression forced them to modify their criticism, silenced them or forced them underground. Today none of these states allows a political opposition in the real sense of the word. Several political parties exist in Uzbekistan, Tajikistan, and Kyrgyzstan, but only in Kyrgyzstan and Tajikistan do parties have some freedom to express disagreement with the government.

Uzbekistan

The international attention being paid to the fight against terrorism after September 2001 gave President Islam Karimov the opportunity to further strengthen his rule but also increased the international focus on violations of human rights in the country. As a close ally of the USA, it might have been expected that Karimov would be under strong pressure to reform. The Uzbek regime also offered the greatest promise of change, for example, in the US-Uzbek Declaration on the Strategic Partnership and Cooperation framework of March 2002.[4]

A referendum in January 2002, criticized internationally for being neither free nor fair, extended Karimov's term of office from five to seven years. This reflected Karimov's major concern to guarantee his continued hold on power. At the same time, the referendum also approved a reorganization of the parliament, replacing the previous legislature with a new bicameral legislature. The Uzbek authorities promised that the parliamentary elections to follow in 2004 would be free and fair.

After the brief flurry of political freedom during the perestroika period and the first months of independence, all opposition movements were suppressed in 1992–93. In 1992 police broke up the Uzbek Islamic Revival Party (IRPU) and detained its leader. The leaders of the secular–nationalist parties—*Birlik* (Unity), and *Erk* (Freedom)—were either imprisoned or went into exile.[5] From the mid-1990s the government increased its repression of opposition groups. In the period after September 2001, the repression against the opposition did not abate.[6] Instead the Uzbek police continued their campaign of harassment against members and supporters of the banned opposition parties of Erk, Birlik and Hizb-ut-Tahrir.[7] Feeling the international pressure for democratization, in particular from the OSCE, the United Nations and the US Government, Karimov called in August 2002 for greater freedom of speech in the country. In a brilliant performance of hypocrisy he asked whether Uzbekistan was not 'capable of creating conditions for freedom of speech, the conditions where people are able to express their ideas freely, without fear, the conditions where people's thoughts are carried in the press freely'.[8] However, he was careful to point out the limits of freedom of speech referring to Islam as the provider of the boundaries which could not be crossed: 'When I said boundaries, I meant there are some values, such as Islamic values, cherished by many generations of our people. Not everything that is allowed in European countries can be accepted here.'

There were a few individual signs of improvement in the Uzbek regime. In April 2002 Birlik managed to hold a number of meetings—including seven regional congresses—without interference from the authorities.[9] In June 2003 Erk managed to hold a party conference for the first time in 10 years.[10] However, its exiled leader, Muhammad Solih, did not dare to return to Uzbekistan because the authorities accused him of participation in the February 1999 bombings. These meetings did not alter the big picture—the Uzbek authorities continued to block the legal development of a political opposition. When in October 2003 these parties tried to register officially, the Uzbek Ministry of Justice turned their applications down.[11]

Although under international pressure to introduce democratic reforms, Karimov continued his previous repressive policy. He pretended to live up to the international expectations of the reforms he had promised, but little changed in reality. In spring 2003 Martha Brill Olcott wrote: 'To date, though, there is little progress in allowing truly independent political groups to freely operate in the country. The same is true of the media'.[12] Uzbekistan remained a repressive system.

The Uzbek opposition, which had started out as a secular–political opposition in the late 1980s but been blocked, instead took on a religious–political form when repression increased in the second half of the 1990s—thus fuelling radical Islamism. In this way, the Uzbek authorities contributed to making the Islamic Movement of Uzbekistan (IMU) and Hizb-ut-Tahrir the two major opposition groups.

Kyrgyzstan

Kyrgyzstan which in the 1990s was regarded as a fairly stable, but weak state erupted into political instability in spring 2002. Here, in contrast to Uzbekistan, a secular-oriented opposition had developed and increased in strenght during the late 1990s. The treatment of the opposition and the main opponent to President Askar Akaev, Feliks Kulov, at the time of the 2000 parliamentary elections reflected the increasingly authoritarian nature of the regime. On 17–18 March 2002 unrest in the south of the country developed over an unexpected issue. A serious political crisis arose when some 1500 people gathered in the village of Kerbent in the Ak-Sui District of the Jalal-Abad Region demanding the release from custody of Azimbek Beknazarov, a member of the Kyrgyz Parliament. In parliament Beknazarov had been active on the issue of Kyrgyzstan's handover of some 95,000 hectares of territory to China as part of a border settlement. Beknazarov had been detained in January on charges of criminal abuse of power in connection with a murder case he handled in 1995, when he was working as an investigator at the district prosecutor's office in Jalal-Abad.[13] The police, called out to restore order, shot dead five demonstrators. Although the conflict initially had the more of the characteristics of a dispute between clans, and the conflict between the south and the north of the country, the demonstrators gained broader support as the political crisis developed. Parts of the political opposition joined forces, calling for the resignation of the president and the whole government, and new elections.[14] In

May a state commission, established to investigate the shooting in March, issued a report criticizing the government and the law enforcement bodies at all levels for the way they handled the events. It stated that the security forces' use of weapons against demonstrators had been illegal. Large demonstrations followed. Several thousand people blocked the main Bishkek–Osh highway at two points, calling for the resignation of Akaev and for the criminal case against Beknazarov to be dropped.[15] As a result of the protests, on 22 May the president dismissed the prime minister and the whole government.

The protests continued, however. In an attempt to divert attention away from the protests, the authorities warned of the threat from Islamist extremism and ordered the strengthening of the southern border. The secretary of the Kyrgyz Security Council repeated his warnings about Hizb-ut-Tahrir, claiming that it was cooperating with the Islamic Movement of Uzbekistan (IMU) and al-Qaeda. Increasingly worried by the security situation in the country, the government on 7 September 2002 issued a decree containing urgent measures to prevent the destabilization of the situation. Two days later Prime Minister Tanaev submitted a bill to parliament imposing a three-month moratorium on all public marches, meetings and rallies.[16] The bill resulted in disagreements within the government and First Deputy Prime Minister Kurmanbek Osmonov urged the lower chamber of parliament not to approve the ban until negotiations with participants in the opposition march to Bishkek had been completed.[17] In the meantime, the ongoing prosecutions of the officials responsible for the shootings at the March demonstration exacerbated the mood of confrontation. The trial not only reignited outrage among long-standing opponents of the government but also antagonized a significant number of law enforcement officials.[18]

The protest, which had developed into a full-scale political crisis, resulted in August 2002 in the Kyrgyz opposition closing ranks. A movement was set up by 22 opposition-oriented parties to seek the resignation of President Akaev and changes to the constitution.[19] In response to the situation, Akaev presented a proposal to amend the constitution—making the bicameral parliament unicameral and transferring some presidential powers to parliament—while at the same time asking for confirmation of his own position. In late December 2002 the former Prosecutor and police chief of the Jalal-Abad Region together with two senior officials were convicted and sentenced to prison terms for the shooting in March.

In February 2003 the referendum took place, and Akaev received support to stay in power until the end of his term of office in 2005. The president had managed to manoeuvre himself out of the crisis situation but the events illustrated the fragility of the system.

Turkmenistan

President Niyazov has maintained his control of the country since Soviet times and had crushed the opposition in the mid-1990s. In the spring of 2002, however, the first serious signs of 'cracks in the marble' became visible in the Turkmen regime.[20] The dismissals of individuals in the top political echelons initiated by Niyazov in March demonstrated that an internal secular–political opposition was establishing itself in secret within the highly repressive Turkmen system. Turkmen opposition was secular, and at no time since independence have there been signs of any radical Islamist activities.

During 2000 criticism of Niyazov's rule developed from within the upper echelons of the state administration. In that year Foreign Minister Boris Shikhmuradov was fired and made ambassador to China. In October the following year he fled to Moscow after losing his post as ambassador. In January 2002, from exile, he created the People's Democratic Movement and became a key figure in the opposition to Niyazov. On 1 April 2002 Niyazov dismissed the head of national security, the head of the border service and the defence minister.[21] Niyazov's request that the US Government extradite Shikhmuradov resulted in tense relations with the USA.[22] In May 2002, Niyazov started cleansing the Ministry of Interior Affairs, removing certain key functions from its jurisdiction, reducing its manpower by nearly one-third, and transferring certain branches to the Defence Ministry (among them the security guard service). The more Niyazov feared the opposition the more people he dismissed, and the more people he turned away from him. The opposition to Niyazov was especially strong within the security service, which Niyazov therefore repeatedly purged. In September 2002 the newly appointed head of the National Security Committee had to leave, and Niyazov ordered another reorganization of the committee into a Ministry of National Security.[23]

International organizations tried to put pressure on the Turkmen authorities to improve their human rights record. In September 2002 the European Bank for Reconstruction and Development (EBRD) urged Turkmenistan to embrace democracy and market reforms as a condition for new loans.[24] The EBRD adopted a new two-year strategy for Turkmenistan by which it would increase its involvement in Turkmenistan 'once the government had demonstrated its commitment to reform and transition'. It criticized the Turkmen authorities for their failure 'to make progress towards the development of a free media and improvement in the dialogue with NGOs, the protection of national minorities' rights and the removal of travel restrictions'.[25]

In the meantime Shikhmuradov had come to the conclusion that the time was ripe for the opposition to go into action against Niyazov and to ask him to step down.[26] In preparation for the forthcoming government meeting on 25 November, Shikhmuradov left Turkey and went to Turkmenistan via Uzbekistan. As reported by sources close to him, he intended to confront Niyazov at the meeting with a request that he step down. Certain of his support among the opposition, Shikhmuradov travelled to Ashgabat. About one month later, in the afternoon of 25 November, Niyazov announced that there had been an attempt on his life. According to reports, the president's motorcade was fired on as he was making his way to work. Niyazov accused Shikhmuradov of being the main organizer of an attempted coup. Turkmen opposition groups denied that there had been any attempt on Niyazov's life, accusing Niyazov of faking the attempt himself to create a pretext for arresting the opposition.[27]

On 5 December Shikhmuradov was arrested in Ashgabat. In front of the television cameras he confessed to various crimes against the state and the president in something reminiscent of a Soviet 'managed' show trial from the

1930s.[28] Looking tired and unshaven, and speaking slowly in Russian, Shikhmuradov declared that he and his accomplices were 'not opposition members but ordinary criminals using drugs and ready to do anything for money'. He was sentenced to 25 years in prison.[29] Altogether, more than 60 people were arrested and sentenced to prison terms.

The Turkmen authorities accused Uzbekistan of involvement in the failed assassination attempt. The Uzbek ambassador in Ashgabat was asked to leave the country and the Turkmen police searched the Uzbek embassy.[30] At first the Turkmen authorities also claimed that Russia was involved,[31] and in January 2003 they turned against the USA, accusing the US Government of being behind the attempted assassination. The editors of Turkmenistan's leading state newspapers sent an 'open letter' to the US State Department protesting against US allegations of human rights abuses during the investigation into the attempt on Niyazov's life.[32]

Russia, anxious to reach agreement on their gas deal and the planned gas alliance, chose to go along with the Turkmen authorities on the issue of the assassination attempt. As reported by the Russian media, Niyazov had a telephone conversation with President Putin during which he informed the latter of the measures he had taken and received his support.[33] When the secretary of the Russian Security Council, Vladimir Rushailo, came to Ashgabat in early January 2003, he promised Russia's help with investigations into the attempt. 'We discussed the issue of fighting international terrorism, and in particular the recent events in Turkmenistan connected with the attempt on the life of the head of state', he told television reporters following talks with Niyazov on 3 January.[34] He continued 'Russia has always stated its position and we would like to stress once again that we regard the incident as a manifestation of terrorism, and we are ready to cooperate in the context of the law-enforcement bodies and secret services'. Rushailo signed a protocol on cooperation between the two countries' security councils with his Turkmen counterpart, which included cooperation in 'apprehending and extraditing criminals'.[35]

Although Niyazov had once again managed to crush the opposition and tighten his control of the country, the events clearly demonstrated a profound discontent with his rule. In September 2003 four opposition groups in exile made the first effort to join forces to topple Niyazov.[36]

In December 1999 Niyazov had the People's Council (Halk Maskhalaty—made up of almost 3000 people) appoint him president for life. In August 2002 he turned down its decision but instead asked them to give him an indefinite term. Niyazov suggested presidential elections some time between 2008 and 2010, and indicated that the People's Council would decide the issue in 2005–06.[37] In August 2003 Niyazov was appointed Chairman of the People's Council for life, while the People's Council was given all power by a constitutional amendment.[38] He seemed to have found an alternative strategy to remain in power after his term of office as president had come to an end.

Tajikistan

Domestic developments in Tajikistan in the immediate aftermath of 11 September 2001 stood in stark contrast to the course of events in the other three Central Asian states. The general instability in society after the civil war, still evident as late as September 2001 when the Minister of Culture, Press and Information was assassinated, came to an end. This murder was the last in a chain of political murders and kidnappings that had dominated life in Tajikistan for many years. In the same month, the government successfully completed its campaign against the warlord Rakhmon Sanginov and his supporters, initiated in early summer 2001. As a result of the new international situation the government's control over the territory was extended to areas which had previously been under the control of non-compliant warlords. When, in early 2002, the president dismissed the whole State Committee on Border Protection and two powerful commanders of the border troops, without any violent reaction on their part, this was interpreted as a sign that the general situation in the country was heading for a dramatic improvement.

In its process of further stabilization during 2002, Tajikistan differed from the other Central Asian states because of its movement towards democratic reform. In 2002 an independent news agency and a TV station were set up. Tajikistan had always had a relatively more pluralistic tradition than its neighbours. The fact that an Islamic political party was allowed gave a larger degree of freedom in Tajik society than in the rest of Central Asia. Yet, as president Rakhmonov consolidated his position, he increased the pressure on parties other than the ruling People's Democratic Party. Authoritarian tendencies showed themselves as soon as the regime felt secure enough of its hold on power. On 22 June 2003 Rakhmonov, in a much criticized referendum, had his term of office extended from five to seven years with the possibility of re-election for two subsequent terms—taking him up to 2020.[39] Under heavy pressure from the government, the parties that had initially criticized the referendum modified their stances before the vote.[40]

The fact that Tajikistan allows an Islamic political party makes the Tajik party system worth a closer look. The Tajik constitution gives strong power to the president—and developments after September 2001 gave him better opportunities to use that power. Although the constitution specifies a division of power between the branches of state, the president dominates the executive branch, the legislative assembly and the judiciary. The constitution prescribes a multiparty system. Five parties were allowed to register in time for the parliamentary elections of 2000 and three of them gained representation in Parliament—the pro-government People's Democratic Party (PDP), the Communist Party (CP) and the Islamic Revival Party (IRP). The parties that did not win representation in Parliament were the Democratic Party, once a partner of the United Tajik Opposition, and the Socialist Party. In December 2002 a Social Democratic Party was allowed to register after three failed attempts.

The political parties continued to work in difficult conditions. Although the IRP, the Democratic Party and the Social Democratic Party each expressed their ambition to act as a 'constructive' opposition, the authorities demonstrated little understanding of this concept. All parties were weak and apart from the CP, which had the remnants of its party organization from Soviet times, their local party branches were badly developed. There was also a general caution about creating tensions in society by missing political demands—the experience of the civil war still lingered. Personal ties, kinship relations and regional affiliations continued to be more important to people than party affiliation. Two major ideological dividing lines separated the three largest parties from each other and produced shifting voting alliances in parliament—the role of religion and the issue of private property. Although ideological differences existed between the parties, there were no developed party policies on specific issues. The PDP dominated the scene and pursued an active policy of co-opting people from the Communist Party and the former UTO. Formally, a multiparty system existed. In reality, the opposition parties found it difficult to survive.

Nevertheless, a slow democratization process was continuing. The by-elections during 2002 to the Majlisi Namoyandagon, the lower chamber of the parliament, demonstrated some progress in this regard although they also reflected the problems. Local authorities were clearly reluctant to register candidates from parties other than the ruling PDP. Their scepticism and mistrust were even stronger than that normally displayed by the central authorities.

The IRP and the Democratic Party could be expected to fulfil the function of major opposition parties since they were both part of the former United Tajik Opposition (UTO). After the 1997 peace agreement was signed, UTO representatives were to have received posts in executive bodies at all administrative levels, according to a 30 per cent quota. As mentioned in a previous chapter the UTO never received its full quota at local levels. After the 2000 parliamentary elections, all the IRP representatives among the UTO representatives from the IRP lost their seats at the local levels. Of those remaining at the national government level, most were co-opted by the pro-government party, or otherwise distanced themselves from the party with which they had previously been associated. For example, Akhbar Turazhonzoda, the First Deputy Prime Minister, and Mirzo Ziyoev, the Minister of emergency situations, previously belonged to the Islamic wing of the UTO but did not join the IRP.

The IRP held many radical views in the early 1990s but modified its political views during the years of the civil war, and developed into a constructive political force after the peace agreement. Party chairman Said Abdullo Nuri acted more as a statesman than a party leader. He was respected by the authorities as the leader of the former UTO but put under heavy pressure as party leader of the IRP. The IRP faced the double threat of being squeezed out by the authorities and marginalized by the voters. In the 2000 parliamentary election the IRP received only 7.3 per cent of the votes and two seats in the lower chamber. Many of its followers were disappointed because they believed the party leadership had given in too much to the Rakhmonov regime. Some of them turned to the radical alternative, Hizb-ut-Tahrir. In the spring of 2002, when the so-called Social Accord was extended for a third time, the IRP signed. The document, which was introduced by the president, had the declared purpose of carrying on a continuous dialogue between the government and the political parties in search of consensus on important issues. No such dialogue took place, but a signature was a symbolic act of belonging to the official consensus.

In the post-11 September situation the IRP feared that its existence was threatened and that the regime would use the international anti-terrorist campaign to clamp down on the party. The IRP continued to exist but in the summer of 2002 it became evident that the party was a target of the government's efforts to gain better control over political and religious life in the republic. The draft of the referendum question in summer 2003 had initially suggested that the clause in the constitution that directly spelled out the right for religious political parties to exist should be deleted. To heavy criticism the president agreed to maintain the original text and not attempt to change it.

Although Tajikistan was an exception among Central Asian states in allowing an Islamic political party, it did not allow any party to develop and articulate popular political demands. Therefore, if popular discontent were to suddenly and dramatically increase, in the way that occurred in Kyrgyzstan in 2002, there would be no channel for it to be expressed and the political situation could erupt in Tajikistan, as it did in Kyrgyzstan.

Thus, the chances for a secular–political opposition to develop into a constructive opposition within the present regimes remain limited in all the Central Asian countries. The regimes did not allow an opposition to develop. Vested interests ensured that the incumbent regimes remained in power. The manner in which the secular opposition was repressed had already resulted in the expansion of religious -political forms of protest, especially in Uzbekistan.

The Religious–Political Dimension

As pointed out above, political Islam has a huge potential in Central Asia. A crucial question therefore is whether a radical form will find support, or whether a more moderate version will prevail.

The general background to the rise of political Islam in Central Asia is the dominance of the tolerant Hanafite school of Sunni Islam, to which the overwhelming majority of the population belong. There is also a strong component of Sufism and a tradition of a separation between religion and the state. When the Russians conquered Central Asia, the region was cut off from ideological and religious debates and developments within Muslim societies in the Middle East and South Asia. As a result, Islam in Central Asia maintained a greater element of popular beliefs than was the case in many other Muslim countries. Perestroika and the relaxation of ideological controls at the end of the 1980s led to a revival of religion and the growth of political Islam. This process accelerated after the break up of the Soviet Union as the societies in Central Asia searched for their heritage, identity, norms and values.[41] Political Islam, in its radical and moderate interpretations, has its history in movements and debates from earlier centuries in Central Asia. In this context, the distinction between the concepts of 'Islamism' and 'political Islam' becomes important. Islamism relates to political activities for the purpose of creating a theocratic state, while 'political Islam' relates only to the use of religion in a general political context. Within Islamism a distinction will be made here between 'moderate' and 'radical' Islamism.

The present constitutions of all the Central Asian states prescribe a secular state and a clear distinction between religious and state affairs. In all of them, religious–political activities provoke the concern of the authorities. The states are trying to control religious activities in order to prevent religion from mixing with politics, and the mosques from propounding political ideas. Nevertheless, they differ in practice over how much freedom they allow to religious communities.

Moderate and Radical Islamism

Moderate Islamism. As part of the revival of political Islam on former Soviet territory, moderate Islamism wants to strengthen Islamic values as a basis for state policies while keeping religious affairs separate from the government of the state. So far only Tajikistan provides the conditions for moderate Islamism to develop, since the other Central Asian states forbid all political Islamic activities.

In the international history of Islamic debate, those advocating a secular state have asserted that the interference of religion in the affairs of the state has the effect of slowing economic development and is therefore intolerable in a modern society. They have argued that what is needed instead is Western civil law and the relegation of Islam to the spiritual system of ontological beliefs about God and man.[42] Tajik moderate Islamists often refer back to Jadidism, the reformist sect in tsarist Russia from the late-19th and early-20th century, which worked to introduce both Western ideas about science and society and a modern reinterpretation of Islam. It was one of the many intellectual Islamic reform movements that swept the colonized Muslim world in the late-19th century. It started as a movement for educational reform but developed as an effort to modernize Central Asian Muslim societies. The Jadidids played an important role in the break up of the Bukhara Emirate.[43]

The IRP of Tajikistan can best be characterized as a 'moderate Islamist' party in the sense that it recognizes the present secular constitution of Tajikistan and works within this framework.[44] This is the result of the political compromise that ended the civil war: if the IRP accepted the constitution it was allowed to function as an Islamic party. Nonetheless, the IRP works to make Islamic values the foundation of state policy. There are no definitive answers to what political role the IRP prescribes for religion in state affairs in a long-term perspective. Different views exist within the party.[45] Among the IRP's grass roots some voices are more in favour of a stronger influence for Islam than the party leadership. Within the IRP leadership a tiny modernist group is attempting to transform the party into a proper political party using the German Christian Democratic Party as its model. This minority wants to blend European political ideas with Islamic values.

Radical Islamism. The radical alternative is part of a long tradition in Islamic discourse in favour of a close relationship between state and religion. This tradition has hitherto had only weak support in Central Asia.

Contemporary Central Asian radical Islamist groups—for example, Hizb-ut-Tahrir and the IMU—are offshoots of the Salafite movement and share its view of the relationship between state and religion. The Salafites belong to a religious movement within Islam dedicated to puritanical reform of religion and society and to restoring the pure Muslim society of the first four Caliphs—the successors of Mohammed.[46] In the seventeenth, eighteenth and nineteenth centuries a number of Salafite cults crystallized into a political force, and became part of a modernization and reformist tendency within Islam, albeit the conservative wing of such a trend. The Salafites do not recognize any separation between state and religion, government and religion or politics and religion. Some experts on Islam have characterized the core of their political programme as 'theocratic authoritarianism'.[47]

Central Asia had theologians who tried to purge Islam of the popular traditions that had entered the rituals of Islam in the region. Such reform efforts ended in failure because they encountered resistance from the majority of people who defended the popular forms of Islam in everyday life.[48] Although this was part of a religious discussion, radical religious leaders were not seldom among the leaders of the struggle against tsarist Russia in the nineteenth century. The armed uprisings at the time, in the Fergana Valley against the Russians in Andizhan, had as their goal the restoration of a 'truly Islamic state' from the time of the first four caliphs. The leader of the revolt, Muhammad-'Ali (Dukchi Ishan), was executed in 1898.[49] Religious leaders played a central role in the *basmachi* movement that fought against Russian and Soviet rule well into the 1930s.[50]

In Soviet times, Islam was strictly controlled and theologians were forbidden to teach if they or their activities did not come under the authority of the official spiritual administration. In spite of this regulation, unofficial teaching began in the late 1950s and early 1960s. One of the most famous of these teachers was Muhammadjan Rustamov, better known as Domulla Hindustani (1892–1989), who was born in Kokand.[51] From the late 1950s he organized illegal instruction (*hujra*) for small groups of believers. His works were disseminated all over the Fergana Valley and he played a major role in the revival of Islam in the 1970s and 1980s. When some of his followers were caught up in the radical trend, Hindustani stood up strongly against what he labelled 'Wahhabites'—the term he applied to all radical 'purifiers' of Islam. Hindustani thus introduced the term to Soviet territory, although in strict terms these people did not belong to the Wahhabite sect. A more correct term would be Salafites.[52] Hindustani upheld the traditional approach of not mixing religion with politics.

The radical pupils of Hindustani, such as Rahmatullah-'allamah and Abduwal-qari Mirzaev from Andizhan, who wanted to reform Islam and cleanse it of 'innovations', became 'wahhabites'. They worked to develop a political position among believers. In the 1970s they set up the Mujaddidiya movement and, with followers among the imams (the heads of mosques) and khatibs (preachers) of several mosques in the Fergana Valley and Tashkent, who had been appointed without the approval of the official religious board (SADUM), they spread their radical message. Thus, when religious literature from Arab countries reached Central Asia in the mid-1980s it became a catalyst for ideas which already existed there.

Under the influence of international events—in particular the Iranian revolution in 1979—radical Islamist ideas spread in Central Asia. The Uzbek scholar Bakhtiar Babadzhanov writes:

> The armed struggle of the Afghan mujahiddin against the Soviet army and the Iranian revolution of 1979 proved profoundly symbolic for the Mujaddidiya. It is possible that under the influence of these events, the Mujaddidiya began to see the possible realization of their ideas only in the event that Islam (of course in a purified form) became the state religion, and the country where it would blossom would bear the name Musulmanabad ('Muslimbad').[53]

Traditional Hanafites opposed the Mujaddidiya, its efforts to purify Islam and its political pretensions. They did not accept involvement in politics and were negative to the very idea of a political party. Although the traditional Hanafites were in a majority among the population, the Mujaddidiya came to dominate the religious–ideological debate and to control many mosques in the Fergana Valley in the late 1980s. The political struggle between the traditionalists and the radicals became especially acute in the main cities of the valley, such as Andizhan, Namangan and Kokand. In Namangan and Margilan the radicals dominated.

The radicals were not united, however. One group did not wish to become directly involved in politics. They only wanted to prepare the conditions for the coming of the caliphate by creating small communities, which would function according to the rules of the four caliphs, thereby providing a moral example.[54] Another group wanted to give Islam political status, and initially tried to achieve legalization by establishing domestic branches of the Party of Islamic Revival in the late-1980s and early-1990s. The Tajik and Uzbek parties of Islamic Revival were examples of this. A third group rejected the idea of legalizing their party and decided to create parallel political structures of their own. Thus in Namangan they established the Adolat and Islom lashkarlari movements (under the leadership of Tahir Yuldash and Juma Namangani), which functioned as parallel Islamic authorities. As these organizations became more active, they tried to replace local government organs.[55] After an incident in Namangan in 1992, when President Karimov was insulted, the state authorities took repressive measures against such radicals.

In Uzbekistan the security forces pursued a steady campaign against religious expression of all kinds during the 1990s. In 1995 an event took place of great importance in the chain of events leading to the formation of a radical religious–political opposition in Uzbekistan.[56] In August 1995 Abduwal-qari Mirzaev, a pupil of Hindustani, friend of Said Abdullo Nuri (Chairman of the IRP) and the imam of the Friday mosque in Andizhan, the biggest in the Fergana Valley, disappeared. After checking in for a flight to Moscow, he was never seen again. His disappearance was feared to have been the work of the security forces, and protests and demonstrations followed. This set off a trend of politicization and radicalization, and in the autumn of 1995 the official Muftiat began a campaign to tighten its grip over the mosques in Uzbekistan. It decreed that every leader of a mosque must sit an examination—mostly about state policy. Those who failed it, or refused to take it, lost their jobs.

The contemporary radical Islamic movements in Central Asia have their roots in the upheaval of radical Islamist thought in the Fergana Valley of the late 1980s and early 1990s. The Islamic Movement of Uzbekistan (IMU), created in 1998 by Juma Namangani and Tahir Yuldash, became the best-known but remained a small organization with few followers.[57] IMU is not only a Salafite organization but is committed to violent struggle in the name of Islam against the secular state. In 2000 in Afghanistan Namangani became deputy defence minister in the Taliban government, and after 11 September IMU members fought together with the Taliban.[58] Namnagani was reported killed in November 2001 in combat in northern Afghanistan but the reports have been contradictory and some believe he is still alive. After the fall of the Taliban in Afghanistan the IMU disappeared but there are indications that the IMU leadership is in hiding in Pakistan.[59]

Since the late 1990s Hizb-ut-Tahrir has been the fastest-growing organization in Tajikistan, Uzbekistan and Kyrgyzstan. At first it did not attract as much attention because it did not advocate violence as a political means.

Hizb-ut-Tahrir shares its ultimate goal with IMU as well as many of the radical groups—the creation of an Islamic state, a caliphate. Beyond this goal these groups differ. Judging from its political objectives—the overthrow of the present regimes and the setting up of a sharia-based caliphate—Hizb-ut-Tahrir is a revolutionary organization. However, it does not advocate violent revolution. Its advocacy of non-violence is thus an important distinction.[60] Nonetheless, a closer look at the organization is justified, especially as it was included on the Russian list of terrorist organizations presented by the Russian Federal Security Service in February 2003.[61]

Although Hizb-ut-Tahrir is officially against the use of force, its confrontational approach to the *kufr*, the infidels—and the *kufr* include in principle everyone with a different view, including fellow Muslims—means that violence seems to be not very far from its thinking. Many observers suspect that the organization may support violence in a critical political situation if violence can be defined as necessary for self-defence. Moreover, one extremely important aspect of Hizb-ut-Tahrir is that its propaganda might prepare the ground or pave the way for more ideologically militant groups. According to some observers, when the US bombing of Afghanistan started, Hizb-ut-Tahrir's attitude to violence seemed to shift towards greater acceptance.[62]

Hizb-ut-Tahrir is an international organization with branches in many countries. There are local variations and the Central Asian branches differ from those in the Middle East. However, they share the same basic convictions, which can be summarized as follows: to fight against the corruption and moral decay of the rulers, imperialism and colonialism, and the ideological influence of the West; to condemn and fight the ideas of the *kufr*; to lead the *umma*—the world community of Muslims—into a struggle with the *kufr*, his systems and thoughts until Islam embraces the whole world; to condemn the concepts of democracy, pluralism, political compromise, the market economy and dialogue as means and instruments intended to cheat the Muslim population into subordination to the West and undermine the true faith by blurring the distinction between what is true and what is false; to oppose the secular state and the secularization of social and political life; to overthrow the governments and regimes of the *kufr* by mobilizing the population; and to create:

> an Islamic society ... where all aspects of life in society are administered according to the rules of the Shari'ah, ... the Khilafah State ... in which Muslims appoint a Khaleefah ... he rules according to the Book of Allah ... and the Sunnah of the Messenger of Allah ... and on condition that he conveys Islam as a message to the world through *da'wah* and *jihad*.[63]

The political programme of Hizb-ut-Tahrir draws on criticism of the severe economic and social conditions in the Central Asian countries—the corruption, injustice and social inequalities. By mobilizing the population against the ruling elite of political and religious leaders it aims to overthrow the governments and install a theocratic state led by a head of state who will rule by the 'true' interpretation of the Koran. The goal is to create a state where the leader runs both state affairs and religious affairs by being the source of the authoritative interpretation of *sharia*. Several experts have therefore made the comparison between Hizb-ut-Tahrir and Leninist groups in the sense that they have in common a long-term vision of a paradisal society; a belief that they have a monopoly on the truth; an understanding of the party as the avant-garde; the idea that they have a special relation to the masses; and are organized structurally as an illegal and conspiratorial party. The ideology of Hizb-ut-Tahrir has the same kind of attraction as all extremist ideologies in the sense that it offers a consistent and closed system of thought with one general, simple solution to all problems. The organization is built on a structure of small cells (*halka*) of between five and seven people that is typical of illegal parties.[64] Members are supposed to know only the other members of the same cell and the leader who prepares them ideologically for membership. In theory, the organization has a well-developed strategy with separate stages for mobilizing and preparing the population for a takeover of power.[65] Yet the reality of Hizb-ut Tahrir in Central Asia still seems far from this description of such an organizational structure.

The message of Hizb-ut-Tahrir receives a degree of sympathy from parts of the population because the organization dares to raise issues that are critical to many Muslims. The idea of creating an Islamic state based on *sharia*—a caliphate—across borders in Central Asia does attract broad groups of the disaffected population. Although the party does not provide solutions to specific problems, its general call for a caliphate is presented as the solution to many practical problems of direct concern to the individual—the caliphate would dissolve state borders and sharia law would eliminate corruption and social inequality.

The first leaflets of Hizb-ut-Tahrir were distributed in mosques in Tashkent as early as the beginning of 1993, according to Uzbek scholar Bakhtiar Babadzhanov.[66] Other sources date the appearance of the organization in Uzbekistan to 1995, when branches were set up in Andizhan, Samarkand, Tashkent, and the town of Fergana.[67] In February 1999 Karimov mentioned Hizb-ut-Tahrir directly by name for the first time, in connection with the terrorist bombings in Tashkent that month.[68] During the four years 1999–2002 some 7000 activists, the majority of them members of Hizb-ut-Tahrir, were imprisoned in Uzbekistan.[69] The first emissaries of Hizb-ut-Tahrir appeared in southern Kyrgyzstan around 1995 but the law enforcement bodies did not pay attention to the group until 1998. At the time of the Batken events in August 1999 and 2000 its activities increased dramatically, particularly in the Jalal-Abad Region, and the authorities intensified their efforts to arrest its members.[70] The first members of Hizb-ut-Tahrir in Kyrgyzstan were radical Islamists who had left Uzbekistan after radical Islamic organizations were outlawed there in 1992. The first Hizb-ut-Tahrir material was printed in Uzbekistan; in April 1999 the Kyrgyz authorities discovered an underground printer in Osh.[71] Penalties for members of Hizb-ut-Tahrir have been exceptionally severe in Uzbekistan: those convicted of membership and of distributing anti-government leaflets were often sentenced to prison terms of 10–25 years. For the same offences in Kyrgyzstan, members received a maximum of five years in prison, and in many cases they were only fined.[72] Hizb-ut-Tahrir came to Tajikistan in the late 1990s, and in 1999 the first legal case was heard against a member of the organization.[73] Even though the organization had its support base in the north, many members were also arrested in Dushanbe and the south. More than 244 members of Hizb-ut-Tahrir were arrested in Tajikistan between 2000 and autumn 2002, and 165 were sentenced to prison terms.[74]

Thus, radical Islamism developed as part of a religious–political trend and the number of followers increased in Uzbekistan, Kyrgyzstan and Tajikistan.

State Control of Islamic Activities

The state regulation of religion is broadly similar in the four countries of Central Asia. The states are secular, the constitutions guarantee the freedom of religion, and there is a state committee on religious affairs with responsibility for the regulation of religious life in the country. The law prescribes that religion should not interfere in state affairs, and state authorities should not interfere in religious affairs. However, the ways in which these laws are applied differ between the four countries.

When the Uzbek authorities carried out campaigns against what they believed to be radical Islamism, they also targeted religious institutions. In early 1998 a rigorous new law on religion was adopted, which severely limited the activities of Uzbek religious organizations. The new legislation was designed to counter the 'threat of aggressive Wahhabi activism' in Uzbekistan:[75] Arrests and trials followed.[76]

Religious organizations in Tajikistan experienced more freedom than their counterparts in Uzbekistan. Tajikistan offers an interesting case study, since the existence of the IRP created a legal channel for political activities. Yet the authorities in Tajikistan also feared radicalization and tried to keep religious institutions under strict control. The post-September 2001 situation illustrates the authorities' dilemma of, on the one hand, guaranteeing the rights of the IRP and the freedom of religion while, on the other hand, controlling the IRP as well as religious institutions.

It is pointed out above that the very existence of a legal IRP makes the scope for religious activity broader in Tajikistan than it is in the other Central Asian countries. Yet Tajik law prohibits the Islamic clergy from joining a political party or using the mosques for political propaganda. The 1994 Law on Religion and Religious Organizations defines the rights of religious organizations, the form and content of their activities and their place in the spiritual and social life.[77] Article 7 of the law defines religious organizations as religious societies and centres, Friday mosques (*jomea*), monasteries, religious brotherhoods, missionary societies, spiritual educational institutions and associations of several religious organizations. All religious organizations have to be officially registered and to receive authorization from the State Committee on Religion.[78] In September 2001 there were more than 3000 ordinary mosques registered as *panjvaqta*—or *pyatikratnye* in Russian—which means places for praying five times a day, and 241 *jomeas*, where the imam is allowed to read a *hutba*, religious lecture, on Fridays. There were also 58 registered non-Islamic religious organizations, most of them Christian, and 10 unregistered non-Islamic organizations.[79] The Committee on Religion, appointed by the president, controls religious activities in the country.[80] Its three main functions are to control the activities of religious organizations, to coordinate the work of all the state authorities involved in controlling religious activities, and to inform ministries and the state institutions about developments on the ground.

Formally, the regular worshippers at the mosque elect the imam. In practice, the elections follow the Soviet tradition, which in this case means that the *Hukumat* (local government) together with the local representative of the State Committee suggest a candidate and have an unofficial but deciding vote. As a result, the heads of the mosques are appointed not because of their qualifications or authority with regard to religious issues but on the basis of their relations with the state authorities. The state authorities appoint the heads of the *jomeas* after consultations with the Sovet Uleimov (the Council of Scholars, composed of 10–15 leading official religious leaders). The state security organs keep control of the Friday lectures given by the *imamkhatibs*. The state does not allow any independent religious hierarchy within the Islamic community. That means that the status of the *jomea* is not above that of the *pyatikratnyi* mosque, and the latter is therefore not subordinated to the *jomea*. Although the Sovet Uleimov is formally the highest Islamic administrative body, it has no right to make statements (*fatwas*) on any topic.[81] Moreover, as mentioned above, it has no formal right to examine or to confirm the professional religious knowledge of the heads of the mosques.

The Tajik Government has thus tried to keep strict control over the official religious leadership and not allowed any unregistered religious activity. However, strict control of the official religious leadership undermines its authority among believers. As a result many people have turned to unofficial leaders for advice and guidance. These leaders remain outside state control and are often more radical in their interpretation of the Islamic texts. Since the Sovet Uleimov has no right to issue *fatwas*, only Hizb-ut-Takhrir takes a clear stand on issues of concern to Islamic believers. Thus, the measures taken by the government are often counter productive.

Although radical Islam did not seem to be a dominant trend in Tajikistan in the immediate post 11-September situation, the government rapidly took action. When the anti-terrorist campaign started in the autumn of 2001, the IRP feared that President Emomali Rakhmonov would exploit it as an opportunity to clamp down on the party, accusing it of indirectly supporting terrorism, and proscribe it. This did not happen. During the spring of 2002 Rakhmonov gave the issue of domestic terrorism and extremism high priority but at the same time stated that the threat to domestic stability came from the underdeveloped state of the economy and the difficult socio-economic conditions in which the majority of the population live. In May 2002, Rakhmonov called for a mobilization against the threats of terrorism and extremism.[82] In his September 2002 speech on the 11th anniversary of Tajikistan's independence the 'fight against terrorism and religious extremism' was declared as 'one of the top priorities for Tajikistan'.[83]

In March 2002 Rakhmonov launched a campaign to increase government control over religious institutions. According to existing legislation all mosques are to be registered, yet, many small mosques remained unregistered. In a speech that month Rakhmonov emphasized registration.[84] This set off a countrywide campaign during which mosques already registered had to re-register, and non-registered mosques to register. Local authorities drastically reduced the number of mosques. For example, in the Leninskii District to the south of Dushanbe the number of mosques was reduced from around 225 to 156. Where previously there had been 13 mosques for 13 villages in Faizabad, there were now three. However, as one observer pointed out, those places for praying which were not allowed to register would continue unofficially as a *pyatikratnyi* mosque, although hidden as ordinary tea-houses. Such had been the practice in Soviet times, and so it would continue, he said.[85]

At the request of the State Committee on Religious Affairs, a nationwide campaign was also initiated to check the imams' knowledge of religious issues as well as of state laws on religious affairs.[86] The procedure was termed a 'regular annual appraisal'. However, in contrast to previous appraisals, the leaders of the country's religious organizations would have to demonstrate their knowledge of the country's laws, particularly the law on the activities of religious organizations. The religious leaders of the northern Sughd Region were the first to undergo appraisal.

In the summer of 2002 the district of Isfara in the Fergana Valley, near the borders of Kyrgyzstan, and Uzbekistan, attracted particular attention from the government. Isfara has always been a stronghold of Islam. In early July 2002 a special meeting of the Tajik Security Council took place in the town of Isfara behind closed doors, attended by the President, the Secretary of the Security Council, the ministers of all the security departments and the chairman of the Sughd Region.[87] A few days later, on 10 July, President Rakhmonov in Isfara, urged the citizens there not to give in to calls by extremist religious figures.[88] He said that he had 'specially chosen Isfara as the venue for meeting the public because two Isfara residents, who were members of the Al-Qa'idah terrorist organization, are currently being held at the US military base in Guantanamo, Cuba'. He complained that there were only 82 schools for 200,000 people in Isfara District but 192 mosques and a religious seminary, although the law stipulated one mosque per 15,000 people. He called this an 'alarm signal'.[89] Rakhmonov also brought up the issue of the return of more than 1500 young Tajik citizens, children of former refugees from the Tajik civil war, including 60 from the Isfara District, who were studying at foreign religious educational establishments, particularly in Saudi Arabia, Iran and Pakistan, where they 'learned Wahhabism'. He added that 'if every graduate of these educational establishments propagates Wahhabism, then this will lead to religious dissent and discord, which may cause the destabilization of the situation in the country'.[90]

When during the summer the campaigns intensified, Rakhmonov used them to target the IRP. Again, the party feared that it would be banned. On 13 July Rakhmonov accused some IRP members of 'indoctrinating people in the spirit of extremism, which may lead to a split of society'. The president specifically cited the activities of IRP members in Isfara District,[91] and claimed that eight clerics in the mosques were IRP members, which was, he said, a 'flagrant violation of the law'.[92] He also hinted that the IRP was engaging in activity similar to that of Hizb-ut-Tahrir and the IMU. Moreover, the president implied that the Tajik nationals at Guantanamo Bay had ties to the IRP. His comments were the harshest criticism he had so far levelled at the IRP since the 1997 peace agreement.

The IRP leaders did not immediately respond to Rakhmonov's attack but, at a news conference on 1 August 2002, party leader Nuri insisted that the IRP should not be equated with Hizb-ut-Tahrir and the IMU. 'We [the IRP] have always acted and will always act only within the framework of laws of the country', Nuri said. He dismissed any suggestion that the IRP had connections to the Tajik detainees at Guantanamo. Nuri acknowledged that recent public comments by 11 IRP-affiliated imams in Isfara could be interpreted as controversial, but stressed that the opinions expressed by the clerics did not represent the official position of the party and suggested that Rakhmonov was blowing this up out of proportion for his own political ends. It would be wrong to accuse the party, he said, when 'It is the fault of its individual members'.[93] As a result of the campaign, the Isfara town prosecutor reported in November 2002, 63 imams were investigated and charged, and four criminal cases were opened against 14 people on suspicion of involvement in Hizb-ut-Tahrir. Ten grand mosques and 144 ordinary mosques were refused legal authorization to continue their activities.

These incidents illustrate the complex domestic situation in Tajikistan after 11 September 2001. The general security situation had improved, and the political situation had stabilized. Yet the government's efforts to strengthen its control over religious institutions and attack the IRP illustrate the risk of the government exploiting the international situation after September 2001 and using the 'anti-terrorist' label to legitimize actions to weaken and remove opponents.

No religious–political opposition had developed in Turkmenistan and President Niyazov seemed to have the religious situation under control. Niyazov had been the first among the Central Asian presidents to do the *hajj* and he built several mosques declaring them to be part of the cultural–religious heritage of the country. As Alexei Malashenko wrote in early 2003, the fact that there were no existing Islamist groups was not a guarantee that none would appear in the future.[94] The measures the Turkmen authorities undertook in October 2003 seemed to indicate that a change was under way in this regard. The president signed a new law on religious freedom and religious organizations, which replaced the previous law from 1991. The law declared all unregistered religious activity illegal, and a new amendment to the Criminal Code made such illegal activity punishable by up to one year of 'corrective labour' or fines of up to 30 times the average monthly wage.[95] When Turkmen authorities in 2003 required all imams in large mosques to put the book by the president, *Ruhnama*, alongside the Koran during prayers they consciously or unconsciously declared 'war' on Islam. Imams who refused to follow the request were detained.[96]

The developments in all four Central Asian countries illustrate the risk that the authorities run when taking measures to increase control over religious institutions—that of provoking the kind of religious–political opposition that they seek to prevent.

The Ethno-National Dimension

Ethno-national divisions have not played the role that many expected at the time of the break up of the Soviet Union. In 1990 there was an outbreak of ethnic violence between Kyrgyz and Uzbeks in the Fergana Valley, the roots of which were found in the uneven distribution of land and water, both scarce. Such outbreaks were not repeated.[97] There were no explicit mobilization of the population on ethno-national lines either by the regimes or by the opposition. Among ordinary people ethnic affiliation continued to play a subordinate role.

Yet, several sources of potential conflict on an inter-ethnic basis exist in Central Asia—on the national and on the interstate levels. There are numerous unresolved problems to which the response could be ethno-national mobilization. The issues of water and land are only two among them. Although interstate tension relaxed in the immediate post-September 2001 situation, tensions between the states remain and these tensions may trigger, or be triggered by, ethno-national issues.

A major factor preparing the ground for an ethno-national form of protest in the future is the ongoing nation- and state-building process in the multi-ethnic Central Asian states. All four states are engaged in creating a national identity, and for this purpose the focus is on the national culture, national history and national language. In formulating a national heritage, the regimes refer to different aspects and times of the history of a partly common territory. As Martha Brill Olcott writes: 'The leaders of each Central Asian nation are looking to the past to write national histories which affirm their claims to statehood. These efforts pose a potential security risk in themselves, because contemporary boundaries and reinterpreted historical ones in no way coincide.'[98] Uzbekistan invokes Timur (Tamerlane) and the Timurid period (1370–1507) in support of national consolidation.[99] Timur ruled an empire that covered Transoxania (the land between the Amudarya and Syrdarya rivers), present-day Afghanistan, Iran and Iraq. Tajikistan relies on Ismail Somoni and the Samanid empire with Bukhara as the capital, which covered Transoxania and Khorasan (to the south of Transoxania) during the ninth and tenth centuries. Tajikistan's references to the Samanid Empire indirectly imply claims on Bukhara and Samarkand located on Uzbek territory, although the Tajik Government does not officially raise such claims. Turkmenistan is a successor of Khwarazm, a historic region in western Central Asia, and of the Khanate of Khiva, and thereby has historical claims on Uzbek territory. The present Central Asian governments do not raise territorial claims, yet their invocations of history could prepare the ground for possible future conflicts.

As the states encourage the heritage of the titular nation, other national groups are defined as minorities. The rights of national minorities are supposed to be guaranteed by law. However, when interstate relations deteriorate, this is reflected in the situation for the minorities, which also deteriorates.

The complex ethnic matrix of Central Asia with large concentrations of different groups makes it sometimes difficult to talk in terms of minorities. The territories of these states belonged to different empires that replaced each other over the centuries. Ethnic groups are therefore scattered over large territories as a kind of historical remnant. Moreover, the oasis cultures of the old Central Asian centres were always multi-ethnic. Today, the share of the Uzbeks of the population in the neighbouring countries has been reduced although they still constitute the largest minority group. They make up 15.3 per cent of the total population in Tajikistan (according to the 2000 census), 13.8 per cent in Kyrgyzstan (1999 census) and 9 per cent in Turkmenistan (the 1989 Soviet census).[100] The Fergana Valley in particular presents a complicated mix. In the Kyrgyz part of the valley there are concentrations of Uzbeks in Jalal-Abad and Osh (in the town of Osh they constitute 50 per cent of the population). In the Tajik part of the valley (Sughd Region) the Uzbeks make up a very large share of the population. Kyrgyz and Tajiks can be found on the Uzbek side of their borders.

There are also large concentrations of ethnic minorities outside the Fergana Valley. In Uzbekistan, Bukhara and Samarkand historically and culturally constitute Tajik cities with a mainly Tajik population. There are Tajiks all over the Samarkand region and in the Surkhandarya and Karshi regions in southern Uzbekistan. Uzbeks live not only in northern Tajikistan but also along the border in the south-west of the country in Hissar, and in the Khatlon region, especially around the towns of Shartuz and Kurgan-Tyube. A concentration of Uzbeks can be found in north-eastern Turkmenistan in the Dashkhnovuz region, and Turkmen in the Uzbek Khorazm region around the town of Urgench on the other side of the border. Kyrgyz concentrations can be found in Pamir, Tajikistan, close to the Kyrgyz border.[101] The existence of exclaves in neighbouring countries further complicates the ethnic picture.

The nation- and state-building process has created state borders on a territory where borders and nationalities played no role for centuries. Border problems are now the worst trigger for inter-ethnic tension. The Fergana Valley constitutes a cultural and economic entity in spite of its ethnic mix and now state borders create obstacles to people's normal life.[102] Laws on state languages were adopted in Central Asia as early as 1989–90 and were fairly relaxed compared with the language laws of the Baltic states. In Central Asia there was a generous timetable for the law to be implemented. Other languages were reduced to languages of national minorities, which were guaranteed the right to their own language. The Russian language maintained its position as the language of the educated strata, although it soon lost its former dominant position among the population as a whole. In December 2001 the Russian language was granted the status of 'official language' in Kyrgyzstan next to the Kyrgyz state language.[103] When a similar suggestion was made in Tajikistan in the spring of 2002, this led to a heated debate.[104] Opponents feared that if the Russian language were granted such a status, the Uzbeks in Tajikistan would soon demand a similar status for the Uzbek language.

National minorities are under pressure in the ongoing nation- and state-building processes. Statistics reflect the situation. Compared with figures of the last Soviet census, of 1989, the share of minority groups in the populations has fallen. The share of the Uzbek population in Tajikistan fell from 24 per cent in 1989 to 15.3 per cent in year 2000. A similar development has taken place in Uzbekistan and other Central Asian countries. The reduction can be partly explained by migration but also by people choosing to define themselves as belonging to the titular nation in order to avoid problems.

Intergovernmental tension adds to the pressure on minority groups. Tensions are reflected when minorities complain that their rights are violated, for example, when Tajiks in Uzbekistan and Uzbeks in Tajikistan complain they have no access to books in their own language or to schools that teach in their own language.[105] For ethnic Tajiks in Uzbekistan the situation dramatically deteriorated in 2000 when 5000 Uzbek residents (most of them ethnic Tajiks) were removed from border villages in the Surkhandarya region and deported to central Uzbekistan.[106]

When Turkmen–Uzbek relations deteriorated after December 2002, Turkmen authorities forcibly relocated ethnic Uzbeks in Turkmenistan living near the border to Uzbekistan. The arrest of Boris Shikhmuradov in Turkmenistan in December 2002 resulted in Turkmen accusations of Uzbek involvement in the coup attempt. In mid-December 2002, Turkmen special forces entered the Uzbek embassy in Askhabad and the Uzbek ambassador was declared *persona non grata,* accused of support for Shikhmuradov, and forced to leave the country. The Uzbek Government denied the accusations. A 'Turkmenization' process of ethnic Uzbeks in Turkmenistan intensified, while there was a parallel process of 'Uzbekization' of ethnic Turkmen in Uzbekistan.[107] Discrimination is felt first and foremost in schools.

Border issues and border policies remain major triggers of interstate tension. There are several aspects to the border problems. Unilateral measures taken by one country with the purpose of defending its security or its economy often have serious consequences for its neighbours. As mentioned above, since 1999 the Uzbek security services have repeatedly persecuted ethnic Uzbeks on Kyrgyz territory, accusing them of 'Wahhabism'.[108] As mentioned in a previous chapter during the events in the Batken district in southern Kyrgyzstan in August 1999, Uzbek aircraft bombed villages on the Tajik side of the border, which led to protests from the Tajik Government.[109] In 2000 Uzbekistan mined the borders with Kyrgyzstan and Tajikistan without informing the authorities in these countries. It closed border crossing points on the border with Tajikistan, introduced strict visa regulations and increased tariffs and taxes on transit goods. Uzbekistan's unilateral security measures, its intrusions into foreign territories and its involvement in the domestic politics of its neighbours have given rise to a fear of Uzbekistan in neighbouring countries.

Developments after September 2001 reinvigorated talks on border demarcation. Such agreements were signed towards the end of 2002 between Tajikistan and Uzbekistan, and between Tajikistan and Kyrgyzstan. Yet disputed areas remain. Four areas in Sughd remained in dispute between Tajikistan and Uzbekistan after an agreement was signed in October 2002. Border talks between Tajikistan and Kyrgyzstan recommenced in December 2002—without final agreement being reached. However, the local authorities from the Kyrgyz Batken and Tajik Sughd regional administrations managed to solve several of the practical problems on the ground.[110] The existence of a Tajik exclave in Vorukh, Kyrgyzstan, complicates the talks. The Uzbek–Kyrgyz talks are even more complicated. No agreement was signed on delimitation of the Uzbek–Kyrgyz border, on which there are 39 disputed points. The most complex section along the 1400-km long border is in the Jalal-Abad Region and the area of the Andizhan water reservoir. The Uzbek exclaves in Kyrgyzstan, Sokh and Shakhimardan, are also contributory problems. Between Uzbekistan and Turkmenistan an agreement demarcating the 1867-km long border was signed in September 2000. In 2001 a 1700-km long fence was installed on the Turkmen side.[111]

The fact that parts of both Kyrgyzstan and Tajikistan territory can be reached only by crossing Uzbek territory gives Uzbekistan the upper hand. A road over Uzbek territory connects the Kyrgyz towns of Osh and Jalal-Abad. Exit roads and railways from Tajikistan run across Uzbekistan. In the winter, when the Anzob Pass is blocked by snow, the only road connection between the north and south of Tajikistan runs across Uzbek territory. An important road runs through the Uzbek exclave of Sokh, in Batken on Kyrgyz territory, connecting different parts of Kyrgyzstan.

In December 2002 Uzbek officials began closing border crossing posts along the frontiers with Kyrgyzstan, Tajikistan, Turkmenistan and Kazakhstan as part of the government's efforts to make the Uzbek currency convertible. In early 2003 the border with Kyrgyzstan was practically sealed in order to stop Uzbek shoppers from taking hard currency out of the country, and tensions between the two states increased.[112] Near the Kyrgyz town of Kara-Sui, on the road between Osh and Jalal-Abad, Uzbek border guards blew up a bridge spanning a border crossing. Uzbekistan's sealing of its borders caused massive disruption to regional trade. Many regional analysts disputed the official explanation from Uzbek authorities at the time that the measures were driven by a desire to protect consumers from shoddily manufactured imports. Instead, observers said, the chief impetus for border closures was Tashkent's own inability to grapple with economic reforms, especially the introduction of currency convertibility.[113] Interstate tension increased when people were fired on at the border.[114] In July 2003 a Kyrgyz man was killed by Uzbek border guards when he tried to cross the border, and an exchange of diplomatic letters followed between the two governments.[115] A similar situation characterized relations between Uzbekistan and Kazakhstan.[116] The situation along the Uzbek-Turkmen border also deteriorated after stricter border controls were introduced in 2001. Shooting incidents at the border started in January 2002 when people tried to cross illegally. The crisis in relations after December 2002 resulted in the deployment of troops from both countries along the border and military exercises followed.[117]

There were no conflicts involving the Russian minorities in the region until Turkmenistan removed the right to dual citizenship in 2003. Instead of protesting at the way their living conditions have changed, Russians have been leaving the Central Asian countries in a regular stream since the late 1970s. They made up 12.5 per cent of the population of Kyrgyzstan in 1999; 9.8 per cent in Turkmenistan in 1989; 8.3 per cent in Uzbekistan in 1999, and only 1.1 per cent of Tajikistan in 1999.[118] Although the Russian Government was concerned about the plight of Russians in Central Asia, and issued statements and declarations, it did not engage directly on this issue in the region.[119] In an effort to encourage Russians to stay, Turkmenistan had introduced the right to dual citizenship in 1993, and Kyrgyzstan and Tajikistan soon followed. The removal of this right by the Turkmen authorities in 2003 may be the signal for a new and more active Russian engagement on the issue of the Russian minority in Central Asia in the future.

Ethno-nationalism has so far played no major role. However, there is a risk that this dimension might become important in the future, if triggered by interstate tensions and exploited for political purposes by groups or governments.

Summary

This chapter deals with the dynamics of domestic protest from within the Central Asian states as a challenge to Russian Central Asian policy. Russia has lost control over the governments as well as the patterns of protest in these societies. The developments on the domestic scenes of Central Asian countries have to be responded to by Russian policy if Russia is to play a political role in these countries in the future. After September 2001 domestic threats to security moved to the forefront. Central Asia is a region with serious problems and will remain so for years to come. A major question for the future is what form and direction protest will take. This chapter discusses three possible dimensions to popular protest: the secular–political, religious–political and ethno-national dimensions.

Although the Central Asian states differ from each other with regard to their degree of political freedom, authoritarian tendencies increased in all these societies after 11 September 2001. All presidents strengthened their power and took measures to secure their positions and extend their terms of office. The expectation that external pressure from international organizations and foreign governments engaging in the region would help domestic reforms was not justified in the short run. The US Government attempted to maintain close relations with Uzbekistan and thereby became cautious about making too strong or direct criticisms of the Uzbek Government for violations of democratic and human rights.

The secular–political form of opposition would have considerable potential if it were allowed to function legally. Critics of the regimes were arrested in all four countries. At the same time, the behaviour of the regimes reflected the fragility of their power and their fear of losing control of the situation. The outbreak of popular discontent in Kyrgyzstan demonstrated how easily a single issue can trigger a broad protest when there is general discontent in society. The repressive cleansing of state structures in Turkmenistan also demonstrated deep 'cracks in the marble' in the Niyazov dictatorship. In Tajikistan, which gained the most from the post-Taliban situation as society was stabilized, authoritarian tendencies were strengthened when the Tajik authorities pushed the IRP almost to extinction. For all four Central Asian regimes, the international anti-terrorist campaign provided a convenient and legitimate way of framing and legitimizing their clampdown on domestic opposition. Under these circumstances, with secular–political protest being blocked, political protest took other forms and the religious-political opposition was strengthened.

While only Tajikistan has the legal framework in place to permit a moderate Islamism to develop, Uzbekistan has witnessed the development of a radical and violent religious–political movement. Although the post-11 September situation seemed, at least temporarily, to have stopped the IMU propounding the violent overthrow of the Uzbek regime, it has not permanently eradicated such movements. The fastest growing movement, Hizb-ut-Tahrir, did not engage in violent acts but its confrontational and uncompromising approach to the *kufr* may pave the way for a radical and violent 'solution' by other groups.

Of the three dimensions of protest discussed in this chapter, the religious–political dimension, primarily radical Islamism, seems to be developing most rapidly. Although the number of followers of radical Islamism seems to be small, all observers agree that it is rising. Especially in Kyrgyzstan, Uzbekistan and Tajikistan, Hizb-ut-Tahrir is growing fast. If the present governments cannot satisfy the demands for a better life for a large part of the population, and at the same time allow criticism and political demands to be articulated, there is a risk that many will turn to radical Islamist groups and support their vision of a paradise-caliphate as the preferred solution to all problems. Central Asian societies would then decline into chaos and turmoil. Continued turmoil in Afghanistan and drug trafficiking—almost twice as high as pre-11 September levels—across Central Asian territory create a dangerous context in which extremist movements may grow. A future disappointment with non-fulfilled promises by the West might encourage the search for a radical Islamist alternative.

The ethno-national form of protest has so far not played a major role but religious–political protest also has an ethnic dimension as radical Islamist movements first gained ground among ethnic Uzbeks. The complex ethnic map of the region adds to the problems when interstate relations deteriorate. Ethnic divisions have a potential for conflict in the future as minorities can easily be used as scapegoats in an atmosphere of growing nationalism. The national identity-building process provides the general background to these processes. Border conflicts and common unresolved problems in the Central Asian states may trigger tensions.

The presidents responded to tensions in their societies by strengthening their hold on power. They all tried to postpone the unavoidable generational transfer of power and to find ways for their continued rule. The international anti-terrorist campaign provided a pretext for taking measures against the opposition. Central Asian societies seem to be building a dangerous potential for conflict and domestic violence.

Nevertheless, as pointed out above, there is also a potential for peaceful reform in these countries in the form of educated and reform-minded people at middle levels within the system. This makes assistance and support from the outside—from international organizations and foreign governments, including the Russian Government—crucial for providing advice, aid, credits and assistance.

The domestic situation in the Central Asian countries is a serious challenge to Russia as well as to every foreign actor engaged in the region. The underlying economic and social problems may risk aggravating the negative trends already discernible. These countries require assistance for their economic development but also with carrying out political reforms. Russia's limited capacity to meet the new domestic challenges to security in these countries after September 2001 is illustrated by the case of Tajikistan, its closest ally. In spite of the large Russian military presence in the country, Russia has few means to help the Tajik economy develop, and what Tajikistan needs more than anything else is support for securing economic development, building democracy and institutionalizing the rule of law. If Russia is to secure a future role for itself in the region, and meet the new challenges, it has to increase its economic presence and level of economic exchange. It must also make more effort to assist these countries to peacefully solve conflicts and build democracy. Assisting democracy-building in Central Asia may seem to be too large a task for Russia, which only started democratic reforms in its own country about 15 years ago. The task of assisting democracy-building also means a policy far beyond the present narrow Russian focus on anti-terrorism, and requires Russia to extend and develop cooperation with international organizations and individual governments engaged in Central Asia. These are major challenges for Russian policy in Central Asia.

PART IV

THE SHAPING OF RUSSIAN
FOREIGN POLICY

8

THE SHAPING OF FOREIGN POLICY

The purpose of this study is threefold: to analyse the changes made to Russia's Central Asian policy in 1999 and 2001, and explain why these changes took place; to analyze Russian policy in the region since then, and discuss the future prospects for Russian influence there; and to consider the implications for the overall revision of Russian foreign policy. Russia's Central Asian policy is studied as a microcosm of Russia's search for a new international role and policy in the modern post-Soviet world.

Why Did Russian Policy Change?

The 1999 and 2001 policy shifts were preceded by dramatic events—the 1999 hostage taking in Batken by Uzbek Islamist rebels and the terrorist attacks on the USA of 11 September 2001. Putin used both occasions as 'policy windows'. Chapter 1 identifies Russian policy change as: (a) changes in the way problems and concerns are defined; (b) changes in the means by which Russia responds to major problems; and (c) changes in its approach to Western states engaging in Central Asia.

In the 1990s Russia continued its traditional emphasis on security aspects and security cooperation as a means of policy in Central Asia. In that respect, Putin's policy of 1999 did not represent a change. The problems for Russia in the region remained both strategic (concern about growing engagement by foreign actors) and security-related (concern about the consequences of the instability in Afghanistan for Central Asia). Yet the way Putin in 1999 made the anti-terrorist struggle first priority on the Russian agenda in Central Asia constituted a dramatic shift compared with the policy of his predecessor. The concept of 'securitization' is applied in the present analysis to highlight the process by which the terrorist threat came to frame Russian Central Asian policy. Thus, under Putin Russian problems and concerns in Central Asia were defined above all in relation to the terrorist threat.

In this regard, Putin's 2001 policy turn brought no change. His anti-terrorist focus remained, and Russian-led security cooperation in the Collective Security Treaty (CTS) became a crucial instrument. What made his 2001 policy change dramatic was the shift of approach to the US engagement in the region. Although Putin's consent to the US military presence in Central

Asia was based on the assumption that it would only be temporary, he accepted its extension when the military operation in Afghanistan was over. The policy turn of 2001 was thus more fundamental than that of 1999, since Russia's overall orientation, that is, its approach to US engagement in the region, radically shifted. The anti-terrorist struggle was inverted in the sense that it was now used as a platform for cooperation with the USA instead of for rallying forces against the US engagement in the region.

Different contributory factors to the changes in foreign policy are analysed throughout this volume—including external factors (the development in Central Asia and on the global scene), and domestic factors of various kinds. This chapter discusses the relationships between these factors and their relative weights. In chapter 1, four possible theoretical explanations are presented: (a) the international structure explanation; (b) the instrumental explanation; (c) the institutional rivalry explanation; and finally (d) the socialization explanation. They each place different emphasis on the capacity of the state to have an influence or an impact on the international system. Employing a term first used by John M. Hobson in his study of the state in international relations, the explanations differ with regard to the degree of 'international agential state power' that they each imply, that is, the capacity of the state to act as an agent in the international arena.[1]

The International Structure Explanation

The first explanation considers international conditions (international structure) to have the greatest explanatory power. Its basic premise is that a state's policy and position in the international system are determined by its powers and capabilities in comparison with those of other states on the global scene. Thus, the relatively weak position of Russia in the present hierarchy of states, both globally and in Central Asia, sets the limits to Russian foreign policy. International conditions force Russia to react in a certain way. The waning of Russia's economic and military power in the Central Asian region, the engagement of other foreign actors in the region, and the efforts by the independent states of Central Asia to 'diversify' their foreign policies and reduce their dependence on Russia, while at the same time exploiting the new interest of other large powers, all forced the Russian Government to adapt its policy. The 'overlay' of Russian dominance in Central Asia, inherited from the Soviet Union, gradually disappeared.

To Russia, the effect of its waning role and influence in Central Asia was felt on two different levels: (a) in the Russian–US balance in the region, and (b) with regard to Russia's influence on the local dynamics in Central Asia.

Although the USA had already started to engage in Central Asia in the mid-1990s, after 11 September there was a qualitative increase in its engagement. The USA focused its attention on Central Asia partly because of the energy resources in the Caspian Sea Basin but also as part of its strategy to contain Russia in Asia. Bilateral and multilateral cooperation on security issues developed within the framework of the North Atlantic Treaty Organization's Partnership for Peace Programme. Before 11 September, several US experts questioned the seriousness of the US commitment in Central Asia if a real threat were to develop.[2] Putin's policy turns of 1999 and 2001 were responses, although different responses, to the reality of a reduced Russian presence and influence and a growing US engagement in Central Asia. While in 1999 he intensified the effort to rally the Central Asian states against the common threat of terrorism and to counter US influence, the 2001 policy turn was a necessary retreat as the USA increased its involvement in the region.

Against this background of the changing balance of forces between Russia and the USA, Putin's consent in 2001 to the US military's use of Central Asian airbases is quite logical. The discrepancy between the US ascendancy and Russia's decline was too great to be ignored. Moreover, the balance of forces on the ground in Central Asia gave Putin no choice. All the Central Asian Governments expected benefits in one form or another from their different levels of participation in the US-led anti-terrorist coalition. Russia would not have received any support from the Central Asian countries if it had tried to prevent or obstruct security cooperation between the USA and the Central Asian states under the anti-terrorist banner.

To this may be added Russia's loss of control over the local dynamics in Central Asia. While Russia in 1999 still seemed to hold certain levers of influence—it was successful in bringing the Tajik civil war to an end in 1997, and managed to engage Uzbekistan in bilateral anti-terrorist cooperation in autumn 1999—this had changed by 2001. The situation in Afghanistan, where the Russian-supported anti-Taliban Northern Alliance was almost wiped out in the spring of 2000, spread instability into Central Asia as the Taliban gave shelter to Uzbek Islamist extremists. Russia's inability to turn the tide of events emanating from Taliban Afghanistan had been demonstrated, in spite of its anti-terrorist focus in the region after 1999. Russia's economic, political, cultural and military exchanges with the Central Asian countries were reduced and the levers with which it could influence relations between them were weakened as a result. The fear of Islamist tendencies and groups developing in Central Asian countries such as Uzbekistan, Kyrgyzstan and Tajikistan demonstrated that Russia had lost control over the local dynamics in these societies.

Putin's policy changes of 1999 and 2001 can be viewed as reactions, albeit different ones, to the long-term changes in the structural conditions of the international system in Central Asia. With this explanation, the 2001 policy shift can be understood as the consequence of the reduced room for manoeuvre for Russian policy compared with the situation in 1999.

The Instrumental Explanation

The second explanation regards the state as an autonomous and unitary actor, and policy as an instrument for influencing the international environment. This perspective also ascribes a certain degree of rationality to the state, and the state is assumed to have a fixed set of preferences and to behave instrumentally in order to maximize the attainment of these preferences. This approach explains policy change as the reformulation by the state's leadership of strategic goals, tactics and instruments.

According to this explanation, Putin's policies in 1999 and 2001 are seen as instruments for improving Russia's international position. A question then arises over which strategic framework best fits the steps taken by Putin. In chapter 1, Robert Gilpin's study *War and Change in World Politics* is suggested as a possible analytical framework in which to place Putin's strategic thinking.[3] Gilpin writes that a state in decline does its utmost to maintain its previous international position. The references in Russian official statements and doctrines to the late nineteenth century Foreign Minister Alexander Gorchakov indicate the present desire to take Russia back to international influence and great-power status. The great-power dream is alive. According to Gilpin, two possible and analytically different courses of action are available to such states—to devote more resources to maintaining its commitments and position in the international system, or to reduce its commitments (and associated costs) while trying not to jeopardize its international position. As demonstrated above, since Mikhail Gorbachev the Russian leadership has had a general strategy of increasing efficiency through domestic reform while trying to reduce costs. The second type of response—to reduce costs—can be attempted in different ways. Most relevant to the discussion here are expansion into more secure and less costly defensive perimeters, and political, territorial or economic retrenchment. With regard to retrenchment, three possible directions present themselves: to unilaterally abandon certain of Russia's economic, political or military commitments; to enter into alliances with or seek rapprochement with less threatening powers; and to make concessions to the rising power and thereby seek to appease its ambitions.

The increased attention Russia paid to Central Asia after 1999 can be viewed as an effort to expand into a 'more secure and less costly defensive perimeter' (Gilpin) as a possible option to reduce costs. Still, retrenchment seems to be the general characteristic of Russian Central Asian policy during the 1990s. Russia abandoned many previous commitments as its presence in the region was reduced. In 1999 it also tried to seek rapprochement with China, a less threatening power in the wider Central Asian region. Between 1999 and 2001 the Shanghai Five (later the Shanghai Cooperation Organization, SCO) was given an anti-US direction as both Russia and China tried to prevent the USA from getting a foothold in Central Asia. Yet neither Russia nor China was prepared to seriously harm its relations with the USA. Gilpin's third option—a policy of appeasement—appears to be an appropriate characterization of Russian policy after September 2001.

It might seem strange to a Western reader to think of Russian–US relations in terms of Russian appeasement of the rising USA as the one and only global power, but the comparison does provide a number of insights. In September 2001 Putin seized the moment and accepted further retrenchment in order to improve relations with the West and create more favourable conditions for domestic reform as part of a long-term strategy to prepare for a Russian return to the international stage. The policy turn of 2001 has to be understood in the context of Russia's search for a strategy to enable it to make its return as a great power. Observers have characterized Putin as a pragmatist and a realist who is well aware of Russia's weakness. Yet this does not exclude the possibility of his maintaining a strategic vision of Russia as a great power and making it his task to create the conditions that will make this vision possible in the future. Since Mikhail Gorbachev, Russia has been engaged in a constant search for an appropriate balance between attempting to maintain international influence, on the one hand, and concentrating on domestic reform and creating favourable external conditions to assist with this process, on the other. Gorbachev took the radical decision to reduce the international role of the Soviet Union from that of a superpower to that of a great power. Both Yeltsin and Putin have tried to maintain Russia's status as a great power and to prevent it from slipping into the position of a second-rate country.

While the long-term strategic goal of a Russian return to great power influence was important to Putin, he had to adapt his tactics to what the international situation allowed at the time. Thus, his consent in 2001 to a US military presence in Central Asia can be understood in the context of Russia's search for a way back to its former status.

The Institutional Rivalry Explanation

Although the third explanation accepts the state as the major actor, it explains policy as the outcome of a contest between different vested interest groups. Throughout the 1990s Russian foreign policy suffered from institutional rivalry and infighting between different interests. Policy shifted back and forth, especially with regard to policy on former Soviet territory and on Russia's involvement in armed conflicts.

Using this explanation, the 1999 anti-terrorist focus in Central Asia can be explained as the result of the security sector strengthening its influence within the Russian Governmental structures during the second half of the 1990s. The intelligence and security sector regained influence when Yevgenii Primakov became foreign minister in 1996 and prime minister in September 1998. Vladimir Putin's background in the security sector was important for his appointment as prime minister in August 1999. Under Putin, the influence of the security sector further increased as, even more drastically, did the proportion of people in the state apparatus who had a professional security background. Early on, the military and security services acted as important lobby groups in pushing forward a security-dominated agenda for the Commonwealth of Independent States (CIS). Putin's approach to the Chechnya conflict influenced his understanding of what was going on in Central Asia. Once appointed prime minister, he pursued the anti-terrorist issue on a grand scale, thereby also strengthening his own power and position.

By September 2001 President Putin had more or less full control over the foreign-policy making mechanisms. The post-11 September foreign policy was formulated by a narrow group of people around the president. Institutional rivalry therefore does not explain Russian foreign policy decision-making at the time of the 11 September terrorist attacks. Putin was met with strong resistance from among the military and the security sector, which he had to overcome, when he allowed US forces access to Central Asia. Disagreement continued within the Russian leadership up until the last minute before Putin made public his consent to a US military presence on 24 September. On 22 September, before his consultations with Central Asian leaders, an extended meeting of the Russian Security Council took place in Sochi, and it took Putin six hours to convince its members.[4]

The policy change in 2001 was not the result of any shift in the balance of power in Moscow. Putin acted to ensure the support of influential interest groups. His pro-Western agenda had strong support among the Russian oligarchs and businessmen, and his anti-terrorist agenda had strong support among the power structures. Thus, neither of Putin's strong constituencies could abandon him. However, Putin's post-11 September 2001 foreign policy favoured the interests of those economic and financial groups which were oriented to the West.

Institutional rivalry does explain the 1999 shift of policy, but not the 2001 shift. In 2001 Putin's policy was heavily criticised but he was in control of the policy-making structures.

The Socialization Explanation

The fourth explanation refers to a process whereby Russia finds it to be in its own interests to be drawn into an international and institutional framework of accepted norms and rules of behaviour. Structures are to be understood here as social institutions in the form of international regimes, norms and rules, which replace material values such as 'military power'. They can alter bureaucratic practices or habits; promote an understanding of cause-and-effect relations; alter ideas about the legitimacy and value of particular practices; become embedded in higher-level normative networks; increase the political salience of certain issues; change the balance of political influence in domestic politics; or enhance the political or administrative capacity of government or non-governmental organizations (NGOs) in countries.[5] States change their values and norms by participating in international cooperation and multilateral institutions. As Martha Finnemore writes: 'Structures of shared knowledge and inter-subjective understandings may also shape and motivate actors. Socially constructed rules, principles, norms of behaviour, and shared beliefs may provide states, individuals, and other actors with understandings of what is important or valuable and what are effective and/or legitimate means of obtaining those valued goods'.[6] This is basically the constructivist perspective on international relations.

Thus, states find that there are potential gains from cooperation as well as possible costs if norms, rules and commitments are violated. On top of this, these specific norms, rules and commitments also influence state behaviour. A state such as Russia makes cost-benefit calculations but may also take into consideration the wider implications or longer-term costs of non-compliance.[7] Once states accept the long-term benefits from participating in an international legal system, the idea of obligation and the normative nature of rules can be given a tangible form. The socialization explanation thus suggests that a state, in this instance Russia, will make decisions to fall into line with what could be expected of it in order to cooperate with Western states and participate as an equal in the international community.

Putin's policy turn in September 2001 can be interpreted as the result of a socialization process—Russia had entered a common value system with the West and wanted to join the USA to combat what was perceived a common threat. Since Gorbachev introduced perestroika and Yeltsin allowed the Soviet system to break down, Russian leaders have tried to introduce Western-oriented values of a market economy and democratic reforms and to adhere to international norms and standards. Russia submitted to the values of the Council of Europe on democratic and human rights issues (although violating them in particular instances, as in Chechnya) and to the demands of global economic organizations such as the World Trade Organization (WTO) and the Group of Eight industrialized countries (G8). In his 'Internet speech' of December 1999, Putin declared his ambition to have Russia integrated into the world economy.[8] The anti-terrorist issue opened the door to intensified cooperation between Russia and NATO, and in May 2002 the Russia–NATO Council was created. With his efforts to embed Russia into an international institutional framework of organizations and cooperation with the West, Putin continued Gorbachev's and Yeltsin's ambitions to integrate with the West.

The 2001 policy turn in particular can be partly viewed as a reflection that Russia had internalized Western values and therefore naturally sided with the USA. Still, this explanation is weak. As several Russian experts pointed out the joint anti-terrorist struggle with the USA after 11 September created a golden opportunity for Russia to play the role of a great power, if only within the very narrow confines of anti-terrorism.[9]

None of the four discussed explanations fully explains Russia's foreign policy turns of 1999 and 2001. They complement each other rather than exclude each other. Yet which of them has the greatest explanatory strength? And which explain the crucial 2001 policy turn? The international structure explanation points to Russia's weak position in the international system, on the global level and in Central Asia. Russia's weakness forced Russia to reconsider its foreign policy. The reduced international influence was a precondition for Putin's acceptance of the US presence. Yet, the instrumental explanation is crucial in order to understand the specific choice of policy. The 2001 change of policy was determined by Russia's strategic goal of returning to its position as a great power. To support the US Administration in the post-11 September situation secured a breakthrough in relations with the West after years of frosty relations since the mid-1990s. Cooperation with the USA was also considered the best way to win international influence. Institutional rivalry, which contributes to an understanding of the 1999 policy change, does not help to explain the 2001 decision. By 2001 Putin was in control of foreign policy making and a narrow group around the president took the decision, in the face of strong opposition from other groups within his own power base. Putin did, however, have the support of oligarchs and economic interests which wanted to develop cooperation with the USA. He was therefore able to balance different groups against each other. His Chechnya policy maintained support from the security sector, while his US policy increased support among economic interest groups. The socialization explanation contributes the least. Although it cannot be excluded that developing cooperation and exchange with the West over the years has resulted in Russia becoming socialized into common values with the West, this cannot explain Putin's 2001 policy turn. Socialization is a long-term process, which may come to have a larger impact on Russian policy making in the future.

The analysis of Russia's policy response to the international disagreement over how to deal with Iraq in 2002–2003 confirms this conclusion.

Iraq: A Test Case of Russian Foreign Policy

Post-September 2001 developments demonstrated a change to a US-centric Russian foreign policy. In the light of the vocal criticism of this policy within Russia, the resilience of this new policy, or whether it would collapse as soon as Russian-US relations came under serious stress, remained open to question.

Russia's response to the growing controversy over how to handle the threat to international peace and security emanating from Saddam Hussein in Iraq, and the US–British invasion of Iraq in March 2003, which took place without a mandate from the UN Security Council, became a test of how far Russia's approach to the USA had actually changed. How did Russia react to this situation when the views of the Russian and US Governments seriously diverged?

Although Central Asian countries were not directly involved in the disagreement over Iraq, they were drawn into it as both Russia and the USA tried to convince the Central Asian Governments of the correctness of their policy. Thus, Central Asia was affected by a souring as well as by an improvement of relations between Russia and the USA.

The Russian Reaction to the Iraq Conflict

The argument over Iraq became a test case of the extent to which Russian foreign policy had changed in at least two regards. First, how did Russia handle an issue on which its own views radically diverged from US views at a time when Russia wanted to improve its relations with the USA? Second, how US-centric was Russian policy on an issue where different views existed between the USA and its allies—France and Germany? Third, would Russia demand loyalty from the Central Asian members of the CST on the Iraq issue when these governments were becoming more understanding of the US view. To Russia, the core issue of the conflict over Iraq was its relationship with the USA.

The question of whether Saddam Hussein had weapons of mass destruction (WMD) and how to make him comply with the demands of UN resolutions that he destroy these weapons became the most burning issue on the international scene from October 2002 until May 2003, when the Iraqi regime fell. The conflict culminated in the US–British military invasion of Iraq in March and April 2003. The twists and turns of the Russian Government reflected disagreement on the Russian domestic scene and in the foreign policy debate, in particular with regard to policy towards the USA.

On the one hand, Iraq was a long-time partner of Russia. Iraq had large debts to Russia and Russian oil companies had large contracts with Iraqi oil businesses. The argument over how to deal with Saddam Hussein also was an issue of principle. The US Administration under President George W. Bush was prepared to resort to unilateral measures to force Iraq to comply, thereby sidestepping the UN and its Security Council. Russia was against sidestepping the UN. The invasion of Iraq also had the potential to drastically reconfigure the international scene, with unpredictable consequences. On the other hand, Putin wanted to maintain good relations with the West, particularly the USA. He was also well aware of Russia's limitations on the international scene.

Russia had for several years tried to act as a mediator in the conflict between the USA and Iraq and to convince Iraq to come to a compromise with the UN Security Council. As late as May 2002 Russia managed to have Resolution 986 and the Oil for Food Programme extended, and part of the trade embargo against Iraq lifted as a result.[10] When disagreement developed in the UN Security Council about how to proceed with regard to suspicions that Saddam Hussein's regime was producing WMD—primarily biological and chemical weapons—a new situation arose. As a first stage in putting pressure on Iraq, the UN Security Council on 8 November 2002 adopted Resolution 1441 to force Iraq to comply with UN conditions concerning nuclear, biological and chemical weapons. During the autumn of 2002 more and more states agreed that Iraq had to comply with the resolution. Resolution 1441 did not include agreement to the use of force to make Iraq comply but, over time, as it became more evident that the US Government was prepared to resort to military force against Iraq, the Russian Government started to waver in its statements on the issue. Russia did not accept US unilateral measures and demanded that the Iraq issue be dealt with within the UN. However, at the same time, it was against the UN legitimizing any US use of force against a member state before the UN weapons inspectors—the UN Monitoring, Verification and Inspection Commission (UNMOVIC)—had had the chance to prove whether Iraq did or did not have WMD.

In the autumn of 2002 disagreement deepened on the issue of the UN sending weapons inspectors to Iraq in order to confirm whether Iraq had access to WMD. France, together with Russia and Germany, demanded a thorough investigation to answer the question, while the US and British Governments were impatient and thought it necessary to take immediate measures to force Saddam Hussein to admit that he had access to such weapons and destroy them. The Russian stand on the Iraq issue can be explained both by Russia's own economic interests in Iraq and by its principled stand with regard to the use of military force against a UN member state without the authority of the UN Security Council. The latter had been a source of disagreement going back to the NATO bombing of Kosovo in April 1999. Russia was defending the role of the UN and multilateral structures, while the US Government was bent on unilateral operations when consensus could not be found in the UN.

At the same time, influential voices in the Russian debate stressed that further cooperation with the USA would benefit Russia's position internationally. Russia's stand against terrorism had opened up prospects for cooperation with the USA in a field where Russia traditionally had experience, knowledge and capacity. The official perception of the threats to Russian security after 11 September had led Russia to view the international situation as radically different. Russia and the USA had common interests against the common enemy—international terrorism—and the dividing lines in the world were no longer East–West. Moreover, they argued that in this specific international situation, when security issues were very much at the forefront, Russia had a good opportunity to improve its position in the world.

The first issue of a new Russian foreign policy journal, *Russia in Global Affairs*, was published in early 2003. Among the members of its editorial board were officials and people in semi-official positions such as Foreign Minister Igor Ivanov, the president's foreign policy adviser Sergei Prikhodko, Sergei Yastrzhembskii from the president's administration, former Prime Minister Yevgenii Primakov and Duma member Alexei Arbatov. *Russia in Global Affairs* stated that Russia had made significant progress in 2002 in its relations with the USA, and much was expected from this relationship in the future. In an excerpt published in the journal and taken from a report by the Foundation for Prospective Studies and Initiatives, which had Primakov, Arbatov and former Prime Minister Yegor Gaidar among the authors, it was stated:

> There are no insurmountable barriers between Russia and the US today for forming a coalition aimed at a future victory over international terrorism. It may also predetermine the progress of relations between them. For Russia, the interest in that coalition is much bigger than for the USA, and the reason is not because Russia is weaker. The format of an antiterrorist coalition provides this country with the opportunity for speeding up its integration into the community of democratic and highly developed nations.[11]

Russia's support for anti-terrorist efforts provides it with an 'important foreign policy resource'. The USA, said the authors, will remain the only superpower and world leader in terms of economic and military might for the foreseeable future regardless of Russia or any group of states. 'All of this means that Russia stands to benefit from maximum use of its opportunities for cooperation with the US.'

Russia was in a better position to handle the new threat of terrorism than Europe was, wrote Sergei Karaganov in the same issue:

> Russia exists in a different geopolitical reality, as it finds itself lodged simultaneously, as it were, on the cusp of two socio-political fractures. On the one hand, it is positioned somewhere between the rich and the poor nations of the world. On the other hand, it is caught between an Islam that is currently losing a cultural–historical battle, and a Western society, which appears to be winning so far. This gives Russia the advantage of being in a better position than most other nations to recognize new challenges and, more importantly, the imperative to cope with them in a decisive manner.[12]

This latter point was especially important, said Karaganov, since 'Russia, by operating on a different geopolitical and historical plane, is better equipped to cope with the latest "recurrence of history", with its instability and bloody conflicts as well as new challenges to international security, the rest of Europe is having a problem accepting such a new reality'.

Putin did not agree with the US Administration on Iraq. He tried to rally the Central Asian CST member states behind a joint position on Iraq, and on 5 November 2002 a meeting of the CST took place at which the issue was debated.[13] Uzbek President Karimov had already declared on 21 October that in principle he was against the use of force over the Iraq issue, but demanded that Iraq's attempt to make WMD be stopped. Peaceful means must be used as far as possible, but if they were not enough the issue should be resolved in the manner proposed by the USA, he said. He also stated that Uzbekistan would allow US troops to use Uzbek territory in the event of an attack on Iraq.[14] Unofficial reports seemed to indicate a more understanding approach by President Rakhmonov towards a possible US invasion of Iraq. Rakhmonov thus seemed prepared to use the moment for his own ends at a point when the Russian leadership seemed not to have made up its mind how to respond to the sharper tone the US Government was using against Iraq.

At a meeting in Moscow on 20 November of the defence ministers of the CST parties, Russian Defence Minister Sergei Ivanov declared that the member states must agree on a united position on Iraq. According to reports in the Russian media, the Kyrgyz, Tajik and Kazakh ministers, who had previously been reported to be prepared to open their airports to US aircraft during operations in Iraq, fell into line with Russia.[15]

On 8 November a compromise resolution was adopted by the UN Security Council ordering Iraq to renounce its WMD or face 'serious consequences'. As UNMOVIC under Hans Blix was sent to Iraq in November to investigate whether Iraq had WMD, discussions in the UN Security Council became more heated. The UK and the USA tried to obtain support for a second, tougher, UN resolution on Iraq which would directly legitimize the use of military force in order to make it comply; France, Germany and Russia joined forces in a temporary alliance in opposition to the idea of the UN using military force against Iraq. For some time these three states managed to delay any US-British action against Iraq. Russian diplomacy seemed successful in the sense that Russia was back in the 'rarefied atmosphere' of the world stage. The peak of its success was reached when Putin in the beginning of 2003 visited Presidents Jacques Chirac of France and Gerhard Schroeder of Germany and a Russian–French–German statement was issued. As the diplomatic tensions intensified, the issue of whether Russia would risk its relations with the USA by using its veto in the UN Security Council became more dramatic.

Russia's siding with France and Germany in opposition to the USA seemed to be in line with the lessons of Alexander Gorchakov: to use the disagreements between the Western powers in order to further Russia's own position. To many Western observers such behaviour seemed reminiscent of the Soviet Union playing on the discord between the USA and Europe. Russian analysts were themselves aware of the risk attached to being perceived as doing this. Thus, as Ivan Safranchuk said: 'Of course the Russian defence minister is trying to use the tough position of Germany and France as well. To use the contradictions between Europe and the USA is normal. It is even desirable. But this has to be done in such a way as not to provoke a negative response'.[16] Safranchuk warned that Russia had to act carefully in order not to make the Europeans wonder whether it was worth it to side with Russia. However, instead of encouraging a split between the USA and its European allies the Russian Government tried to act as a 'bridge' to the USA and overcome the transatlantic disagreement. In Sergei Karaganov's words: 'Russian politicians and intellectuals are beginning to worry about the deepening of the cultural, ideological, and political disparities between the US and Western Europe. Moreover, as unthinkable as this would have been in the recent past, there are calls in Russia today for the country to start working toward overcoming such contradictions, and to assume the role as "an integrator" in the transatlantic relationship'.[17]

Opinion remained divided within the Russian political establishment on whether Russia should give priority to its relations with Europe or with the USA. Europe was divided on the Iraq issue and the EU common foreign and security policy had broken down—at least temporarily. To Russia, 'Europe' was represented by France and Germany. When Putin announced that Russia would veto any proposal brought to the UN Security Council that intended to legitimize the use of military force against Iraq, many observers were surprised and worried that he was overplaying his hand. The Deputy Speaker of the Duma, Vladimir Lukin warned of the consequences if Russia should veto the proposed UN Security Council resolution on Iraq: 'We might get caught in an old trap... When Europe is unhappy with the United States, they push Russia to the forefront while they stand behind, settling their differences with the United States in a quiet way. ... Russia does not need a serious conflict with either Europe or the United States.'[18]

Lukin believed Russia would be better off acting within a framework of cooperation with the USA. He said:

> Playing the role of political–diplomatic integrator of two Atlantic poles, Russia will, in my understanding, attain the most important thing—a relatively stable and calm development for two or three decades. Moreover, this goal can be attained not through refusing to participate in international activities but on the contrary through a more active foreign policy on a really pivotal direction. This way Russia is using the unique chance to become a factor which leads to a balance of interests and views within her kindred (and in this sense 'unipolar') Atlantic space, united in its plurality.[19]

Lukin was joined by the chairman of the Federal Council Foreign Affairs Committee, Mikhail Margelov, who claimed that Russia now had a historic chance to find its niche as an 'international integrator' located in the space between two Atlantic poles and take on the mission of becoming a catalyst and initiator of joint political activities.[20]

By early March 2003, just before the US–British military operation against Iraq was launched, the Central Asian states had taken their positions on the forthcoming war. President Karimov expressed strong support for US military action in Iraq, even playing down the need for a second Security Council resolution on the crisis. He said that Uzbekistan unequivocally supported the US position on resolving the Iraq problem.[21] 'If you ask me about the motives for Uzbekistan's position, I would like to draw a comparison. Just imagine a genie sitting in a vessel with a narrow neck. Once the genie is let out of the bottle, it will not be possible to put it back in.' 'If there are programmes to develop chemical, biological and bacteriological weapons in Iraq, and they are not stopped in time, tomorrow these weapons will fall into the hands of terrorists and religious extremists, and then, believe me, the whole world will tackle this problem, but it will be too late, and the situation will be uncontrollable.' Karimov went on to say that the USA had grounds for a military campaign even if it meant going ahead without a UN resolution. 'We support the position of the United States to resolve the Iraq problem. It is all we want to say. There is no need to clarify this point.' Turkmenistan was initially vague on its position. President Niyazov had said to the Organization for Security and Co-operation in Europe (OSCE) Chairman-in-Office and Dutch Foreign Minister, de Hoop Scheffer, that Turkmenistan supported the US position.[22] To Iranian representatives, however, he said that he supported Iran's critical stance towards the USA. Tajikistan and Kyrgyzstan kept a low profile.[23] When Iraq was discussed at the CST meeting in Moscow on 21 March they joined in the criticism that the USA and UK had sidestepped the UN but refrained from further comments.[24]

When the US-led military invasion of Iraq was launched on 17 March, Putin's reaction, on 20 March, was harsh. His strong words—that military action could 'not be justified', that there was no need for military action, that Iraq did not constitute a threat to its neighbours or other states, and finally that 'military action against Iraq was a great political mistake'[25]—were met with international surprise. It had been expected that Putin would avoid using strong words against the US Government.

As a result of Putin's criticism, Russian–US relations soured. The US Government accused Russia of delivering arms and military equipment to Iraq—anti-tank rockets, night vision devices, and electronic systems for jamming radio signals. According to Russian media on 27 March US Secretary of State Colin Powell warned that if the Russian Government could not stop Russian firms exporting to Iraq the issue would become a 'major problem' in Russian–US relations and Russia would have no chance of participating in the post-war reconstruction of Iraq.

The increased tensions in relations between Russia and the USA during the first two weeks of the military intervention in Iraq set off a wave of anti-Americanism in Russia. Quite apart from such sentiments among the general public, the head of the Spiritual Administration of Russia, Mufti Talgat Tadzhiddin, declared a jihad against the USA.[26] A similar wave went through the political establishment. Both chambers of parliament made statements condemning the US–British military operation. The upper chamber, the Federation Council, which was usually more cautious than the Duma changed the wording of its statement on the Iraq war from US 'military action' in Iraq to 'US aggression' against Iraq, reflecting the sudden flaring up of anti-Americanism. Both the foreign minister and the chairman of the Federal Council Foreign Affairs Committee, Margelov, tried in vain to convince the delegates of the Federation Council that they had to work in close concert with the Russian President and the UN Security Council in this very delicate international situation.[27]

The Russian Government wanted to avoid too far-reaching damage to relations with the USA. Although Putin had criticized the US–British invasion of Iraq, he tried to maintain the previously good relations with the USA. In early April, therefore, he made clear 'that for political and economic considerations Russia is not interested in a US defeat'. This was perceived as a signal to the world and to the US Government in particular.[28] The International Institute for Strategic Studies concluded its analysis of Russian policy during the Iraq war:

> 'For Russia the price of a serious break in bilateral relations with the US was too high to pay in terms of both integration and longterm security. Therefore, unlike France and Germany, which severed high-level contacts with Bush and senior administration officials, Moscow continued to conduct a careful diplomacy and kept many channels of communication open to Washington and London.'[29]

Putin played the 'European card' with France and Germany in relation to the USA, and according to some commentators he even overplayed it. Yet, he prevented a rising wave of anti-Americanism in Russia from destroying relations with the USA. On 12 May 2003 Foreign Minister Igor Ivanov declared that Russian–US relations could be restored to the level they were at before the Iraqi crisis 'since the dialogue never stopped even when the Iraqi crisis reached its climax'.[30]

The diplomatic game around Iraq had demonstrated that the Russian Government remained strongly US-centric. Only the USA could help Russia to achieve economic growth and national security and give it recognition as a major actor in international politics. In the end this was what determined Putin's policy on the Iraq issue. The conflict over Iraq also reflected the fact that Russia under Putin had found a new identity as a great power, aware of its limitations but at the same time determined to play an international role. Moreover—and most important to the Central Asian countries—Russia had accepted their somewhat divergent views on Iraq.

Explaining Russia's Policy on Iraq

Russia's response to the increasingly heated debate over how to handle Saddam Hussein and the issue of Iraq's access to weapons of mass destruction demonstrated that Putin wanted to maintain good relations with the West but also that his policy was US-centric, which was an outcome of his 2001 policy. The conflict over Iraq was a decisive event in 2003, demonstrating not only the USA's political and military superiority as the strongest power in the world but also the new and proactive US foreign and security policy after 11 September 2001.

Applying the four alternative theoretical explanations to the Iraq conflict in March–April 2003 suggests that Russia's role in the international system remained very weak. The USA was intensifying its security cooperation with the states in Central Asia. After the terrorist attacks in 2001 US foreign policy had become highly activist and oriented towards changing the status quo in Western Asia and the Middle East. The US military build up around Iraq in preparation for its invasion changed the balance in favour of the USA in the whole region of Western and Central Asia. Uzbekistan explicitly supported the US-led invasion of Iraq; Kyrgyzstan, Kazakhstan and Tajikistan did not declare support but neither did they directly condemn the USA. Central Asian leaders did not follow up on Putin's harsh words prior to the fall of Baghdad

Official Russian behaviour during the Iraq war proved that Putin was maintaining his previous priority of maintaining good relations with the West in general, and the USA in particular, as well as his long-term ambition to restore Russia to a position of influence in world politics. A low Russian profile on US policy in Iraq raised the possibility that Russia would be able to exploit the common US–Russian interest in fighting international terrorism and give Russia—at least temporarily and in the specific issue area of anti-terrorism—the status of a great power. Moreover, a low profile on US policy in Iraq would give Russia access to the US oil market while also guaranteeing US support for Russian membership of international organizations and a greater US understanding of Russia's problems in Chechnya. Thus, the government acted in line with its strategic vision in trying to make the best of the situation.

Different institutions and interests tried to influence Putin's position on the Iraq crisis. Putin did follow a 'double track' up to the time that Baghdad fell, trying to satisfy domestic critics of his foreign policy by siding with France and Germany.[31] The Russian state had given large credits to Iraq, and Russian oil companies had acquired concessions on oilfields in Iraq and were selling part of Iraq's oil under the UN oil-for-food programme. There was therefore a direct interest in not abandoning Saddam Hussein. As the fall of Baghdad approached, however, it was the Russian oil companies oriented towards the West, and towards the US market in particular, that had a definite influence over Russian Government policy. These Russian companies played an important role behind the scenes in preserving cooperation with the USA during the operation in Iraq.

Finally, it may be argued that Russia's support for the norms and values of the United Nations system has increased over the years and did play a role in the Iraq conflict. Russia defends the traditional values of the UN system such as state sovereignty and the supreme authority of the UN Security Council. Russia called for UN involvement during the Iraq crisis and was an uncompromising supporter of the Security Council, while the USA selectively brushed the Security Council aside when it expected a veto. On issues of multilateralism and the role of the UN the Russian Government and the Bush Administration are far apart. Yet on the Iraq issue Russia behaved as a member of a transatlantic community where disagreement runs high but still takes place within 'a family of states'.

All four perspectives contribute to explain Russia's reaction in 2003. Yet Russia's weak position in the international system seems to have been the major precondition for Russian behaviour.

Central Asian Security: A New Situation

The US-led anti-terrorist campaign in Afghanistan and the fall of the Taliban regime improved the general security situation for the Central Asian states. The reduction of the external security threat, the attention now being paid to the region by the international community and the new US—Russian cooperation—all contributed to the improved security situation.

Althoug, Afghanistan was not brought to peace, the negative influence on Central Asia was reduced as a result of (a) a stabilization process in Afghanistan through the engagement of the International Security Assistance Force (ISAF) according to UN Security Council Resolution of December 2001); and (b) a more effective protection of the Central Asian states through better border control and, as in the case of Tajikistan, improved government control of its territory.

The new situation in Afghanistan brought favourable prospects to Central Asian states through their participation in the reconstruction of Afghanistan. Many international organizations (such as the UN and the OSCE) viewed the Central Asian states as crucial to the stabilization of Afghanistan. Afghanistan's Central Asian neighbours saw potential benefits arising from developing economic cooperation with Afghanistan. Projects for energy cooperation in oil, gas, water, and above all electricity were drawn up along with projects for developing the transport infrastructure.[32] The Central Asian states had already demonstrated their importance by virtue of their geographical location for the delivery of international humanitarian and reconstruction assistance to Afghanistan.

The situation in Afghanistan remained unstable, however, in spite of the peace process supported by the international community. Attacks on international troops intensified during 2003, and small groups of Taliban and al-Qaeda fighters were regrouping. With the warlords strengthening their hold on different regions, ethnic and clan rivalry seemed to be intensifying once again. Although the government of President Hamid Karzai included representatives of different ethnic groups, the dominance of Tajiks increased Pushtun discontent. The disarmament and demobilization process prescribed in the 2001 Bonn Agreement, due to commence in July 2003, was delayed by staunch resistance from the warlords.[33] Although the Constitution was adopted in January 2004, the elections planned for 2004 were postponed. Afghanistan maintained its position as a hub for the production of drugs and their export across Central Asia. The export of opium increased after the fall of the Taliban compared to its level in the final year of the regime. The proliferation of small arms and light weapons remained a major problem in Afghanistan and increased the flow of weapons into Central Asia.

On 22 December 2002 Afghanistan's closest neighbours signed the Kabul Declaration of Good Neighbourly Relations in which they pledged not to interfere in the internal affairs of Afghanistan. However, the declaration did not prevent these states from continuing their support for different factions on the Afghan scene.[34] Russia continued to support the ethnic-Tajik Afghan Defence Minister, Mohammed Fahim, and in September 2002 promised to provide military equipment to the Afghan Army.

As a result of the fall of the Taliban regime in Afghanistan the dynamics of Central Asia changed, in particular with regard to Uzbekistan and Tajikistan. Tensions between the two were reduced after 11 September 2001. Border delimitation talks were restarted and border crossing checkpoints reopened. The situation improved even though Uzbekistan's fear of Islamist insurgents remained strong and continued to affect relations with its neighbours. Relations between Uzbekistan and Tajikistan are a long way from what could be described as 'normal' (Uzbekistan has mined the border), and Uzbek security forces are still regularly accused of intervening in neighbouring countries to target ethnic Uzbeks believed to be in opposition to the Karimov regime.[35]

Tajikistan, viewed as the weakest link in the chain of Central Asian states, gained the most by the post-September 2001 situation. The disappearance of Islamic Movement of Uzbekistan (IMU) fighters, the simultaneous elimination of several warlords who had challenged and threatened the Rakhmonov regime (Khudoberdiev, Sanginov and others) and the extensive international attention now being paid to Tajikistan helped to strengthen government control over Tajik territory and strengthen the position of the president. With international support for the implementation of the peace agreement that ended the civil war, Tajikistan in many ways had a better psychological platform from which reforms could take off than other Central Asian states. With a legal Islamic opposition party (the Tajik Islamic Revival Party) and Tajik media enjoying comparatively more freedom of speech, Tajikistan was a stark contrast to Uzbekistan. Tajikistan, in common with the other Central Asian states, faced the challenge of Islamist radicalism from within the country, but the general security situation improved and it no longer functioned as a transit area for Islamist insurgents from Afghanistan.

Under a new UN mandate for the reconstruction of Afghanistan, NATO took over responsibility for the international peacekeeping force in Afghanistan in September 2003. On 13 October 2003 the UN Security Council decided to expand the remit of the 5500-strong ISAF beyond Kabul. The international community's increased willingness to take on responsibilities in Afghanistan, and to handle the situation in a Central Asian context, was demonstrated when in April 2003 the OSCE granted Afghanistan the status of a 'Cooperation Partner'. NATO's willingness to take on responsibility for security in Central Asia was demonstrated when, in September 2003, an agreement was reached on the creation of a NATO–OSCE centre in Dushanbe for the training of personnel from the border services and law enforcement agencies of the Central Asian countries to counter the illegal arms trade and illegal immigration.[36]

Since 2001 the geopolitical situation in Central Asia is characterized by five overlapping security arrangements, in the making or, in other words, overlapping layers of bilateral and multilateral agreements.[37] The first is the Russian-led security arrangement CSTO based on the 1992 Collective Security Treaty in which Tajikistan, Kyrgyzstan and Kazakhstan are members. The second is the US/NATO-led arrangement based on NATO, the PFP, and NATO's Euro-Atlantic Partnership and Cooperation Council (EAPC), in which all the Central Asian states participate. The third is cooperation based on the UN and the OSCE, of which all the Central Asian states are members. The fourth is regional cooperation based on the SCO including the two major powers of Russia and China, of which all the Central Asian states except Turkmenistan are members. The fifth is the regional cooperation of the Central Asian states based on the Central Asian Cooperation Organization (CACO) (also not including Turkmenistan).

Although regional security was added to the agenda of the CACO, and the heads of state in summer 2003 recognized the common tasks of fighting terrorism, religious extremism and drug trafficking, the organization has little prospect of developing as a security organization. Caution and mutual suspicion between the member states are effective barriers to cooperation.[38] The SCO, meanwhile, was developing more in the direction of regional economic and energy cooperation, in spite of its efforts to develop anti-terrorist structures. The Russian-led arrangement remains the most developed, while the arrangement led by the USA and NATO represents a strong new trend.

Present security arrangements in the making partly overlap. Uzbekistan which is a crucial country for any security arrangement, is the most willing partner for the USA and NATO in the region, although it is also active in the SCO, and hosts the SCO Anti-Terrorism Centre since early 2004. Still, closer bilateral cooperation between major external powers and individual Central Asian states, primarily Uzbekistan, could increase fear and suspicion among neighbouring states. Such major power involvement has the potential to cause tension. The presence of Russian-led and US/NATO-led arrangements may seem anomalous and a potential source of great power rivarly and instability. So far, this situation has not been destabilizing.

Prospects for Russian Policy in Central Asia

Russian Policy towards the Central Asian States

From mid-2002 Russian policy towards the Central Asian states was reactivated in spite of the growing US/Western engagement. Although the previous strong emphasis on security was maintained, a shift towards economic cooperation was simultaneously discernible, primarily in the energy sector aimed at the restoration of previously common grid and pipeline systems. The most striking feature was that Russia's previous interest in energy resources expanded from Turkmenistan to the much smaller gas resources of Uzbekistan, Kyrgyzstan and Tajikistan, and to the hydro-energy resources of the latter two. A more active Russian policy should not be mistaken for increased influence.

How successful was Putin's policy? Even if the CSTO and the Eurasian Economic Community (EEC) seem to consolidate since 2002, they were not rigorous. The CST was reorganized into the CSTO in 2002, a rapid reaction force was set up the same year, a Russian military base (formally under CSTO), became operational in 2003, and a CSTO Joint Staff was created in January 2004. The CIS set up its Anti-Terrorism Centre in Moscow with a subdivision in Bishkek. The EEC continued to negotiate on a free trade-zone. Nonetheless these organizations could not turn the trend of Russia losing influence.

These CSTO structures did not exist in the immediate post-11 September period, and they played no direct role in anti-terrorist activities in the region in the following two years. Many commentators therefore question the value of the CSTO and consider it to be no more effective than other Russian-led multilateral organizations on former Soviet territory. Nevertheless, it is gradually building up its institutions, and therefore may play a role in the future. With the CSTO Russia gets a forum for its efforts to coordinate policy on UN-related issues. With the agreements on security and energy cooperation during 2002–2003 Russia improved bilateral cooperation with both Kyrgyzstan and Turkmenistan.

Russia's interest in the energy sector beyond Turkmenistan's gas sector was a new element of its policy in Central Asia. Russia intensified its efforts to make a long-term, 25-year, gas deal with Turkmenistan, which was finally signed in April 2003; Russian energy companies (primarily Gazprom) expanded into Uzbekistan, Tajikistan and Kyrgyzstan. Gazprom signed agreements for the exploitation of gas resources, running pipelines and export. In March 2002 Russia initiated a gas alliance between Russia, Kazakhstan, Turkmenistan and Uzbekistan to export gas to Europe. Agreements were signed for Russian companies to increase the capacity of the pipeline infrastructure connecting Turkmenistan and Uzbekistan with Kazakhstan and Russia. The Russian electricity monopoly (UES) took on the task of reconstructing hydro-energy stations in Tajikistan and Kyrgyzstan, although the question of financing was not resolved. The UES also took over responsibility for the Central Asian electricity grid.

Thus, there was a more active Russian interest in developing the Russian presence in Central Asia and a larger emphasis on economic cooperation than previously had been the case. Putin in his speeches emphasized the role of companies in Russian foreign policy in general and a close link between Russian foreign policy and the interests of Russian business (not only energy companies). His speech to the Russian Parliament in April 2002 about economic competition as a new characteristic of the contemporary world indicated his new emphasis on economic relations in general but also in Central Asia. Yet, trade between Russia and Uzbekistan, Kyrgyzstan, Tajikistan and Turkmenistan has not recovered from it slump in the early 1990s. Even if issues of trade and capital investment were given more attention at the meetings of the EEC as well as at the meetings of bilateral intergovernmental economic commissions after 2001, there has been little progress in this regard. Russian interest in economic projects in Central Asia remained mainly geo-strategic.

The new Russian emphasis on economic cooperation is an important step towards the economization of relations with Central Asia. So far, however, economic or commercial interests do not constitute the driving force behind Russia's new engagement in the energy sector. The companies and the government think strategically and share the same interest in securing a hold in the area for the future. Dmitrii Trenin wrote in spring 2003:

> Over the last decade, both security and economic considerations have driven Russia's policy toward Central Asia. While the former essentially puts Russia on the defensive, the latter presents it with new opportunities. Russia needed to construct working relationships with the ruling elites in the Central Asian states to protect its national security and to promote its material interests. By and large it has succeeded.[39]

Trenin's words were wishful thinking and events have not transpired in the way he hoped. A restructuring of Central Asian policy with a stronger focus on economic issues has only just started. So far Russia's interest in economic issues is way below the expectations of its allies in Central Asia, as President Rakhmonov of Tajikistan, for example, has repeatedly made clear.

By relating Russia's post-11 September policy to the major problem of the Central Asian region, defined by Moscow in terms of international terrorism, the Russian anti-terrorist project is limited to cooperation between the military, security, intelligence and law-enforcement agencies. Viewed against the real problems of the region—such as underdevelopment and severe socio-economic conditions which provide breeding ground for different kinds of political radicalism—the focus on international terrorism has obvious weaknesses. There seems to be a crisis situation in the making in Central Asia in the sense that domestic protest is building up in response to the many domestic and regional problems while at the same time a generational transfer of power is approaching in these states. All these states are to different extents authoritarian and corrupt and the authorities are afraid of allowing discontent to be articulated through legal opposition in the political system.

Three dimensions of protest—religious–political, secular–political, and ethno-national—represent possible trajectories for the future. Most analysts observe the revival of Islamic values in these countries. This is an entirely normal phenomenon especially given the political–ideational vacuum in these societies, but the growth of radical Islamism could well become the most dangerous threat to a democratic course of development. The violent movements of radical Islamism have—at least temporarily—left the scene. Yet non-violent but confrontational radical movements such as Hizb-ut-Tahrir are growing in number and support, and this is a reminder that the domestic situation is rife with problems. If a solution to the burning social and economic problems of the Central Asian countries is not found, representatives of the political radical underground will be ready to do their best to channel popular discontent. Continued instability in Afghanistan and the return of the Taliban as a strong force in society, together with other extreme political–religious forces in that country, suggest a scenario for the radicalization of Central Asia. When the authorities block the formation of open political opposition, that opposition uses other channels of expression. Political repression and lack of reform constitute sources of tension and conflict in these societies.

Secular–political protest is represented by demands for democratic reforms. The authorities in both Turkmenistan and Uzbekistan have resorted to harsh repression to silence the opposition. The numerous arrests in Turkmenistan in early 2003 demonstrated President Niyazov's nervousness as well as the fragility of the system. The outbreak of unrest in Kyrgyzstan in 2002 reflected how easily a single issue can set off a chain of events with roots in general popular discontent. In Tajikistan authoritarian traits are being strengthened. The ethno-national dimension of protest has played only a minor role so far. Yet this dimension should not be underestimated since it is directly linked to the relations between the states of the region. Tensions between states easily spill over into domestic tensions in relation to ethnic diaspora groups, and vice versa. In all four states of Central Asia the nation- and state-building process is ongoing, and national themes and topics are becoming more relevant. The unresolved issues of water, borders, and the use and cultivation of land could take on a nationalistic tone if interstate negotiations stall, with repercussions for the diaspora groups in these countries.

The general trend since the mid-1990s is for a decline in the Russian presence and its influence in Central Asia. If Russia is to play a role in the future of the Central Asian countries, it must therefore make itself more relevant to these countries in contributing to social and economic development and to the democratization of their societies. Although Russian policy in the region was activated after September 2001 it is not ready to take on this broader engagement.

Russia can no longer rely on its historical role in Central Asia as the centre of an empire to which border states naturally look. Nevertheless, Russia continues to attract hundreds of thousands of Central Asian migrant workers. Yet the long-term trend of Russia losing influence on the ground in Central Asia was demonstrated when the Tajik Government, Russia's closest ally in the region, in late 2001 so clearly showed its interest in expanding relations with the USA and the NATO countries. For Tajikistan, expectations of economic cooperation and foreign investment were the determining factors when its government opened up the country by expanding relations with the USA. Russia's Central Asian allies no longer expect Russia to provide economic assistance and investment.

Russia's Attitude towards US Engagement in Central Asia

The Russian Government maintained a low profile with regard to the US engagement in Central Asia although individual officials from time to time pointed out that the US military presence was intended to last only as long as operations in Afghanistan. The Russian Government gradually accommodated itself to the changes in the political landscape. When NATO in August 2003 was given the responsibility for the UN-led international assistance force in Afghanistan, Russia welcomed this development. Defence Minister Sergei Ivanov declared that Russia was prepared to cooperate with NATO by providing intelligence, back-up services, and search and rescue operations in the north of Afghanistan.[40] The same month Nikolai Bordyuzha, the Secretary-General of the CSTO, said that he would be happy if cooperation developed between NATO and the CSTO since they were facing similar tasks in fighting terrorism and drug trafficking.[41] Nonetheless,

Russia was concerned about the growing US/NATO engagement and the way Central Asian states sought ways to develop relations with the West. First Deputy Prime Minister Vyacheslav Trubnikov called for greater transparency in the US military's role in Central Asia and in the Western cooperation with Central Asian states in the security field.[42]

One concern for Russia was to find a formula or a framework that would guarantee it a role in Central Asia even as US/Western engagement increased. Russia had raised the issue of its role in the anti-terrorist struggle on former Soviet territory at the 2003 Evian G8 Summit. Russia wanted recognition of its leading role in this regard and also to have the CSTO recognized as the legitimate organization for such cooperation in Central Asia.

During his visit to the USA in September 2003 Putin called for a 'strategic alliance' with the USA on fighting terrorism. He also stressed Russia's readiness to continue cooperating with the USA to resolve the problems of Central Asia. 'We intend to continue interacting with the United States to resolve the problems of the region', he said.[43] Presidents Putin and Bush at their press conference on 27 September used the term 'allies in fighting terrorism'.[44] However, Russia wanted to avoid falling into the trap of being a junior partner to the USA in Central Asia.

The position paper presented to Putin the day before he left for the USA and which he was said to have incorporated in his talks with President Bush was therefore especially significant.[45] The 'Doctrine for Forming a Strategic Alliance between Russia and the USA' was drafted by, among others, the adviser to the deputy head of the Presidential Administration with responsibility for foreign affairs. The paper, which vigorously argued in favour of close partnership with the USA, suggested a kind of division of labour between the two states on former Soviet territory in the sense that Russia would recognize US interests in the region on condition that Russia became the 'operator' of these interests. The paper suggested that 'The USA ought to realize and acknowledge a role for Russia as the major partner of Washington on post-Soviet territory'.[46] It was also said that 'Russia aims not to squeeze out the USA from post-Soviet states but to further Russian interests in the region while leaning on the support from and cooperation with the USA. Mutual support on each other's capacity is a guarantee for success.' Suggesting that Russia be recognized as the leader and integrator on post-Soviet territory in order to regulate the US presence, the paper was a reminiscent of Yeltsin's 1993 request to the UN to recognize Russia as responsible for upholding peace and security on former Soviet territory.[47]

Although Russia seemed to have come to terms with NATO and even accepted NATO taking on responsibility in Afghanistan, Defence Minister Ivanov directed heavy criticism against NATO in the draft document on a new Russian military doctrine presented at a meeting, on 2 October, between Putin, the military leadership, members of the Federation Council and the Duma.[48] For Putin it was important to bridge the diverging opinions and appease the critical voices among the military. This became especially important as the parliamentary and presidential elections came closer.

The draft document of the new Russian military doctrine claimed rights for Russia similar to those the USA had assumed for itself. Ivanov did not rule out the pre-emptive use of force in any region of the world if Russia's interests or its commitments to its allies so dictated. Russia is facing new challenges, he said, having in mind primarily former Soviet territory, mentioning interference in Russia's internal affairs by foreign countries or organizations supported by them, and instability in countries bordering Russia engendered by the weakness of their own governments or by others.[49] He singled out Central Asia as a 'potentially dangerous area'—unstable and in the near neighbourhood of Afghanistan. 'If internal instability of either inter-ethnic or political nature in the CIS occurred or if some political regime attempted to phase out democratic reforms', Ivanov said, Russia could be prompted to make significant changes to the deployment of its military units or other security agencies. His words indicated a possible future scenario in which the domestic situation in a Central Asian country would be regarded by Russia as a cause for intervention in support of stability and democracy or in defence of the Russian minority in the country concerned. Turkmenistan was not referred to directly, but the worst-case scenario outlined seemed to fit a situation in which the rights of the Russian minority in that country were seriously violated and Russia intervenes.

The draft doctrine and Ivanov's statements reflected the widespread discontent among the military with the situation in Central Asia. This discontent was also in the background when Ivanov in late September gave a new interpretation of the two military bases in Kyrgyzstan. He stated that 'The two bases perform completely different tasks', and he explained that while the US base was set up to support operations on Afghan territory, the Kant base 'acts in the interests of our allies from the Collective Security Treaty Organization and provides support for army units and stability and security for the countries in the region'.[50] Thus, he implicitly said that Manas is a temporary base while Kant is a permanent one. Ivanov expressed the general dissatisfaction within the military but he spread uncertainty in CIS countries about the intentions of the Russian leadership. He had no constructive policy to offer.

A more specific plan of action was suggested by Anatolii Chubais, one of the leaders of the Union of Rightist Forces political party, who attracted a great deal of attention with his article 'The mission of Russia in the 21st century', published on 1 October 2003.[51] Chubais argued that Russia's mission is to create a 'liberal empire' consisting of Russia and the states on former Soviet territory, and claimed that Russia, with the strongest economy and the highest standard of living of all the former Soviet republics, has to 'develop, strengthen and enforce its leading positions in this part of the world for the next 50 years'. Chubais did not want to restore the former Soviet Union. Instead, he argued that Russia should be guided by the liberal values of democracy, a market economy and economic cooperation between these states. His recommendations for the Russian state and the mechanisms and channels it can use to influence its neighbours include: (a) encouraging the development of Russian culture and the cultures of the different nations within Russia, and defending Russians and Russian-speaking citizens of neighbouring countries; (b) promoting the expansion of Russian business into neighbouring countries with regard to trade as well as the acquisition and development of assets; and (c) supporting freedom, democracy and the rights of the citizens of neighbouring countries. This programme, according to Chubais, is valid for the 'near as well as the distant abroad'.

Chubais wrote this article as part of the campaign for the forthcoming Duma election. In choosing the phrase 'a liberal empire', which could only too easily be misused in politics, he was giving in to populism. Chubais was articulating both the existing trend in the Russian public debate of dissatisfaction with the present international situation, and the developing trend of an economization of Russian foreign policy. His recommendations included a stronger emphasis on economic means while at the same time seeming to provide a framework of democratic values to legitimize an active Russian involvement in Central Asian domestic affairs.

In sum, the official Russian approach to the US engagement in Central Asia had undergone radical change and the Russian Government was accommodating to the fact of the US engagement in the region. At the same time there was a strong undercurrent of criticism of Putin's foreign policy and the US military presence in Central Asia. The search for a kind of regulation of the US presence, which would guarantee Russia a future role, reflected this mood.

Prospects for the Further Revision of Russian Foreign Policy

In the Duma elections of December 2003 the voters awarded Putin's party, United Russia, a sweeping victory. At the same time populist-nationalist views were drastically strenghened by an increased number of seats for the Liberal Democratic Party and the newcomer, the Rodina Party under Dimitrii Rogozin and Sergei Glaziev. These parties loudly argued in favour of a tougher Russian foreign policy. The liberal pro-Western parties of the Union of Rightist Forces (SPS) and Yabloko did not pass the five per cent threshold for parties in parliament and received no representation in the Duma. The Duma does not have a direct influence over foreign policy making. With its present composition of Putin's supporters, and all chairmen of the Duma committees appointed by United Russia, Putin does not have to fear serious criticism. Still it can not be excluded that the general tone adopted in foreign policy debate would be slightly harder compared with the previous Duma.

Most western commentators pointed to the increasing authoritarian tendencies in Russian domestic politics. The arrest of one of Putin's harshest critics, the oligarch Mikhail Khodorkovskii, in October 2003 and the reductions in media freedom during the election campaigns raised Western concern. When two weeks before the presidential election of 14 March 2004 Putin replaced Prime Minister Kasyanov with Mikhail Fradkov, there was astonishment but also relief in the West. The composition of the new government signalled a continuation of previous domestic and foreign policy priorities. Economic reform and close cooperation with the West seemed guaranteed by the liberal economists Alexei Kudrin, German Gref, and Viktor Khristenko, and the new foreign minister Sergei Lavrov. The choice of Lavrov, Russian Ambassador to the UN since 1994 and a professional diplomat, also seemed to secure Putin's control of the foreign ministry.

Thus, already before his first term of office had come to an end Putin had set the stage for his second term, and he seemed at the peak of his power. It could not be excluded that during the second term his support party might break down into several factions in the Duma. Yet, he had control of the government and the presidential administration. By replacing the two most influential members of the 'Family', Prime Minister Kasyanov and before him the head of the presidential administration, Alexei Voloshin (November 2003), Putin strengthened his hold of power. Re-elected on 14 March 2004 Putin had even better conditions than previously to tune policy according to his own desire.

Putin had used the policy window opened by the 11 September events to improve relations with the USA. By exchanging his consent to a US military presence in Central Asia for improved relations with the West, he had created a direct linkage between Russian policy towards Central Asia and that towards Europe or the West. Central Asia became part of Russia's policy towards the West, and first and foremost the USA. In the long-term perspective his consent was part of the process of Russia adapting to the new conditions in the post-Soviet world.

Central Asia therefore came to play an extremely important role in the shaping of Russian foreign policy. With Russia's historical bonds with Central Asia and interest in maintaining a presence in the region, accompanied by its desire to improve relations with the West, Russian Government had to adjust its policy. Moreover, 11 September 2001 made Russian policy extremely US-centric, and, as long as it remains so, and the US Administration upholds its engagement in Central Asia, Russia will accept the US presence there. This situation of 'forced acceptance' is a crucial component in the revision of Russian foreign policy in the defined post-Soviet era. The US engagement in Central Asia thus triggered a further revision of overall Russian foreign policy since it forced the Russian Government to rethink its policy in the region.

The priority given to good relations with the USA and the West should not be viewed in isolation from Russia's efforts to promote its state interests. The promotion of Russia's state interests is the motor behind the foreign policy revision. Part of this logic is that it is better to maintain a low profile vis-à-vis US policy if Moscow disagrees with the US Administration but is unable to counter its policy. This insight contributed to an improvement in relations with the West in general. Although highly critical of US policy during the Iraq crisis and of the US–British invasion of Iraq in March–April 2003, Putin, at the end of the day, declared that a US defeat in Iraq would not be in the interest of Russia. Diverging Russian and US views on the role of the UN and its Security Council for international conflict resolution did not prevent the Russian Government from continuing its cooperation with the USA, as demonstrated by Defence Minister Ivanov's preparedness to cooperate with NATO.[52] In July 2003 Russian Deputy Foreign Minister Alexander Losyukov said that neither Russia nor China was happy about the USA's military presence in Central Asia, but Russia thought it was justified.[53] When the US Government declared that it was to include the UN in the post-war reconstruction of Iraq and the setting up of an international force, Defence

Minister Ivanov responded that Russia might contribute troops.

Tension and competition remained in relations between Russia and the USA, and were reflected in Central Asia. While both Russia and the USA define terrorism as a major threat in Central Asia, institutionalized cooperation was not initiated between them. Dmitrii Trenin argued in early 2003 that Central Asia constitutes 'a convincing case' for security cooperation.[54] His recommendations for Russian–US security cooperation in Central Asia are highly relevant, but the fact that such cooperation has not materialized indicates the element of strategic competition between them.

There are serious disagreements on several international issues between the Russian and US Governments, in spite of Putin's US orientation after 2001. A major issue of disagreement remains their different views on multilateralism and the role of the UN. While the USA is in general in favour of multilateralism, after September 2001 it took upon itself the right to act unilaterally. The trend of unilateralism is part of a USA's traditional view of its rights and duties, which had strengthened during the 1990s and was clearly reflected in the US National Security Document of September 2002.[55] US foreign and security policy under President Bush exploded in an activist approach, which excluded waiting for a consensus to take shape in the UN Security Council. The supreme authority of the UN Security Council on issues of war, peace and the use of force in international relations is an important issue where Russia, the Central Asian states and many European states share similar critical views of US policy. The issue is at the core of the future of the UN system and the handling of threats to security, conflicts and crises. Russia, which shares its opinions on the UN and the handling of international crises with France and Germany, will continue to criticize US policy. US policy towards what it nowadays called 'the wider Middle East' may open a Pandoras's box of disagreements on the handling of conflicts.

Important contradictions remain in Putin's foreign policy. One important aspect is the self-image of Russia, which reflects a strong desire to be internationally recognized as a great power and an equal of the USA. Putin has not accepted the idea of Russia as an 'ordinary and normal European state'. On the contrary, after September 2001 Russia tried to base a great power status upon cooperation with the USA in fighting international terrorism. Both states shared the conviction that terrorism is the major threat to their own societies as well as to the world and interpret the problem in the narrow sense, as a matter first and foremost for the military and security services. The issue of terrorism created the illusion of great power status for Russia which hampers the further revision of Russian foreign policy.

Russian–US relations stagnated in 2003. The position paper of September 2003 on a strategic Russian–US alliance, mentioned above, reflected Russia's sense of insecurity in its relations with the USA and its concern with the increasing US influence on former Soviet territory. The authors of the paper suggested that the new US–Russian partnership be confirmed in a joint Russian–US document, and that Russia's international relations with the USA should be regulated on post-Soviet territory, in particular, but also globally. Russia's status would be defined as an 'Essential Non-NATO Ally' of the USA, which would allow for access to US intelligence information, US military technology and foreign policy consultations.[56] Even if the document might best be understood in the context of the approaching parliamentary elections, it hit on a fundamental issue—the growing unease within the Russian political establishment about the degradation of Russia's status in the world and on former Soviet territory. It also argued that Russia would carry out this mission in pursuit of a common Russian–US agenda of fighting terrorism and strengthening democracy.

In sum, the document reflected Russia's difficulty in coming to terms with its new role and reduced influence in the world, and the contradictory views in Russian foreign policy debate. There is a belief in the world of globalization into which Russia entered in order to develop, but also a parallel belief in traditional thinking in terms of spheres of influence. The existence of competing political interests within the political establishment, which Putin has to bridge, contributes, at times, to a certain lack of political consistency.

At present there are no signs that Russia's pro-Western orientation will be abandoned. Putin remains in control of policy making mechanisms, although he is bound to listen to the voices of strong interest groups. These voices come from the large energy companies with their primary interests in the Western market. Putin's offensive against oil oligarch Mikhail Khodorkovskii, who was arrested in the summer of 2003, changes nothing in this regard. There are no serious alternatives to Putin or to his foreign policy agenda, in spite of the criticism of his policy. In theory it is possible that the Russian Government could radically change its foreign policy, build up its military capacity and turn against the West and the USA, but this could happen only at a very high political and economic costs.

The different views on international issues between the Russian Government and the US Administration will lead to ups and downs in the relations between the two countries, but these can be expected to remain within the spectrum of what good relations allow, as was demonstrated during the Russian–US disagreement over Iraq. The present international system and Russia's weak position in it are major factors determining future Russian policy.

If the USA was to withdraw its troops from Western and Central Asia and turn inward, the international situation would change. Although intended to bring peace and democracy into Iraq US policy in Iraq could result in chaos, disorder, and an escalation of terrorist acts and violence, with possible implications for development in the Islamic world, including Central Asia. Growing chaos in what the West now calls 'the wider Middle East' may call the US military engagement in Central Asia into question. In early 2003 some analysts claimed that because the war against the Taliban was winding down the USA and its NATO allies have little further interest in deepening their involvement in Uzbekistan, Kyrgyzstan, Tajikistan, Turkmenistan.[57] Nevertheless, in early autumn 2003 the USA extended the agreement on the use of the Manas International Airbase for a further three years. Half a year later it could not be excluded that deep US involment in fighting in Iraq could result in a reduction of the US military presence in Central Asia. Although it is impossible to predict US policy, by 2004 it seems most likely that the Western engagement will remain in Central Asia. The same holds true for international organizations, including the UN, the OSCE, NATO, the EU, the PFP, the International Monetary Fund (IMF), the World Bank, the Asian Development Bank, the Islamic Development Bank and a range of NGOs. The USA's direct engagement with troops after 11 September 2001 opened the gate wide for foreign actors in Central Asia. This international presence in Central Asia has come to stay.

The historical memory of the Russian conquest of Central Asia indicates that Russia will remain interested in and concerned about developments in Central Asia. The main factors behind the Russian expansion in the late nineteenth century have been described as political–strategic and domestic (mainly economic). The political–strategic factor can be understood in its security aspect—to defend Russia's borders, which eventually moved to the south–east. The strategic aspect meant first of all the concern that prevailed at the time about British expansion into an area with which Russia had long-term contacts, although not yet control over. This also included a psychological urge for compensation in the sense that Russia wanted to replace the influence it had lost in European politics with expansion into Central Asia. The self-image of Russia at the time was that of a great power, temporarily weak after defeat in the Crimean War but bound to recover its great-power influence. The economic factor did play a role because there were expectations of economic benefits that Russian control of Central Asia would bring and of how economic exchange with the region could strengthen Russia. No strong groups existed in Russian society at the time with direct commercial interests of their own in Central Asia, but the economic argument was frequently used in the Russian debate.

Today, more than a decade after the break up of the Soviet Union, Russia is internationally weak but still regards itself as a great power that is bound to return to international influence. Although the security threats and geopolitical challenges are different from those of the late nineteenth century, Central Asia is considered to be an area of Russian concern. At present Russia is not capable of undertaking a deeper engagement. Nevertheless, it is pursuing a policy of the long-term build up of structures for cooperation with CIS states, in the hope that that this will guarantee it a role and an influence in Central Asia in the future. As in the late nineteenth century, economic interests do not yet constitute the major driving force behind the Russian interest in Central Asia—but they do play a role. Gazprom, Unified Energy Systems, Lukoil and its offshoots constitute the major Russian corporate interests in Central Asia today. The interests of these companies overlap to a great extent with those of the government (in contrast to the situation of the late 1990s when major divergences were demonstrated between Gazprom and the Russian Government on the issue of Turkmen gas). Gradually, expectations are evolving in Russia that a commercial expansion of Russian business into Central Asia would be of great benefit to Russian interests.

The Central Asian region, however, is changing fundamentally. The new international engagement provides a completely different political context. Taking into consideration the fact that the larger part of the territories of the four Central Asian countries were latecomers to the Russian Empire and that they contain populations whose cultural affinities are primarily with their neighbours to the south, they will without doubt try to orient themselves in directions other than that of Russia. The way the Russian language is losing ground among the younger generation in Tajikistan is a sign of this. To the young Tajik generation, English is becoming a language of more interest than Russian. In contrast to the nineteenth century, when Britain had to accept Russian power in Central Asia, Russia today has to accept that Central Asia is becoming a global arena. Therefore, if the Russian Government is determined not to become marginalized by events in Central Asia, it has to rethink its policy in the region. A narrow military–security perspective on Russian–Central Asian relations is far from enough. A restructuring is necessary to make Russian policy more relevant to Central Asian societies.

In revising foreign policy to fit the present international situation, President Putin, like Alexander Gorchakov, seeks to strengthen Russia's future role and influence in the international system. However, the world is changing rapidly, and he may therefore have to further revise Russian foreign policy, make more far-reaching revisions than he originally intended, and thereby adapt to a lower profile and lesser international role than Russia has had historically.[58] Putin has an interest in maintaining good relations with the US Government, although profound disagreements exist. This creates a chance for the USA and the West to contribute to multilateral structures for international cooperation being created between the large powers engaging in Central Asia. The active Western engagement in Central Asia may prove to be the most important factor for stimulating the Russian leadership to adjust foreign policy to the realities of the post-Soviet world and to transform Russian policy into a constructive force in the region in support of peace, stability, and sustainable economic development.

NOTES

Chapter 1

INTRODUCTION

[1] On the definition of Central Asia and the coverage of this book, see chapter 7 below.

[2] There are numerous books and articles on Russian foreign policy during the first years after the break up of the Soviet Union. See, for example, Mark Webber, *The International Politics of Russia and the Successor States* (Manchester and New York: Manchester University Press, 1996); Robert H. Donaldson and Joseph L. Nogee, *The Foreign Policy of Russia: Changing Systems, Enduring Interests* (Armonk and London: M. E. Sharpe, 1998); Leszek Buszynski, *Russian Foreign Policy after the Coldk War* (Westport, Connecticut and London: Praeger, 1996); Peter Shearman (ed), *Russian Foreign Policy Since 1990* (Boulder, San Fransisco, Oxford: Westview Press, 1995); Jeffrey Checkel, 'Structure, institutions, and process: Russia's changing foreign policy', in Adeed Dawisha and Karen Dawisha (eds), *The Making of Foreign Policy in Russia and the New States of Eurasia* (Armonk and London: M. E. Sharpe, 1995). Later studies include for example, Margot Light, 'Post-Soviet Russian foreign policy: the first decade', in Archie Brown (ed.), *Contemporary Russian Politics: A Reader* (Oxford: Oxford University Press, 2001); Dmitri Trenin, 'From pragmatism to strategic choice: is Russia's security policy finally becoming realistic?', Andrew C. Kuchins (ed.), *Russia after the Fall.* (Washington, DC: Carnegie Endowment for International Peace, 2002); Dale R. Herspring and Peter Rutland, 'Putin and Russian Foreign Policy', in Dale R. Herspring (ed.), *Putin's Russia: Past Imperfect, Future Uncertain* (Lanham, Boulder, New York, London: Rowman and Littlefield Publishers, Inc., 2003); in Gabriel Gorodetsky (ed.), *Russia Between East and West: Russian Foreign Policy on the Threshold of the Twenty-First Century* (London, Portland: Frank Cass, 2003); Bobo Lo, *Russian Foreign Policy in the Post-Soviet Era: Reality, Illusion and Mythmaking* (London: Palgrave, 2002); Bobo Lo, *Vladimir Putin and the Evolution of Russian Foreign Policy* (London: Royal Institute of International Affaits and Blackwell, 2003).

[3] See, for example, Amin Saikal and William Maley (eds), *Russia in Search of Its Future* (Cambridge: Cambridge University Press, 1995); Roy Allison and Cristoph Bluth (eds), *Security Dilemmas in Russia and Eurasia* (London: Royal Institute of International Affairs, 1998); Rajan Menon, 'After empire: Russia and the Southern 'Near Abroad'", in Michael Mandelbaum (ed.), *The New Russian Foreign Policy* (New York: Council on Foreign Relations, 1998); Martha Brill Olcott, Anders Åslund and Sherman W. Garnett, *Getting It Wrong: Regional Cooperation and the Commonwealth of Independent States* (Washington, DC: Carnegie Endowment for International Peace, 1999); *Vneshnyaya politika Rossii. 1991–*

2000. Chast I, *Pro et Contra* (Carnegie Endowment for International Peace). Winter/Spring 2001; *Vneshnyaya politika Rossii: 1991–2000*, Chast II, *Pro et Contra* (Carnegie Endowment for International Peace). Autumn 2001; Roy Allison, 'The network of new security policy relations in Eurasia', and Roy Allison, 'Russia and the New States of Eurasia', in Archie Brown (ed.), *Contemporary Russian Politics: A Reader* (Oxford: Oxford University Press, 2001).

[4] See, for example, Mark Khroustalev, *Central Asia in Russia's Foreign Policy*. Occasional Papers of the Centre of International Studies, MGIMO, no. 5 (Moscow, 1994); Irina Zvyagelskaia, *The Russian Policy Debate on Central Asia* (The Royal Institute of International Affairs, London, 1995); Sergei Gretzky, *Russia's Policy Toward Central Asia* (Moscow: Carnegie Moscow Center, 1997); Lena Jonson, *Russia and Central Asia: A New Web of Relations* (London: Royal Institute of International Affairs, 1998); Mehdi Mozaffari (ed.), *Security Politics in the Commonwealth of Independent States: The Southern Belt.* (London: Macmillan Press Ltd, 1999); Rajan Menon, Yuri E. Fedorov and Ghia Nordia (eds), *Russia, the Caucasus and Central Asia: The 21st Century Security Environment* (Armonk and London: EastWest Institute/M. E. Sharpe, 199; Roy Allison and Lena Jonson (eds), *Central Asian Security: The New International Context* (Washington and London: Brookings Institution Press and Royal Institute of International Affairs, 2001); Boris Rumer, *Central Asia: A Gathering Storm?* (New York and London: M. E. Sharpe, 2002).

[5] Lena Jonson, *Russia and Central Asia: A New Web of Relations* (London: Royal Institute of International Affairs, 1998).

[6] Ivan Ilin, *Osnovy borby za natsionalnuyu Rossii* [The fundamentals of the struggle for a national Russia] (1938), quoted by Dmitri Trenin, *The End of Eurasia: Russia on the Border Between Geopolitics and Globalization* (Washington, DC and Moscow: Carnegie Endowment for International Peace, 2002), p. 77.

[7] See, for example, K. J. Holsti, *Why Nations Realign: Foreign Policy Restructuring in the Postwar World* (London: George Allen and Unwin, 1982); and Kjell Goldmann, *Change and Stability in Foreign Policy: The Problems and Possibilities of Détente* (New York, London, Toronto, Sydney and Tokyo: Harvester Wheatsheaf, 1988).

[8] Charles Hermann, 'Changing course: when governments choose to redirect foreign policy', *International Studies Quarterly* 34/1 (1990), pp. 5–6.

[9] Robert Gilpin, *War and Change in World Politics* (Cambridge, London and New York: Cambridge University Press, 1981), p. 187.

[10] According to Gilpin, this often explains the use of the 'turbulent frontier' thesis, for example, by Britain in India. There is a serious risk of further over extension of commitments, however. Gilpin, *War and Change in World Politics*, p. 191.

[11] Gilpin, *War and Change in World Politics*, pp. 193–4.

[12] Gilpin, *War and Change in World Politics*, p. 194.

[13] Mikhail Gorbachev, *Perestroika: New Thinking for Our Country and the World* (New York: Harper and Row Publishers, 1987); Vilho Harle and Jyrki Ivonen (eds), *Gorbachev and Europe* (London: Pinter Publishers, 1990); Lena Jonson, 'Russia and Europe: the emergence of a new Russian foreign policy', in Bo Huldt and Gunilla Herolf (eds), *Towards a New European Security Order: Yearbook 1990–91* (Stockholm: Swedish Institute of International Affairs, 1991).

[14] Dov Lynch, *Russian Peacekeeping Strategies in the CIS: The Cases of Moldova, Georgia and Tajikistan* (London: Royal Institute of International Affairs and Macmillan, 2000); Pavel Baev, *Russia's Policies in the Caucasus* (London: Royal Institute of International Affairs, 1997); Lena Jonson and Clive Archer (eds), *Peacekeeping and the Role of Russia in Eurasia* (Boulder, Colo.: Westview Press, 1996).

[15] This issue is discussed in Lena Jonson, 'In search of a national interest: the foreign policy debate in Russia', *Nationalities Papers* 22/1 (Spring 1994).

[16] Mark Webber, *CIS Integration Trends: Russia and the Former Soviet South* (London: Royal Institute of International Affairs, 1996).

[17] Primakov introduced Gorchakov's policy as a model for contemporary Russian policy in a speech during the celebrations of Gorchakov's 200th anniversary in 1998. Yevgenii Primakov, 'Rossiya v mirovoi politike (k 200-letiyu A. M.Gorchakova)' [Russia in world politics. Lecture at the Gorchakov bicentenary proceedings 28 April 1998], *Diplomaticheskii vestnik* 7 (July 1998), pp. 76–9. A number of conferences and studies celebrating Gorchakov's diplomatic efforts followed, as did the annual Gorchakov lectures by the foreign minister and the annual distribution of the Gorchakov medal.

[18] A. V. Ignatev (ed.), *Istoriya vneshnei politiki Rossii: Vtoraya polovina XIX veka* [History of Russian foreign policy: the second half of the nineteenth century] (Moscow: Mezhdunarodnye otnosheniya, 1997).

[19] Quoted by William C. Fuller, Jr, *Strategy and Power in Russia 1600–1914* (New York and Toronto: The Free Press, 1992), p. 270.

[20] Fuller, *Strategy and Power in Russia 1600–1914*, p. 269.

[21] Flemming Spidsboel-Hansen, 'Past and future meet: Aleksandr Gorchakov and Russian foreign policy', *Europe–Asia Studies*, 54/3 (2002), pp. 377–8.

[22] Barry Buzan, *People, States and Fear*, 2nd edition (New York: Harvester Wheatsheaf, 1991), p. 300.

[23] The author discusses this in Lena Jonson, 'Russia and European security: old wine in new bottles?', in William E. Ferry and Roger Kanet (eds), *Post-Communist States in the World Community* (London: Macmillan, 1998).

[24] http://www.pravitelstvo.gov.ru/data/news_print.html?he_id=15&news_id=53.

[25] Lena Jonson, 'Russian policy in Northern Europe', in Vladimir Baranovsky (ed.), *Russia and Europe: The Emerging Security Agenda* (Oxford: Oxford University Press for the Stockholm International Peace Research Institute, 1997).

[26] Lena Jonson and Clive Archer (eds), *Peacekeeping and the Role of Russia in Eurasia* (Boulder, Colo.: Westview Press, 1996).

[27] Hermann's formulation of problems and goals as an aspect of change is not fully clear and has been interpreted here as problems of concern and their solution rather than the goals of Russian policy.

[28] F. Fischer and J. Forester, *The Argumentative Turn in Policy Analysis and Planning* (London: University College London, 1993), quoted in Johan Eriksson (ed.), *Threat Politics: New Perspectives on Security, Risk and Crisis Management* (Aldershot, Burlington USA, Singapore and Sydney: Ashgate, 2001), p. 8.

[29] Cf. Jonson, *Russia and Central Asia: A New Web of Relations*.

[30] Bobo Lo, *Russian Foreign Policy in the Post-Soviet Era: Reality, Illusion, and Mythmaking* (London: Palgrave, 2002); and Bobo Lo, *Vladimir Putin and the Evolution of Russian Foreign Policy*.

[31] Lo, *Russian Foreign Policy in the Post-Soviet Era*, pp. 52–3.

[32] Lo, *Russian Foreign Policy in the Post-Soviet Era*, p. 158.

[33] See, in particular the works by Ole Waever, e.g., in Barry Buzan, Ole Waever and Jaap de Wilde, *Security: A New Framework for Analysis* (London: Lynn Rienner Publishers, Inc., 1998). Securitization may involve a country breaking the normal rules of the political game 'in the form of secrecy, levying taxes or conscription, placing limitations on otherwise inviolable rights, or focusing society's energy and resources on a specific task' (p. 24).

[34] The theoretical implications for using Waever's concept of securitization has been drastically reduced in this study. Here, it only indicates the process of moving an issue up to top priority while referring to it as the most dangerous security threat.

[35] Cf. Jonson, *Russia and Central Asia: A New Web of Relations*.

[36] The concept of a 'policy window' is useful in this context, and has been used in the academic literature on domestic reform processes, referring to the moment of opportunity that can be used to introduce reforms. R. Kingdon, *Agendas, Alternatives, and Public Policies* (Boston, Mass.: Little, Brown & Co., 1984). See the discussion in Jakob Gustavsson, *The Politics of Foreign Policy Change: Explaining the Swedish Reorientation on EC Membership* (Lund: Lund University Press, 1998).

[37] Holsti gives the following sets of variables for foreign policy change: external factors (military threats, non-military threats, structure of previous relationship); domestic factors (internal threats, economic conditions, political factionalization); and background historical and cultural factors (attitudes to foreigners, colonial experience). As intervening variables Holsti added policy makers' perceptions and calculations, the policy-making process, personality factors and elite attitudes. Holsti, *Why Nations Realign: Foreign Policy Restructuring in the Postwar World*. See also Goldmann, *Change and Stability in Foreign Policy*; Walter Carlsnaes, 'On analysing the dynamics of foreign policy change: a critique and reconceptualization', *Cooperation and Conflict* 28/1 (1993); and Jakob Gustavsson, 'How should we study foreign policy change?', *Cooperation and Conflict* 34/1 (1999).

[38] See Bobo Lo, *Vladimir Putin and the Evolution of Russian Foreign Policy*, pp. 60–1. Emphasis in the original.

[39] Cf. the discussion about the 'international agential power' of the state in John M. Hobson, *The State and International Relations* (Cambridge: Cambridge University Press, 2000).

[40] Kenneth Waltz, *Theory of International Politics* (New York: Random House, 1979).

[41] Kenneth Waltz, 'Another gap', in Robert Osgood et al. (eds), *Containment, Soviet Behavior and Grand Strategy*, Policy Papers in International Affairs no. 16 (Berkeley, Calif.: Institute of International Studies, University of California at Berkeley, 1981), pp. 74–86, quoted by Christer Pursiainen, *Russian Foreign Policy and International Relations Theory* (Aldershot: Ashgate, 2000), p. 118.

[42] Graham T. Allison, *Essence of Decision: Explaining the Cuban Missile Crisis* (Boston, Mass.: Little, Brown & Co., 1971).

[43] Joseph S. Nye, 'Nuclear learning and US–Soviet security regimes', *International Organization* 41/3 (Summer 1987), pp. 371–402.

[44] Robert Keohane, 'The analysis of international regimes: Towards a European–American research programme', in Volker Rittberger (ed.), *Regime Theory and International Relations* (Oxford: Clarendon Press, 1993), pp. 29, 30, quoted by Pursiainen, *Russian Foreign Policy and International Relations*, p. 120. See also Pursiainen's discussion of Russian studies and international relations theory in his *Beyond Sovietology: International Relations Theory and the Study of Soviet/Russian Foreign and Security Policy* (Helsinki: Finnish Institute of International Affairs, 1998).

[45] Christer Pursiainen, 'The impact of international security regimes on Russia's behavior', in Ted Hopf (ed.), *Understandings of Russian Foreign Policy* (University Park, Pa.: Pennsylvania State University Press, 1999), pp. 126–7.

[46] Andrew Hurell, 'International society and the study of regimes: a reflective approach', in Rittberger (ed.), *Regime Theory*.

[47] Alexander Wendt, 'Collective identity formation and the international state', *American Political Science Review* 88 (June 1994), pp. 384–96.

[48] See the different definitions of Central Asia in Olivier Roy, *The New Central Asia: The Creation of Nations* (New York: New York University Press. 2000) pp. 1–2.

[49] Buzan, *People, States and Fear*, 2nd edition, p. 190.

Chapter 2

CENTRAL ASIA GAINED

[1] Dietrich Geyer, *Russian Imperialism: The Interaction of Domestic and Foreign Policy 1860–1914* (Leamington Spa, Hamburg and New York: Berg, 1987) (German edition 1977), p. 86.

[2] For the history of Central Asia see e.g. Svat Soucek, *A History of Inner Asia* (Cambridge and New York: Cambridge University Press, 2000).

[3] Khaigarsho Pirumshoev, *Rossiisko-sredneaziatskie otnosheniya XV–srediny XIX vekov v Russkoi istoriografii* [Russian–Central Asian relations from the fifteenth to the mid-nineteenth century in Russian historiography] (Dushanbe: Academy of Science of Tajikistan/Izdatelstvo Maolif, 2000), p. 170; and N. A. Khalfin, *Politika Rossii v Srednei Azii (1857–1868)* [Russian policy in Central Asia, 1857–68] (Moscow: Izdatelstvo vostochnoi literatury, 1960), p. 19.

[4] Seymour Becker, *Russia's Protectorates in Central Asia: Bukhara and Khiva, 1865–1924* (Cambridge, Mass.: Harvard University Press, 1968), p. 12.

[5] Otto Hoetzsch, *Russland in Asien: Geschichte einer Expansion* [Russia in Asia: the history of an expansion] (Stuttgart: Deutsche Verlags-Anstalt, 1966); and Pirumshoev, *Rossiisko-sredneaziatskie otnosheniya*, pp. 185, 256–64.

[6] V. V. Bartold, *Istoriya izucheniya Vostoka v Evrope i Rossii: Sochineniya T. IX* [History of the study of the East in Europe and Russia: Works, vol. 10] (Moscow: Nauka, 1977), pp. 197–482. See reference in Pirumshoev, *Rossiisko-sredneaziatskie otnosheniya*, p. 186.

[7] These categories are used in A. V. Ignatiev et al. (eds), *Istoriya vneshnei politiki Rossii: Vtoraya polovina XIX veka* [History of Russian foreign policy: the second half of the nineteenth century] (Moscow: Mezhdunarodnye otnosheniya, 1997), p. 98.

[8] Quoted by Firuz Kazemzadeh, *Russia and Britain in Persia, 1864–1914: A Study in Imperialism* (New Haven, Conn., and London: Yale University Press, 1968), pp. 8–9; and by Hoetzsch in *Russland in Asien*, p. 27.

[9] Khalfin, *Politika Rossii v Srednei Azii*, p. 163.

[10] John P. LeDonne, *The Russian Empire and the World 1700–1917: The Geopolitics of Expansion and Containment* (New York and Oxford: Oxford University Press, 1997), p. 130.

[11] Geyer, *Russian Imperialism*, p. 86.

[12] E.g. one of the heads of the Russian Foreign Ministry, I. A. Zinovev, in V. M. Lamsdorf, *Dnevnik 1891–1892* [Diary, 1891–1892]. Quoted by Khalfin, *Politika Rossii v Srednei Azii*, p. 89, footnote 95.

[13] Ignatiev et al. (eds), *Istoriya vneshnei politiki*; and Peter Hopkirk, *The Great Game: The Struggle for Empire in Central Asia* (London: Murray, 1990).

[14] Khalfin, *Politika Rossii v Srednei Azii*, p. 114.

[15] Ignatiev et al., *Istoriya vneshnei politiki Rossii*, pp. 87–8.

[16] The Kokand Khanate tried to conquer Kazakh territory, Bukhara tried to incorporate parts of Kokand Khanate, and Bukhara and Khiva competed.

[17] Peter Hopkirk, *The Great Game: The Struggle for Empire in Central Asia* (London: Murray, 1990).

[18] Khalfin, *Politika Rossii v Srednei Azii*, p. 52.

[19] Geyer, *Russian Imperialism*, p. 113.

[20] See, e.g., William C. Fuller, *Strategy and Power in Russia 1600–1914* (New York and Toronto: The Free Press), p. 290.

[21] Geyer, *Russian Imperialism*, pp. 91–3. Geyer writes that the treaties with Bukhara (1868) and Khiva (1873) included preferential tariffs for Russian caravans, but this was

mainly for military purposes since the Russian military had to maintain themselves on these territories.

[22] Ignatiev et al., *Istoriya vneshnei politiki Rossii*, p. 98.

[23] Becker, *Russia's Protectorates in Central Asia: Bukhara and Khiva*, p. 13.

[24] Becker, *Russia's Protectorates in Central Asia: Bukhara and Khiva*, p. 13.

[25] See in particular the Soviet Russian scholar N. A. Khalfin.

[26] Becker, *Russia's Protectorates in Central Asia: Bukhara and Khiva*, p. 11.

[27] Pirumshoev, *Rossiisko-sredneaziatskie otnosheniya*, p. 170.

[28] By the 1850s Russian canvas had been gradually ousted by non-Russian producers, mainly British. Khalfin, *Politika Rossii v Srednei Azii*, p. 32.

[29] G. P. Nebolsin points in his study from 1850, *Statisticheskoe obozrenie o vneshnei torgovle Rossii* [Statistical overview of Russia's foreign trade] to the distinction between Russian exports to the West and those to the East. Grain, different raw materials and half-processed goods accounted for 96 per cent of Russia's exports to the European market, and processed articles only 4 per cent, while processed goods made up almost 60 per cent of exports to Central Asia. Khalfin, *Politika Rossii v Srednei Azii*, p. 37.

[30] Khalfin, *Politika Rossii v Srednei Azii*, p. 33.

[31] Pirumshoev, *Rossiisko-sredneaziatskie otnosheniya*, p. 223.

[32] In 1849 the geographer and explorer P. A. Chikhachev published *O issledivanii vershin Syr i Amu-Dary i nagornoi ploshchadi Pamir* [Explorations of the peaks of the Syr- and Amu-Darya and the Pamir mountain areas] (Moscow, 1849). See also Ya. V. Khanykov, *Poyasnitelnaya zapiska k karte Aral'skogo morya i Khvinskogo Khanstva* [Explanatory notes on the map of the Aral Sea and the Khiva khanate], 1850; G. P. Nebolsin, *Statisticheskoe obozrenie o vneshnei torgovle Rossii* [Statistical survey of Russia's foreign trade] (St Petersburg, 1850); P. I. Nebolsin, *Ocherki torgovli Rossii s Srednoi Aziei* [Outline of Russia's trade with Central Asia] (St Petersburg, 1855); and F. G. Terner, *Dvizhenie vneshnei torgovli Rossii s 1853 po 1856 g.* [The movement of Russia's foreign trade, 1853–56] (St Petersburg, 1856).

[33] Nebolsin, *Statisticheskioe obozrenie o vneshnei torgovle Rossii*, quoted by Khalfin, *Politika Rossii v Srednei Azii*, p. 36.

[34] Khalfin, *Politika Rossii v Srednei Azii*, p. 41.

[35] Khalfin, *Politika Rossii v Srednei Azii*, p. 118.

[36] Khalfin, *Politika Rossii v Srednei Azii*, p. 151.

[37] Pirumshoev, *Rossiisko-sredneaziatskie otnosheniya*, p. 283 refers among others to V. V. Grigorev (Zailestskii), *Sredneaziatskie dela* [Central Asian affairs] (Moscow, 1865).

[38] Becker, *Russia's Protectorates in Central Asia: Bukhara and Khiva*, p. 23.

[39] Pirumshoev, *Rossiisko-sredneaziatskie otnosheniya*, p. 184.

[40] Geyer, *Russian Imperialism*, p. 94.

[41] Fyodor Dostoevskii, *Geok-Tepe. Chto takoe dlya nas Aziya?* [What is Asia to us?], 1881. Geok-Tepe was a Turkoman fortress. In 1879 the Russians failed to take it but in December 1880 General Skobelev took it by storm.

[42] Geyer, *Russian Imperialism*, p 86.

[43] Khalfin, *Politika Rossii v Srednei Azii*, p. 62.

[44] *Moskovskie vedomosti*, 16 August 1879, quoted in Hoetzsch, *Russland in Asien*, p. 116.

[45] Ignatiev et al., *Istoriya vneshnei politiki Rossii*, p. 330.

[46] Vera Tolz, *Inventing the Nation: Russia* (London and New York: Arnold and Oxford University Press, 2001), pp. 135–40. Such values later became a ground for criticism of the brutality of the Russian conquest and behaviour. The Russian Revolutionary Democrats were to develop ideas and values critical of Russian colonialism towards the end of the century. Russian censorship removed all critical articles on Central Asia from the press, and the underground press printed rely to a large extent on the studies of Khalfin and Pirumshoev.

47 Geyer, *Russian Imperialism*, p. 31.

48 Becker, *Russia's Protectorates in Central Asia: Bukhara and Khiva*, p. 20.

49 In the following analysis I rely to a large extent on the studies of Khalfin and Pirumshoev.

50 Khalfin, *Politika Rossii v Srednei Azii*, pp. 76-8.

51 Khalfin, *Politika Rossii v Srednei Azii*, p. 89.

52 Pirumshoev, *Rossiisko-sredneaziatskie otnosheniya*, p. 273.

53 Khalfin, *Politika Rossii v Srednei Azii*, p. 88.

54 Khalfin, *Politika Rossii v Srednei Azii*, p. 94.

55 Katenin wrote to the Foreign Ministry at about the same time as Ignatiev, on 6 July 1858, with similar demands. Khalfin, *Politika Rossii v Srednei Azii*, p. 95.

56 Khalfin, *Politika Rossii v Srednei Azii*, p. 103.

57 Khalfin, *Politika Rossii v Srednei Azii*, p. 105.

58 Khalfin, *Politika Rossii v Srednei Azii*, p. 121.

59 Khalfin, *Politika Rossii v Srednei Azii*, p. 121.

60 Khalfin, *Politika Rossii v Srednei Azii*, p. 123.

61 'Zapiska polk. N. P. Ignatieva o politike nashei v Srednoi Azii' [Memorandum of Col. N. P. Ignatiev on our Central Asia policy], 5 January 1859, quoted in Khalfin, *Politika Rossii v Srednei Azii*, pp. 123–4.

62 Khalfin, *Politika Rossii v Srednei Azii*, p. 137.

63 Richard A. Pierce, *Russian Central Asia 1867–1917: A Study in Colonial Rule* (Berkeley and Los Angeles, Calif.: University of California Press, 1960), p. 7. Abroad was therefore the only source of information about the negative aspects of the Russian presence in Central Asia. See Ignatiev et al., *Istoriya vneshnei politiki Rossii*, p. 340.

64 D. A. Milyutin, *Moi starcheskie vospominaniya* [My oldest recollections], quoted by Khalfin, *Politika Rossii v Srednei Azii*, p 143.

65 While Khalfin draws the conclusion that there was no government plan for military–political measures with regard to Central Asia, Pirumshoev comes to the opposite conclusion from his reading of the same Russian documents.

66 Khalfin, *Politika Rossii v Srednei Azii*, p. 163.

67 Becker, *Russia's Protectorates in Central Asia: Bukhara and Khiva*, p. 26.

68 Pirumshoev, *Rossiisko-sredneaziatskie otnosheniya*, p. 140.

69 Eugene Scuyler, *Turkestan: Notes of a Journey in Russian Turkistan, Khokand, Bukhara and Kuldja* (London, 1876), quoted in Pierce, *Russian Central Asia 1867–1917*, p. 25.

70 Khalfin, *Politika Rossii v Srednei Azii*, p. 232.

71 Tsentralnyi gosudarstvennyi istoricheskii arkhiv UzSSR [Central State Archive of the Uzbek Soviet Socialist Republic], quoted by Khalfin, *Politika Rossii v Srednei Azii*, p. 232.

72 Ignatiev et al., *Istoriya vneshnei politiki Rossii*, p. 109.

73 Namoz Khotamov, *Sverzhenie emirskogo rezhima v Bukhare* [The overthrow of the emirate regime in Bukhara] (Dushanbe: Academy of Sciences of Tajikistan, 1997), p. 12.

74 Hélène Carrère d'Encausse, *Islam and the Russian Empire: Reform and Revolution in Central Asia* (London: I. B. Tauris, 1988), p. 38.

75 Khalfin, *Politika Rossii v Srednei Azii*, p. 230.

76 Becker, *Russia's Protectorates in Central Asia: Bukhara and Khiva*, p. 41.

77 Becker, *Russia's Protectorates in Central Asia: Bukhara and Khiva*, p. 56.

78 Khotamov, *Sverzhenie emirskogo rezhima v Bukhare*, p. 12.

79 Ignatiev et al., *Istoriya vneshnei politiki Rossii*, pp. 119–20.

80 Pierce, *Russian Central Asia 1867–1917*, pp. 34–7.

81 Becker, *Russia's Protectorates in Central Asia: Bukhara and Khiva*, p. 90.

82 Becker, *Russia's Protectorates in Central Asia: Bukhara and Khiva*, p. 92.

[83] Carrère d'Encausse, *Islam and the Russian Empire*, p. 38.

[84] Khotamov, *Sverzhenie emirskogo rezhima v Bukhare*, p. 16.

[85] Becker, *Russia's Protectorates in Central Asia: Bukhara and Khiva*, pp. 152–3.

[86] Becker, *Russia's Protectorates in Central Asia: Bukhara and Khiva*, p. 157.

[87] Becker, *Russia's Protectorates in Central Asia: Bukhara and Khiva*, p. 171.

[88] Becker, *Russia's Protectorates in Central Asia: Bukhara and Khiva*, p. 173.

[89] Becker, *Russia's Protectorates in Central Asia: Bukhara and Khiva*, p. 175.

[90] Becker, *Russia's Protectorates in Central Asia: Bukhara and Khiva*, p. 176.

[91] Becker, *Russia's Protectorates in Central Asia: Bukhara and Khiva*, p. 176.

[92] Becker, *Russia's Protectorates in Central Asia: Bukhara and Khiva*, p. 180.

[93] Ignatiev et al., *Istoriya vneshnei politiki Rossii*, p. 115.

[94] Becker, *Russia's Protectorates in Central Asia: Bukhara and Khiva*, p. 107.

[95] Becker, *Russia's Protectorates in Central Asia: Bukhara and Khiva*, p. 121.

[96] Khalfin, *Politika Rossii v Srednei Azii*, p. 50.

[97] By then a Khorezmi People's Soviet Republic had also been established in Khiva.

[98] Khotamov, *Sverzhenie emirskogo rezhima v Bukhare*.

[99] Ignatiev et al., *Istoriya vneshnei politiki Rossii*, p. 130.

[100] Ignatiev et al., *Istoriya vneshnei politiki Rossii*, p. 130.

[101] Alexandre Bennigsen and S. Enders Wimbush, *Muslims of the Soviet Empire* (Bloomington: Indiana University Press, 1986) p. 33.

[102] Alexandre Bennigsen, Paul B. Henze, George K. Tanham, and S. Enders Wimbush, *Soviet Strategy and Islam* (London: Macmillan, 1989), p. 14.

[103] S. M. Akimbekov, *Afganskii uzel i problemy bezopasnosti Tsentralnoi Azii* [The Afghan knot and problems of security in Central Asia] (Almaty: Kontinent, 2003) p. 44.

[104] Bennigsen, Henze, Tanham and Wimbush, *Soviet Strategy and Islam*, p. 14.

[105] Akimbekov, *Afganskii uzel i problemy bezopasnosti Tsentralnoi Azii* (Almaty: Kontinent, 2003) p. 44.

Chapter 3

CENTRAL ASIA LOST

[1] See the prediction by the Moscow State Institute of International Relations in 1992. 'In its policy Russia faces a serious challenge. The differentiated pattern of the evolution of the CIS provokes its growing fragmentation. Given the emergence of a core within the CIS, the Eurasian community wight well become transformed into an alliance between Russia and the ex-Soviet Central Asian states and Kazakhstan.' *The Commonwealth of Independent States: Developments and Prospects*. Report of the Centre of International Studies. Moscow State Institute of International Relations (MGIMO), 1992, p. 10. See also Irina Zviagelskaia, *The Russian Policy Debate on Central Asia* (London: Royal Institute of International Affairs, 1995).

[2] 'Strategiya dlya Rossii' [Strategy for Russia], *Nezavisimaya gazeta*, 19 August 1992, pp. 4–5.

[3] On the Russian debate during the first eight months after the dissolution of the Soviet Union see Lena Jonson, 'In Search of a national interest: the foreign policy debate in Russia', *Nationalities Papers* 22/1 (Spring 1994).

[4] *Rossiiskaya gazeta*, 24 February 1994.

[5] See, for example, the analysis in *Posle raspada SSR: Rossiya v novom mire. Doklad tsentra mezhdunarodnykh issledovanii MGIMO* [After the fall of the Soviet Union: Russia in a new

world. Report of the MGIMO Centre for International Studies] (Moskva: MGIMO, February 1992).

[6] 'Osnovnye polozheniya voennoi doktriny Rossiiskoi Federatsii' [The basic provisions of the military doctrine of the Russian Federation], *Krasnaya zvezda*, 19 November 1993.

[7] 'Rossiya–SNG: Nuzhdaetsya li v korrektirovke pozitsiya zapada?' [Russia and the CIS: does the position of the West need correcting?], *Rossiiskaya gazeta*, 22 September 1994, p. 6.

[8] Lena Jonson, *Russia and Central Asia in a New Web of Relations* (London: Royal Institute of International Affairs, 1998).

[9] Jonson, 'Russia and Central Asia', p. 106.

[10] Jonson, 'Russia and Central Asia', p. 106.

[11] Russian capital investment played a minor role in the region except in the energy sector. Yu. Yudanov, 'Tsentralnaya Aziya: novyi favorit inostrannykh investorov' [Central Asia: the new favourite of foreign investors], *Mirovaya ekonomika i mezhdunarodnye otnosheniya* 3–4 (2000).

[12] Vyacheslau Paznyak, 'The Customs Union of five and the Russia–Belarus Union', in Renata Dwan and Oleksandr Pavliuk (eds), *Building Security in the New States of Eurasia* (New York and London: M. E. Sharpe, 2000).

[13] R. S. Grinberg et al., 'Sodruzhestvo nezavisimykh gosudarstv: sostoyanie i perspektivy razvitiya. Doklad podgotovlen dlya mezhdunarodnoi nauchnoi konferentsii "Sodruzhestvo Nezavisimykh Gosudarstv: Sostoyanie i Perspektivy"' [The Commonwealth of Independent States: the state of and prospects for development. Paper prepared for the international scientific conference on The Commonwealth of Independent States: Current State and Prospects], Moscow, 30–31 March 2000 (Avtorskii kollektiv R. S. Grinberg, L. Z. Zevin, L. S. Kosikova and A. V. Shurubokich, Moscow, 2000).

[14] Natalya Pulina and Ekaterina Tesëmnikova, 'Integratsionnye itogi' [Integration: the achievements], *Nezavisimaya gazeta* 28 December 1999.

[15] 'Itogi zasedaniya Soveta glav gosudarstv SNG' [Results of the meeting of CIS heads of state], *Diplomaticheskii vestnik* 5 (May 1998), pp. 21–2.

[16] Yevgenii Primakov, 'Rossiya v mirovoi politike (k 200-letiyu A. M. Gorchakova)' [Russia and world politics: on the 200th anniversary of A. M. Gorchakov], *Diplomaticheskii vestnik* 7 (July 1998), p. 78.

[17] See, e.g., Lev Rokhlin (Chairman of the Duma Defence Committee), 'Rossiya utrachivaet svoe vliyanie v stranakh SNG' [Russia loses its influence in the CIS countries], *Nezavisimaya gazeta*, 4 March 1997, p. 2.

[18] Igor Korochenko, 'Igor Rodionov vystupil za sozdanie oboronnogo soyuza stran SNG' [Igor Rodionov comes out in favour of the creation of a defence union of the CIS countries], *Nezavisimaya gazeta*, 26 December 1996, p. 1.

[19] [Proposals at the CIS Defence Ministerial Council on 26 March 1997], *Krasnaya zvezda* 28 March 1997, quoted in Roy Allison, *Security Dilemmas in Russia and Eurasia* (London: Royal Institute of International Affairs, 1998), p. 27.

[20] *Krasnaya zvezda*, 28 March 1997.

[21] Richard Pomfret, *Central Asia Turns South? Trade Relations in Transition* (London: Royal Institiute of International Affairs, 1999).

[22] Lena Jonson, 'Russia, NATO and the handling of conflicts at Russia's southern periphery: at a cross roads?', *European Security* 9/4 (Winter 2000).

[23] See, for example, articles by Dmitrii Gornostaev and Mekhman Gafarli, 'Nachav s Balkan, SshA zaimutsya stranami SNG' [Starting with the Balkans, the USA engages in the CIS countries], *Nezavisimaya gazeta*, 23 April 1999, pp. 1, 6; and Aleksandr Ruzskii,

'Prelyudiya k novumu pokhodu na vostok' [Prelude to a new march towards the east], *Nezavisimoe voennoe obozrenie* 18 (14–20 May 1999), p. 3.

24 Quoted in Stephen Blank, 'Russia rises to perceived threats', *Jane's Intelligence Review* 12/2 (February 2000), p. 25.

25 Anatolii Kvashnin, 'Alternativy vozobnovleniyu sotrudnichestva s NATO net' [There is no alternative to renewal of cooperation with NATO], *Nezavisimoe voennoe obozrenie* 45 (19–25 November 1999).

26 Vyacheslav Belokrenitsky, 'Russian–Afghan relations', in Gennady Chufrin (ed.), *Russia and Asia: The Emerging Security Agenda* (Oxford: Oxford University Press, 1999), p. 199.

27 Amin Saikal, 'Russia and Central Asia', in Amin Saikal and William Maley (eds), *Russia in Search of its Future* (Cambridge: Cambridge University Press, 1995), p. 145.

28 A. D. Davydov (ed.), *Afganistan: Problemy voiny i mira* [Afghanistan: problems of war and peace], (Moscow: Institut Vostokovedeniya RAN, 1996), p. 144.

29 Lena Jonson, *The Tajik War: A Challenge to Russian Policy* (London: Royal Institute of International Affairs, 1998), pp. 37–8.

30 'Osnovnye polozheniya voennoi doktriny Rossiiskoi Federatsii' [The basic provisions of the military doctrine of the Russian Federation], *Krasnaya zvezda*, 19 November 1993.

31 Vladimir Lukin, 'Our Security Predicament', *Foreign Policy* 88 (Fall 1992), p. 62.

32 Shirin Akiner, *Tajikistan: Disintegration or Reconciliation?* (London: Royal Institute of International Affairs, 2001).

33 Reuters, 27 July 1993.

34 Andrei Kozyrev, [What does Russia want in Tajikistan?] *Izvestiya*, 4 August 1993.

35 'Rossiya–SNG: Nuzhdaetsya li v korrektirovke pozitsiya zapada?' [Russia and the CIS: does the position of the West need correcting?], *Rossiiskaya gazeta*, 22 September 1994, p. 6.

36 'Rossiya–SNG: Nuzhdaetsya li v korrektirovke pozitsiya zapada?', p. 6.

37 Interview in 'Worst-case Afghan scenario comes to pass: a Foreign Intelligence Service (SVR) official grants MN an exclusive interview', *Moscow News* 21 (31 May–6 June 2000), pp. 1, 4.

38 For an analysis of the change of Russian policy in the Tajik conflict see Jonson, *The Tajik War*. The analysis includes Russian peacekeeping policy. See also Jonson, *Keeping the Peace in the CIS: The Evolution of Russian Policy* (London: Royal Institute of International Affairs, 1999).

39 Jonson, *The Tajik War: A Challenge to Russian Policy*.

40 Walentin Buschkow, 'Der innere konflikt Tadschikistans als regionales Sicherheitsproblem' [The internal conflict in Tajikistan as a regional security problem] *Berichte des Bundesinstitut fur Ostwissenschaftliche und Internationale Studien*, 1996 no. 35, p. 11.

41 See Jonson, *The Tajik War*, pp. 35–6.

42 *Sotsialno-politicheskaya situatsiya v post-sovetskom mire*, 1996 no. 9 (53) September, p. 34.

43 'Sovmestnoe zayavlenie prezidentov RF i Respubliki Uzbekistan' [Joint statement of the presidents of the Russian Federation and Uzbekistan], *Diplomaticheskii vestnik* 6 (June 1998), pp. 30–1.

44 For an analysis of Russia and the Uzbek, Tajik and Afghan factors in the security dynamics of Central Asia see Lena Jonson, 'Russia and Central Asia', in Roy Allison and Lena Jonson (eds), *Central Asian Security Dynamics: The New International Context* (Washington, DC and London: Brookings Institution Press and Royal Institute of International Affairs, 2001).

[45] Anara Tabyshalieva, *The Challenge of Regional Cooperation in Central Asia: Preventing Ethnic Conflict in the Ferghana Valley* (Washington, DC: United States Institute of Peace, 1999). Tabyshalieva mentions the figure of 45,000 Tajik refugees in Kyrgyzstan.

[46] In an interview Kyrgyz President Askar Akaev commented on this behaviour by Uzbekistan in terms of a small country which has no alternative but to accept such acts by a larger neighbour. Igor Rotar, 'Neprostoe sosedstvo' [Not a straightforward neighbourhood], *Nezavisimaya gazeta*, 2 July 1999, p. 5. Similar problems along the Uzbek–Kazakh border led the authorities of a border region of Kazakhstan, the Makhtaralskii region, to request that a military unit be deployed there. Igor Rotar, 'Mezhdu otvergnutym proshlym i tumannym budushchim' [Between a repudiated past and an unclear future], *Sodruzhestvo NG* 7 (July 1999). See also Vladimir Georgiev, 'Moskva obrela novogo soyuznika' [Moscow finds a new ally], *Nezavisimaya gazeta*, 17 April 1999, pp. 1, 5.

[47] Gulfira Gayeva and Yuri Chubchenko, 'Russia names its principal ally in Central Asia', *Kommersant Daily*, 26 February 1999, p. 3; *Former Soviet Union Fifteen Nations: Policy and Security*, February 1999, p. 85.

[48] Vitaly V. Naumkin, *Militant Islam in Central Asia: The Case of the Islamic Movement of Uzbekistan*. Berkely Program in Soviet and Post-Soviet Studies. Working Paper series. Spring 2003, pp. 40-42

[49] Ahmed Rashid, *Jihad: The Rise of Militant Islam in Central Asia* (New Haven and London: Yale University Press, 2002), p. 162.

[50] Vitaly V. Naumkin, *Militant Islam in Central Asia: The Case of the Islamic Movement of Uzbekistan*, pp. 40–2.

[51] Kyrgyzstan's National Security Minister, Tashtemir Aytbaev, responded that Kyrgyzstan had taken 'very correct steps'. 'We did not let them drag us into a long drawn-out war.' BBC, *Inside Central Asia* 301 (15–21 November 1999).

[52] BBC, *Inside Central Asia/BBC* 294 (27 September–3 October 1999).

[53] The independent Tajik journalist with experience from the Tajik opposition and Afghanistan Sultan Khamadov, 'Mezhdunarodnyi kontekst–afganskii faktor' [The international contact: the Afghan factor], in *Religioznyi ekstremizm v Tsentralnoi Azii* [Religious extremism in Central Asia] (Dushanbe: OSCE Mission to Tajikistan, 2002) pp. 140–1.

[54] Khamadov, 'Mezhdunarodnyi kontekst–afganskii faktor', p. 143.

[55] *Sotsialno-politicheskaya situatsiya v post-sovetskom mire*, 1996 no. 10 (54) October, p. 38.

[56] Yurii Golotyuk, 'Rossiya poka ne usilivaet svoi kontingent v Tadzhikistane' [Russia is not reinforcing its contingents in Tajikistan], *Segodnya*, 15 October 1996.

[57] This is the general view of the Russian military in Tajikistan. See Dmitrii Nikolaev and Ilya Kedrov, 'Talibam poka khvataet del v Afganistane' [For the time being the Taliban have their hands full in Afghanistan], *Nezavisimoe voennoe obozrenie* 36 (29 September–5 October 2000), p. 1. On 20 February 2001, Konstantin Totskii, Director of the Russian Federal Border Guard Service, repeated that: 'The Taleban will not go into Tajikistan … They have many internal problems, and the war with the Northern Alliance is continuing'. Interfax 20 February 2001. Never theless, in October 2000 units from the tactical groups of the 201st MRD complemented the Russian border troops in order to support them with artillery fire and tanks (*bronetekhnika*), and, if necessary, in direct combat. The border troops and these units along the border are currently in an increased state of readiness.

[58] *Krasnaya zvezda*, 1 November 1996, p. 1.

[59] Vladimir Mukhin (Professor of the Russian Academy of Military Sciences), 'Extension of the zone of Taleban's influence may significantly infringe upon Russia's

interests in Central Asia', *Former Soviet Union Fifteen Nations: Policy and Security*, August 1998, pp. 18–23.

[60] Signed during President Yeltsin's visit to Tashkent in October 1998. 'Deklaratsiya o vsestoronnem sotrudnichestve Rossiiskoi Federatsii, Respubliki Tadzhikistan i Respubliki Uzbekistan' [Declaration of comprehensive cooperation between the Russian Federation, the Republic of Tajikistan and the Republic of Uzbekistan], *Diplomaticheskii vestnik* 11 (November 1998), pp. 33–4. During Yeltsin's visit to Uzbekistan in 1998 the 'troika' declaration on mutual military assistance against aggression by religious extremism or terrorism was signed, together with a treaty on economic cooperation for the period 1998–2007. The latter replaced an earlier agreement from 1994.

[61] Interview in *Moscow News* 41 (29 October–4 November 1998).

[62] Edmund Herzig, 'Islam, transnationalism and subregionalism in the CIS', in Renata Dwan and Oleksandr Pavliuk (eds), *Building Security in the New States of Eurasia*, p. 246.

[63] See also the joint declaration on Afghanistan from Yeltsin's visit in Uzbekistan, which expressed concern about the situation in Afghanistan and the possible negative consequences for Central Asia and Russia in the context of increased fighting in Afghanistan. *Diplomaticheskii vestnik* 11 (November 1998), p. 35.

[64] 'Iz poslaniya prezidenta Rossiisskoi Federatsii Federalnomu Sobraniyu' [From the message of the President of the Russian Federation to the Federal Assembly], *Diplomaticheskii vestnik* 4 (April 1999), p. 3 (italics in original).

Chapter 4

THE POLICY CHANGE OF 1999

[1] On the Batken incursions, see chapter 3 in this volume.

[2] 'O natsionalnoi bezopasnosti: Poslanie Prezidenta RF Federalnomu Sobraniyu' [On national security: message from the president to the Federal Assembly], *Nezavisimaya gazeta*, 14 June 1996, pp. 7-8. The draft prepared by presidential adviser on national security, Yurii Baturin.

[3] 'Kontseptsiya natsionalnoi bezopasnosti Rossiiskoi Federatsii' [The national security concept of the Russian Federation], *Diplomaticheskii vestnik* 2 (February 1998), pp. 8–9.

[4] See Foreign Minister Primakov's speech on the basic directions of Russian foreign policy in 1997, 23 December 1997. *Diplomaticheskii vestnik* 1 (1998), pp. 3-5.

[5] This is clear from the meetings as reported in the Russian diplomatic bulletin, *Diplomaticheskii vestnik*.

[6] 'Zasedanie Soveta glav pravitelstv SNG v Bishkeke, 9 oktyabrya 1997' [Meeting of the Council of the CIS Heads of State in Bishkek, 9 October 1997], *Diplomaticheskii vestnik* 11 (1997), pp. 32-33.

[7] 'Zasedanie SMID SNG' [Meeting of the CIS Council of Ministers of Foreign Affairs], *Diplomaticheskii vestnik* 4 (1998), p. 43.

[8] 'Ocherednoe zasedanie Soveta Ministrov inostrannykh del SNG' [Regular meeting of the CIS Council of Ministers of Foreign Affairs], *Diplomaticheskii vestnik*, 3 (1998), p. 19.

[9] See Vladimir Zemskii, General Secretary of the Council of Collective Security of the CST, in consultations with the signatories of the CST on 7 September 1999: 'Konsultatsii predstavitelei gosudarstv uchastnikov dogovora o kollektivnoi bezopasnosti' [Consultations of representatives of the parties to the Collective Security Treaty], *Diplomaticheskii vestnik* 10 (1999), p. 19.

[10] 'On the situation in the Central Asian region' of 15 September 1999. Referred to in 'Konsultatsii v Bishkeke' [Consultations in Bishkek], *Diplomaticheskii vestnik* 12 (1999), p. 19.

[11] Yu. Golotyuk, [Russia is in no hurry to open a 'second front'], *Izvestiya*, 22 September 1999, p. 3.

[12] 'Osnovnye napravleniya vneshnei politikoi Rossii na sovremennom etape' [Main directions of Russian foreign policy at the present stage], *Diplomaticheskii vestnik* 10 (1999), p. 54. Sredin gave his speech at the Academy of State Service.

[13] Nadezhda Alekseeva, 'Vizit rossiiskogo premera v Tadzhikistan' [Visit by the Russian Premier to Tajikistan], *Nezavisimaya gazeta*, 17 November 1999, p. 1.

[14] *Jamestown Monitor* 6 (January 2000).

[15] Leonid Panin, Yuri Stepanov and Igor Shestakov, 'Uzbek servicemen armed with Russian weapons to conduct operations in Kyrgyzstan', *Kommersant Daily*, 2 September 1999.

[16] Leonid Ivashov (Main Directorate for International Cooperation of the Defence Ministry), 'Rol Rossii v uregulirovanii konfliktov usilivaetsya' [Russia's role in the settlement of conflicts strengthens], *Nezavisimaya gazeta*, 15 September 1999, p. 3.

[17] Viktoriya Panfilova, 'Grazhdane Yaponii obreli svobodu' [Citizens of Japan find freedom], *Nezavisimaya gazeta*, 26 October 1999, p. 5.

[18] This translation is taken from Alexei Arbatov, *The Transformation of Russian Military Doctrine: Lessons Learned from Kosovo and Chechnya*, Marshall Center Papers, no 2, 2000. For the full text in Russian see http://www.scrf.gov.ru/Documents/Decree/2000/706-1.html References in Russian official declarations to 'religious extremism' imply primarily Islamism. Islamism is usually defined along the lines of the following words by Russian Islam specialist Aleksander Ignatenko as 'efforts to create political conditions in order to apply Islamic (Sharia) norms in all spheres of human life'.

[19.] The text says that international terrorism is linked to a campaign to destabilize the situation in Russia. Thus, mainly the situation in Chechnya is referred to. The full Russian text of the National Security Doctrine of 2000 can be found at http://www.scrf.gov.ru/Documents/Decree/2000/24-1.html

[20] For full text of document in Russian, see http://www.scrf.gov.ru/Documents/Decree/2000/07-10.html

[21] 'Vstrecha Prezidenta RF s rukovodyashchim sostavom diplomaticheskoi sluzhby MID Rossii' [Meeting of the President of the Russian Federation with the senior members of the diplomatic service of the Ministry of Foreign Affairs of the Russian Federation], *Diplomaticheskii vestnik*, 2 (2001), pp. 7–13.

[22] *Vedomosti*, 6 April 2000/Reuters, 10 April 2000.

[23] Previously the Botanlyk district was part of Kazakhstan.

[24] Ahmed Rashid, *Jihad: The Rise of Militant Islam in Central Asia* (New Haven and London, Yale University Press, 2002) p. 172.

[25] The members of the CIS were Armenia, Azerbaijan, Belarus, Georgia, Kazakhstan, Kyrgyzstan, Moldova, Russia, Tajikistan, Turkmenistan, Ukraine and Uzbekistan. The CST signatories at this point were Armenia, Belarus, Kyrgyzstan, Russia, Tajikistan and Kazakhstan.

[26] 'Zasedaniya vyshykh organov SNG' [Meetings of the supreme organs of the CIS], *Diplomaticheskii vestnik* 7 (2000), pp. 47–8.

[27] 'Vystuplenie pervogo zamestitelya ministra inostrannykh del Rossii V.I. Trubnikova na mezhdunarodnoi nauchno-prakticheskoi konferentsii "Mezhdunarodnyi terrorizm"', S.-Peterburg, 18–19 Aprelya' [Speech by First Deputy Foreign Minister of Russia V. I. Trubnikov at the international scientific–practical conference on

International Terrorism, St Petersburg, 18–19 April], *Diplomaticheskii vestnik* 5 (2001), p. 125.

[28] The intention to include terrorism as one of the new, non-traditional security threats covered by the treaty had been indicated in Russian documents as early as 1997.

[29] 'Memorandum on increasing the effectiveness of the Treaty and its *adaptation* to *the* contemporary geopolitical situation', *Diplomaticheskii vestnik* 6 (2000).

[30] 'Sessiya Soveta kollektivnoi bezopasnosti gosudarstv: uchastnikov DKB' [Meeting of the Collective Security Council of the parties to the Collective Security Treaty], *Diplomaticheskii vestnik* 6 (2000), p. 30.

[31] 'Zayavlenie zasedaniya ministrov' [Declaration from the ministerial meeting], *Diplomaticheskii vestnik* 6 (2000), p 31.

[32] 'Zayavlenie Glav gosudarstv: uchastnikov DKB' [Declaration of the heads of state of the parties to the CST], *Diplomaticheskii vestnik* 6 (2000), p. 31. Among the documents issued there was also (a) a position (*polozhenie*) about the principles governing the adoption and implementation of collective decisions on the use of force and instruments of the system of collective security, and (b) a polozhenie on the creation of a Committee of the Secretaries of the Security Councils of the parties, and a Council of Defence Ministers.

[33] 'Sessiya Soveta kollektivnoi bezopasnosti gosudarstv: uchastnikov DKB' [Session of the Council of Collective Security Council of the parties to the CST], *Diplomaticheskii vestnik* 11 (2000), pp. 55–6.

[34] Thus the agreement On Creating Forces and Installations of the Collective Security System provides a basis for introducing and stationing 'collective troops' on the territories of the signatory countries. Under the agreement, each of the six signatories is to earmark national military units for use as part of CST forces. The allocated units are to participate in exercises and, if necessary, in military operations on the territories of signatory countries under 'joint' command. The signatory countries will in future make collective decisions regarding the deployment, size, composition and mission of joint forces and the duration of their stay in a particular country. Any operation will require a decision by the heads of state-in their collective capacity as the CIS Collective Security Council-and the consent of the 'host' country. *Jamestown Monitor* 192 (16 October 2000).

[35] Vladimir Mukhin, 'Dogovor o kollektivnoi bezopasnosti obretaet konkretnye ochertaniya' [The Collective Security Treaty takes concrete form], *Nezavisimaya gazeta*, 19 October 2000, p 5.

[36] Lena Jonson, *Keeping the Peace in the CIS: The Evolution of Russian Policy*. Discussion Paper 81 (London: Royal Institute of International Affairs), 1999, pp. 29–31.

[37] *Jamestown Monitor* 104 (30 May 2001).

[38] Mukhin, 'Dogovor o kollektivnoi bezopasnosti', p. 5.

[39] *Nezavisimaya gazeta*, 12 October 2000, p 1.

[40] Ekaterina Tesemnikova and Armen Khanbabyan, '"Shesterka" protiv "pyaterki"' [The 'six' against the 'five'], *Nezavisimaya gazeta*, 14 October 2000, p 5.

[41] *Jamestown Monitor* 84 (1 May 2001).

[42] *Jamestown Monitor* 100 (23 May 2001).

[43] It is interesting to note that in May 2001 Tajikistan joined the NATO Partnership for Peace (PFP) programme, the last of the CIS countries to do so. Viktoriya Panfilova, 'Tadzhikistan v fokuse mezhdunarodnogo vnimaniya' [Tajikistan at the centre of international attention], *Nezavisimaya gazeta*, 19 May 2001, p 5.

[44] The chief of the Defence Ministry's Main Department for International Military Cooperation, Leonid Ivashov, said that the Defence Ministry was not considering additional aid to Kyrgyzstan and Uzbekistan. Ilya Bulavinov, 'Sergeyev sends Putin to the front line', *Kommersant Daily*, 2 September 2000, p 1.

[45] 'Strategiya bezopasnosti Rossii' [Russia's security strategy], *Nezavisimoe voennoe obozrenie* 45 (1–7 December 2000), pp. 1, 4.

[46] *Jane's Defence Weekly*, 22 December 1999.

[47] ITAR-TASS (Moscow), 11 December 1999, 1126 GMT (in Russian); and BBC Worldwide Monitoring, 11 December 1999.

[48] On 5 April the CIS anti-aircraft defence system held unprecedented headquarters command training exercises. Over 50 aircraft took off in Belarus, Armenia, Kyrgyzstan, Kazakhstan, Uzbekistan and Ukraine. It was the first time that joint operating control of the anti-aircraft defence systems of these countries had been practised in a situation where national capacity and resources were applied to detain hijacked planes. About 20,000 servicemen took part in the exercises. *Kommersant Daily*, 6 April 2000/Reuters, 7 April 2000.

[49] See Chapter 3.

[50] 'Ukreplyaetsya dogovornaya baza' [Agreed base strengthened], *Krasnaya zvezda*, 16 March 2001.

[51] Yurii B. Chernogaev, *Kommersant Daily*, 2 March 2001. Uzbekistan participated in Southern Shield 2000 but only on its own territory and not with the troops from Tajikistan, Kazakhstan, Kyrgyzstan and Russia, which were at Tigrovaya balka in Tajikistan. Vladimir Georgiev, 'Unichtozhat' terroristov budut poka na kartakh' [Eliminating terrorists remains on the map for the time being], *Nezavisimoe voennoe obozrenie* 10 (23–29 March 2001).

[52] In 2000 their bilateral trade increased by 17 per cent, but Russia's negative balance of trade with Uzbekistan increased by more than US$350 million. On his visit to Moscow in May 2001 Karimov invited Russian capital investment in Uzbekistan. At that time there were 520 Russian–Uzbek joint ventures and Russian companies for Uzbekistan. Mekhman Gafarli, 'Rossiya–Uzbekistan: nastupaet epokha potepleniya' [Russia and Uzbekistan: start of an era of warmer relations], *Nezavisimaya gazeta*, 5 May 2001, p. 5.

[53] 'Vizit V. V. Putina v Uzbekistane' [V. Putin's visit to Uzbekistan], *Diplomaticheskii vestnik* 6 (2000), p. 29.

[54] Ahmed Rashid, *Jihad: The Rise of Militant Islam in Central Asia* (New Haven and London: Yale University Press, 2002) p. 172.

[55] The Russian press expected Uzbekistan to support these warnings. Aleksei Mironov, 'Plany Moskvy nikogo ne udivili v Tashkente' [Moscow's plans surprise no one in Tashkent], *Nezavisimaya gazeta*, 25 May 2000, p. 5.

[56] Lena Jonson, 'Russia and Central Asia under Putin: the Afghan factor', in Michael H. Crutcher (ed.), *Russian National Security: Perceptions, Policies, and Prospects*, 4–6 December 2000 (US Army War College, Carlisle Barracks, Pa., 2001).

[57] Quoted in Konstantin Zatulin and Ekaterina Tesemnikova, 'Rossiya v sodruzhestve i vne ego' [Russia in the Commonwealth and out of it], *Nezavisimaya gazeta*, 27 October 2000, p. 5.

[58] Afghan Islamic Press News Agency (Peshawar), 14 October 2000/BBC, *Summary of World Broadcasts*, SU/3973 G/1.

[59] See Chapter 3.

[60] According to their commander, Major General Aleksandr Markin. Interfax, 22 July 1999/BBC, *Inside Central Asia* 284 (19–25 July 1999), p. 2. Patrolling functions along parts of the Tajik–Afghan border were transferred in 1999 to the Tajik national border guard service.

[61] Lyudmila Romanova, 'Sozdayutsya sily bystrogo reagirovaniya' [Rapid reaction forces set up], *Nezavisimaya gazeta*, 12 October 2000, p. 1.

[62] In November 2000 Kazakh leaders stated publicly that they had been in contact with the Taliban for more than a year, described the Taliban as a major, legitimate

political force, and called for an urgent end to the fighting and an end to outside interference in the conflict. Prime Minister Kasymzhomart Tokaev declared that 'in no way should the Taliban be made into an object of ostracism'. *Jamestown Monitor* 211 (10 November 2000).

[63] Stated when Pakistan's President, General Pervez Musharraf, conferred with President Nazarbaev and senior Kazakh officials in Astana. *Jamestown Monitor* 210 (9 November 2000).

[64] Viktoriya Panfilova, 'Osnovnoi tsentr terrorizma peremestilsya k yuzhnym rubezham SNG' [Key centre of terrorism moves to the southern border of the CIS], *Nezavisimaya gazeta*, 26 October 2000, p. 5.

[65] Russian Ambassador to Tajikistan Maksim Peshkov explained that: 'We have never refused to have contacts with the Talebans. They have taken place in our country periodically, so to speak, and we have never said that we would categorically never have any contacts with them. One must talk to any side because it is our fundamental principle that the Afghan problem can only be resolved by political methods.' NTV International, 18 October 2000/BBC, *Summary of World Broadcasts*, SU/3976 B/2 (18 October 2000).

[66] RIA News Agency (Moscow), 'Pakistan refuses to have "direct" discussions of Taleban with Russia', 26 September 2000/BBC, *Worldwide Monitoring*/Reuters, 26 September 2000.

[67] Concerning the politicians see Viktoriya Panfilova, 'Osnovnoi tsentr terrorizma peremestilsya k yuzhnym rubezham SNG', p. 5. See also the article by independent researcher Semen Bagdasarov, who suggested negotiations with the Taliban about an end to the fighting along the Tajik–Afghan border and a normalization of Russian–Afghan bilateral relations. 'Mify o talibakh' [Myths about the Taliban], *Nezavisimaya gazeta*, 18 November 2000, p. 6.

[68] 'SB OON o situatsii v Afganistane' [UN Security Council on the situation in Afghanistan], *Diplomaticheskii vestnik* 8 (2000), pp. 68–8.

[69] Vadim Solovev, 'Preodolenie afganskogo sindroma' [Overcoming the Afghan syndrome], *Nezavisimaya gazeta*, 27 October 2000, p. 1.

[70] Massoud's force had been using multiple rocket launchers of recent vintage, freshly supplied from Russian Army stocks, which probably required the presence of Russian instructors on the ground with Massoud's forces. Russian military helicopters, almost certainly flown by Russian crews, were shown in action with Massoud's troops on Russian Public Television (ORT). Pavel Felgengauer, 'Afghan conflict revisited', *Moscow Times*, 2 November 2000 /*Jamestown Monitor* 210 (9 November 2000).

[71] *Jamestown Monitor* 203 (31 October 2000).

[72] Sergei Fedotov (CIS Headquarters for Coordination of Military Cooperation), 'War in Afghanistan makes situation in Central Asia explosive', *Former Soviet Union Fifteen Nations: Policy and Security* September 2000, pp. 3–4.

[73] *Jamestown Monitor* 211 (10 November 2000). Ivanov's statement was the first publicly uttered threat of Russian sanctions on CIS member countries whose foreign policy diverges from Russia's. ITAR-TASS, *Komsomolskaya pravda*, 9 November 2000.

[74] It included sanctions on the sale, delivery and transport of weapons and military goods, munitions and arms to military groups in areas of Afghanistan under Taliban control; forbade the provision of technical assistance, training or specialists in any sphere of military operations; prohibited civil flights to territories under Taliban control; and proposed that UN member states close all offices of the Taliban movement as well as the Afghan airline, Arian.

[75] Sultan Akimbekov, 'The conflict in Afghanistan: conditions, problems, and prospects', in Boris Rumer (ed.), *Central Asia: A Gathering Storm?* (New York and London: M. E. Sharpe, 2002), p. 101.

[76] See, e.g., the declarations from the CIS meeting of the commanders of border troops on 19 February 2001 (*Interfax*, 20 February 2001).

[77] See, e.g., the press conference with Putin on 23 July 2000. *Diplomaticheskii vestnik* 8 (2000), p. 101.

[78] The fact that at the CIS summit of January 2000 the issue was transferred to the ministries of defence reflected the narrow approach to terrorism.

[79] Andrei Mikhailov, 'Geopoliticheskaya lovushka dlya Moskvy' [Geopolitical trap for Moscow], *Nezavisimoe voennoe obozrenie* 24 (7–13 July 2000), pp. 1–2.

[80] Mekhman Gafarli, 'Narkobiznes i islamskii ekstremizm' [Drug trafficking and Islamic extremism], *Nezavisimaya gazeta*, 23 October 1999, p. 5.

[81] Mekhman, 'Narkobiznes i islamskii ekstremizm', p. 5.

[82] Igor Rotar, 'Neprostoe sosedstvo' [Not a straightforward neighbourhood], *Nezavisimaya gazeta*, 2 July 1999, p. 5.

[83] Valerii Popov, 'Ukhodit iz Tadzhikistana nelzya' [It is impossible to leave Tajikistan], *Nezavisimoe voennoe obozrenie* 5 (11–17 February 2000), p. 2.

[84] Mikhail Pereplesnin, 'Taliby pytayutsya poluchit priznanie mira' [The Taliban seek international recognition], *Nezavisimaya gazeta*, 18 February 2000, p. 6.

[85] 'Basic Principles, Objectives and Tasks for Russian Policy in Relation to the CIS at the Present Stage' and 'Main Directions of the Development of Russia's Relations with CIS States at the Present Stage'. See the reference and comments by Deputy Foreign Minister Vasilii Sredin a year later in 'Vneshnyaya politika Rossii na sovremennom etape: Vystuplenie stats-sekretarya: zamestitelya ministra inostrannykh del Rossii V. D. Sredina v Rossiiskoi akademii gossluzhby, 29 marta' [The foreign policy of Russia at the present stage: speech of Deputy Foreign Minister V. D. Sredin at the Russian Academy of State Administration, 29 March], *Diplomaticheskii vestnik* 4 (2001), pp. 137–42.

[86] http://www.pravitelstvo.gov.ru/data/news_print.html?he_id=15&news_id=53

[87] ITAR-TASS, 29 February 2000.

[88] Stephen Blank, 'American grand strategy and the Transcaspian region', Paper presented at the conference on Central Asia in a New Security Context, Swedish Institute of International Affairs, Stockholm, September 1999; and Anthony Richter, 'Great expectations on the Caspian: can US policy live up to them?', in Caspian Studies Program Experts Conference Report 'Succession and long-term stability in the Caspian region', Harvard University, John F. Kennedy Shool of Government, October 1999.

[89] ITAR-TASS *World Service*, 8 April 2000/Reuters, 8 April 2000.

[90] Interfax, 7 April 2000/BBC Monitoring, *Newsfile*, 7 Apr. 2000.

[91] Dmitri Trenin, 'Russia–NATO relations: time to pick up the pieces', *NATO Review* 49 (Spring/Summer 2000).

[92] Roy Allison, 'Structures and frameworks for security policy cooperation in Central Asia', in Roy Allison and Lena Jonson (eds), *Central Asian Security: The New International Context* (Washington, DC and London: Brookings Institution Press and Royal Institute of International Affairs, 2001), p. 225.

[93] *Nezavisimaya gazeta*, 5 August 2000.

[94] Sultan Akimbekov, 'The conflict in Afghanistan: conditions, problems, and prospects', in Boris Rumer (ed.), *Central Asia: A Gathering Storm?* (New York and London: M. E. Sharpe, 2002), p. 101.

[95] *Renmin Ribao*, 4 July 1998, referred to by Guangcheng Xing, 'China and Central Asia', in Roy Allison and Lena Jonson (eds), *Central Asian Security Dynamics: The New International Context*.

[96] For the joint declaration by the summit see ITAR-TASS, 25 August 1999.

[97] 'Sovmestnoe kommyunike po itogam vstrechi ministrov inostrannykh del respubliki Kazakhstan, Kitaiskoi Narodnoi Respubliki, Kyrgyzskoi Respubliki, Rossiiskoi

Federatsii i Respubliki Tadzhikistan' [Joint communiqué from the meeting of the foreign ministers of the Republic of Kazakhstan, the People's Republic of China, the Republic of Kyrgyzstan, the Russian Federation and the Republic of Tajikistan], Dushanbe, 4 July 2000, *Diplomaticheskii vestnik* 8 (2000), pp. 14–16.

[98] For a more detailed presentation of the organization see the analyses by Roy Allison on sub-regional security cooperation in Central Asia. Roy Allison, 'Policy cooperation in Central Asia', in Allison and Jonson (eds), *Central Asian Security: The New International Context*; and Jyotsna Bakshi, 'Sino-Russian strategic partnership in Central Asia: implications for India', *Strategic Analysis* 35/2 (May 2001).

[99] BBC, *Inside Central Asia* 379 (11–17 June 2001).

[100] See e.g. the evaluation in International Crisis Group (ICG), *Central Asia: Islamist Mobilisation and Regional Security*, ICG Asia Report no. 14 (Osh/Brussels: ICG, 1 March 2001). Amin Saikal wrote in 1995: 'It is important not to exaggerate the potential for ethno-nationalist conflicts and Islamic radicalism in Central Asia'. Amin Saikal, 'Russia and Central Asia', in Amin Saikal and William Maley (eds), *Russia in Search of its Future* (Cambridge: Cambridge University Press, 1995), p. 151.

Chapter 5

POST-SEPTEMBER 2001

[1] 'Korotko: Politika: Prezident' [In brief: politics: the president], *Nezavisimaya gazeta*, 13 September 2001.

[2] Andrey Fedorov (Programme Director at the Council for Foreign and Defence Policy), 'Rossiya stoit pered vyborom: Podderzhav antiterroristicheskie mery SshA, Moskva mozhet uskorit sblizhenie s ES i NATO' [Russia faces a choice: in supporting the USA's anti-terrorist measures, Moscow can speed up rapprochement with the EU and NATO], *Nezavisimaya gazeta*, 14 September 2001.

[3] Vladimir Mukhin, 'SshA ishchut voennye bazy v SNG: Uzbekistan, Tadzhikistan i severnyi Afganistan mogut stat zalozhnikami antiterroristicheskoi operatsii' [USA seeks military bases in the CIS: Uzbekistan, Tajikistan and northern Afghanistan may be hostages to anti-terrorist operations], *Nezavismaya gazeta*, 15 September 2001.

[4] ORT Vremya Programme, 14 September 2001/ITAR-TASS, 14 September 2001; and *Jamestown Monitor* 170 (18 September 2001).

[5] 'Rossiya mozhet sygrat svoyu partiyu: Eksperty "NG" uvereny, chto vneshnyaya politika dostatochno pragmatichna' [Russia may play a trick in its favour: NG experts confident that foreign policy is pragmatic enough], *Nezavisimaya gazeta*, 15 September 2001.

[6] 'Rossiya mozhet sygrat svoyu partiyu: Eksperty "NG" uvereny, chto vneshnyaya politika dostatochno pragmatichna' [Russia may play a trick in its favour: NG experts confident that foreign policy is pragmatic enough], *Nezavisimaya gazeta*, 15 September 2001.

[7] See, for example, Igor Bunin from the Centre for Political Technology in 'Rossiya mozhet sygrat svoyu partiyu: Eksperty "NG" uvereny, chto vneshnyaya politika dostatochno pragmatichna' [Russia may play a trick in its favour: NG experts confident that foreign policy is pragmatic enough], *Nezavisimaya gazeta*, 15 September 2001.

[8] Marina Volkova, 'Prezident reshaet filosofskie voprosy: V Kremle dumayot nad tem, kakie mery po borbe s terrorizmom mozhet predlozhit' Rossiya' [The president resolves philosophical questions: the Kremlin considers what measures Russia can propose in the fight against terrorism], *Nezavisimaya gazeta*, 20 September 2001.

[9] *Jamestown Monitor* 170 (18 September 2001).

[10] *Jamestown Monitor* 170 (18 September 2001).

[11] http://www.kremlin.ru/actions/2001/09/17.shtml

[12] 'Rushailo otpravilsya v poezdku po stranam Tsentralnoi Azii' [Rushailo sets off on a trip to the countries of Central Asia], *Nezavisimaya gazeta*, 18 September 2001.

[13] Alan Kasaev and Armen Khanbabyan, 'Den velikogo peredela: Ot segodnyashego resheniya Vladimira Putina zavisit sud'ba SNG' [The day of the great re-division: the fate of the CIS depends on Vladimir Putin's decision today], *Nezavisimaya gazeta*, 20 September 2001.

[14] Marina Volkova, 'Prezident reshaet filosofskie voprosy: V Kremle dumayot nad tem, kakie mery po borbe s terrorizmom mozhet predlozhit Rossiya' [The president resolves philosophical questions: the Kremlin considers what measures Russia can propose in the fight against terrorism], *Nezavisimaya gazeta*, 20 September 2001.

[15] Marina Volkova, 'Putin sozyvaet politelitu' [Putin calls together the political elite], *Nezavisimaya gazeta*, 25 September 2001; BBC, *Inside Central Asia* 393 (17–23 September 2001).

[16] http://www.kremlin.ru/actions/2001/09/23.shtml

[17] Statement by Putin, 24 September 2001, http://www.kremlin.ru/text/appears/2001/09/28639.shtml

[18] See statement by Foreign Minister Igor Ivanov: 'President Putin reached agreement on this issue with the leaders of the five Central Asian countries over the weekend' and 'only flights with humanitarian cargo are meant here'. Interfax, 26 September 2001.

[19] See Putin's speech in German Bundestag, Berlin, 25 September 2001, http://www.kremlin.ru/text/appears/2001/09/28641.shtml.

[20] *Diplomaticheskii vestnik* 11 (2001), p. 26.

[21] BBC, *Inside Central Asia* 395 (1–7 October 2001).

[22] BBC, *Inside Central Asia* 392 (10–16 September 2001), p. 2.

[23] Vladimir Mukhin, 'Vashington i Moskva uzhe planiruet poslevoennoe ustroistvo mira' [Washington and Moscow are already planning the post-war structure of the world], *Nezavisimaya gazeta*, 21 September 2001. See also BBC, *Inside Central Asia* 393 (17–23 September 2001). Kvashnin and Fahim also met 18 October. BBC, *Inside Central Asia* (15–21 October 2001).

[24] Vladimir Georgiev, 'Uzbekistan prodalsya Vashingtonu za 8 mld. dollarov' [Uzbekistan for sale to Washington for 8$ billion], *Nezavisimaya gazeta*, 19 October 2001, p. 1. The military complained that the US Air Force only bombed those targets which would benefit Dostum and his troops, not the Tajik troops.

[25] 'War in Afghanistan', *Strategic Survey 2001/2002* (London: The International Institute for Strategic Studies, 2002), p. 236.

[26] 'War in Afghanistan', *Strategic Survey 2001/2002* (London: The International Institute for Strategic Studies, 2002), p. 243.

[27] Aleksandr Umnov, 'Rossiya i Pakistan na afganskom pole' [Russia and Pakistan on the Afghan battlefield], *Nezavisimaya gazeta*, 17 October 2001, p. 6.

[28] *Jamestown Monitor* 202 (30 November 2001). The official intention was to set up a Russian hospital and a Russian embassy in Kabul.

[29] Charles Fairbanks, 'Being there', *The National Interest* 68 (2002).

[30] BBC, *Inside Central Asia* 396 (8–14 October 2001).

[31] BBC, *Inside Central Asia* 420 (1–7 April 2002).

[32] *Nezavisimaya gazeta*, 9 April 2002.

[33] Uzbek Radio First Programme (Tashkent), 29 August 2002, 1120 GMT (in Russian)/BBC Monitoring, *Central Asia*, 29 August 2002.

³⁴ *Jamestown Monitor* 227 (11 December 2002). The first four US military transport planes landed at Manas international airport on 18 December 2001. BBC, *Inside Central Asia* 406 (17 December 2001–1 January 2002).

³⁵ *Asia Plus*, 17 January 2002.

³⁶ Interfax/*Asia Plus*, 15 March 2002.

³⁷ *Jamestown Monitor* 170 (18 September 2001).

³⁸ ITAR-TASS, 14 September 2001.

³⁹ At the end of September President Rakhmonov told US Secretary of State Colin Powell that Tajikistan would cooperate with the USA to fight terrorism. BBC, *Inside Central Asia* 395 (1–7 October 2001).

⁴⁰ DPA, 18 October 2001; and *Jamestown Monitor* 204 (6 November 2001).

⁴¹ *Jamestown Monitor* 204 (6 November 2001).

⁴² Raffi Khatchadourian, 'US eyes bases in Tajikistan', Eurasia Insight, 6 November 2001.

⁴³ BBC, *Inside Central Asia* 414 (18–24 February 2002).

⁴⁴ *Asia Plus*, 24 September 2002.

⁴⁵ BBC, *Inside Central Asia* 394 (24–30 September 2001).

⁴⁶ According to the Tajik Ministry of Economy and Trade, the volume of exports and imports fell because of the introduction of real restrictions by Kazakhstan and Uzbekistan for the movement of Tajik traffic through their territory. *Biznes i Politika*, 15 March 2002.

⁴⁷ BBC, *Inside Central Asia* 394 (24–30 September 2001).

⁴⁸ Chairman of the State Border Protection Committee of Tajikistan Saidanvar Kamolov, Dushanbe, 2002. As reported, most of those killed were from the Asht, Shahriston, Isfara and Panjakent districts of Sughd Province

⁴⁹ *Asia Plus*, 13 February 2002

⁵⁰ *Asia Plus*, 27 August 2002.

⁵¹ Iskandar Asadullaev, 'O kornyakh terrorizma' [On the roots of terrorism], *Biznis i politika*, 1 March 2002, pp. 1–2.

⁵² *Asia Plus*, 31 July 2002.

⁵³ BBC, *Inside Central Asia* 446 (30 September–6 October 2002, Internet edition).

⁵⁴ Varorud News Agency (Sughd), 4 October 2002 (in Russian)/BBC Monitoring, 7 October 2004.

⁵⁵ Interfax/*Asia Plus*, 30 September 2002.

⁵⁶ 'Zasedanie Soveta glav pravitelstv SNG' [Session of the CIS heads of government], *Diplomaticheskii vestnik* 10 (October 2001), p. 62.

⁵⁷ See, e.g., the CST meetings of 2 October 2001 and 23 October 2001: 'Konsultatsii polnomochnykh predstavitelei gosudarstv-uchastnikov dogovora o kollektivnoi bezopasnosti' [Consultations of the plenipotentiaries of the governments of the CST participating states], *Diplomaticheskii vestnik* 11 (2001), p. 81.

⁵⁸ BBC, *Inside Central Asia* 395 (1–7 October 2001).

⁵⁹ 'Vneocherednoe zasedanie Komiteta Sekretarei Sovetov bezopasnosti gosudarstv uchastnikov dogovora o kollektivnoi bezopasnosti' [Extraordinary session of the Committee of the Secretaries of the National Security Councils of the CST participating states], *Diplomaticheskii vestnik* 11 (2001), p. 81.

⁶⁰ As reported in March 2002, although documents on weapons and equipment had been ratified, for a number of practical reasons no deliveries of weapons had so far taken place. Georgiev, Vladimir, 'Nash otvet "Kerzonu"' [Our answer to Kerzon], *Nezavisimaya gazeta*, 23 March 2002, p. 5.

⁶¹ *Diplomaticheskii vestnik* 12 (2001), pp. 68–9.

⁶² *Diplomaticheskii vestnik* 2 (2002), pp. 57–8.

[63] Russia TV (Moscow), 15 March 2002, 1400 GMT (in Russian)/BBC Monitoring, *Former Soviet Union–Political*, 15 March 2002.

[64] 'Sessiya Soveta kollektivnoi bezopasnosti gosudarstv-uchastnikov Dogovora o kollektivnoi bezopasnosti' [Session of the Collective Security Council of the CST participating states], *Diplomaticheskii vestnik* 6 (2002), pp. 76–8.

[65] 'Sessiya Soveta kollektivnoi bezopasnosti gosudarstv-uchastnikov Dogovora o kollektivnoi bezopasnosti', *Diplomaticheskii vestnik* 6 (2002), pp. 76–8.

[66] RFE/RL, *Newsline*, 8 October 2002.

[67] ITAR-TASS, 7 October 2002 1203 GMT (in Russian)/BBC Monitoring, *Former Soviet Union–Political*, 7 October 2002.

[68] V. Lukin, 'Russia's indispensable role in the fight against terrorism', *International Affairs* 48/1 (2002), p. 59.

[69] The anti-terrorist centre makes monthly analytical reports on the situation in the CIS territory, which contain information about terrorism, and conclusions and forecasts about possible developments. The materials are supplied to all the secret services of the CIS, including the Russian Federal Security Service (FSB). Under bilateral agreements the FSB sends its materials and reports from the CIS anti-terrorist centre to the related services of the United States. Interfax (Moscow), 13 June 2002, 1152 GMT (in English)/BBC Monitoring, *Former Soviet Union–Political*, 13 June 2002.

[70] RFE/RL, *Central Asia Report* 2/44 (21 November 2002).

[71] Karimov visited the USA on 11–14 March, Akaev on 23–29 September and Rakhmonov in early December.

[72] BBC, *Inside Central Asia* 456 (9–15 December 2002).

[73] Vladimir Mukhin, 'Rossiya vernulas v Tsentralnuyu Aziyu' [Russia has returned to Central Asia], *Nezavisimaya gazeta*, 24 October 2003, p. 2.

[74] Viktoriya Panfilova, 'Rossiya zanovo osvaivaet Tsentralnuyu Aziyu' [Russia approaches Central Asia again], *Nezavisimaya gazeta*, 23 September 2003, p. 5.

[75] According to the Russian Ministry of Defence there will be 4 SU-27 fighters, 5 SU-25 attack planes (including one combat plane), 1 An-26 military transport plane, and 2 Mi-8 helicopters. See BBC, *Inside Central Asia*, 12 October 2003. According to Russian sources at Manas in October 2003 there were 25 F-16 fighters and military transport planes C-130 and about 2000 men from the US-led international anti-terrorist coalition (among them US soldiers). See Vladimir Mukhin, 'Rossiya vernulas v Tsentralnuyu Aziyu', *Nezavisimaya gazeta*, 24 October 2003, p. 2.

[76] See, for example, Viktoriya Panfilova, 'Rossiya zanovo osvaivaet Tsentralnuyu Aziyu', *Nezavisimaya gazeta*, 23 September 2003, p. 5.

[77] BBC, *Inside Central Asia* 456 (9–15 December 2002).

[78] Associated Press, 12 December 2002.

[79] According to the Secretary-General of the CST, in November 2002 the CST had already developed mechanisms for initiating operations by the Rapid Reaction Force. 'If the situation in Central Asia aggravates, the Collective Rapid-Deployment Forces are ready to act immediately upon receiving a corresponding directive and decision of the collective leadership of the ... signatories to the Collective Security Treaty. A mechanism [for] making such a decision within a short period of time at the level of heads of state and an agreement on the relocation of corresponding forces and assets of the Collective Rapid-Deployment Forces have been worked out.' AVN, 21 November 2002.

[80] 'Sessiya Soveta kollektivnoi bezopasnosti uchastnikov DKB' [Session of the CST Council of Collective Security], *Diplomaticheskii vestnik* 5 (2003), p. 58.

[81] 'Za bezopasnost nado platit' [Security has to be paid for], *Nezavisimaya gazeta*, 20 May 2003.

[82] *Asia Plus*, 28 April 2003. The Joint Staff/Unified HQ is due to start operating on 1 January 2004. RFE/RL, *Newsline*, 30 April 2003.

[83] Interviews with Nikolai Bordyuzha: 'Za bezopasnost nado platit', *Nezavisimaya gazeta*, 20 May 2003; and 'Vo imya kollektivnoi bezopasnosti' [In the name of collective security], *Krasnaya zvezda*, 21 May 2003.

[84] Russia began its deliveries in 2004 taking upon itself the task of ensuring that no re-export takes place to third countries.

[85] See, e.g., Vladimir Mukhin, 'Rakety dlya diktatury Turkmenbashi' [Rockets for the dictator Turkmenbashi], *Nezavisimaya gazeta*, 12 November 2003, p. 1.

[86] This fear is reflected in Sergei Sorkut, 'Grozit terroristam budem iz Bishkeka' [We will threaten the terrorists from Bishkek], *Nezavisimoe voennoe obozrenie* 43 (6–13 December 2002), p 3.

[87] Vladimir Mukhin, 'Moskva pokupaet soyuznikov' [Moscow buys allies], *Dipkurer NG*, 21 April 2003, p. 9.

[88] 'Vystuplenie ministra inostrannykh del RF I. S. Ivanova v Gosudarstvennoi Dume v ramkakh "pravitelstvennoga chasa" 13 marta' [Speech of the Foreign Minister of the Russian Federation, I. S. Ivanov, in the State Duma during the 'Government's Hour', 13 March], *Diplomaticheskii vestnik* 4 (2002), p. 57.

[89] 'Vystuplenie V. V. Putina' [Speech of V. V. Putin, 12 July 2002], *Diplomaticheskii vestnik* 8 (2002), pp. 10–13.

[90] BBC, *Inside Central Asia* 437 (29 July–4 August 2002). Russia invited all the Caspian littoral states to participate in the exercise, but Turkmenistan—the only Central Asian state with a Caspian coast—only sent an observer.

[91] It is interesting to note that the hardliner Colonel General Leonid Ivashov was among those who warned Putin against carrying out the threat to bomb the Pankisi Gorge. He and several other Russian press commentators argued that Russia did not have the capacity to become involved in the hopeless task of bombing a mountainous area in order to prevent the movement of Chechen rebels. They also warned about negative reaction from the West. Leonid Ivashov, 'Opasnye igry na Kavkaze' [Dangerous games in the Caucasus], *Nezavisimaya gazeta*, 9 October 2002, p. 7.

[92] Tatyana Rubleva, 'Moskva stala Vashingtonom' [Russia becomes like Washington], *Dipkurer NG* 12 (2 December 2002), p. 10.

[93] See Putin's annual State of the Nation address to the Russian Parliament, 18 April 2002. BBC Monitoring, *Former Soviet Union–Political*, 18 April 2002.

[94] Putin's annual State of the Nation address to the Russian Parliament, 18 April 2002. BBC Monitoring, *Former Soviet Union–Political*, 18 April 2002.

[95] Bobo Lo calls this practice the 'myth-making of CIS integration'. Bobo Lo, *Vladimir Putin and the Evolution of Russian Foreign Policy* (London: Royal Institute of International Affairs and Blackwell, 2003).

[96] Grinberg, R. S., 'Vektory strukturivaniya postsovetskogo ekonomicheskogo pravitelstva' [Vectors of the structuring of the post-Soviet economic space], Paper presented at a conference on 'Rossiya i SNG v noveisheikh evropeiskikh integratsionnykh protsessakh' [Russia and the CIS in the latest European integration processes], Moscow, October 2002.

[97] During these years the level of investment in Russia itself was very low.

[98] The membership is the same as that of the CST—Armenia, Belarus, Kazakhstan, Kyrgyzstan, Russia and Tajikistan.

[99] Lyudmila Romanova, Elena Lashkina and Andrei Polevoi, 'Provokatsiya nakanune sammita' [Provocation on the eve of the summit], *Nezavisimaya gazeta*, 1 June 2001, pp. 1 and 5. The Inter-State Council of the EEC was structured in such a way as to give the member states a voting capacity based on the economic strength and financial

contribution of each. Russia will have 40 per cent of the votes, Kazakhstan and Belarus 20 per cent each, and Kyrgyzstan and Tajikistan 10 per cent each. Decisions are taken by a two-thirds majority. In theory Russia is able to block proposals which it dislikes but unable to force through something against the will of the other member states.

[100] Lena Jonson, *Russia and Central Asia: A New Web of Relations* (London: Royal Institute of International Affairs, 1998), p. 76.

[101] S. Z. Zhiznin and P. I. Rodionov, 'Energicheskaya diplomatiya v Kaspiisko-Chernomorskom regione (gazovye aspekty)' [Energy diplomacy in the Caspian–Black Sea region: gas aspects], *Diplomaticheskii vestnik* 6 (June 2000), pp. 79–87.

[102] *Asia Plus*, 'Priorities of development of the Eurasian Economic Community (EAEC) for the coming four years', 28 April 2003. The summit also discussed the creation of a free trade zone by 2006, a transport union, a common agricultural market, joint efforts to combat drug trafficking, a common migration policy, and coordination for dates of accession to the WTO.

[103] On 22 April 2003 the Collegium at the Foreign Ministry discussed 'The role of the energy factor in Russian foreign policy' at a special meeting. *Diplomaticheskii vestnik* 5 (2003), p. 122.

[104] Sergei Blagov, 'Efforts to produce "Eurasian OPEC" fall short at CIS summit', Eurasianet, 1 March 2002.

[105] 'Russia's alliance with Central Asian gas could serve Europe', UzReport.com, 6 November 2002, Document uzrepe0020021106dyb60005m

[106] 'Russia's alliance with Central Asian gas could serve Europe', UzReport.com, 6 November 2002, Document uzrepe0020021106dyb60005m.

[107] Isabel Gorst, 'Focus: Russia gas alliance', *Platts Oilgram News* 80/205 (24 October 2002).

[108] On 17 October Russian Deputy Foreign Minister Andrei Denisov stated that Russia 'supports major economic projects in the area, including the construction of a Trans-Afghan gas pipeline via Turkmenistan, Afghanistan and Pakistan'. BBC, *Inside Central Asia* 448 (21–27 October 2002).

[109] RFE/RL, *Newsline*, 31 May 2002; and RFE/RL, *Newsline*, 21 October 2002.

[110] BBC, *Inside Central Asia* 448 (21–27 October 2002).

[111] Turkmen. RU Internet newspaper web site, 17 July 2002/BBC, *Inside Central Asia* 435 (15–21 July 2002).

[112] ITAR-TASS, 17 October 2002/BBC, *Inside Central Asia* 448 (21–27 October 2002).

[113] BBC, *Inside Central Asia* 458 (23–29 December 2002).

[114] BBC, *Inside Central Asia* 437 (29 July–4 August 2002).

[115] According to Kyrgyz Finance Minister Bolot Abildayev. BBC, *Inside Central Asia* 455 (2–8 December 2002).

[116] Nabi Ziyadullaev, 'SNG: natsionalnaya bezopasnost i ekspansiya SshA' [The CIS: national security and the expansion of the USA], *Svobodnaya Mysl* 6 (2002), pp. 73–87.

[117] RFE/RL, *Newsline*, 12 March 2003.

[118] Vechernyi Bishkek web site (Bishkek), 23 October 2002 (in Russian)/BBC Worldwide Monitoring, 23 October 2002.

[119] *Asia Plus*, 28 April 2003.

[120] Interfax, 3 September 2003. Proven gas reserves are 5.7 billion cubic metres. Kyrgyzstan has bought 1 billion cubic metres of gas per annum. Interfax/BBC, *Inside Central Asia*, 18 May 2003.

[121] Marika S. Karayianni, 'Russia's Foreign policy for Central Asia Through Energy Agreements', *Central Asia and the Caucasus* 4 (2003), p. 93.

[122] Angela Sikamova, 'Chubais dotyanetsya do Yaponii' [Chubais reaches to Japan], *Nezavisimaya gazeta*, 18 September 2003, p. 3.

[123] Interview with the Kyrgyz Deputy Prime Minister Dzhoomart Otorbaev in Viktoriya Panfilova, 'My vlezli v dolgi, no my vyzhili' [We got into debt, but we made it], *Nezavisimaya gazeta*, 17 October 2003, p. 5. He also said Kyrgyzstan is attractive for investments in six sectors: hydro-energy, metals (gold, stibium, tin, volfram), tourism, agricultural products, information technology, and services in the broad sense (including transport, financing, banking, and so on).

[124] Russian experts interpreted the energy agreements with Kyrgyzstan as mainly political in nature and a compensation for the general reduction of Russian influence. See for example Viktoriya Panfilova, 'Ne gazom edinym' [They unite not because of the gas], *Nezavisimaya gazeta*, 12 May 2003.

[125] *Asia Plus*, 24 April 2003.

[126] Russia would buy about 6 billion cubic metres of Turkmen gas in 2004, and this figure could increase to 80 billion cubic metres per year by 2009. BBC, *Inside Central Asia*, 13 April 2003.

[127] Jonson, *Russia and Central Asia: A New Web of Relations*, pp. 63–4.

[128] *Jamestown Fortnight in Review*, 26 May 2000.

[129] BBC, *Inside Central Asia* 439 (12–18 August 2002).

[130] BBC, *Inside Central Asia* 444 (16–22 September 2002).

[131] Aleksei Grivach and Arkadii Dubnov, '"Gazprom" vernulsya v Turkmeniyu' [Gazprom returns to Turkmenistan], *Vremya vedomosti*, 3 April 2003, p 7. However, since 50 per cent of the price is payable in kind, actual export revenues will be half the notional amount. After 2006 the price will be determined by world market prices. Arkadii Dubnov, 'Turkmenbashi boosted by Moscow deal'. RCA 199 (17 April 2003).

[132] BBC, *Inside Central Asia* 423 (22–28 April 2002).

[133] BBC, *Inside Central Asia*, 15 April 2003.

[134] Arkadii Dubnov, Russian Regional News, May 2003.

[135] Viktoriya Panfilova, *Nezavisimaya gazeta*, 10 April 2003. Both men (former Central Bank chief Hudayberdi Orazow and former ambassador to Turkey Nurmuhammet Hanamow) now have Russian citizenship.

[136] RFE/RL, *Central Asia Report* 3/16 (1 May 2003).

[137] Igor Torbakov, 'Russia set to toughen position on Turkmenistan over dual citizenship dispute', Eurasia Insight, 17 June 2003 www.eurasianet.org

[138] BBC, *Inside Central Asia*, 22 June 2003.

[139] Elena Baikova, 'Strasti po turkmenskomu gazu' [Passions for Turkmen gas], *Nezavisimaya gazeta*, 13 October 2003, p. 6.

[140] ITAR-TASS, 8 August 2003. In April 2003 Tajik media reported that in talks on regulating the status of the Russian 'Window' radar station in Tajikistan, built in Soviet times, the Tajik side wanted the Russians to write off their debt, and to relieve the situation of Tajiks in Russia as a kind of compensation. Varorud News Agency, 30 April 2003.

[141] BBC, *Inside Central Asia*, 21 September 2003.

[142] Interfax, 25 September 2003.

[143] In July 2002 the Russian military inaugurated a sophisticated optical tracking facility in Tajikistan that is capable of monitoring objects in space. See 'Russia: Moscow seen as moving to increase military ties with Central Asia', rferl.org, 6 August 2002. On Russian plans to reorganize the 201st Motorized Infantry Division into a regular army base see RFE/RL, *Newsline*, 28 July 2003.

[144] Economist Intelligence Unit, *Country Profile Kyrgyzstan/Tajikistan 2002* (London, 2002), p. 80.

¹⁴⁵ *Asia Plus*, 4 March 2002.

¹⁴⁶ *Asia Plus*, 17 April 2003.

¹⁴⁷ Russian NTV, 26 April 2003/BBC, *Inside Central Asia*, 27 April 2003.

¹⁴⁸ *Asia Plus*, 28 April 2003.

¹⁴⁹ The Head of the Dushanbe office of the International Organization for Migration, Igor Bosc, to ITAR-TASS, 19 November 2002.

¹⁵⁰ BBC, *Inside Central Asia* 424 (29 April–5 May 2002).

¹⁵¹ BBC, *Inside Central Asia* 454 25 (November–1 December).

¹⁵² R. Ghani (political scientist), in *Biznes i Politika*, 18 March 2002. In June, the Russian Ambassador to Tajikistan, Maxim Peshkov, reaffirmed the Russian plans for cooperation with Tajikistan, mentioning the construction of the Sang Tuda hydroelectric power station and the transmission of electricity produced by the Dushanbe thermal electric power station to Afghanistan. 'Both projects are very beneficial. Russia has technical and personnel opportunities for implementing them, but it does not always have financial opportunities.' Work had to be done to drum up foreign investment, Peshkov said.

¹⁵³ BBC, *Inside Central Asia* 450 (28 October–3 November 2002). It is planned to generate up to 13 billion kWh of electricity per year.

¹⁵⁴ Tajik Radio, 30 October 2002/BBC, *Inside Central Asia* 450 (28 October–3 November 2002). The first stage was to consist of the construction of a 150–160-metre-high dam and the commissioning of two units, and the second stage the construction of another 335-metre high dam and the commissioning of four units. The Tajik–Russian agreement was estimated to be worth US\$ 100 million.

¹⁵⁵ *Asia Plus*, 13 March 2003.

¹⁵⁶ *Asia Plus*, 28 April 2003.

¹⁵⁷ Total estimated resources are about 1000 billion cubic metres. Interfax/BBC, *Inside Central Asia*, 18 May 2003. Rangun, located 20 km from Dushanbe, would be able to provide central Asia with gas, while northern Tajikistan imports from Uzbekistan, and the southern part has its own production.

¹⁵⁸ Marika S. Karayanni, 'Russia's Foreign policy for Central Asia passes through energy agreements', *Central Asia and the Caucasus*, 4 (2003), pp. 93–4.

¹⁵⁹ Among them the Agreement on Interstate Relations, Friendship and Cooperation, an agreement on developing economic relations in 1998–2007, an agreement between the governments on cooperation between their administrative regions of May 2000 and, finally, the agreement between the city of Moscow and Uzbekistan of September 2001.

¹⁶⁰ Economist Intelligence Unit, *Country Profile Uzbekistan 2002* (London: EIU, 2002), p. 53.

¹⁶¹ Interfax News Agency (Moscow), 7 June 2002, 1512 GMT (in English)/BBC Monitoring, *Former Soviet Union–Political*, 7 June 2002.

¹⁶² This made it possible to sell six Il-78MKIs to India with deliveries over a three-year period. Konstantin Lantrapov, 'Rossiya i Uzbekistan podelili "Ily"' [Russia and Uzbekistan divide Ilyushins], *Kommersant daily*, 28 March 2003, p 14.

¹⁶³ 1.86 trillion cubic metres (2001). Gas production was 55.21 bcm per year by 2000, almost 30 per cent higher than the 1992 level.

¹⁶⁴ ITAR-TASS, 16 January 2003/BBC, *Inside Central Asia*, 19 January 2003.

¹⁶⁵ Faruk Turaev, 'Prickly Uzbekistan comes closer to Russia', Transitions Online, 19 August 2003.

¹⁶⁶ 'Russia: Lukoil leads in external investment', *APS Review of Oil Market Trends (Factiva)*, 23 September 2002. The explored reserves in Bukhara–Khiva and Gissar are estimated at 250 bcm of gas and 10 million tons of condensate.

[167] Lukianchikov interviewed in Dosym Satpaev, 'Russia pushes for Central Asian OPEC', *Institute of War and Peace Reporting* 108 (15 March 2003).

[168] On the SCO see chapter 4.

[169] A statement by the prime ministers of the SCO of 14 September 2001.

[170] Xin Guangcheng, 'The Shanghai Cooperation Organization: fighting terrorism, extremism and separatism', *Central Asia and the Caucasus* 4 (2002), p. 14.

[171] Charter of the Shanghai Cooperation Organization, signed on 7 June 2002 in St Petersburg.

[172] BBC, *Inside Central Asia* 429 (3–9 June 2002).

[173] RIA News Agency (Moscow), 31 October 2002, 1644 GMT (in Russian)/BBC Monitoring, *Former Soviet Union–Political*, 31 October 2002.

[174] ITAR-TASS (Moscow), 5 November 2002, 0841 GMT (in Russian)/BBC Monitoring, *Former Soviet Union–Political*, 5 November 2002.

[175] BBC, *Inside Central Asia* 428 (27 May–2 June 2002).

[176] BBC, *Inside Central Asia* 428 (27 May–2 June 2002).

[177] BBC, *Inside Central Asia* 429 (3–9 June) 2002).

[178] BBC, *Inside Central Asia* 429 (3–9 June 2002).

[179] Herspring and Rutland, pp. 238–9.

[180] Reproduced in DNB, IPD, MID, Moscow, 15 November 2001.

[181] For an analysis of Russian–US relations after 2001 see Alex Pravda, 'Putin's foreign policy after 11 September: radical or revolutionary?', in Gabriel Gorodetsky (ed.), *Russia Between East and West: Russian Foreign Policy on the Threshold of the Twenty-First Century* (London and Portland, Oreg.: Cummings Center Series/Frank Cass, 2003); Dov Lynch, *Russia Faces Europe*, Chaillot Papers no. 60 (Paris: European Union Institute for Security Studies, May 2003); and Ingmar Oldberg, 'Foreign policy priorities under Putin: A tour d'horizon', in Bertil Nygren and Christer Pursiainen (eds), *Dimensions of Russian Security Policy* (forthcoming).

[182] Prezident Rossiiskoi Federatsii (official Web site of the President of the Russian Federation), 'Rossiisko-amerikanskaia vstrecha na vysshem urovne' [Russian–US meeting at the highest level], 24 May 2002, http://www.president.kremlin.ru/summit8, retrieved 31 May 2002.

[183] Dov Lynch, *Russia Faces Europe*, Chaillot Papers no. 60 (Paris: European Union Institute for Security Studies, May 2003).

[184] See www.nato.int/docu/basictxt/bo2052e.pdf.

[185] The working group on Afghanistan of first deputy foreign minister Trubnikov and deputy secretary of state Armitage had its fifth meeting on 1 November 2002. 'Sovmestnoe zayavlenie rossiisko-amerikanskoi rabochei gruppy po Afganistanu' [Joint statement of the Russian–American working group on Afghanistan], *Diplomaticheskii vestnik*, 12 (2001), p. 19.

[186] Trenin developed a detailed programme for Russian–US security cooperation including: (a) establishing a permanent liaison between Russian and US forces' headquarters in Central Asia and between the Russian General Staff and the US Central Command headquarters; (b) engaging in intensive intelligence-sharing on international terrorism, weapons of mass destruction proliferation and other major security threats to the region, along with regular joint threat assessments; (c) strengthening cooperation among US, Russian, European, and Central Asian law enforcement agencies dealing with drug trafficking; (d) harmonizing national military and security doctrines for dealing with current and future threats, including exchanges of students and instructors in anti-terrorist operations; (e) holding periodic joint exercises with Central Asian military and security services; (f) extending US equipment support for Russian border guards, especially those on the Afghan–Tajik border; and (g) engaging China, to the extent

appropriate and at the right level, in the aforementioned activities while inviting the United States to join SCO as an observer. Dmitri Trenin, 'Southern watch: Russia's policy in Central Asia', *Journal of International Affairs* 56/2 (Spring 2003), pp. 130–1.

Chapter 6

RUSSIAN DOMESTIC FACTORS

[1] Ekaterina Stepanova, 'Russia's Approach to the Fight Against Terrorism', in Ingmar Oldberg et al., *Russia–a Great Power? Security Aspects.* (forthcoming).

[2] First Deputy Foreign Minister Trubnikov referred to the law in his speech, 'Vystuplenie pervogo zamestitelya ministra inostrannykh del Rossii V. I. Trubnikova na mezhdunarodnoi nauchno-praktichesko] konferentsii "Mezhdunarodnyi terrorizm: istoki i protivodeistvie", Sankt Peterburg, 18–19 April' [Speech by the First Deputy Minister of Foreign Affairs of Russia, V. I. Trubnikov, to the international scientific–practitioner conference on International Terrorism: sources and counteraction, St Petersburg, 18–19 April], *Diplomaticheskii vestnik* 5 (2001), p. 126.

[3] Federalnyi Zakon Rossiiskoi Federatsii o borbe s terrorizmom [Federal law of the Russian Federation on the Anti-Terrorist Struggle], 9 July 1998. Reproduced in K. V. Zharinov, *Terrorizm i terroristy: Istoricheskii ocherk* [Terrorism and terrorists: a historical outline] (Minsk: Kharvest, 1999), p. 580.

[4] This is referred to by Trubnikov, 'Vystuplenie pervogo zamestitelya ministra inostrannykh del, p. 126.

[5] See e.g. Zharinov, *Terrorizm i terroristy.*

[6] Interfax, 22 January 2001; See also Lena Jonson, 'Russian Chechnya policy: Is this how to square a circle?', *Brown Journal of World Affairs* 8/1 (Winter/Spring 2001).

[7] Gail Lapidus, 'Russia's second Chechnya war: ten assumptions in search of a policy', in Lena Jonson and Murad Esenov (eds), *Chechnya: The International Community and Strategies for Peace and Stability*, Conference Papers 27 (Stockholm: Swedish Institute of International Affairs, 2000).

[8] RFE/RL, *Newsline*, 30 October 2002.

[9] V. Putin, 'Vstupitelnoe slovo Prezidenta RF V. V. Putina na zasedanii Soveta Bezopasnosti' [Introduction by V. V. Putin, President of the Russian Federation, to the session of the Security Council], 31 October 2002.

[10] The continuing dominance of the old perspective among the military was evident at a seminar on fighting terrorism organized by the Academy of the Russian General Staff. See Vadim Solovev, 'Nash Genshtab otvechaet NATO' [Our General Staff's reply to NATO], *Nezavisimoe voennoe obozrenie* 2 (24–30 January 2003), pp. 1, 3.

[11] Putin, 'Vstupitelnoe slovo Prezidenta RF V. V. Putina na zasedanii Soveta Bezopasnosti'.

[12] Vadim Udmantsev, 'SNG stanet antiterroristicheskoi koalitsiei' [The CIS becomes an anti-terrorist coalition], *Nezavisimaya gazeta*, 1 November 2002.

[13] The main issue at the meeting was, however, the US-led invasion of Iraq. *Diplomaticheskii vestnik* 4 (2003), pp. 54–6.

[14] 'Strategicheskii kurs Rossii s gosudarstvami-uchastnikami Sodruzhcstva Nezavisimykh Gosudarstv' [Russia's strategy towards the CIS member-states], *Sobranie zakonodate'lstva Rossiiskoi Federatsii* [Collection of laws of the Russian Federation], no. 38, 1995, pp. 6844/9.

[15] Aleksei Salmin, 'Vnutripoliticheskie aktery i vneshynaya politika Rossiiskoi Federatsii' [Internal policy actors and the foreign policy of the Russian Federation], in

Sergei Medvedev, Alexander Konovalov, and Sergei Oznobishev (eds), *Rossiya i Zapad v novom tysyacheletii* [Russia and the West in the new millennium], (George C. Marshall European Center for Security Studies).

[16] Fred W. Riggs, 'Bureaucrats and political development: a paradoxical view', in Joseph LaPalombara (ed.), *Bureaucracy and Political Development* (Princeton, N.J.: Princeton University Press, 1963), p. 129, quoted by Eugene Huskey, *Presidential Power in Russia* (Armonk, NY and London: M. E. Sharpe, 1999), p. 124.

[17] In April 1998 Yeltsin abolished the Ministry for Cooperation with CIS States. In September the same year the Ministry of CIS Affairs was, however, restored. As soon as Putin had been elected president in May 2000 he again abolished the Ministry for CIS Affairs and transferred its functions to the Foreign Ministry. See reports in *Diplomaticheskii vestnik.*

[18] In May 1998 Yeltsin blamed the two ministries directly for the failures of Russia's CIS policy: 'It is important to admit: the CIS gives no dividends, either with regard to economic interests or to political. I am not now going to delve into an analysis of the reasons for the present situation. They are known to you. I just say that the fault is our own indecisiveness, slowness, interdepartmental disunity and formalism.' 'Prezident Rossiiskoi federatsii v MID Rossii: Mesto i rol Rossii v period formiruyushchegosya mnogopolyarnogo mira' [The President of the Russian Federation to the Ministry of Foreign Affairs: the place and role of Russia in the period of formation of a multipolar world], *Diplomaticheskii vestnik* 6 (1998), pp. 3–5.

[19] Primakov took control of Russian policy on conflicts in the CIS, and a reduced role for the Defence Ministry was an important consequence. See Pavel Baev, 'The influence of the Balkan crisis on Russia's peacekeeping in its "near abroad"', in Lena Jonson and Clive Archer (eds), *Peacekeeping and the Role of Russia in Eurasia* (Boulder, Colo.: Westview Press, 1996); and Lena Jonson, *The Tajik War: A Challenge to Russian Policy* (London: Royal Institute of International Affairs, 1998).

[20] See chapter 3.

[21] Huskey, *Presidential Power in Russia*, p. 41.

[22] Huskey, *Presidential Power in Russia*, p. 50.

[23] Within the Counsellors' Service individual aides had a certain influence on policy because they had direct access to the president. There was one person responsible for foreign policy and one for national security. Dmitrii Ryurikov was for many years responsible for foreign policy, and Yurii Baturin for national security. Yet, as individuals without an institutional basis, their influence remained limited.

[24] In late 1996 an Administration for Foreign Policy was created, headed by Alexander Manzhosin.

[25] In March 1997 when Anatolii Chubais left to join the government he was replaced by Sergei Yumashin, another reformist.

[26] Carolina Vendil, 'The Russian Security Council', *European Security* 2 (Summer 2001), p. 81. Bordyuzha fell as a result of the Skuratov scandal.

[27] Under Alexander Lebed (1996), Ivan Rybkin (1996–98) and Andrei Kokoshin (1998).

[28] Huskey, *Presidential Power in Russia*, p. 96.

[29] International Institute for Strategic Studies (IISS), *Strategic Survey 1998/99* (London: Oxford University Press, 1999), pp. 132–3. Primakov was replaced as prime minister by Interior Minister Sergei Stepashin who, with a background in the Ministry of Interior Affairs, had become head of domestic intelligence, and as such one of those responsible for the first Chechnya war of 1994–96. International Institute for Strategic Studies (IISS), *Strategic Survey 1999/2000* (London: Oxford University Press, 1999), p. 120.

30 'The continuing underlying power of the security services' is mentioned in the analysis by the International Institute for Strategic Studies as one key factor behind the appointment of Putin in August 1999. *Strategic Survey 1999/2000*, p. 120.

31 'It is possible that the "Family" wanted to incorporate the Director of the FSB— one of the best-informed people in the state. Furthermore, they believed that Putin in particular would be able to guarantee the security of the "Family"'. Yevgenii Primakov, *Vosem mesyatsev plyus* [Eight months plus] (Moscow: Mysl, 2001), p. 222.

32 Trubnikov had replaced Primakov at the SVR in January 1996 when the latter became foreign minister. *Diplomaticheskii vestnik* 9 (2000), p. 49.

33 'Bishkekskaya vstrecha' [The Bishkek meeting], *Diplomaticheskii vestnik* 9 (2000), pp. 22–3.

34 'Rabochaya vstrecha sekretarei sovetov bezopasnosti gosudarstv: uchastnikov DKP' [Working meeting of the secretaries of the security councils of the parties to the Collective Security Treaty], *Diplomaticheskii vestnik* 5 (2000), p. 28.

35 'Pervoe zasedanie Komiteta sekretarei sovetov bezopasnosti gosudarstv: uchastnikov DKB' [First session of the Committee of Secretaries of the Security Councils of the parties to the Collective Security Treaty], *Diplomaticheskii vestnik* 10 (2000), p. 43.

36 The new commission was given a wide range of issues to deal with. Among its members were representatives of Russian energy interests—Gazprom, RAO EES Rossii and Transneft. The deputy secretary of the Security Council, O. D. Chernov, became its head. He described the main functions of the commission as to analyse and forecast Russia's relations with other CIS states and to prepare recommendations for the Russian Security Council. Among the priority directions of work in the immediate future, said Chernov, would be the implementation of the Union agreement with Belarus, the programme of measures to guarantee Russia's strategic interests in the Caspian region, counteracting (*protivodeistvie*) negative tendencies in the CIS, regulating conflicts on CIS territory, and activating Russian policy in the Caucasus. He stressed that Russia's relations with the other CIS states were one of the basic priorities of Russian foreign policy but also that it was important to give preference to integration which gives the best returns to Russia and best corresponds with its interests 'Pervoe zasedanie mezhvedomstvennoi komissii Soveta Bezopasnosti Rossiiskoi Federatsii po problemam SNG' [First meeting of the Russian Security Council's Interdepartmental Commission on the Problems of te CIS], *Diplomaticheskii vestnik* 11 (2000), p. 48.

37 'Bishkekskaya vstrecha', pp. 22–3.

38 In Putin's government reshuffle in March 2001 Sergei Ivanov was appointed defence minister. The former defence minister, Igor Sergeev, who had been a major competitor to Ivanov for influence in the traditional security sphere, became an adviser to the president. However, as a minister Ivanov would be more vulnerable to future criticism. The new secretary of the Security Council was former Minister of Interior Affairs Vladimir Rushailo.

39 Compare the discussion of the Foreign Ministry in Bobo Lo, *Vladimir Putin and the Evolution of Russian Foreign Policy* (London: Royal Institute of International Affairs and Blackwell, 2003), pp. 33–4.

40 For example, on the Defence Committee, Andrei Nikolaev (Narodnyi Deputat), a former director of the Federal Border Service; on the Committee on Security, Aleksandr Gurov, a member of Putin's party, Edinstvo; and on the Duma Committee on CIS Affairs and Relations with Russian Compatriots, Ambassador Boris Pastukhov (Otechestvo–Vsya Rossiya) with experience from Central Asia and the Tajik conflict.

41 After the 1995 election Lev Rokhlin took over the Duma Defence Committee until his murder in 1998, when Roman Popkovich became chairman.

[42] See Denis Myuller, 'Na sterzhne derzhavnoi idei' [At the pivot of the great power idea], *Figury i litsa: Obozrenie* (supplement to *Nezavisimaya gazeta*), 17 May 2001, pp. 11, 12.

[43] Myuller, 'Na sterzhne derzhavnoi idei'. On 'multi-vector policy' see below. In this chapter.

[44] On Prince Alexander Gorchakov see chapter 1.

[45] Lilia Shevtsova, *Putin's Russia* (Washington, DC: Carnegie Endowment for International Peace, 2003) p. 149.

[46] Vadim Dubnov, 'The new Putin: a third way to dress up as reformer', *New Times*, January 2002, pp. 8–11.

[47] See, e.g., Vadim Solvyev, 'Generaly ukhodyat v oppozitsiyu Kremlyu' [The generals come out in opposition to the Kremlin], *Nezavisimaya gazeta*, 13 November 2001, p. 1.

[48] Solovev, 'Generaly ukhodyat v oppozitsiyu Kremlyu'.

[49] Igor Korochenko, 'Armeiskoe dvoevlastie' [The army diarchy], *Nezavisimaya gazeta*, 6 March 2002, p. 2.

[50] Interfax, 17 January 2002.

[51] The Kremlin's own foreign policy team 'was more concerned with protocol and logistics than policy planning' wrote *The Economist*. 'The president's ear', *The Economist*, 16 February 2002, p. 32.

[52] Lilia Shevtsova, *Putin's Russia* (Washington, DC: Carnegie Endowment for International Peace, 2003) p. 206.

[53] More than a year later a *Moscow Times* editorial claimed that Voloshin had been the main architect behind Putin's policy turn after 11 September. When Voloshin in February 2003 went to Washington a month before the US invasion of Iraq the paper wrote: 'A reassuring sign that Putin may know what he is doing after all is the presence in Washington this week of presidential chief of staff Alexander Voloshin, as odd as that may sound. Voloshin may not have the nicest reputation in Moscow, but he is said to have been an architect of the post-Sept. 11, pro-US line, and if anyone in the Kremlin knows how to drive a bargain it is Voloshin'. 'Walking a fine line to drive a hard bargain', *Moscow Times*, 27 February 2003.

[54] Putin's reorganization of the security services in the spring of 2003 had no impact on his foreign policy. It was interpreted by commentators as an effort to strengthen the security services and his own grip on power in preparation for the coming parliamentary and presidential elections.

[55] Peter Reddaway, 'Russia–Putin: formal or real power?', *The Banker*, 1 October 2002.

[56] Gazeta/WPS (What Papers Say) reported the following on 30 September 2002: Gazprom is the largest gas corporation and accounts for more than 20 per cent of world and 94 per cent of Russian natural gas extraction. Currently, Gazprom provides about 8 per cent of Russia's gross domestic product (GDP) and a quarter of tax accruals to the federal budget, and produces up to 8 per cent of Russian industrial goods.

MGK Itera is the largest company dealing with extraction and delivery of natural gas to consumers in Russia and all the largest countries of the former Soviet Union, including the Baltic countries. According to information released by MGK Itera, its annual turnover amounts to US$ 3 billion, the volume of agreements for gas delivery in 2000 reached almost 83.5 billion cubic metres, and the gas stock of the companies where MGK Itera has shareholdings amounts to more than 1 trillion cubic metres. In 2000 Itera again became active in the transport and sale of Turkmenistan's gas. The company is involved in the delivery of 20 billion cubic metres of gas from Turkmenistan along the 'Northern route' (Uzbekistan–Kazakhstan–Russia).

Lukoil is the largest oil company. It owns 18 per cent of all Russian oil processing and more than 24 per cent of all oil extracted in Russia, and currently produces up to

1.57 million barrels a day. The largest company shareholders are the state (13.5 per cent of shares), portfolio investors (65.5 per cent of shares), and the company management and employees (21 per cent of shares). On the Forbes 2002 list Lukoil ranked 168th (180th in 2001). It is very active outside Russia. Currently, it is mostly active in the Kazakhstan and Azerbaijan markets.

NK Yukos is the second-largest Russian oil company. Currently it produces about 1.3 million barrels of oil a day and investors call it the most dynamically developing Russian corporation.

[57] 'Vstrecha prezidenta Rossiiskoi Federatsii s rukovodyaschim sostavom diplomaticheskoi sluzhby MID Rossii' [Meeting of the President of the Russian Federation with senior officials of the Diplomatic Service of the Russian Foreign Ministry], *Diplomaticheskii vestnik* 2 (2001), p. 11.

[58] Reddaway, 'Russia–Putin: formal or real power?'.

[59] Vagit Alekperov, 'U biznesa i armii odni tseli: vozrozhdenie Rossii' [Business and the army have a single goal—the revival of Russia], *Krasnaya zvezda*, 6 December 2002.

[60] Some Russian oil companies played a highly important role in preserving cooperation with the USA during the Iraq war in April 2003. For example, Mikhail Khodorkovskii seemed to have had a determining influence before Putin's declaration that he did not want a US defeat in Iraq. Thus the Communist paper *Sovetskaya Rossiya* wrote: 'To the overwhelming majority of Russians it is clear with whose voice the Russian President sings at present. He sings with the voice of the oligarchs, which are connected by many bonds to American and British oil companies—of Khodorkovskiis, Alekperovs, Abramovichs and others. But they are only small partners of the American oil barons'. Although *Sovetskaya Rossiya* had an interest of its own in exaggerating the influence of the oil oligarchs, most of the oligarchs had clear interests in trying to influence the government. Vasilii Safronchuk, 'Putin ne khochet porazheniya SshA' [Putin does not want US defeat], *Sovetskaya gazeta*, 8 April 2003, p. 3.

[61] 'The president's ear', *The Economist*, 16 February 2002, p. 32.

[62] Two deputy foreign ministers were responsible for policy towards the CIS. While Trubnikov was responsible for policy in general and most of all multilateral cooperation, Vladimir Loshchinin had responsibility for bilateral relations. Under them there were two departments for CIS affairs.

[63] Angela Stent, 'Farewell to empire?', *World Policy Journal*, 1 October 2002.

[64] Grigory Yavlinsky, 'Domestic and foreign policy challenges in Russia', Carnegie Endowment for International Peace, http://www.ceip.org/files/events/Yavlinsky transcripts013102.asp.

[65] Marina Volkova, 'Putin sozyvaet politelitu' [Putin calls together the political elite], *Nezavisimaya gazeta*, 25 September 2002.

[66] 'Sovmestnoe zasedanie Kollegii MID Rossii i Komiteta po mezhdunarodnym delam Gosudarstvennoi Dumy Federalnogo sobraniya RF' [Joint session of the Collegium of the Foreign Ministry and the Russian State Duma Committee on International Affairs], *Diplomaticheskii vestnik* 11 (2001), p. 145.

[67] 'Vystuplenie ministra inostrannykh del RF I. S. Ivanova v Gosudarstvennoi Dume v ramkakh "pravitelstvennoga chasa" 13 marta' [Speech of the Foreign Minister of the Russian Federation, I. S. Ivanov, in the State Duma during the 'Government's Hour', 13 March], *Diplomaticheskii vestnik* 4 (2002), pp. 55–60.

[68] Yevgenii Primakov, 'Rossiya v mirovoi politike (k 200-letiyu A. M. Gorchakova)' [Russia and world politics: on the 200th anniversary of A. M. Gorchakov], *Diplomaticheskii vestnik* 7 (1998), pp. 76–9.

[69] David MacKenzie, 'Russia's Balkan policies under Alexander II, 1855–1881', in Hugh Ragsdale (ed.), *Imperial Russian Foreign Policy* (Cambridge, Mass.: Woodrow Wilson Center Press and Cambridge University Press, 1993), p. 227.

[70] Igor Ivanov, 'Novizna i preemstvennost' v rossiiskoi vneshnei politike' [Novelty and continuity in Russian foreign policy], *Nezavisimaya gazeta*, 15 June 2001, p. 6.

[71] Viktor Sheinis, 'Rossiya i Evropa: interesy protiv mifov' [Russia and Europe: interests vs myths], *Nezavisimaya gazeta*, 20 December 2000; and Viktor Sheinis, 'Eshche raz o mifakh i interesakh' [Myths and interests, again], *Nezavisimaya gazeta*, 16 June 2001, p. 8.

[72] 'Russia and the West are different civilizations, the contradictions between them were laid down long ago and will never disappear, and the basic law of geopolitics is "either we or they".' Aleksandr Dugin at the Founding Congress of the 'Eurasia' All-Russian Political and Social Movement, 21 April 2001. See Aleksandr Dugin, 'Evraziistvo: ot filosofii k politike' [Eurasianism: from philosophy to policy], *Nezavisimaya gazeta*, 30 May 2001, p. 8.

[73] See the analysis in Jacob Kipp, 'Alexander Dugin and the ideology of National Revival: geopolitics, Eurasianism, and the conservative revolution', unpublished paper, 2001.

[74] *Komsomolskaya pravda*, 23 April 2002.

[75] 'Statement by President V. V. Putin at the extended meeting of Russian Ambassadors at the Russian Foreign Ministry', 12 July 2002, http://www.gov.ru.

[76] Aleksandr Yanov, 'Kak ostanovit rossiiskii "mayatnik"' [How to stop the Russian 'pendulum'], *Nezavisimaya gazeta*, 13 March 2002, p. 11.

[77] In this context, Yanov also wrote that Russia has no top-ranking national interests in Central Asia.

[78] Yu. Fyodorov, 'Krizis vneshnoi politiki Rossii: kontseptualnyi aspekt' [Russia's foreign policy crisis: the conceptual aspect], *Pro et Contra* 6/1–2 (2001), pp. 31–49; and Dmitri Trenin, *The End of Eurasia: Russia on the Border Between Geopolitics and Globalization* (Washington, DC and Moscow: Carnegie Endowment for International Peace, 2002).

[79] Igor Ivanov, 'Traditions of the past and foreign policy today', *International Affairs* 48/4 (2002), p. 10.

[80] Alexei Arbatov, 'Russian foreign policy thinking in transition', in Vladimir Baranovsky (ed.), *Russia and Europe: The Emerging Security Agenda* (Oxford: Oxford University Press for the Stockholm International Peace Research Institute, 1997), p. 152.

[81] The Liberal-Democrats wanted a Russian retreat from Tajikistan, but there was no difference between liberal-minded reform parties such as Yabloko or even the Union of Rightist Forces, on the one hand, and the government, on the other.

[82] Neil Malcolm and Alex Pravda, 'Introduction', in Neil Malcolm, Alex Pravda, Roy Allison and Margot Light (co-authors), *Internal Factors in Russian Foreign Policy* (Oxford: Oxford University Press and Royal Institute of International Affairs, 1996).

[83] *Nezavisimaya gazeta*, 26 December 2001.

[84] Interfax, 18 January 2002.

[85] General Vladimir Kulakov in Interfax/*Asia Plus*, 23 January 2002.

[86] *Krasnaya zvezda*, 24 January 2002.

[87] Anatolii Adamyshin, *Nezavisimaya gazeta*, 16 March 2002.

[88] *Nezavisimaya gazeta*, 11 March 2002.

[89] Vystuplenie ministra inostrannykh del RF I. S. Ivanova v Gosudarstvennoi Dume v ramkakh "pravitelstvennoga chasa" 13 marta', pp. 55–60. In order to calm down the reaction in the Duma and explain official policy, the deputy foreign minister responsible for CIS affairs, Trubnikov, had met the Duma Committee on International Affairs on 5 March. See 'Mezhdunarodnye voprosy v Federalnom Sobranii RF' [International

questions at the Russian Federation Federal Assembly], *Diplomaticheskii vestnik* 4 (2002), p. 62.

[90] 'Rossiya-SshA: nevnyatnyi dialog' [Russia–USA: incomprehensible dialogue], *Nezavisimaya gazeta*, 8 April 2002, p. 10.

[91] Lidiya Andrusenko and Olga Tropkina, 'Mezalyans s Amerikoi' [Mésalliance with America], *Nezavisimaya gazeta*, 11 September 2002, pp. 1 and 2.

[92] Leonid Ivashov, 'V ozhidanii bolshikh potryasenii v Rossii' [Waiting for major convulsions in Russia], *Nezavisimaya gazeta*, 20 January 2003.

[93] Alex Pravda, 'Putin's foreign policy after 11 September: radical or revolutionary?', Gabriel Gorodetsky (ed.), *Russia Between East and West. Russian Foreign Policy on the Threshold of the Twenty-First Century* (London and Portland: Frank Cass, 2003), p. 40.

Chapter 7

FACTORS WITHIN CENTRAL ASIA

[1] On the problems of economic development in Central Asia see Eshref Trushin and Eskender Trushin, 'Challenges to economic policy in Central Asia: Is a miracle possible?' and Stanislav Zhukov, 'Development under conditions of globalization', in Boris Rumer (ed.), *Central Asia: A Gathering Storm?* (New York and London: M. E. Sharpe, 2002); and International Crisis Group (ICG), *Tajikistan: A Roadmap for Development*, ICG Asia Report 51 (Osh/Brussels: International Crisis Group, 24 April 2003); and Anders Aslund, 'Sizing up the Central Asian economies', *Journal of International Affairs* 56/2 (Spring 2003).

[2] The adjective I will use for Islamism is 'Islamist' while for Islam in general I will use 'Islamic'. Compare Edward Walker, 'Islam, Islamism and Political Order', *Journal of International Affairs* 2/56 (Spring 2003).

[3] http://www.freedomhouse.org.

[4] www.state/gov/r/pa/prs/ps/2002/873bpf.htm

[5] Monica Whitlock, *Beyond the Oxus: The Central Asians* (London: John Murray, 2002).

[6] Aaron Rhodes and Paula Tscherne-Lempiäinen, 'Human rights and terrorism in the Central Asian OSCE states', *Helsinki Monitor* 1 (2002).

[7] BBC, *Inside Central Asia* 424 (29 April–5 May 2002).

[8] BBC, *Inside Central Asia* 441 (26 August–1 September 2002).

[9] Josh Machleder, 'Alternative political voices in Uzbekistan', *Eurasia Insight*, 27 January 2003, www.eurasianet.org

[10] Farangis Najibullah, 'Uzbek opposition meets openly for the first time in 10 years', *Eurasia Insight*, 12 June 2003, www.eurasianet.org

[11] BBC, *Inside Central Asia*, 2 November 2003.

[12] Martha Brill Olcott, 'Taking stock of Central Asia', *Journal of International Affairs* 2/56 (Spring 2003).

[13] Interfax/*Asia Plus*, 19 March 2002.

[14] *Asia Plus*, 26 March 2002.

[15] *Asia Plus*, 22 May 2002.

[16] RFE/RL, *Newsline*, 10 September 2002.

[17] *Asia Plus*, 13 September 2002.

[18] Alisher Khamidov, 'Ak-Sui trial in Kyrgyzstan causes rift between president and law-enforcement officials', http://www.Eurasianet.com, 18 October 2002.

[19] BBC, *Inside Central Asia* 439 (12–18 August 2002).

[20] See the report of the International Crisis Group (ICG) with the same title, *Cracks in the Marble: Turkmenistan's Failing Dictatorship* (Osh/Brussels: ICG, 21 January 2003).

21 BBC, *Inside Central Asia* 420 (1–7 April 2002).

22 BBC, *Inside Central Asia* 425 (6–12 May 2002).

23 BBC, *Inside Central Asia* 443 (9–15 September 2002).

24 Interfax, 11 September 2002.

25 BBC, *Inside Central Asia* 443 (9–15 September 2002).

26 The Turkmen opposition in exile fell into the quarrelling that is usual among such groups. Shikhmuradov in October 2002 voiced doubts that the unification of the various opposition groups would yield any tangible benefit. Gundogar web site 29 October 2002/BBC, *Inside Central Asia* 450 (28 October–3 November 2002).

27 BBC, *Inside Central Asia* 454 (25 November–1 December 2002).

28 Altogether Niyazov accused four people of being the 'main organizers of the terrorist attack'—Shikhmuradov; a former chairman of the Central Bank, Hudayberdi Orazow; a former first deputy agriculture minister, Ymamberdi Yklymow; and a former ambassador to Turkey, Nurmuhhamet Hanamow—all of them in exile. BBC, *Inside Central Asia* 455 (2–8 December 2002).

29 BBC, *Inside Central Asia* (5 January 2003).

30 BBC, *Inside Central Asia* 457 (16–22 December 2002).

31 Russian Information Agency, 26 November 2002.

32 BBC, *Inside Central Asia*, 12 January 2003.

33 Viktoriya Panfilova, 'Pod prikrytiem Putina' [Under cover of Putin], *Nezavisimaya gazeta*, 19 December 2002, p. 5.

34 BBC, *Inside Central Asia*, 5 January 2003.

35 ITAR-TASS, quoting the Turkmen presidential office. BBC, *Inside Central Asia*, 5 January 2003.

36 'Turkmenistan's Embattled Opposition Forges a United Front', Eurasia Insight, 30 September 2003 www.eurasianet.org

37 BBC, *Inside Central Asia* 438 (5–11 August 2002).

38 See Niyazov's speech 'My reshili korennye voprosy', www.turkmenistan.ru/index.cfm?r=3&d=3121&op=viw

39 BBC, *Inside Central Asia*, 22 June 2003.

40 Kambiz Arman, 'Islamic Party Reduces Tension in Tajikistan by Moderating Stance on Upcoming Referendum', Eurasia Insight, 12 June 2003 www.eurasianet.org

41 Aleksei Malashenko, 'Islam and politics in Central Asian States', in Lena Jonson and Murad Esenov (eds), *Political Islam and Conflicts in Russia and Central Asia* (Stockholm: Swedish Institute of International Affairs, 1999).

42 Ismael and Ismael, *Government and Politics in Islam*, p. 39.

43 Hélène Carrère d'Encausse, *Islam and the Russian Empire: Reform and Revolution in Central Asia* (London: I. B. Tauris, 1988).

44 Anna Kreikemeyer and Arne Seifert (eds), *Zur Vereinbarkeit von politischen Islam und Sicherheit im OSZE Raum: Dokumente eines islamisch-säkularen Dialogs in Tadschikistan* [On the compatibility of Islam and security in the OSCE space: documents of an Islamic–secular dialogue] (Baden-Baden: Nomos Verlagsgesellschaft, 2002/2003).

45 Saodat Olimova, 'Political Islam and conflict in Tajikistan', in Lena Jonson and Murad Esenov (eds), *Political Islam and Conflicts in Russia and Central Asia*, and Shirin Akiner, *Tajikistan. Disintegration or Reconciliation?* (London: Royal Institute of International Affairs, 2001).

46 For an introduction see Tareq Y. Ismael and Jaqueline S. Ismael, *Government and Politics in Islam* (London: Frances Pinter, 1985).

47 'This basically derives from the fact that the moral order pursued by the Brotherhood is perceived as being dictated by God and imposed by government. In effect, the function of the state is to maintain a mystical moral order. By its nature, then,

government must oppose any tendency towards an increase in moral choice or moral pluralism. The doctrine is mystical, repressive, dictatorial and intolerant—characteristics which were, in a European context, labelled fascist.' Ismael and Ismael, *Government and Politics in Islam*, p. 77.

[48] Ashirbek Muminov, 'Traditsionnye i sovremennye religiozno-teologicheskie shkoly v Tsentralnoi Azii', *Tsentralnaya Aziya i Kavkaz*, 4/5 (1999); Bakhtiar Babadzhanov, 'Islam in Uzbekistan: from the struggle for "religious purity" to political activism', in Rumer (ed.), *Central Asia: A Gathering Storm?*, p. 303.

[49] Babadzhanov, 'Islam in Uzbekistan', p. 303.

[50] Richard A. Pierce, *Russian Central Asia 1867–1917: A Study in Colonial Rule* (Berkeley and Los Angeles, Calif.: University of California Press, 1960), pp. 221 ff.

[51] On Hindustani see, Monica Whitlock, *Beyond the Oxus: The Central Asians* (London: John Murray, 2002); *Musulmanskie lidery: sotsialnaya rol i avtoritet* (Dushanbe: Friedrich Ebert Stiftung and 'Shark' Independent Research Institute, 2003)

[52] Wahhabism is a Saudi Arabian sect whose ideas stem from Ibn Abd al-Wahhab (1703–97).

[53] Babadzhanov, 'Islam in Uzbekistan', p. 311.

[54] Babadzhanov, 'Islam in Uzbekistan', p. 318–9.

[55] Babadzhanov, 'Islam in Uzbekistan', p. 315.

[56] Monica Whitlock, *Beyond the Oxus*, p. 211.

[57] On the IMU see Ahmed Rashid, *Jihad: The Rise of Militant Islam in Central Asia*, New Haven and London: Yale University Press, 2002, p. 148; Vitaly V. Naumkin, *Militant Islam in Central Asia: The Case of the Islamic Movement of Uzbekistan* (Berkeley Program in Soviet and Post-Soviet Studies Working Paper Series, Spring 2003).

[58] Vitaly V. Naumkin, *Militant Islam in Central Asia: The Case of the Islamic Movement of Uzbekistan* (Berkeley Program in Soviet and Post-Soviet Studies Working Paper Series, Spring 2003), p. 48.

[59] Vitaly V. Naumkin, *Militant Islam in Central Asia: The Case of the Islamic Movement of Uzbekistan*, p. 58.

[60] See the web site of the organization, http://www.hizb-ut-tahri.org. The best scholarly study is Suha Taji-Farouki, *A Fundamental Quest: Hizb-ut-Tahrir and the Search for the Islamic Caliphate* (London: Grey Seal, 1996); Ahmed Rashid, *Jihad: The Rise of Militant Islam in Central Asia* (London and New Haven, Conn.: Yale University Press, 2002).

[61] Nadezhda Kerovkova, 'Spiski terroristov' [The lists of terrorists], *Smysl* 28 February 2003, pp. 34–5.

[62] See, e.g., the analysis in Bakhtiar Babadzhanov, *Religiozny ekstremizm v Tsentralnoi Azii. Problemy i perspektivy. Materialy konferentsii, Dushanbe, 25 aprelya 2002* [Religious extremism in Central Asia: problems and prospects. Materials from a conference held in Dushanbe, 25 April 2002] (Dushanbe: OSCE Mission to Tajikistan, 2002), p. 58.

[63] See e.g. three Hizb-ut-Tahrir documents, 'The American campaign to suppress Islam'; 'Dangerous concepts to attack Islam and consolidate Western culture'; and 'The system of Islam' on the web site of Hizb-ut-Tahrir, http://www.hizb-ut-tahri.org.

[64] Compare the organizational structure of the Bolshevik Party in tsarist Russia as well as the Front National de Libération (FNL) in Algeria against French colonial rule.

[65] Taji-Farouki, *A Fundamental Quest*, pp. 76–113.

[66] Bakhtiar Babadzhanov, 'O deyatelnosti "Hizb-ut-Tahrir al-Islami" v Uzbekistane' [The activity of Hizb-ut-Tahrir-al-Islami in Uzbekistan], in Aleksei Malashenko and Martha Brill Olcott (eds), *Islam na postsovetskom prostranstve: Vzglyad iznutri* [Islam in the post-Soviet space: a look from within] (Moscow: Art-Biznes-Tsentr, 2001), p. 161.

[67] V. Ponomarov, 'Islam Karimov protiv "Hizb-ut-Tahrir"' [Islam Karimov against Hizb-ut-Tahrir], Moscow, 1999, pp. 18–9, quoted by Uran Botobekov, 'Vnedrenie idei

partii "Hizb-ut-Tahrir al-Islami" na yuge Kirgizii' [Introduction of the idea of the Hizb-ut-Tahrir-al-Islami party in southern Kyrgyzstan], in Malashenko and Brill Olcott (eds), *Islam na postsovetskom prostranstve: Vzglyad iznutri*, p. 139.

[68] Botobekov, 'Vnedrenie idei partii "Hizb-ut-Tahrir al-Islami"', pp. 144–5.

[69] Zamira Eshanova, 'Central Asia: Uzbekistan, Kyrgyzstan differ in approach to Hezb ut-Tahrir', RFE/RL,
http://www.rferl.org/nca/features/2002/07/12072002171856.asp.

[70] Botobekov, 'Vnedrenie idei partii "Hizb-ut-Tahrir al-Islami"', p. 140.

[71] Botobekov, 'Vnedrenie idei partii "Hizb-ut-Tahrir al-Islami"', p. 141.

[72] Saniya Sagnaeva, 'Religiozno-oppozitsionnye gruppy v Kyrgyzstane: Hizb-ut-Tahrir', *Religioznyi ekstremizm v Tsentralnoi Azii. Problemy i perspektivy* [Religious extremism in Central Asia: problems and prospects] (Dushanbe, 2002), p. 68.

[73] Kurbonali Mukhabbatov, 'Religiozno-oppozitsionnye gruppy v Tadzhikistane: Hizb-ut-Tahrir' [Religious opposition groups in Tajikistan: Hizb-ut-Tahrir], in Organization for Security and Co-operation in Europe, Mission to Tajikistan, *Religiozny ekstremizm v Tsentralnoi Azii: Problemy i perspektivy* [Religious extremism in Central Asia: problems and prospects] (Dushanbe, 2002). They were mainly sentenced under the articles in the Criminal Law that cover attempts to seize power by force, overthrow of the constitutional system, and stirring up national and religious dissent.

[74] BBC, *Inside Central Asia* 443 (9–15 September 2002). According to the Prosecutor of the Sughd Region, Kurbonali Mukhabbatov, up to April 2002, 108 members had been sentenced in the northern Sughd Region alone. Kurbonali Mukhabbatov, 'Religiozno-oppozitsionnye gruppy v Tadzhikistane: Hizb-ut-Tahrir'.

[75] *The Europe World Year Book 2003*, vol. II. 44th edition (London and New York: Europe Publications. Taylor and Francis Group, 2003), p. 4519.

[76] The car bombs in February 1999 increased the persecutions, and in May 1999 legislation was adopted under an amendment to the Criminal Code on harsher punishment of members of 'religious, extremist, separatist, and fundamentalist organizations'.

[77] Said Akhmedov (Chairman of the Committee on Religion at the Government), *Biznes i Politika*, 27 September 2001.

[78] To register a *pyatikratnyi* mosque there has to be a request from at least 10 people, while a Friday mosque can be registered as a *jomea* only in areas where at least 15,000 people live. There is no charge for registration of mosques. In November 2003 it was reported that a draft of a new law on religion is under preparation, which might increase the number of believers from 10 people to 70 for registering a pyatikratnyi mosque. See Igor Rotar, 'Tajikistan: Religious Freedom Survey, November 2003', F18News, 20 November 2003 www.forum18.org/Archive.php?article_id=190

[79] Gholib Goibov, 'Stroitel'stvo svetskogo kharaktera obshchestva i ustanovleniye otnosheniya religioznoi terpimosti v Tadzhikistane' [Establishing a secular society and religious tolerance in Tajikistan], *Religiozny ekstremizm v Tsentralnoi Azii: Problemy i perspektivy. Materialy konferentsii, Dushanbe, 25 aprelya 2002* [Religious extremism in Central Asia: Problems and prospects. Materials from a conference held in Dushanbe, 25 April 2002] (Dushanbe: OSCE Mission to Tajikistan, 2002).

[80] Under the Committee on Religion there is a Coordinating Consultative Council of 38 leading representatives of the different religious communities active in Tajikistan. The purpose of the council, which was founded in April 2001, was to encourage religious tolerance between different confessions.

[81] Interviews made by the author in Dushanbe, spring 2002.

[82] His call was made on 31 March. *Narodnaya gazeta* (the official newspaper of the Tajik government), 23–24 (2002).

[83] *Asia Plus*, 10 September 2001.

[84] 'Speech to the Intelligentsia' of 20 March 2002.

[85] Interview by the author, Dushanbe, February 2002.

[86] The chairman of the government Committee on Religious Affairs, Said Akhmadov, stated that 'a total of some 250 mosques and 20 religious schools would undergo appraisal. Imams (pontiffs), khatibs (preachers), muezzins (who call the people to prayer) and lecturers will sit examinations on the canons of Islam, rituals, teaching methods and other subjects. The appraisal will be conducted by the Council of Ulemas (religious scholars) jointly with the Committee on Religious Affairs'. *Asia Plus*, 6 August 2002/ BBC, *Inside Central Asia* 438 (August 2002).

[87] BBC, *Inside Central Asia* 434 (8–14 July 2002).

[88] *Asia Plus*, 12 July 2002.

[89] BBC, *Inside Central Asia* 436 (22–28 July 2002).

[90] BBC, *Inside Central Asia* 434 (8–14 July 2002).

[91] Eurasia Insight, http://www.eurasianet.com, 29 August 2002.

[92] BBC, *Inside Central Asia* 436 (22–28 July 2002).

[93] BBC, *Inside Central Asia*, 437 (29 July-4 August).

[94] Aleksei Malashenko, 'Islam, politika i bezopasnost Tsentralnoi Azii' [Islam, politics and the security of Central Asia], *Svobodnaya mysl* 3 (2003), pp. 26–35.

[95] Antoine Blua, 'Ashgabat takes further steps to suppress religious faiths', RFE/RL/Eurasia Insight, 15 November 2003 www.eurasianet.org

[96] Felix Corley, 'Turkmenistan: Secret police close down mosque refusing to go against Islam', F18 News, 19 November 2003 www.forum18.org/Archive.php?article_id=187

[97] On the water problem in Central Asia see: Philip Micklin, *Managing Water in Central Asia* (London: Royal Institute of International Affairs, 2000); Stuart Horsman, 'Water in Central Asia: regional cooperation or conflict?', in Roy Allison and Lena Jonson (eds.), *Central Asian Security: The New International Context* (London and Washington: Royal Institute of International Affairs and Brookings Institution Press, 2001).

[98] Martha Brill Olcott, 'Common Legacies and Conflicts', in Roy Allison and Lena Jonson (eds.), *Central Asian Security: The New International Context* (London and Washington: Royal Institute of International Affairs and Brookings Institution Press, 2001), p. 38.

[99] Svat Soucek, *A History of Inner Asia* (Cambridge: Cambridge University Press, 2000).

[100] *The Europe World Year Book 2003*, vol. II. 44th edition (London and New York: Europe Publications. Taylor and Francis Group, 2003).

[101] See the map 'Major ethnic groups in Central Asia' http://www.lib.utexas.edu/maps/middle_east_and_asia/casia_ethnic_93.jpg

[102] Saodat Olimova, 'Natsionalnye gosudarstva i etnicheskie territorii', in Martha Brill Olcott and Alexei Malashenko (eds), *Mnogomernye granitsy Tsentralnoi Azii*, (Moscow: Carnegie Centre, 2000) electronic version http://pubs.carnegie.ru/books/2000/04am

[103] BBC, *Inside Central Asia*, 2002 issue 406 (17 December 2001–1 January 2002).

[104] Ghayur Qahhorov in *Biznes i Politika* 6 (2002).

[105] For example in 2001 books in Tajik were removed from libraries and schools in Buchara and Samarkand. *The Europe World Year Book 2003*, vol. II. 44th edition (London and New York: Europe Publications. Taylor and Francis Group, 2003).

[106] 'Inter-ethnic tensions threaten fragile Tajik-Uzbek relations', Eurasia Insight, 14 February 2003 www.eurasianet.org

[107] Kamol Kholmuradov, 'Turkmen-Uzbek tension easing, but ethnic minorities in both countries continue to suffer', Eurasia Insight, 15 May 2003 www.eurasianet.org

108 Igor Rotar, 'Neprostoe sosedstvo' [A non-simple neighbour], *Nezavisimaya gazeta*, 2 July 1999, p. 5. See also Vladimir Georgiev, 'Moskva obrela novogo soyuznika' [Moscow finds a new ally], *Nezavisimaya gazeta*, 17 April 1999, pp. 1 and 5.

109 BBC, *Inside Central Asia* 294 (September–3 October 1999).

110 Varorud News Agency (Soghd), 4 October 2002 (in Russian).

111 *The Europe World Yearbook 2003*, vol. II, 44th edition (London and New York: Europe Publications. Taylor and Francis Group, 2003), p. 4170.

112 RFE/RL, *Central Asia Report* 11 (13 March 2003).

113 'Uzbek border row introduces new element of tension in Central Asia', Eurasianet, 27 January 2003, http://www.eurasianet.org/departments/business/articles/eav012703.shtml

114 'Uzbek obrder row introduces new element of tension in Central Asia', Eurasianet, 27 January 2003, http://www.eurasianet.org/departments/business/articles/eav012703.shtml

115 Interfax, 24 July 2003.

116 'Kazakhstan, Uzbekistan Clash over Border Policy', Eurasia Insight, 29 September 2003, http://www.eurasianet.org/departments/insight/articles/eav092903a.shtml

117 RFE/RL reported on 14 August 2003 that Uzbekistan's mountain troops, including Interior Ministry troops and border guards, are conducting operational–tactical exercises in mountainous areas of Kashkadarya Oblast on the Uzbek–Turkmen border, uzreport.com reported on 13 August. The objective of the exercises, in addition topracticing the coordination of joint operations in mountainous terrain, is reported to be a study of the territory bordering Turkmenistan.

118 *The Europe World Yearbook 2003*, vol II, 44th edition (London and New York: Europe Publications. Taylor and Francis Group, 2003).

119 On the situation of the Russians in Central Asia see, for example, Paul Kolstoe, *Russians in the Former Soviet Republics* (London: Hurst & Co., 1995).

Chapter 8

THE SHAPING OF FOREIGN POLICY

1 John Hobson uses the term 'the international agential power' of a state. See John M. Hobson, *The State and International Relations* (Cambridge: Cambridge University Press, 2000), pp. 217–35.

2 See e.g. Stephen Blank, 'The United States and Central Asia', in Roy Allison and Lena Jonson (eds), *Central Asian Security: The New International Context* (London and Washington, DC: Royal Institute of International Affairs and Brookings Institution Press, 2001).

3 Robert Gilpin, *War and Change in World Politics* (Cambridge, London and New York: Cambridge University Press, 1981), p. 187. See also the references to Gilpin in Flemming Splidsboel-Hansen, 'Past and future meet: Aleksandr Gorchakov and Russian foreign policy', *Europe–Asia Studies* 54/3 (2002), pp. 377–8.

4 BBC, *Inside Central Asia* 393 (17–23 September 2001).

5 Robert O. Keohane, 'The analysis of international regimes: towards a European–American research programme', in Volker Rittberger (ed.), *Regime Theory and International Relations* (Oxford: Clarendon Press, 1993), pp. 29, 30. Quoted by Christer Pursiainen, *Russian Foreign Policy and International Relations Theory* (Aldershot: Ashgate, 2000), p. 120. See also Christer Pursiainen on the discussion of Russian studies and international

relations theory in his study, *Beyond Sovietology: International Relations Theory and the Study of Soviet/Russian Foreign and Security Policy* (Helsinki: Finnish Institute of International Affairs, 1998).

[6] Martha Finnemore, *National Interests in International Society* (Ithaca, NY and London: Cornell University Press, 1996), p. 15.

[7] Christer Pursiainen, 'The impact of international security regimes on Russia's behavior', in Ted Hopf (ed.), *Understandings of Russian Foreign Policy* (Pennsylvania: Pennsylvania State University, 1999), pp. 126–7.

[8] See http://www.pravitelstvo.gov.ru/data/news_print.html?he_id=15&news_id=53.

[9] A report by the Foundation for Prospective Studies and Initiatives with Primakov, Alexei Arbatov and former Prime Minister Yegor Gaidar among the authors stated in early 2003: 'There are no insurmountable barriers between Russia and the US today for forming a coalition aimed at a future victory over international terrorism. It may also predetermine the progress of relations between them. For Russia, the interest in that coalition is much bigger than for the USA, and the reason is not because Russia is weaker. The format of an antiterrorist coalition provides this country with the opportunity for speeding up its integration into the community of democratic and highly developed nations'. ('Russia in 2003 and its foreign policy: Excerpts from the report by the Foundation for Prospective Studies and Initiatives', *Russia in Global Affairs* 1/1 (January–March 2003), pp. 96–7.) Anti-terrorism was seen as giving Russia the chance to proceed with its domestic economic agenda while still playing a role on the international scene. Russia's support for anti-terrorist efforts provided it with an 'important foreign policy resource'.

[10] A. Gusher, 'Otrezvlenie Rossii i konflikty na Vostoke' [The sobering up of Russia and conflicts in the East], *Aziya i Afrika* 10 (2002), pp. 2–5.

[11] 'Russia in 2003 and its foreign policy: Excerpts from the report by the Foundation for Prospective Studies and Initiatives', *Russia in Global Affairs* 1/1 (January–March 2003), pp. 96–7.

[12] Sergei Karaganov, 'Russia, Europe, and new challenges', *Russia in Global Affairs* 1/1 (January–March 2003), p. 27.

[13] Oleg Yelenskii, 'Moskva davit na DKB: Strany-chleny Dogovora o kollektivnoi beopasnosti gotovy podderzhat' pozitsiyu SshA po Iraku' [Moscow presses the CST: Members of the Collective Security Treaty ready to support the position of the USA on Iraq], *Nezavisimaya gazeta*, 6 November 2002.

[14] President Karimov, answering questions at a joint news conference held with visiting Polish President Aleksander Kwasniewski, after talks in Tashkent. Uzbek Radio, 21 October 2002/Reuters, 22 October 2002.

[15] Rubleva, 'Moskva stala Vashingtonom', p. 10.

[16] Ivan Safranchuk (Director of the Centre for Military Information), 'Ispolzovat protivorechiya Evropy i SshA—normalno: Dazhe ochen zhelatelno' [Exploiting the clash between Europe and the USA is normal—even very desirable], www.Polit.ru, 25 September 2002.

[17] Karaganov, 'Russia, Europe and new challenges', p. 29.

[18] Vladimir Lukin, 'Desyatiletka mira' [A decade of peace], *Moskovskie novosti* 9 (2003).

[19] Vladimir Lukin, 'Prishla pora igrat v komandnuyu igru' [The time for playing the command game has passed], *Dipkurer NG* 49/5 (24 March 2003), p. 15.

[20] Margelov gave assurances that the new 'entente' was not aimed against the USA and the UK. The USA does not demand absolute unanimity with its partners. 'We also can have different opinions.' Interview in *Zhurnal* 10/61 (18 March 2003), p. 9.

[21] Uzbek Television, 6 March 2003/BBC, *Inside Central Asia*, 9 March 2003.

[22] BBC, *Inside Central Asia*, 9 March 2003.

23 According to Viktoriya Panfilova, Tajikistan and Kyrgyzstan supported Russia's position on the Iraq issue. 'Slozhnaya rol statista' [The intricate role of the 'extra'], *Dipkurer NG* 49/5 (24 March 2003).

24 Vladimir Mukhin, 'Moskva pokupaet soyuznikov', *NG Dipkurer*, 21 April 2003, p. 9–10.

25 Vladimir Putin, 'Zayavlenie na soveshchanii v Kremle' [Declaration at the conference in the Kremlin], 20 March 2003, www.gov.ru.

26 Konstantin Kazenin and Ivan Sukhov, 'Dzhikhad Svyatoi Rusi' [Jihad of Holy Russia], *Vremya novostei*, 4 April 2003, p. 1.

27 Svetlana Ofitova, 'V Sovete Federatsii vozobladali "yastreby"' [Hawks prevail in the Council of the Federation], *Nezavisimaya gazeta*, 27 March 2003, p. 1.

28 'President vstretilsya s regionalnymi zhurnalistami' [The president meets regional journalists], *Izvestiya*, 4 April 2003, p. 2.

29 *Strategic Survey 2002/3* (London and Oxford: International Institute for Strategic Studies, Oxford University Press, 2003) p. 124.

30 Interfax, 12 May 2003.

31 Peter B. Evans, Harold K. Jacobson and Robert D. Putnam (eds), *Double-Edged Diplomacy: International Bargaining and Domestic Politics* (Berkeley and Los Angeles, Calif., and London: University of California Press, 1993).

32 Tajikistan, Uzbekistan and Turkmenistan have signed agreements on the transfer of electricity to Afghanistan. Akhmed Rashid, 'The Great Trade Game', *Far Eastern Economic Review*, 30 January 2003.

33 Ahmed Rashid, 'Eyes wide shut', *Far Eastern Economic Review*, 5 June 2003.

34 Ahmed Rashid, 'Dangerous neighbours', *Far Eastern Economic Review*, 9 January 2003.

35 The disappearance of Mullah Sadykhzhan Rakhmanov of Uzgen in southern Kyrgyzstan on 7 September 2003 was blamed on the Uzbek security services. BBC, *Inside Central Asia*, 28 September 2003.

36 Interfax, 24 September 2003.

37 Compare the situation in the South Caucasus. Lena Jonson, 'The new geo-political situation', in Gennady Chufrin (ed.), *The Security of the Caspian Sea Region* (Oxford: Oxford University Press, 2001).

38 Roy Allison, 'Structures and frameworks for security policy cooperation in Central Asia', in Roy Allison and Lena Jonson (eds), *Central Asian Security: The New International Context* (London and Washington, DC: Royal Institute of International Affairs and Brookings Institution Press, 2002).

39 Dmitri Trenin, 'Southern Watch: Russia's policy in Central Asia', *Journal of International Affairs* 56/2 (Spring 2003), p. 128.

40 Prime-TASS, 23 May 2003. See also Mikhail Khodarenok, 'Moskva-Kabul: povorot na 180 gradusov', *Nezavisimaya gazeta*, 26 May 2003, p. 1 and 2.

41 Interview with Nikolai Bordyuzha in 'Vo imya kollektivnoi bezopasnosti' [In the name of collective security], *Krasnaya zvezda* 6 (2003), p. 72.

42 Vyacheslav Trubnikov, 'Vneshnepoliticheskii front Rossii' [Russia's foreign policy front], *Dipkurer NG*, 15 September 2003, p. 9 and 14.

43 Interfax, 26 September 2003.

44 Interfax, 27 September 2003.

45 *Izvestiya*, 26 September 2003. The document, entitled 'The Doctrine of Forming a Strategic Union Between the United States and Russia', was presented at a meeting held in Moscow on 24 September and attended by Sergei Karaganov, Chairman of the Council for Foreign and Defense Policy, Gleb Pavlovskii, Director of the Foundation for Effective Politics, and Mikhail Nosov, Director of the Institute of the USA and Canada,

as well as political scientists Sergei Kurginyan, Viktor Tretyakov and Viktor Kuvaldin. US, British and French diplomats also attended the discussion. RFE/RL *Newsline* 185 (29 September 2003). See also Evgenii Berlin, Vashingtonu predlozhili strategicheskii soyuz' [Strategic alliance offered to Washington], *Nezavisimaya gazeta*, 29 September 2003, p. 6.

[46] 'Amerika kak strategicheskii soyuznik Rossii' [America as Russia's strategic ally], *Nezavisimaya gazeta*, 29 October 2003, p. 11.

[47] Lena Jonson and Clive Archer (eds), *Peacekeeping and the Role of Russia in Eurasia* (Boulder, Colo.: Westview Press, 1996).

[48] Vladimir Mukhin, 'Atomnaya bomba vse eshche zorko sterezhet bezopasnost strany' [The atomic bomb still protects the country's security], *Nezavisimaya gazeta*, 3 October 2003; Pavel Felgengauer 20 October 2003 http://www.gazeta.ru/comments/2003/10/a_58928.shtml

[49] Interfax, 2 October 2003.

[50] Interfax, 22 September 2003.

[51] Anatolii Chubais, 'Missiya Rossii v XXI veke' [Russia's mission in the 21st century], *Nezavisimaya gazeta*, 1 October 2003.

[52] He ruled out the stationing of Russian troops on the ground in Afghanistan, saying that the question 'is not even being contemplated in theory'. 'Ivanov says Russia to cooperate with NATO in Afghanistan', Prime-TASS, 23 May 2003 (FACTIVA); and 'Russia ready to help avert threat from Afghanistan: defence minister', Agence France Press, 9 June 2003.

[53] Interfax, 24 July 2003.

[54] Trenin, 'Southern Watch', pp. 130–1.

[55] See the discussion of Bush's foreign and security policy agenda in Edward Rhodes, 'The imperial logic of Bush's liberal agenda', *Survival* 45/1 (Spring 2003).

[56] Australia, New Zeeland, Japan, South Korea, Israel and Argentina have such status.

[57] Martin Spechler, 'Economy and security in Central Asia since 9/11: a sceptical look', *Central Asia and the Caucasus* 1 (2003).

[58] Cf. Roy Allison on the 'limited partnership' based on 'Moscow's formal acceptance of a reduced and lower-profile long-term Western strategic presence in Central Asia'. Roy Allison, 'Strategic reassertion in Russia's Central Asia policy', *International Affairs* 80/2 (2004), pp. 277–93.

SELECTED BIBLIOGRAPHY

Books and Articles

Akimbekov, S. M., *Afganskii uzel i problemy bezopasnosti Tsentralnoi Azii* [The Afghan knot and problems of security in Central Asia] (Almaty: Kontinen, 2003).

Akimbekov, Sultan, 'The conflict in Afghanistan: conditions, problems, and prospects', in Boris Rumer (ed.), *Central Asia: A Gathering Storm?* (New York and London: M. E. Sharpe, 2002).

Akiner, Shirin, *Tajikistan: Disintegration or Reconciliation?* (London: Royal Institute of International Affairs, 2001).

Allison, Graham T., *Essence of Decision: Explaining the Cuban Missile Crisis* (Boston, Mass.: Little, Brown & Co., 1971).

Allison, Roy, 'Russia and the new states of Eurasia', in Archie Brown (ed.) *Contemporary Russian Politics: A Reader* (Oxford: Oxford University Press, 2001).

Allison, Roy, 'Structures and frameworks for security policy cooperation in Central Asia', in Roy Allison and Lena Jonson (eds), *Central Asian Security: The New International Context* (Washington, DC and London: Brookings Institution Press and Royal Institute of International Affairs, 2001).

Allison, Roy, 'The network of new security policy relations in Eurasia', in Roy Allison and Christoph Bluth (eds), *Security Dilemmas in Russia and Eurasia* (London: Royal Institute of International Affairs, 1998).

Allison Roy and Cristoph Bluth (eds), *Security Dilemmas in Russia and Eurasia* (London: Royal Institute of International Affairs, 1998).

Allison Roy and Lena Jonson (eds), *Central Asian Security: The New International Context* (Washington, DC and London: Brookings Institution Press and Royal Institute of International Affairs, 2001).

Arbatov, Alexei, *The Transformation of Russian Military Doctrine: Lessons Learned from Kosovo and Chechnya*, Marshall Center Papers, no. 2, 2000.

Arbatov, Alexei, 'Russian foreign policy thinking in transition', in Vladimir Baranovsky (ed.), *Russia and Europe: The Emerging Security Agenda* (Oxford: Oxford University Press for the Stockholm International Peace Research Institute, 1997).

Aslund, Anders, 'Sizing up the Central Asian economies', *Journal of International Affairs* 56/2 (Spring 2003).

Babadzhanov, Bakhtiar, 'Islam in Uzbekistan: from the struggle for "religious purity" to political activism', in Boris Rumer (ed.), *Central Asia: A Gathering Storm?* (New York and London: M. E. Sharpe, 2002).

Babadzhanov, Bakhtiar, *Religiozny ekstremizm v Tsentralnoi Azii: Problemy I perspektivy. Materialy konferentsii, Dushanbe, 25 aprelya 2002* [Religious extremism in Central Asia: problems and prospects. Materials from a conference held in Dushanbe] (Dushanbe: OSCE Mission to Tajikistan, 2002).

Babadzhanov, Bakhtiar, 'O deyatelnosti "Hizb-ut-Tahrir al-Islami" v Uzbekistane' [The activity of Hizb-ut-Tahrir-al-Islami in Uzbekistan], in Aleksei Malashenko and Martha Brill Olcott (eds), *Islam na postsovetskom prostranstve: Vzglyad iznutri* [Islam in the post-Soviet space: a look from within] (Moscow: Art-Biznes-Tsentr, 2001).

Baev, Pavel, 'Russia's policies in the Caucasus', in Lena Jonson and Clive Archer *Peacekeeping and the Role of Russia in Eurasia* (Boulder, Colo.: Westview Press, 1996).

Bakshi, Jyotsna, 'Sino-Russian strategic partnership in Central Asia: implications for India', *Strategic Analysis* 35/2 (May 2001).

Becker, Seymour, *Russia's Protectorates in Central Asia: Bukhara and Khiva, 1865–1924* (Cambridge, Mass.: Harvard University Press, 1968).

Belokrenitsky, Vyacheslav, 'Russian–Afghan relations', in Gennady Chufrin (ed.), *Russia and Asia: The Emerging Security Agenda* (Oxford: Oxford University Press, 1999).

Bennigsen, Alexandre, Paul B. Henze, George K. Tanham, and S. Enders Wimbush, *Soviet Strategy & Islam* (London: Macmillan, 1989).

Benningsen, Alexandre and S. Enders Wimbush, *Muslims of the Soviet Empire* (Bloomington: Indiana University Press, 1986).

Blank, Stephen, 'Russia rises to perceived threats', *Jane's Intelligence Review* 12/2 (February 2000).

Blank, Stephen, 'The United States and Central Asia', in Roy Allison and Lena Jonson (eds), *Central Asian Security: The New International Context* (Washington, DC: Brookings Institution Press and Royal Institute of International Affairs, 2001).

Botobekov, Uran, 'Vnedrenie idei partii "Hizb-ut-Tahrir al-Islami" na yuge Kirgizii' [Introduction of the idea of the Hizb-ut-Tahrir-al-Islami party in southern Kyrgyzstan], in Martha Brill Olcott and Aleksei Malashenko (eds), *Islam na postsovetskom prostranstve: Vzglyad iznutri.* [Islam in the post-Soviet space: a look from within] (Moscow: Art-Biznes-Tsentr, 2001).

Brill Olcott, Martha, 'Taking stock of Central Asia', *Journal of International Affairs* 56/2 (Spring 2003).

Brill Olcott, Martha, 'Common legacies and conflicts', in Roy Allison and Lena Jonson, *Central Asian Security: The New International Context* (Washington, DC and London: Brookings Institution Press and Royal Institute of International Affairs, 2001).

Brill Olcott, Martha, Anders Åslund, and Sherman W. Garnett, *Getting It Wrong: Regional Cooperation and the Commonwealth of Independent States* (Washington DC: Carnegie Endowment for International Peace, 1999).

Buschkow, Walentin, 'Der innere konflikt Tadschikistans als regionales Sicherheitsproblem', *Berichte des Bundesinstitut fur Ostwissenschaftliche und Internationale Studien* 35 (1996).

Buszynski, Leszek, *Russian Foreign Policy after the Cold War* (Westport, Connecticut and London: Praeger, 1996).

Buzan, Barry, Ole Waever and Jaap de Wilde, *Security: A New Framework for Analysis* (London: Lynn Rienner Publishers, Inc., 1998).

Buzan, Barry, *People, States and Fear*, second edition (New York: Harvester Wheatsheaf, 1991).

Carlsnaes, Walter, 'On analysing the dynamics of foreign policy change: A critique and reconceptualization', *Cooperation and Conflict* 28/1 (1993).

Carrère d'Encausse, Hélène, *Islam and the Russian Empire: Reform and Revolution in Central Asia* (London: I. B. Tauris, 1988).

Central Asia: Islamist Mobilisation and Regional Security, International Crisis Group (ICG), ICG Asia Report no.14 (Osh/Brussels: ICG, 1 March 2001).

Checkel, Jeffrey, 'Structure, Institutions, and Process: Russia's Changing Foreign Policy', in Adeed Dawisha and Karen Dawisha (eds), *The Making of Foreign Policy in Russia and the New States of Eurasia* (Armonk and London: M. E. Sharpe, 1995).

Country Profile Kyrgyzstan/Tajikistan 2002, (London: Economist Intelligence Unit, 2002).

Country Profile Uzbekistan 2002, (London: Economist Intelligence Unit, 2002).

Cracks in the Marble: Turkmenistan's Failing Dictatorship. International Crisis Group (Osh/Brussels: ICG, 21 January 2003).

Davydov, A. D. (ed.), *Afganistan: Problemy voiny i mira* [Afghanistan: problems of war and peace] (Moscow: Institut Vostokovedeniya RAN, 1996).

Donaldson, Robert H. and Joseph L. Nogee, *The Foreign Policy of Russia: Changing Systems, Enduring Interests* (Armonk. and London: M. E. Sharpe, 1998).

Eriksson, Johan (ed.), *Threat Politics: New Perspectives on Security, Risk and Crisis Management* (Aldershot, Burlington USA, Singapore and Sydney: Ashgate, 2001).

Evans, Peter B., Harold K. Jacobson and Robert D. Putnam (eds), *Double-Edged Diplomacy: International Bargaining and Domestic Politics* (Berkeley, Los Angeles and London: University of California Press, 1993).

Fairbanks, Charles, 'Being there', *The National Interest* 68 (2002).

Finnemore, Martha, *National Interests in International Society* (Ithaca, NY and London: Cornell University Press, 1996).

Fuller, Jr, William C., *Strategy and Power in Russia 1600–1914* (New York and Toronto: The Free Press, 1992).

Fyodorov, Yu., 'Krizis vneshnoi politiki Rossii: kontseptualnyi aspekt' [Russia's foreign policy crisis: the conceptual aspect], *Pro et Contra* 6/1–2 (2001).

Geyer, Dietrich, *Russian Imperialism: The Interaction of Domestic and Foreign Policy 1860–1914* (Leamington Spa, Hamburg and New York: Berg, 1987) (German edition 1977).

Gilpin, Robert, *War and Change in World Politics* (Cambridge, London and New York: Cambridge University Press, 1981).

Goibov, Gholib, 'Stroitelstvo svetskogo kharaktera obshchestva i ustanovleniye otnosheniya religioznoi terpimosti v Tadzhikistane' [Establishing a secular society and religious tolerance in Tajikistan], *Religiozny ekstremizm v Tsentralnoi Azii: Problemy i perspektivy. Materialy konferentsii, Dushanbe, 25 aprelya 2002* [Religious extremism in Central Asia: problems and prospects. Materials from a conference held in Dushanbe] (Dushanbe: OSCE Mission to Tajikistan, 2002).

Goldmann, Kjell, *Change and Stability in Foreign Policy: The Problems and Possibilities of Détente* (New York, London, Toronto, Sydney and Tokyo: Harvester Wheatsheaf, 1988).

Gorbachev, Mikhail, *Perestroika: New Thinking for Our Country and the World* (New York: Harper & Row Publishers, 1987).

Gorodetsky, Gabriel (ed.), *Russia between East and West: Russian Foreign Policy on the Threshold of the Twenty-First Century* (London, Portland: Frank Cass, 2003).

Gretzky, Sergei, *Russia's Policy toward Central Asia* (Moscow: Carnegie Moscow Center, 1997).

Grinberg, R. S. et al., 'Sodruzhestvo nezavisimykh gosudarstv: sostoyanie i perspektivy razvitiya. Doklad podgotovlen dlya mezhdunarodnoi nauchnoi konferentsii "Sodruzhestvo Nezavisimykh Gosudarstv: Sostoyanie i Perspektivy"' [The Commonwealth of Independent States: the state of and prospects for development. Paper prepared for the international scientific conference on The Commonwealth of Independent States: Current State and Prospects], Moscow, 30–31 March 2000 (Avtorskii kollektiv R. S. Grinberg, L. Z. Zevin, L. S. Kosikova and A. V. Shurubokich, Moscow, 2000).

Grinberg, R. S., 'Vektory strukturivaniya postsovetskogo ekonomicheskogo pravitelstva' [Vectors of the structuring of the post-Soviet economic space], Paper presented at conference on 'Rossiya i SNG v noveisheikh evropeiskikh integratsionnykh protsessakh' [Russia and the CIS in the latest European integration processes], Moscow, October 2002.

Gusher, A., 'Otrezvlenie Rossii i konflikty na Vostoke' [The sobering up of Russia and conflicts in the East], *Aziya i Afrika* 10 (2002).

Gustavsson, Jakob, 'How should we study foreign policy change?', *Cooperation and Conflict* 34/1 (1999).

Gustavsson, Jakob, *The Politics of Foreign Policy Change: Explaining the Swedish Reorientation on EC Membership* (Lund: Lund University Press, 1998).

Harle, Vilho and Jyrki Ivonen, *Gorbachev and Europe* (London: Pinter Publishers, 1990).

Hermann, Charles, 'Changing course: when governments choose to redirect foreign policy', *International Studies Quarterly* 34/1 (1990).

Herspring, Dale R. and Peter Rutland, 'Putin and Russian foreign policy', in Dale R. Herspring (ed.), *Putin's Russia. Past Imperfect, Future Uncertain* (Lanham, Boulder, New York and London: Rowman & Littlefield Publishers, Inc., 2003.

Herzig, Edmund, 'Islam, transnationalism and subregionalism in the CIS', in Renata Dwan and Oleksandr Pavliuk (eds), *Building Security in the New States of Eurasia: Subregional Cooperation in the Former Soviet Space* (Armonk and London: EastWest Institute and M. E. Sharpe, 2000).

Hobson, John M., *The State and International Relations* (Cambridge: Cambridge University Press, 2000).

Hoetzsch, Otto, *Russland in Asien: Geschichte einer Expansion* [Russia in Asia: the history of an expansion] (Stuttgart: Deutsche Verlags-Anstalt, 1966).

Holsti, K. J., *Why Nations Realign: Foreign Policy Restructuring in the Postwar World* (London: George Allen and Unwin, 1982).

Hopkirk, Peter, *The Great Game: The Struggle for Empire in Central Asia* (London: Murray, 1990).

Horsman, Stuart 'Water in Central Asia: regional cooperation or conflict?', in Roy Allison and Lena Jonson (eds), *Central Asian Security: The New International Context* (Washington, DC and London: Brookings Institution Press and Royal Institute of International Affairs, 2001).

Huskey, Eugene, *Presidential Power in Russia* (Armonk, NY and London: M. E. Sharpe, 1999).

Ignatev, A. V. (ed.), *Istoriya vneshnei politiki Rossii: Vtoraya polovina XIX veka* [History of Russian foreign policy: the second half of the nineteenth century] (Moscow: Mezhdunarodnye otnosheniya, 1997).

Ismael, Tareq Y. and Jaqueline S. Ismael, *Government and Politics in Islam* (London: Frances Pinter, 1985).

Ivanov, Igor, 'Traditions of the past and foreign policy today', *International Affairs* 48/4 (2002).

Jonson, Lena, 'Russia and Central Asia', in Roy Allison and Lena Jonson (eds), *Central Asia in a New Security Context* (Washington, DC and London: Brookings Institution Press and Royal Institute of International Affairs, 2001).

Jonson, Lena, 'Russian Chechnya policy: Is this how to square a circle?', *Brown Journal of World Affairs* 8/1 (Winter/Spring 2001).

Jonson, Lena, 'Russia and Central Asia under Putin: the Afghan factor', in Michael H. Crutcher (ed.), *Russian National Security: Perceptions, Policies, and Prospects* 4–6 December 2000 (US Army War College, Carlisle Barracks, Pa., 2001).

Jonson, Lena, 'The new geo-political situation', in Gennady Chufrin (ed.), *The Security of the Caspian Sea Region* (Oxford: SIPRI/Oxford University Press, 2001).

Jonson, Lena, 'Russia, NATO and the handling of conflicts at Russia's southern periphery: at a crossroads?', *European Security* 9/4 (Winter 2000).

Jonson, Lena, *Keeping the Peace in the CIS: The Evolution of Russian Policy*. Discussion Paper 81 (London: The Royal Institute of International Affairs, 1999).

Jonson, Lena, *Russia and Central Asia in a New Web of Relations* (London: Royal Institute of International Affairs, 1998).

Jonson, Lena, *The Tajik War: A Challenge to Russian Policy* (London: Royal Institute of International Affairs, 1998).

Jonson, Lena, 'Russia and European security: old wine in new bottles?', in William E. Ferry and Roger Kanet (eds), *Post-Communist States in the World Community* (London: Macmillan, 1998).

Jonson, Lena, 'Russian policy in Northern Europe', in Vladimir Baranovsky (ed.), *Russia and Europe: The Emerging Security Agenda* (Oxford: Oxford University Press for the Stockholm International Peace Research Institute, 1997).

Jonson, Lena, 'In search of a national interest: the foreign policy debate in Russia', *Nationalities Papers* 22/1 (Spring 1994).

Jonson, Lena, 'Russia and Europe: the emergence of a new Russian foreign policy', in Bo Huldt and Gunilla Herolf (eds), *Towards a New European Security Order: Yearbook 1990–91* (Stockholm: Swedish Institute of International Affairs, 1991).

Jonson, Lena, and Clive Archer (eds), *Peacekeeping and the Role of Russia in Eurasia* (Boulder, Colo.: Westview Press, 1996).

Karaganov, Sergei, 'Russia, Europe, and new challenges', *Russia in Global Affairs* 1/1 (January–March 2003).

Karayianni, Marika S., 'Russia's foreign policy for Central Asia through energy agreements', *Central Asia and the Caucasus* 4 (2003).

Kazemzadeh, Firuz, *Russia and Britain in Persia, 1864–1914: A Study in Imperialism* (New Haven, Conn. and London: Yale University Press, 1968).

Keohane, Robert, 'The analysis of international regimes: towards a European–American research programme', in Volker Rittberger (ed.), *Regime Theory and International Relations* (Oxford: Clarendon Press, 1993).

Khalfin, N. A., *Politika Rossii v Srednei Azii (1857–1868)* [Russian policy in Central Asia, 1857–68] (Moscow: Izdatelstvo vostochnoi literatury, 1960).

Khamadov, Sultan, 'Mezhdunarodnyi kontekst-afganskii faktor', *Religiozny ekstremizm v Tsentralnoi Azii: Problemy I perspektivy. Materialy konferentsii, Dushanbe, 25 aprelya 2002* [Religious extremism in Central Asia: problems and prospects. Materials from a conference held in Dushanbe] (Dushanbe: OSCE Mission to Tajikistan, 2002).

Khotamov, Namoz, *Sverzhenie emirskogo rezhima v Bukhare* [The overthrow of the emirate regime in Bukhara] (Dushanbe: Academy of Sciences of Tajikistan, 1997).

Khroustalev, Mark, *Central Asia in Russia's Foreign Policy*. Occasional Papers of the Centre of International Studies, MGIMO, no. 5 (Moscow, 1994).

Kingdon, R., *Agendas, Alternatives, and Public Policies* (Boston, Mass.: Little, Brown & Co., 1984).

Kolstoe, Paul, *Russians in the Former Soviet Republics* (London: Hurst & Co., 1995).

Kreikemeyer, Anna and Arne Seifert (eds), *Zur Vereinbarkeit von politischen Islam und Sicherheit im OSZE Raum: Dokumente eines islamisch-säkularen Dialogs in Tadschikistan* [On the compatibility of Islam and security in the OSCE space: documents of an Islamic–secular dialogue] (Baden-Baden: Nomos Verlagsgesellschaft, 2002/2003).

Lapidus, Gail, 'Russia's second Chechnya war: ten assumptions in search of a policy', in Lena Jonson and Murad Esenov (eds), *Chechnya: The International Community and Strategies for Peace and Stability*, Conference Papers 27 (Stockholm: Swedish Institute of International Affairs, 2000).

LeDonne, John P., *The Russian Empire and the World 1700–1917: The Geopolitics of Expansion and Containment* (New York and Oxford: Oxford University Press, 1997).

Light, Margot, 'Post-Soviet Russian foreign policy: the first decade', in Archie Brown (ed.), *Contemporary Russian Politics: A Reader.* (Oxford: Oxford University Press, 2001).

Lo, Bobo, *Russian Foreign Policy in the Post-Soviet Era: Reality, Illusion, and Mythmaking* (London: Palgrave, 2002).

Lo, Bobo, *Vladimir Putin and the Evolution of Russian Foreign Policy* (London: Royal Institute of International Affairs and Blackwell, 2003).

Lukin, Vladimir, 'Our security predicament', *Foreign Policy* 88 (Fall 1992).

Lynch, Dov, *Russia Faces Europe*, Chaillot Papers no. 60 (Paris: European Union Institute for Security Studies, May 2003).

Lynch, Dov, *Russian Peacekeeping Strategies in the CIS: The Cases of Moldova, Georgia and Tajikistan* (London: Royal Institute of International Affairs and Macmillan, 2000).

MacKenzie, David, 'Russia's Balkan policies under Alexander II, 1855–1881', in Hugh Ragsdale (ed.), *Imperial Russian Foreign Policy* (Cambridge, Mass.: Woodrow Wilson Center Press and Cambridge University Press, 1993).

Malashenko, Aleksei, 'Islam and politics in Central Asian States', in Lena Jonson and Murad Esenov (eds), *Political Islam and Conflicts in Russia and Central Asia* (Stockholm: Swedish Institute of International Afffairs, 1999).

Malcolm, Neil, and Alex Pravda, 'Introduction', in Neil Malcolm, Alex Pravda, Roy Allison and Margot Light (co-authors), *Internal Factors in Russian Foreign Policy* (Oxford: Oxford University Press and Royal Institute of International Affairs, 1996).

Menon, Rajan, 'After Empire: Russia and the Southern "Near Abroad"', in Michael Mandelbaum (ed.), *The New Russian Foreign Policy* (New York: Council on Foreign Relations, 1998).

Menon, Rajan, Yuri E. Fedorov and Ghia Nordia, *Russia, the Caucasus and Central Asia: The 21st Century Security Environment* (Armonk, NY and London: EastWest Institute and M. E. Sharpe, 1999).

Micklin, Philip, *Managing Water in Central Asia* (London: Royal Institute of International Affairs, 2000).

Mozaffari, Mehdi (ed.), *Security Politics in the Commonwealth of Independent States: The Southern Belt* (London: Macmillan, 1999).

Mukhabbatov, Kurbonali, 'Religiozno-oppozitsionnye gruppy v Tadzhikistane: Hizb-ut-Tahrir' [Religious opposition groups in Tajikistan: Hizb-ut-Tahrir], in *Religiozny ekstremizm v Tsentralnoi Azii: Problemy i perspektivy. Materialy konferentsii, Dushanbe, 25 aprelya 2002* [Religious extremism in Central Asia: problems and prospects. Materials from a conference held in Dushanbe] (Dushanbe: OSCE Mission to Tajikistan, 2002).

Muminov, Ashirbek, 'Traditsionnye i sovremennye religiozno-teologicheskie shkoly v Tsentralnoi Azii', *Tsentralnaya Aziya i Kavkaz* 4/5 (1999).

Naumkin, Vitaly V., *Militant Islam in Central Asia: The Case of the Islamic Movement of Uzbekistan*. Berkely Program in Soviet and Post-Soviet Studies. Working Paper series. Spring 2003.

Nye, Joseph S., 'Nuclear learning and US-Soviet security regimes', *International Organization* 41/3 (Summer 1987).

Oldberg, Ingmar, 'Foreign policy priorities under Putin: a tour d'horizon', in Bertil Nygren and Christer Pursiainen (eds), *Dimensions of Russian Security Policy* (forthcoming).

Olimova, Saodat, 'Natsionalnye gosudarstva i etnicheskie territorii' [Nation-states and ethnic territories], in Martha Brill Olcott and Alexei Malashenko (eds), *Mnogomernye granitsy Tsentralnoi Azii* [Multidimensional borders of Central Asia] (Moscow: Carnegie Centre, 2000) (electronic version http://pubs.carnegie.ru/books/2000/04am).

Olimova, Saodat, 'Political Islam and conflict in Tajikistan', in Lena Jonson and Murad Esenov (eds), *Political Islam and Conflicts in Russia and Central* (Stockholm: Swedish Institute of International Affairs, 1999).

'Osnovnye polozheniya voennoi doktriny Rossiiskoi Federatsii' [The basic provisions of the military doctrine of the Russian Federation], *Krasnaya zvezda*, 19 November 1993.

Paznyak, Vyacheslau 'The Customs Union of five and the Russia–Belarus Union', in Renata Dwan and Oleksandr Pavliuk (eds), *Building Security in the New States of Eurasia* (New York and London: M. E. Sharpe, 2000).

Pierce, Richard A., *Russian Central Asia 1867–1917: A Study in Colonial Rule* (Berkeley and Los Angeles: University of California Press, 1960).

Pirumshoev, Khaidarsho, *Rossiisko-sredneaziatskie otnosheniya XV–serediny XIX vekov v Russkoi istoriografii* [Russian–Central Asian relations from the fifteenth to the mid-nineteenth century in Russian historiography] (Dushanbe: Academy of Science of Tajikistan/Izdatelstvo Maolif, 2000).

Pomfret, Richard, *Central Asia Turns South? Trade Relations in Transition* (London: Royal Institute of International Affairs, 1999).

Posle raspada SSR: Rossiya v novom mire: Doklad tsentra mezhdunarodnykh issledovanii MGIMO [After the break up of the Soviet Union: report by the Centre for International Studies at MGIMO] (Moskva: MGIMO, February 1992).

Pravda, Alex, 'Putin's foreign policy after 11 September: radical or revolutionary?', in Gabriel Gorodetsky (ed.), *Russia Between East and West: Russian Foreign Policy on the Threshold of the Twenty-First Century* (London and Portland, Oreg.: Cummings Center Series/Frank Cass, 2003).

Primakov, Yevgenii, 'Rossiya v mirovoi politike (k 200-letiyu A.M.Gorchakova)' [Russia in world politics. Lecture at the Gorchakov bicentenary proceedings 28 April 1998], *Diplomaticheskii vestnik* 7 (July 1998).

Primakov, Yevgenii, *Vosem mesyatsev plyus* [Eight months plus] (Moscow: Mysl, 2001).

Pursiainen, Christer, 'The impact of international security regimes on Russia's behavior', in Ted Hopf (ed.), *Understandings of Russian Foreign Policy* (Pennsylvania: Pennsylvania State University, 1999).

Pursiainen, Christer, *Beyond Sovietology: International Relations Theory and the Study of Soviet/Russian Foreign and Security Policy* (Helsinki: Finnish Institute of International Affairs, 1998).

Pursiainen, Christer, *Russian Foreign Policy and International Relations Theory* (Aldershot: Ashgate, 2000).

Rashid, Ahmed , *Jihad: The Rise of Militant Islam in Central Asia* (New Haven and London: Yale University Press, 2002).

Rhodes, Aaron and Paula Tscherne-Lempiäinen, 'Human rights and terrorism in the Central Asian OSCE states', *Helsinki Monitor* 1 (2002).

Rhodes, Edward, 'The imperial logic of Bush's liberal agenda', *Survival* 45/1 (Spring 2003).

Richter, Anthony, 'Great expectations on the Caspian: can US policy live up to them?', in *Caspian Studies Program Experts Conference Report* 'Succession and long-term stability in the Caspian region', Harvard University, John F. Kennedy School of Government, October 1999.

'Rossiya–SNG: Nuzhdaetsya li v korrektirovke pozitsiya zapada?' [Russia and the CIS: does the position of the West need correcting?], *Rossiiskaya gazeta*, 22 September 1994.

Roy, Olivier, *The New Central Asia: The Creation of Nations* (New York: New York University Press, 2000).

Rumer Boris (ed.), *Central Asia: A Gathering Storm?* (New York and London: M. E. Sharpe, 2002).

'Russia in 2003 and its foreign policy: excerpts from the report by the Foundation for Prospective Studies and Initiatives', *Russia in Global Affairs* 1/1 (January–March 2003).

Sagnaeva, Saniya, 'Religiozno-oppozitsionnye gruppy v Kyrgyzstane: Hizb-ut-Tahrir' [Religious-oppositional groups in Kyrgyzstan: Hizb-ut-Tahrir], in *Religiozny ekstremizm v Tsentralnoi Azii: Problemy i perspektivy. Materialy konferentsii, Dushanbe, 25 aprelya 2002* [Religious extremism in Central Asia: Problems and prospects. Materials from a conference held in Dushanbe] (Dushanbe: OSCE Mission to Tajikistan, 2002).

Saikal, Amin, 'Russia and Central Asia', in Amin Saikal and William Maley (eds), *Russia in Search of its Future* (Cambridge: Cambridge University Press, 1995).

Saikal Amin and William Maley, *Russia in Search of Its Future* (Cambridge: Cambridge University Press, 1995).

Salmin, Aleksei, 'Vnutripoliticheskie aktery i vneshnaya politika Rossiiskoi Federatsii' [Domestic Actors in Russian Foreign Policy], in Sergei Medvedev, Alexander Konovalov and Sergei Oznobishev (eds.), *Rossiya i Zapad v novom tysyacheletii*, [Russia and the West in the new millenium] (George C. Marshall European Center for Security Studies, 2003).

Shearman Peter (ed.), *Russian Foreign Policy Since 1990* (Boulder, San Fransisco and Oxford: Westview Press, 1995).

Shevtsova, Lilia, *Putin's Russia* (Washington, DC: Carnegie Endowment for International Peace, 2003).

Soucek, Svat, *A History of Inner Asia* (Cambridge and New York: Cambridge University Press, 2000).

Spechler, Martin, 'Economy and security in Central Asia since 9/11: a sceptical look', *Central Asia and the Caucasus* 1 (2003).

Spidsboel-Hansen, Flemming, 'Past and future meet: Aleksandr Gorchakov and Russian foreign policy', *Europe–Asia Studies* 54/3 (2002).

Stent, Angela, 'Farewell to empire?', *World Policy Journal*, 1 October 2002.

Stepanova, Ekaterina, 'Russia's approach to the fight against terrorism', in Ingmar Oldberg et al. (eds), *Russia—a Great Power? Security Aspects* (forthcoming).

'Strategiya dlya Rossii', *Nezavisimaya gazeta*, 19 August 1992.

Tabyshalieva, Anara, *The Challenge of Regional Cooperation in Central Asia: Preventing Ethnic Conflict in the Ferghana Valley* (Washington, DC: United States Institute of Peace, 1999).

Taji-Farouki, Suha *A Fundamental Quest: Hizb-ut-Tahrir and the Search for the Islamic Caliphate* (London: Grey Seal, 1996).

Tajikistan: A Roadmap for Development, International Crisis Group (ICG), ICG Asia Report 51 (Osh/Brussels: International Crisis Group, 24 April 2003).

The Commonwealth of Independent states: Developments and Prospects. Report of the Centre of International Studies. Moscow State Institute of International Relations (MGIMO), 1992.

Tolz, Vera, *Inventing the Nation: Russia* (London and New York: Arnold and Oxford University Press, 2001).

Trenin, Dmitri, 'From pragmatism to strategic choice: is Russia's security policy finally becoming realistic?', in Andrew C. Kuchins (ed.), *Russia After the Fall* (Washington, DC: Carnegie Endowment for International Peace, 2002).

Trenin, Dmitri, 'Southern watch: Russia's policy in Central Asia', *Journal of International Affairs* 56/2 (Spring 2003).

Trenin, Dmitri, *The End of Eurasia: Russia on the Border Between Geopolitics and Globalization* (Washington, DC and Moscow: Carnegie Endowment for International Peace, 2002).

Trushin, Eshref and Eskender Trushin, 'Challenges to economic policy in Central Asia: Is a miracle possible?', in Boris Rumer (ed.), *Central Asia: A Gathering Storm?* (New York and London: M. E. Sharpe, 2002).

Vendil, Carolina 'The Russian Security Council', *European Security* 2 (Summer 2001).

'Vneshnaya politika Rossii: 1991-2000. Chast I', [Russian Foreign Policy], *Pro et Contra* (Carnegie Endowment for International Peace). Winter/Spring 2001.

'Vneshnaya politika Rossii: 1991-2000. Chast II', [Russian Foreign Policy], *Pro et Contra* (Carnegie Endowment for International Peace). Autumn 2001.

Walker, Edward, 'Islam, Islamism and political order', *Journal of International Affairs* 56/2 (Spring 2003).

Waltz, Kenneth, *Theory of International Politics* (New York: Random House, 1979).

Waltz, Kenneth, 'Another gap', in Robert Osgood et al. (eds), *Containment, Soviet Behavior and Grand Strategy*, Policy Papers in International Affairs no. 16 (Berkeley, Calif.: Institute of International Studies, University of California at Berkeley, 1981).

Webber, Mark, *CIS Integration Trends: Russia and the Former Soviet South* (London: Royal Institute of International Affairs, 1996).

Webber, Mark, *The International Politics of Russia and the Successor States* (Manchester and New York: Manchester University Press, 1996).

Wendt, Alexander, 'Collective identity formation and the international state', *American Political Science Review* 88 (June 1994).

Whitlock, Monica, *Beyond the Oxus: The Central Asians* (London: John Murray, 2002).

Xing, Guangcheng, 'China and Central Asia', in Lena Jonson and Roy Allison (eds), *Central Asian Security Dynamics: The New International Context* (Washington, DC and London: Brookings Institution Press and Royal Institute of International Affairs, 2001).

Yavlinsky, Grigory, 'Domestic and foreign policy challenges in Russia', Carnegie Endowment for International Peace,
http://www.ceip.org/files/events/Yavlinsky transcripts013102.asp

Yudanov, Yu., 'Tsentralnaya Aziya: novyi favorit inostrannykh investorov' [Central Asia: the new favourite of foreign investors], *Mirovaya ekonomika i mezhdunarodnye otnosheniya* 3-4 (2000).

Zharinov, K. V., *Terrorizm i terroristy: Istoricheskii ocherk* [Terrorism and terrorists: a historical outline] (Minsk: Kharvest, 1999).

Zhukov, Stanislav, 'Development under conditions of globalization', in Boris Rumer (ed.), *Central Asia: A Gathering Storm?* (New York and London: M. E. Sharpe, 2002).

Ziyadullaev, Nabi, 'SNG: natsionalnaya bezopasnost i ekspansiya SshA' [The CIS: national security and the expansion of the USA], *Svobodnaya Mysl* 6 (2002).

Zviagelskaia, Irina, *The Russian Policy Debate on Central Asia* (London: Royal Institute of International Affairs, 1995).

Newspapers and News Magazines

Asia Plus (Dushanbe)
Biznes i Politika (Dushanbe)
Dipkurer NG
Diplomaticheskii vestnik
Far Eastern Economic Review
Former Soviet Union Fifteen Nations: Policy and Security
Izvestiya
Jamestown Fortnight in Review
Jamestown Monitor
Jane's Defence Weekly
Kommersant Daily
Komsomolskaya pravda
Krasnaya zvezda
Moscow News
Moscow Times
Narodnaya gazeta (Dushanbe)

NATO Review
New Times (Moscow)
Nezavisimaya gazeta
Nezavisimoe voennoe obozrenie
Rossiyskaya gazeta
Segodnya
Smysl
Sodrushchestvo NG
Sotsialno-politicheskaya situatsiya v post-sovetskom mire
Sovetskaya gazeta
The Economist
Zhurnal

News Agencies and News Services

Asia Plus News Agency (Tajikistan)
BBC Inside Central Asia
BBC Summary of World Broadcasts
BBC World Monitoring Service
FACTIVA
Interfax (Russia)
ITAR-TASS (Russia)
Radio Free Europe/Radio Liberty Central Asia Report
Radio Free Europe/Radio Liberty Newsline
Radio Free Europe/Radio Liberty Russian Political Weekly
Reuters
Varorud news agency (Tajikistan)

Index